Act. 15

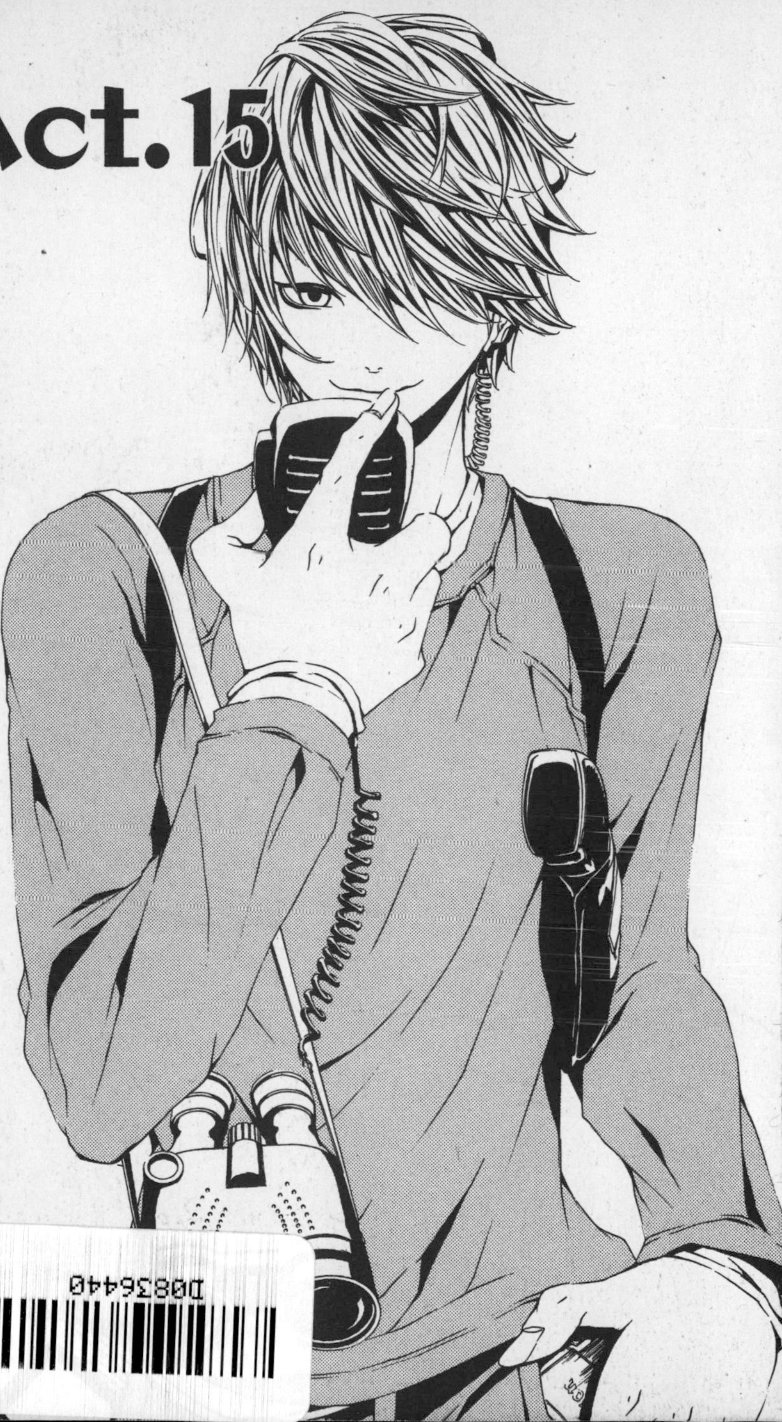

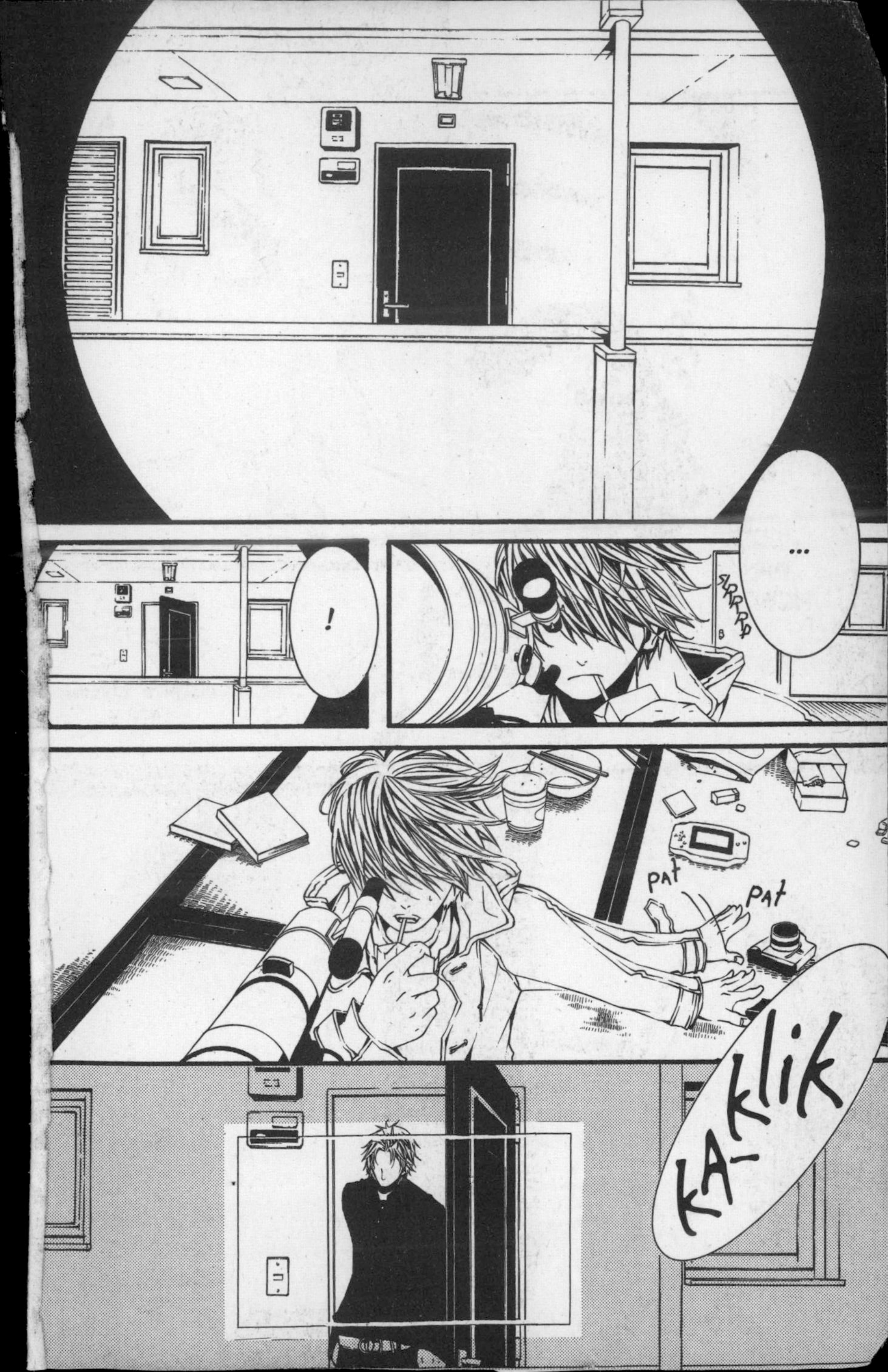
...
SLRRRP
!
PAT
PAT
KA-KLIK

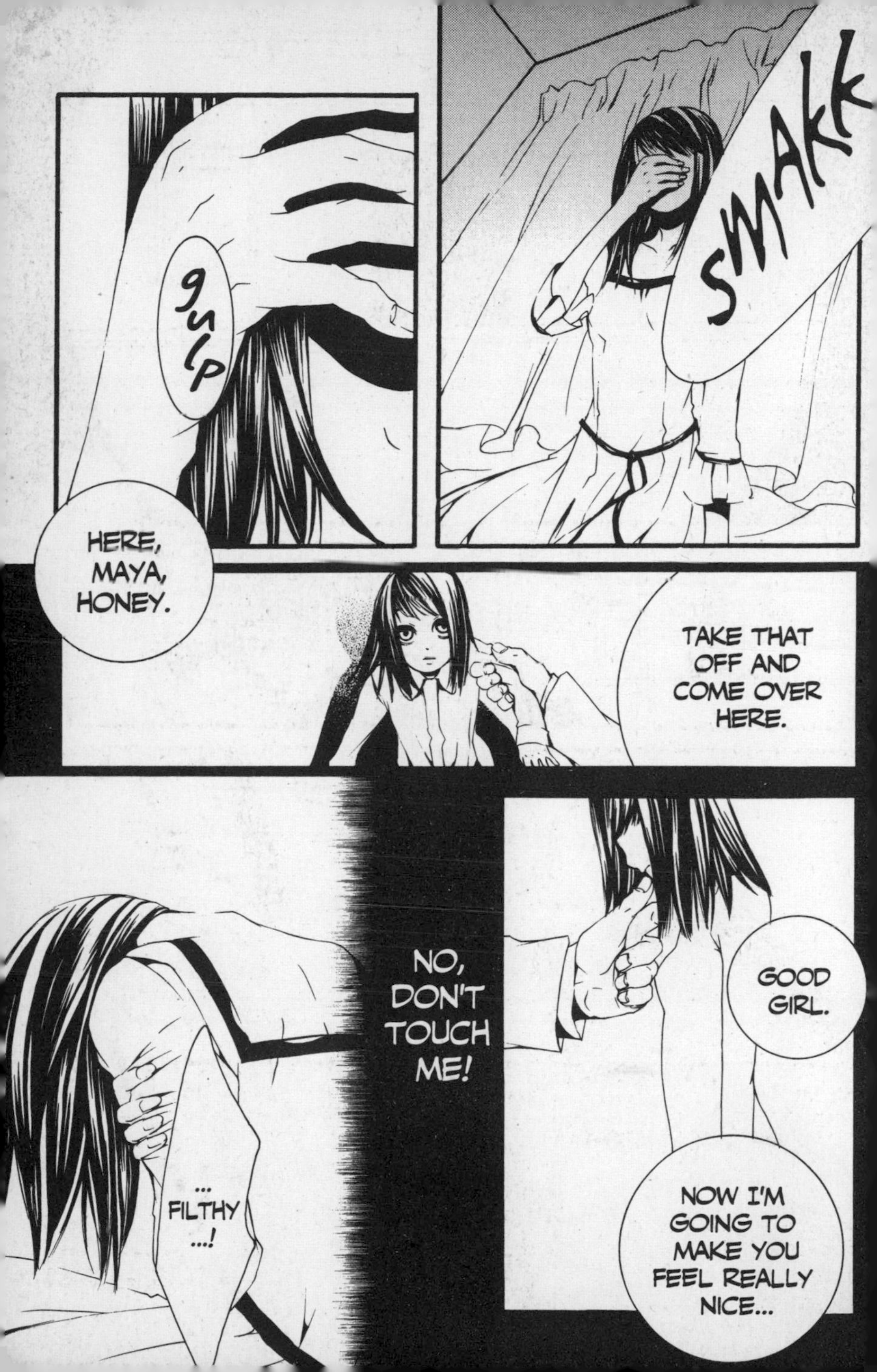
SMAKK
gulp
HERE, MAYA, HONEY.
TAKE THAT OFF AND COME OVER HERE.
GOOD GIRL.
NOW I'M GOING TO MAKE YOU FEEL REALLY NICE...
NO, DON'T TOUCH ME!
...FILTHY...!

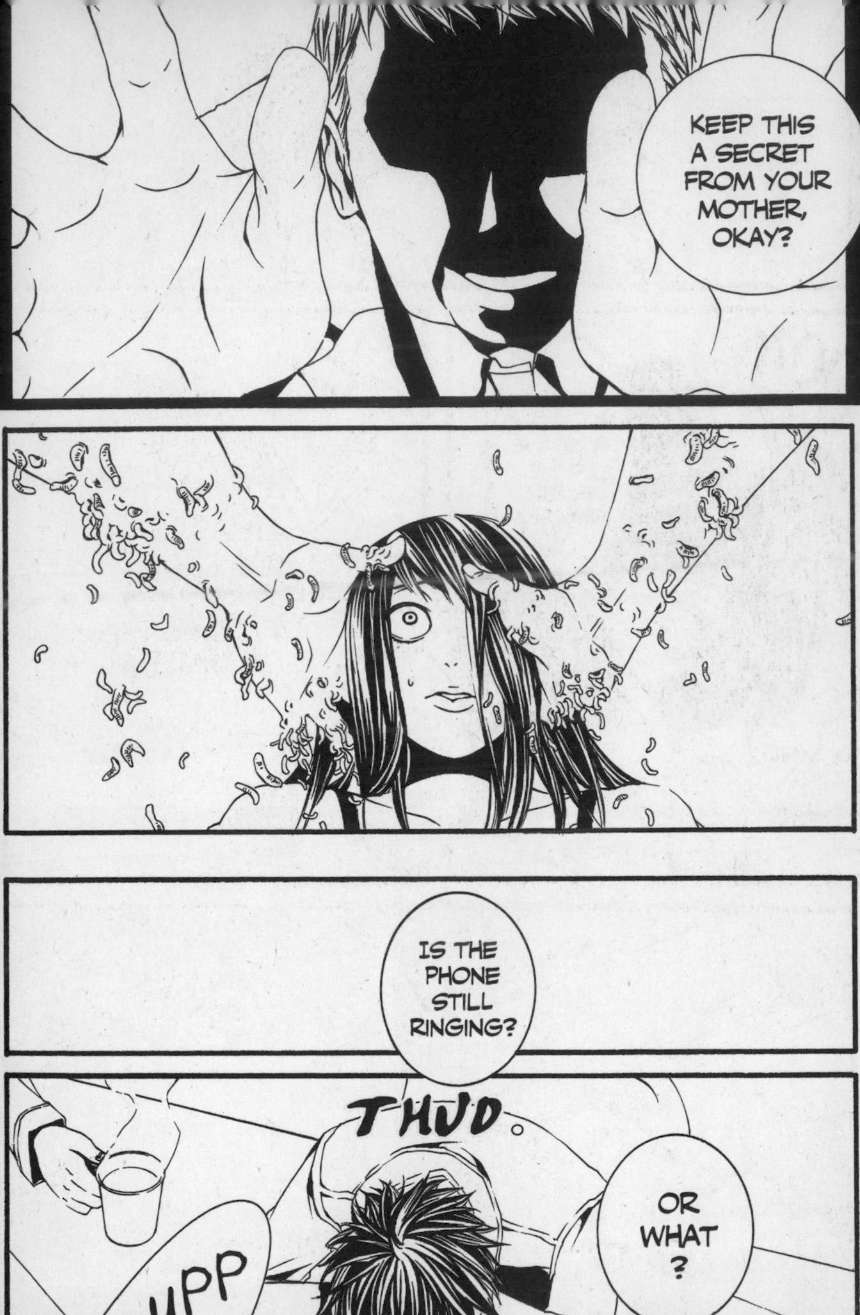
KEEP THIS A SECRET FROM YOUR MOTHER, OKAY?
IS THE PHONE STILL RINGING?
OR WHAT ?
THUD
TUPP

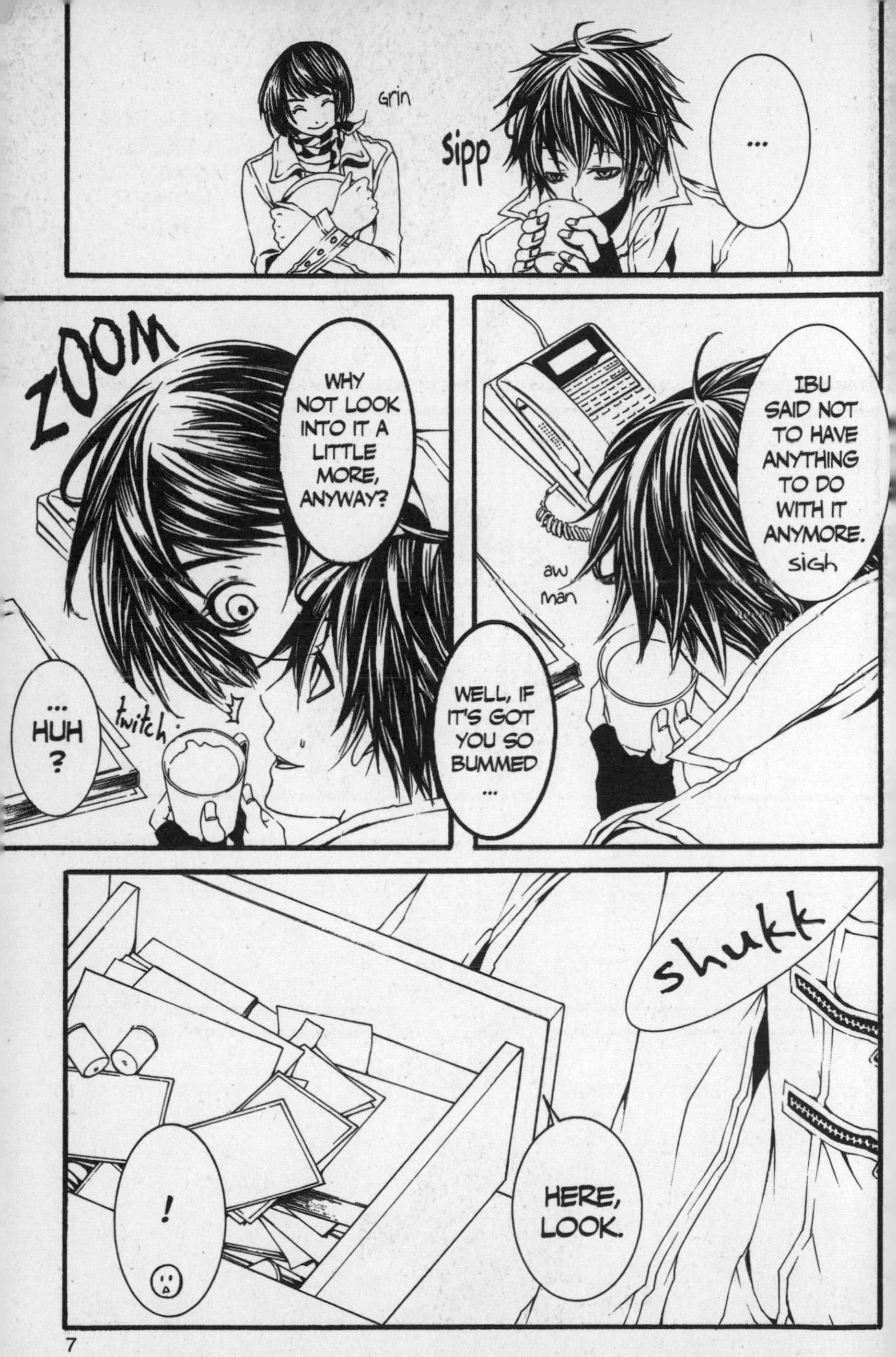
...
Sipp
Grin
IBU SAID NOT TO HAVE ANYTHING TO DO WITH IT ANYMORE.
sigh
aw man
WELL, IF IT'S GOT YOU SO BUMMED ...
WHY NOT LOOK INTO IT A LITTLE MORE, ANYWAY?
ZOOM
twitch
... HUH ?
shukk
HERE, LOOK.
!

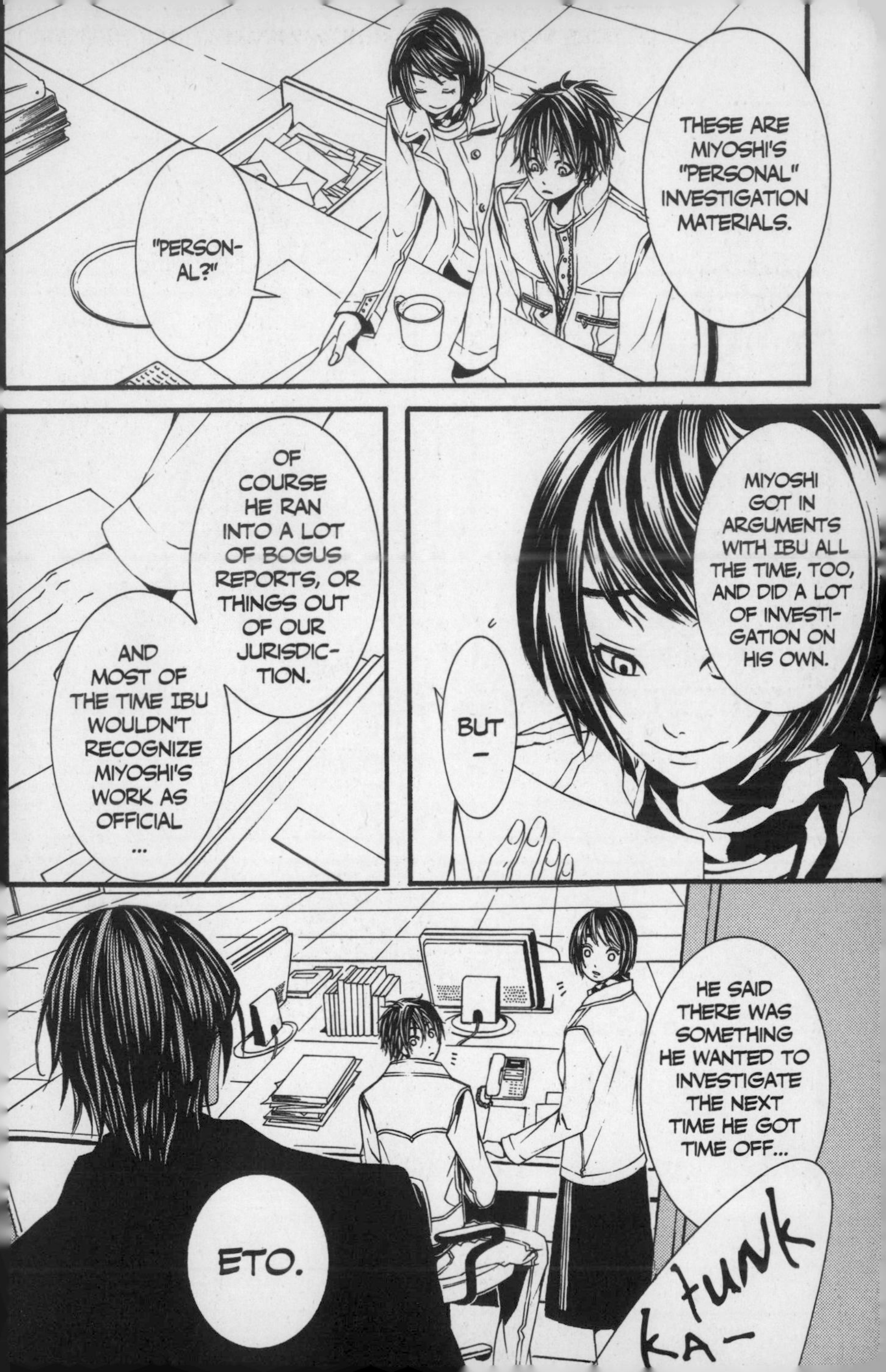
THESE ARE MIYOSHI'S "PERSONAL" INVESTIGATION MATERIALS.
"PERSON-AL?"
MIYOSHI GOT IN ARGUMENTS WITH IBU ALL THE TIME, TOO, AND DID A LOT OF INVESTI-GATION ON HIS OWN.
BUT —
OF COURSE HE RAN INTO A LOT OF BOGUS REPORTS, OR THINGS OUT OF OUR JURISDIC-TION.
AND MOST OF THE TIME IBU WOULDN'T RECOGNIZE MIYOSHI'S WORK AS OFFICIAL ...
HE SAID THERE WAS SOMETHING HE WANTED TO INVESTIGATE THE NEXT TIME HE GOT TIME OFF...
KA-tunk
ETO.

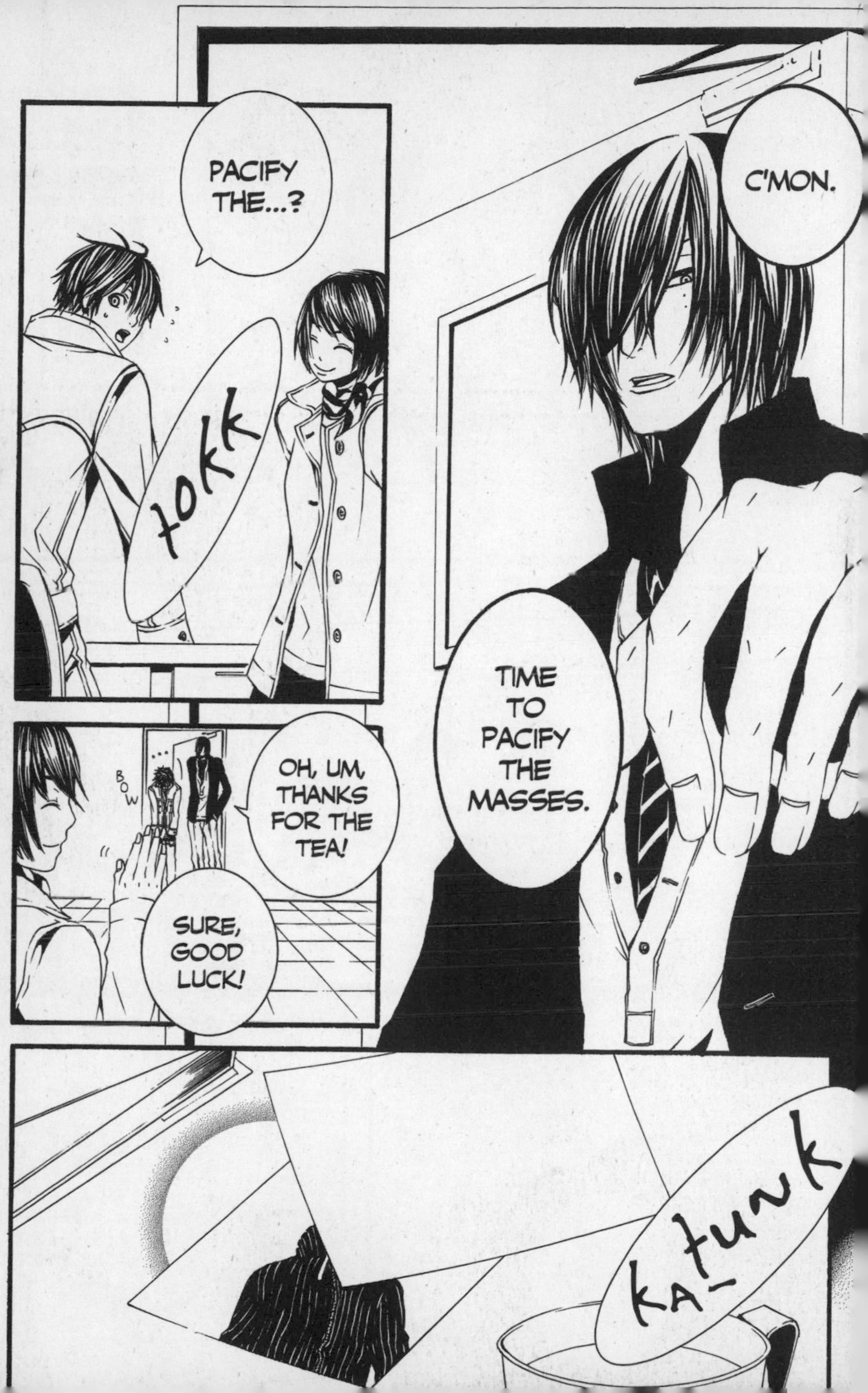
C'MON.
TIME TO PACIFY THE MASSES.
PACIFY THE...?
tokk
OH, UM, THANKS FOR THE TEA!
BOW
SURE, GOOD LUCK!
ka-tunk

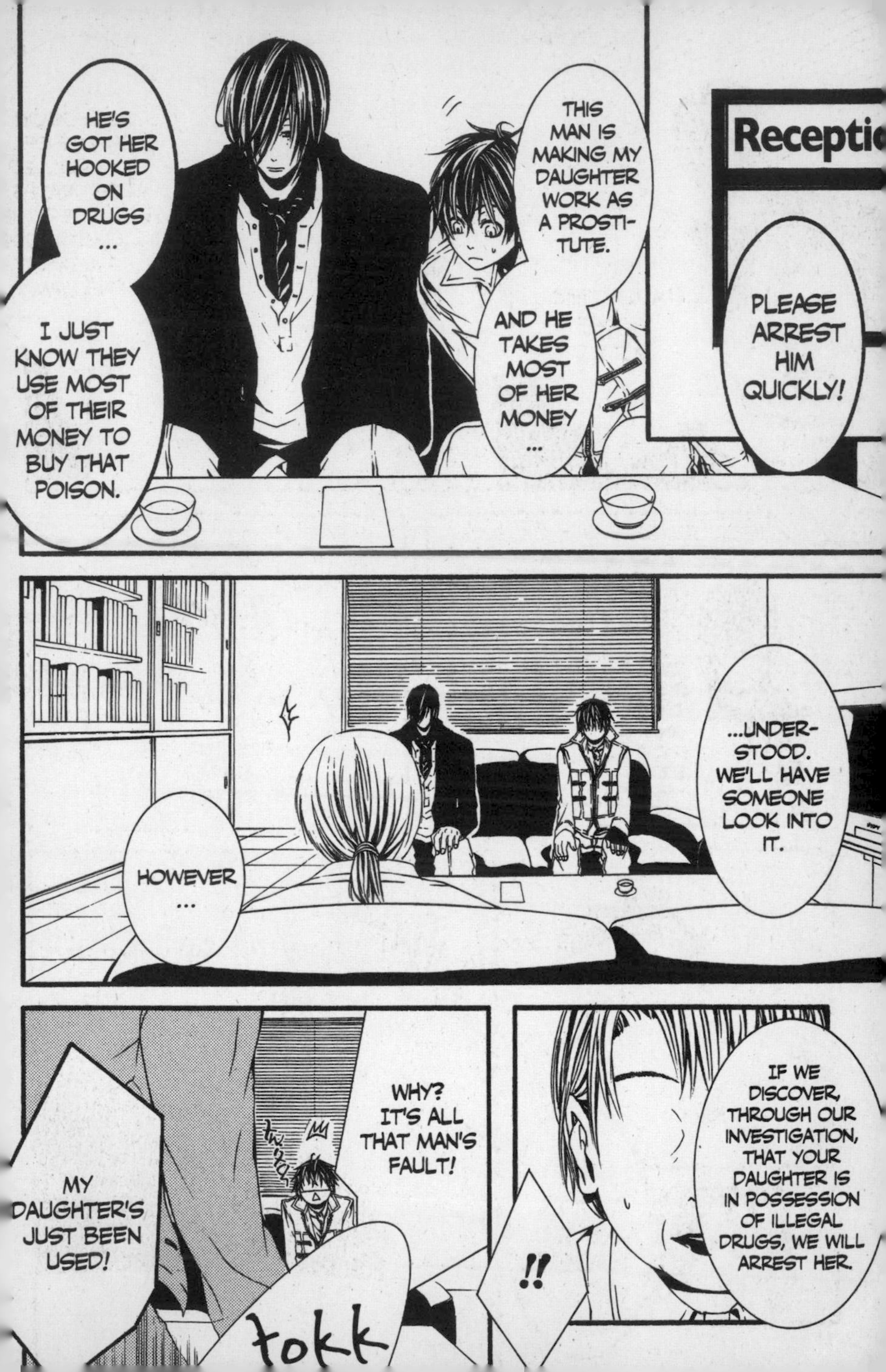
Recepti
THIS MAN IS MAKING MY DAUGHTER WORK AS A PROSTI-TUTE.
AND HE TAKES MOST OF HER MONEY ...
HE'S GOT HER HOOKED ON DRUGS ...
I JUST KNOW THEY USE MOST OF THEIR MONEY TO BUY THAT POISON.
PLEASE ARREST HIM QUICKLY!
...UNDER-STOOD. WE'LL HAVE SOMEONE LOOK INTO IT.
HOWEVER ...
IF WE DISCOVER, THROUGH OUR INVESTIGATION, THAT YOUR DAUGHTER IS IN POSSESSION OF ILLEGAL DRUGS, WE WILL ARREST HER.
!!
WHY? IT'S ALL THAT MAN'S FAULT!
MY DAUGHTER'S JUST BEEN USED!
tokk

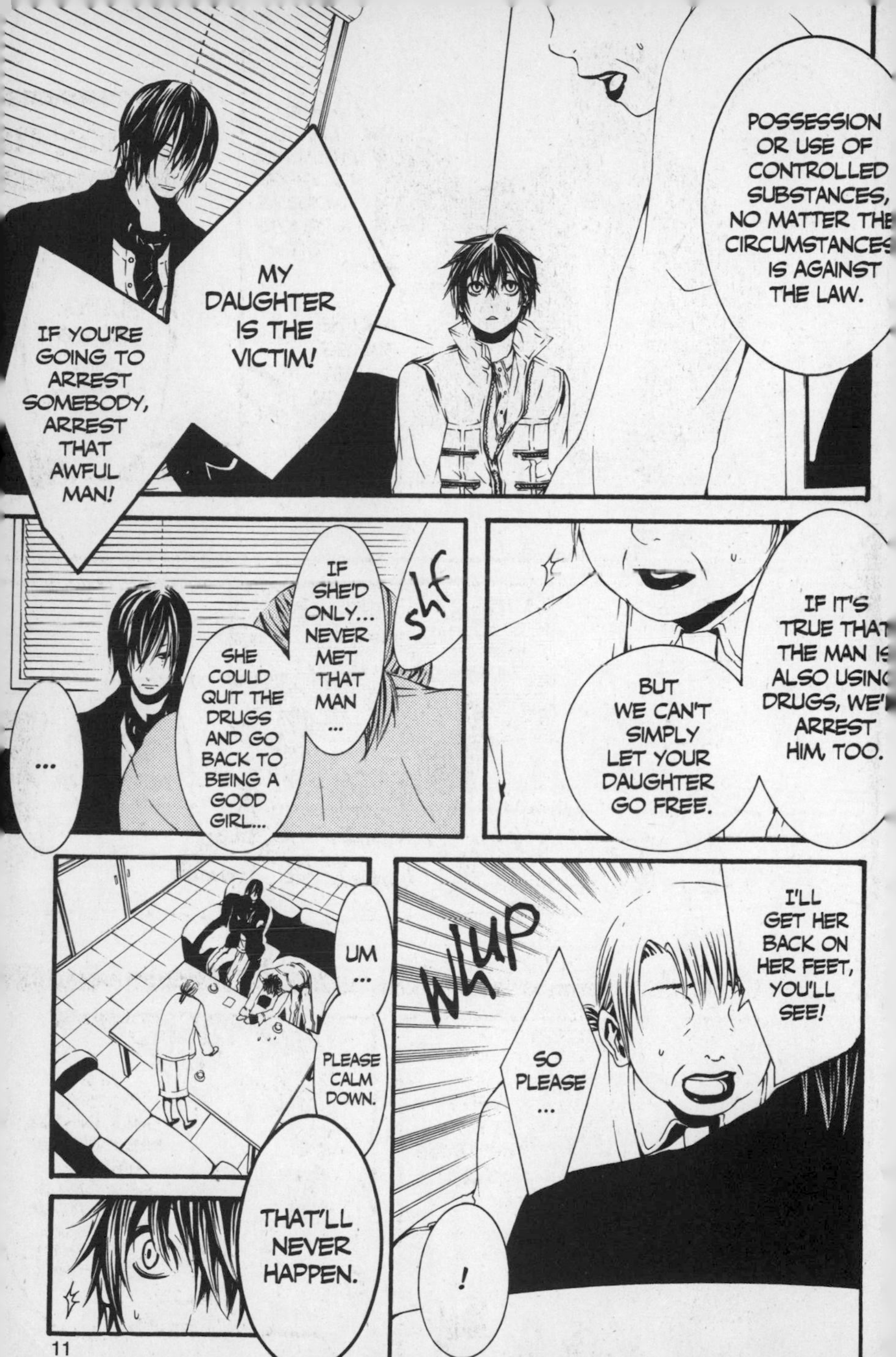

POSSESSION OR USE OF CONTROLLED SUBSTANCES, NO MATTER THE CIRCUMSTANCES IS AGAINST THE LAW.
MY DAUGHTER IS THE VICTIM!
IF YOU'RE GOING TO ARREST SOMEBODY, ARREST THAT AWFUL MAN!
IF IT'S TRUE THAT THE MAN IS ALSO USING DRUGS, WE'LL ARREST HIM, TOO.
BUT WE CAN'T SIMPLY LET YOUR DAUGHTER GO FREE.
SHF
IF SHE'D ONLY... NEVER MET THAT MAN ...
SHE COULD QUIT THE DRUGS AND GO BACK TO BEING A GOOD GIRL...
...
I'LL GET HER BACK ON HER FEET, YOU'LL SEE!
WHUP
SO PLEASE ...
!
UM ...
PLEASE CALM DOWN.
THAT'LL NEVER HAPPEN.

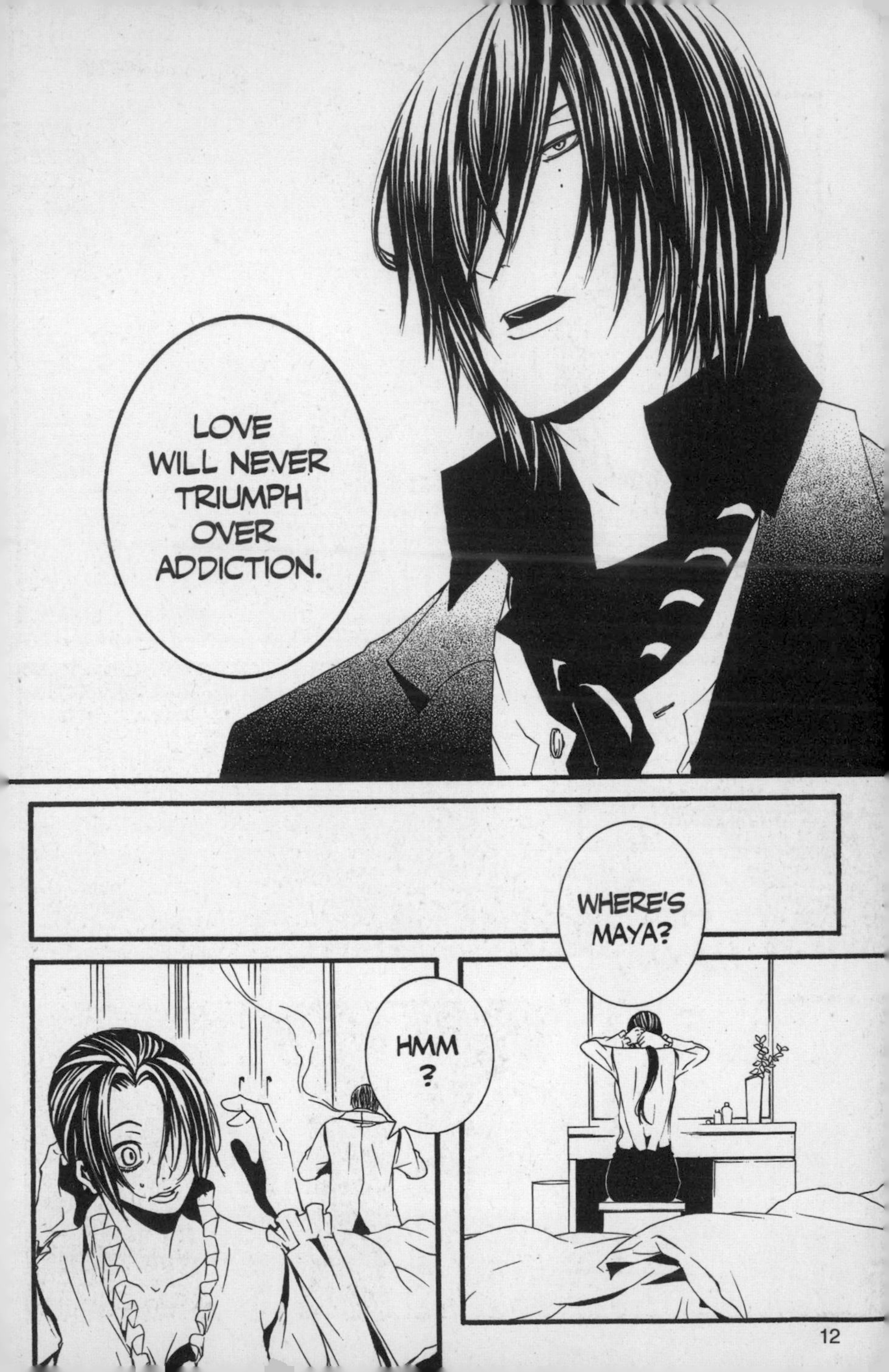
LOVE WILL NEVER TRIUMPH OVER ADDICTION.
WHERE'S MAYA?
HMM ?

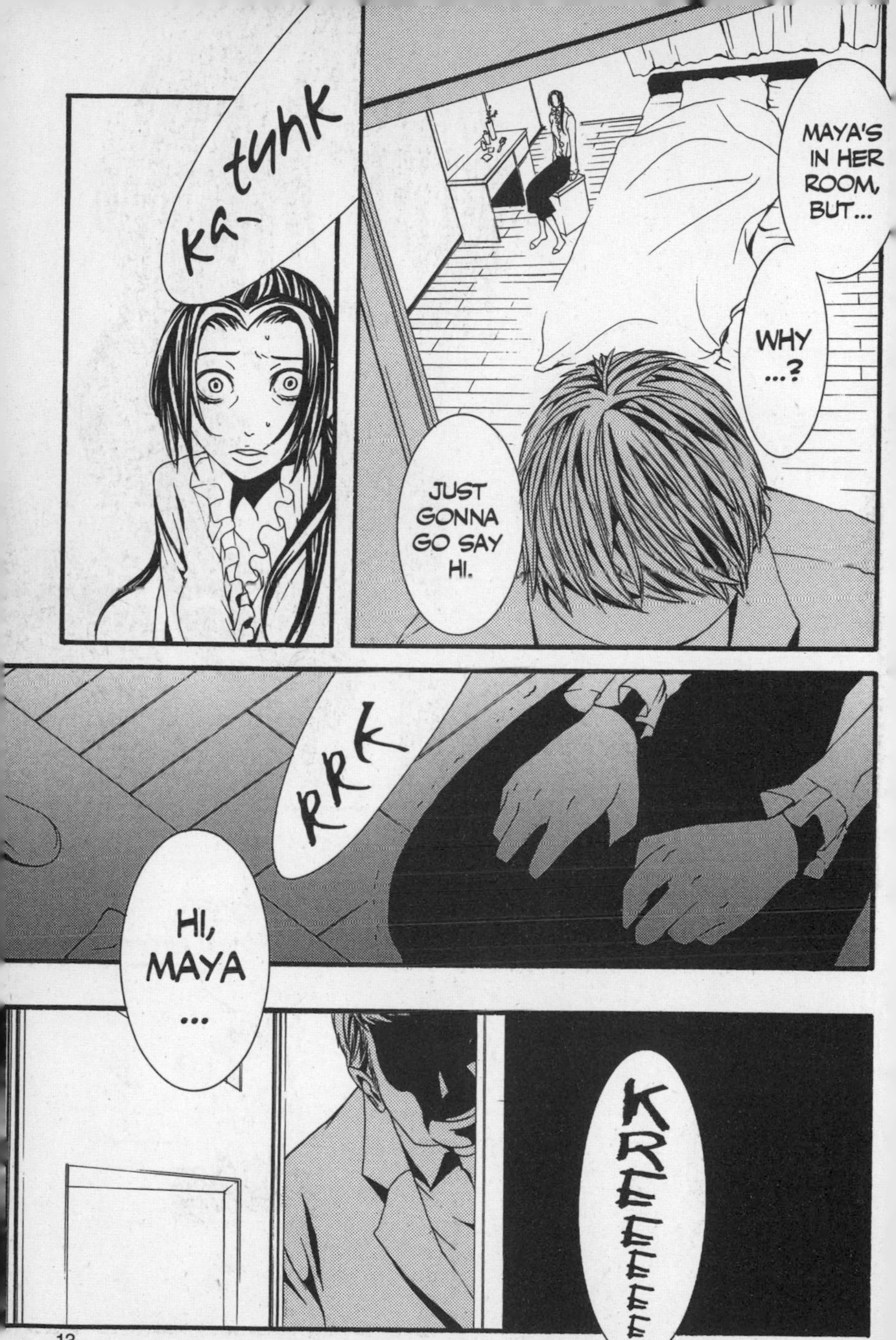
MAYA'S IN HER ROOM, BUT...
WHY ...?
JUST GONNA GO SAY HI.
KA-TUNK
RRK
HI, MAYA ...
KREEEEEE

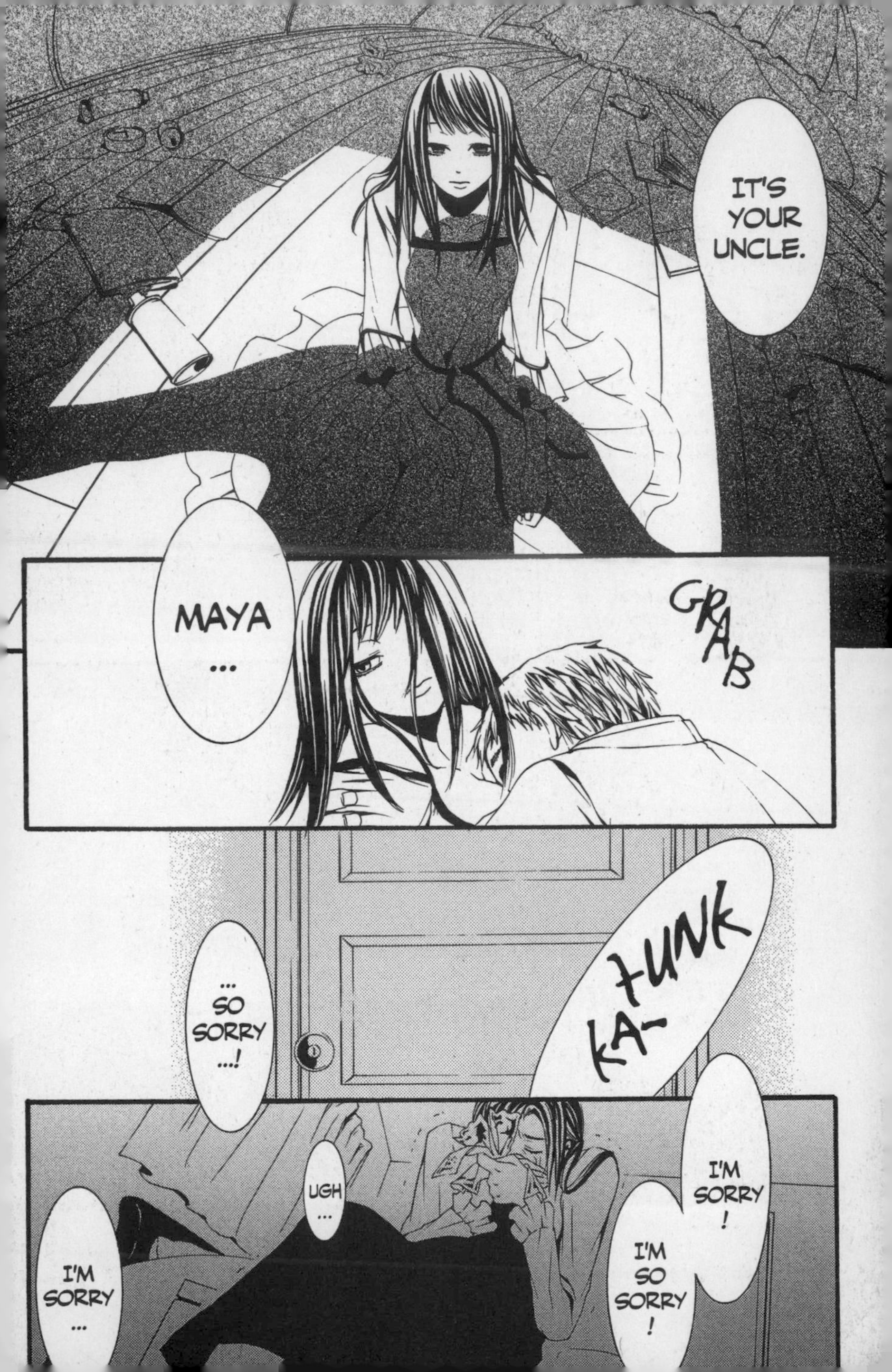
IT'S YOUR UNCLE.
GRAB
MAYA ...
KA-TUNK
... SO SORRY ...!
I'M SORRY!
I'M SO SORRY!
UGH ...
I'M SORRY ...

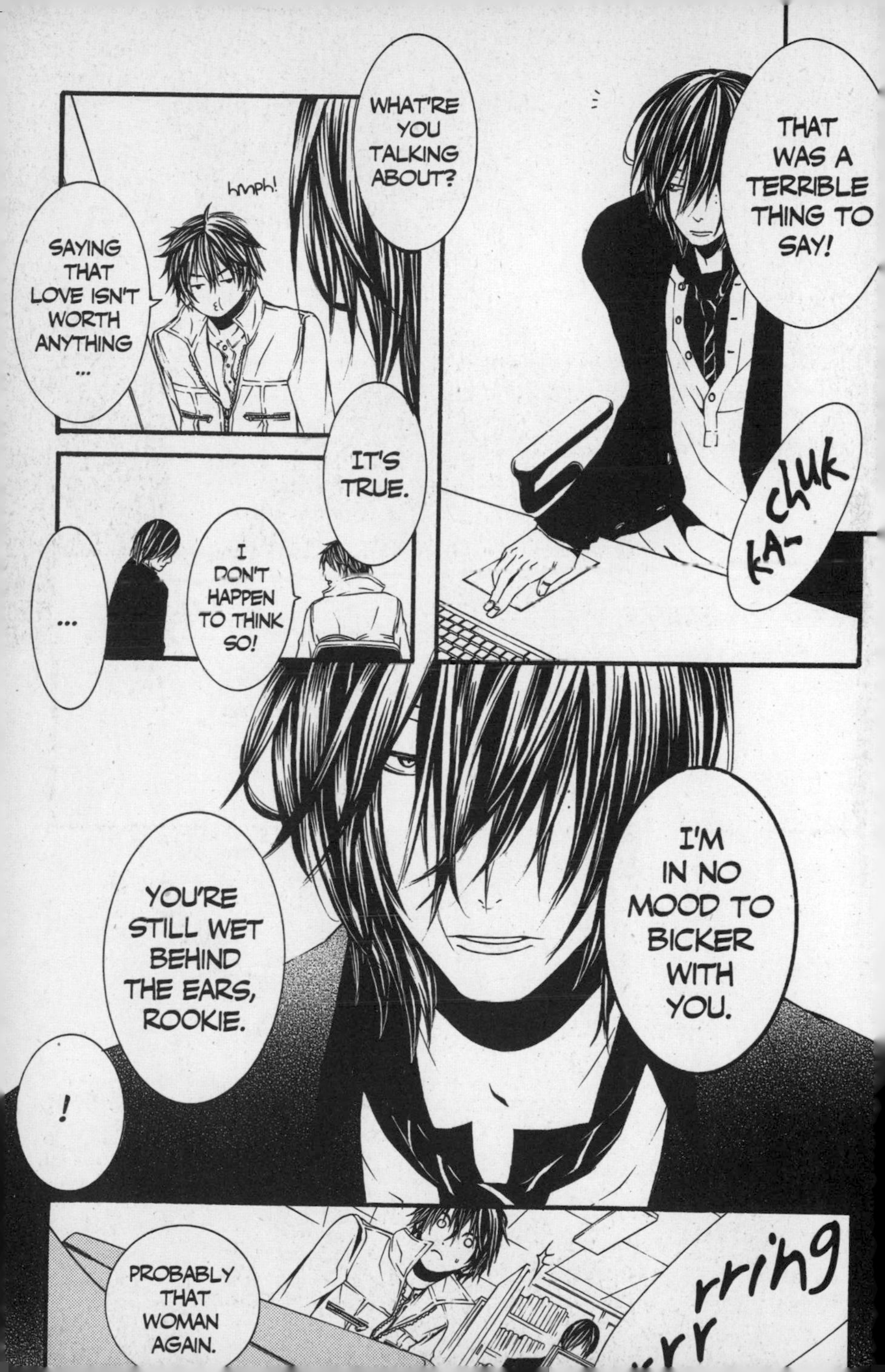

THAT WAS A TERRIBLE THING TO SAY!
KA-CHUK
WHAT'RE YOU TALKING ABOUT?
hmph!
SAYING THAT LOVE ISN'T WORTH ANYTHING ...
IT'S TRUE.
I DON'T HAPPEN TO THINK SO!
...
I'M IN NO MOOD TO BICKER WITH YOU.
YOU'RE STILL WET BEHIND THE EARS, ROOKIE.
!
rrring
rr
PROBABLY THAT WOMAN AGAIN.

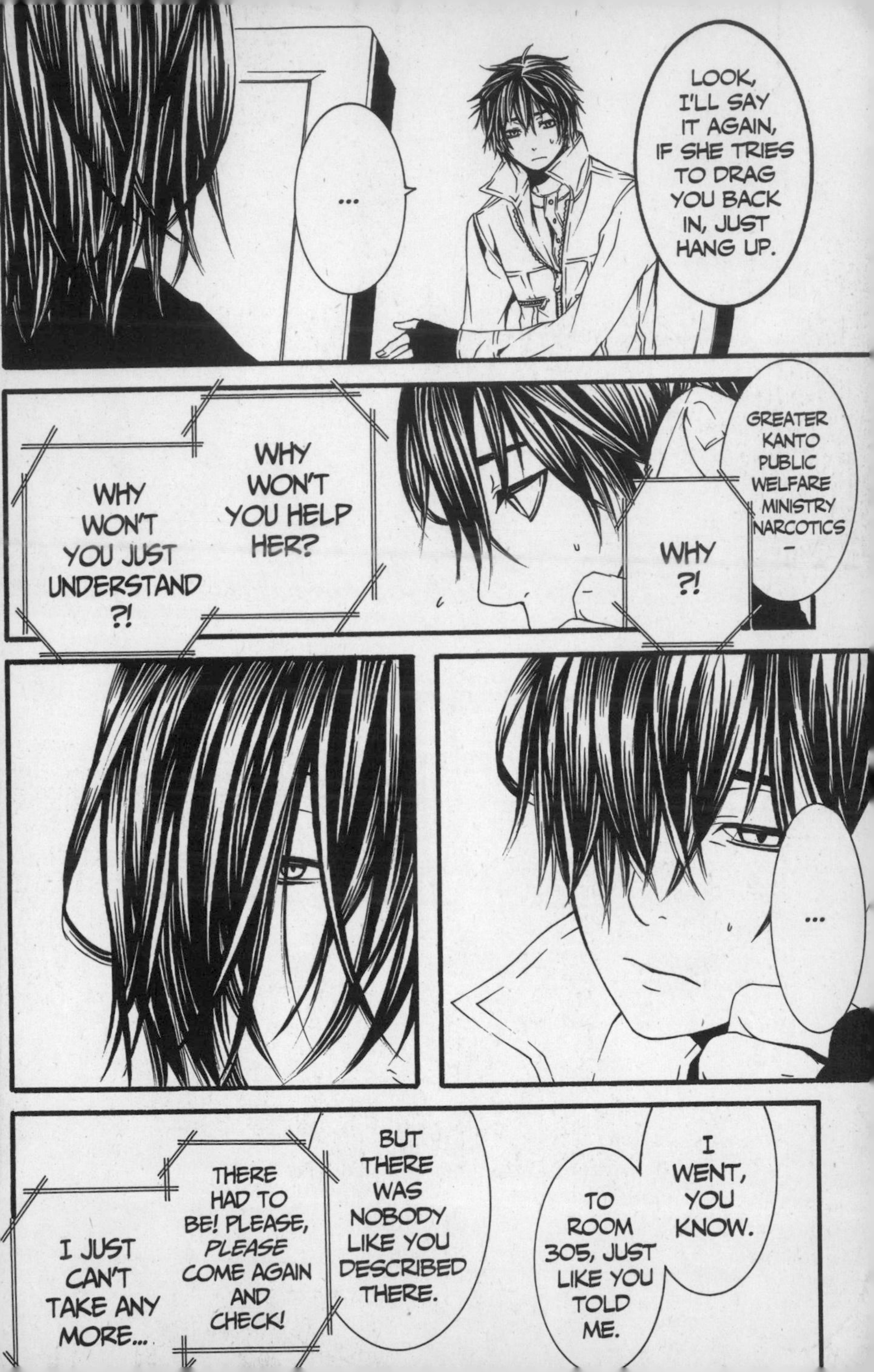
LOOK, I'LL SAY IT AGAIN, IF SHE TRIES TO DRAG YOU BACK IN, JUST HANG UP.
...
GREATER KANTO PUBLIC WELFARE MINISTRY NARCOTICS –
WHY ?!
WHY WON'T YOU HELP HER?
WHY WON'T YOU JUST UNDERSTAND ?!
...
I WENT, YOU KNOW.
TO ROOM 305, JUST LIKE YOU TOLD ME.
BUT THERE WAS NOBODY LIKE YOU DESCRIBED THERE.
THERE HAD TO BE! PLEASE, *PLEASE* COME AGAIN AND CHECK!
I JUST CAN'T TAKE ANY MORE...

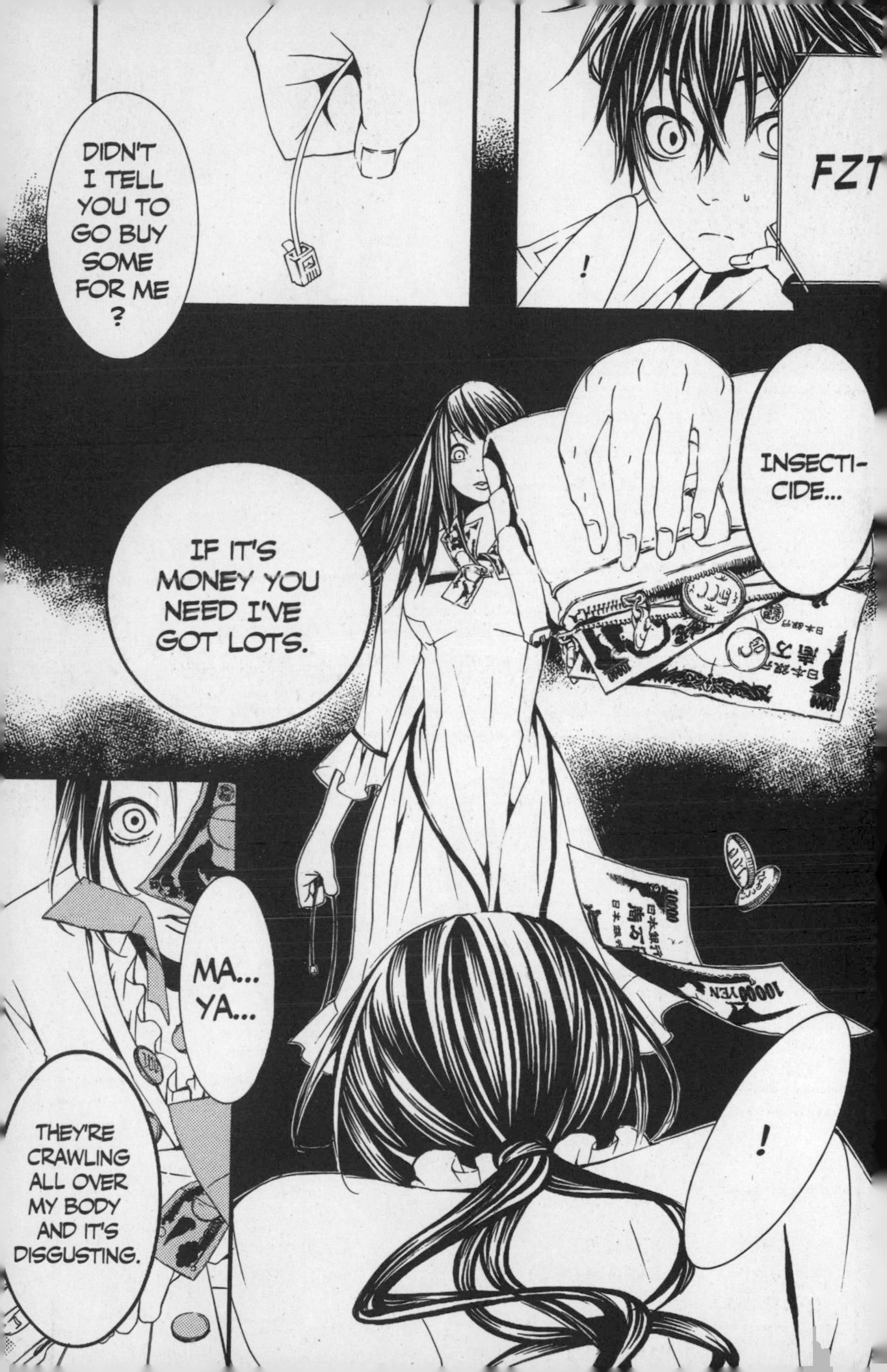
FZT
!
DIDN'T I TELL YOU TO GO BUY SOME FOR ME ?
INSECTI-CIDE...
IF IT'S MONEY YOU NEED I'VE GOT LOTS.
!
MA... YA...
THEY'RE CRAWLING ALL OVER MY BODY AND IT'S DISGUSTING.

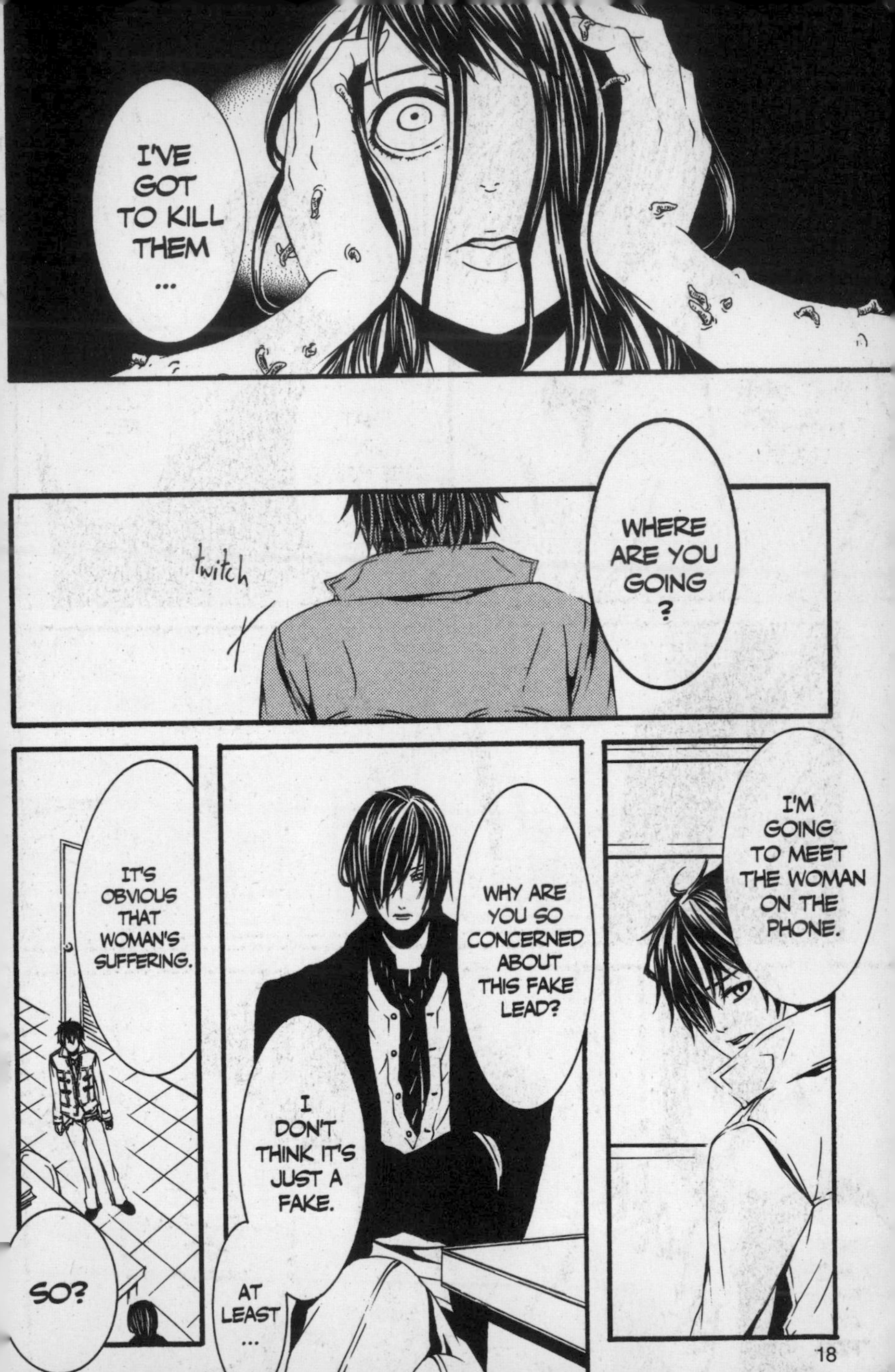
I'VE GOT TO KILL THEM ...
twitch
WHERE ARE YOU GOING ?
I'M GOING TO MEET THE WOMAN ON THE PHONE.
WHY ARE YOU SO CONCERNED ABOUT THIS FAKE LEAD?
I DON'T THINK IT'S JUST A FAKE.
AT LEAST ...
IT'S OBVIOUS THAT WOMAN'S SUFFERING.
SO?

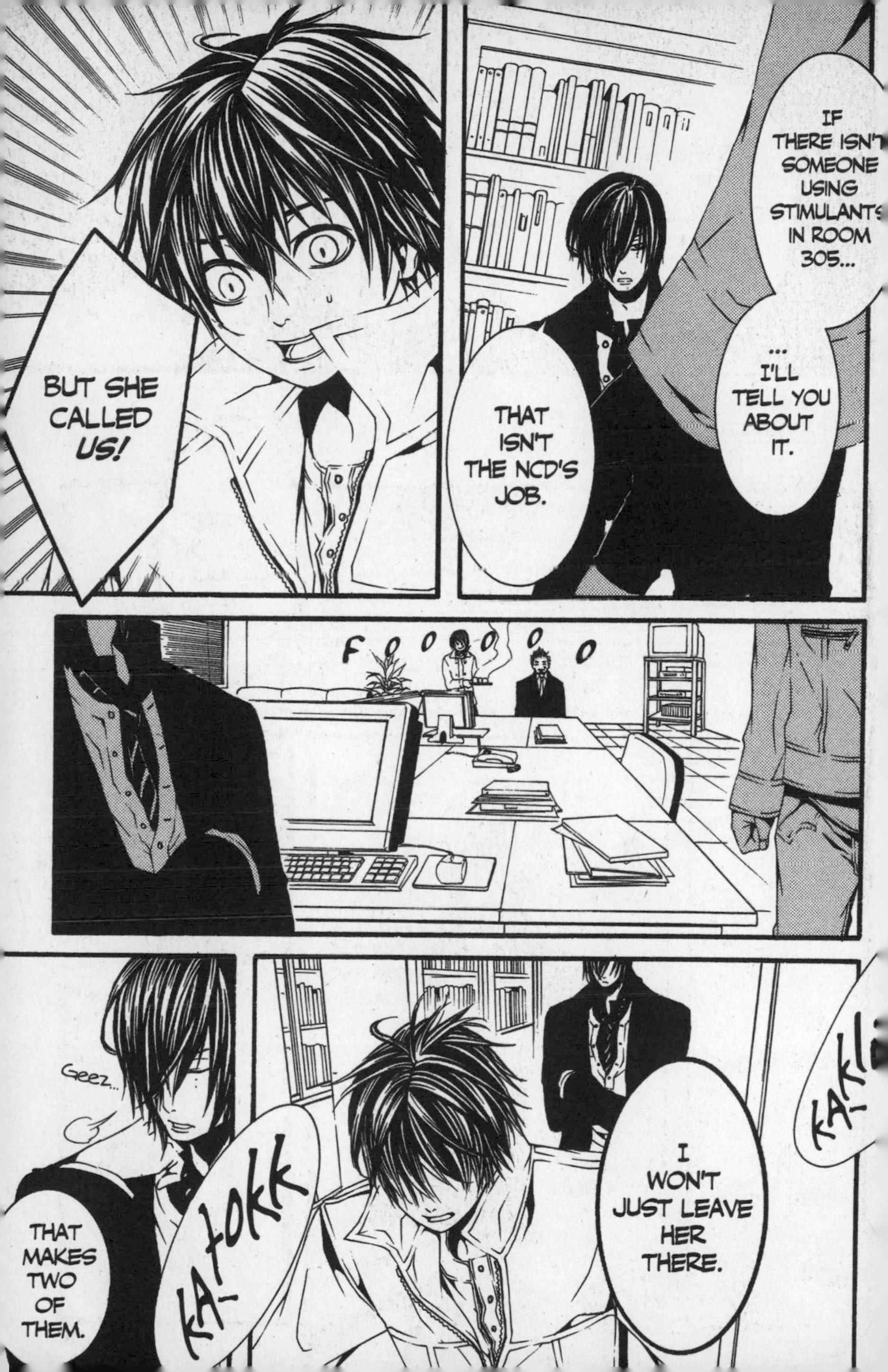
IF THERE ISN'T SOMEONE USING STIMULANTS IN ROOM 305...
...I'LL TELL YOU ABOUT IT.
THAT ISN'T THE NCD'S JOB.
BUT SHE CALLED US!
FOOOOOO
KA-KL
I WON'T JUST LEAVE HER THERE.
KA-TOKK
Geez...
THAT MAKES TWO OF THEM.

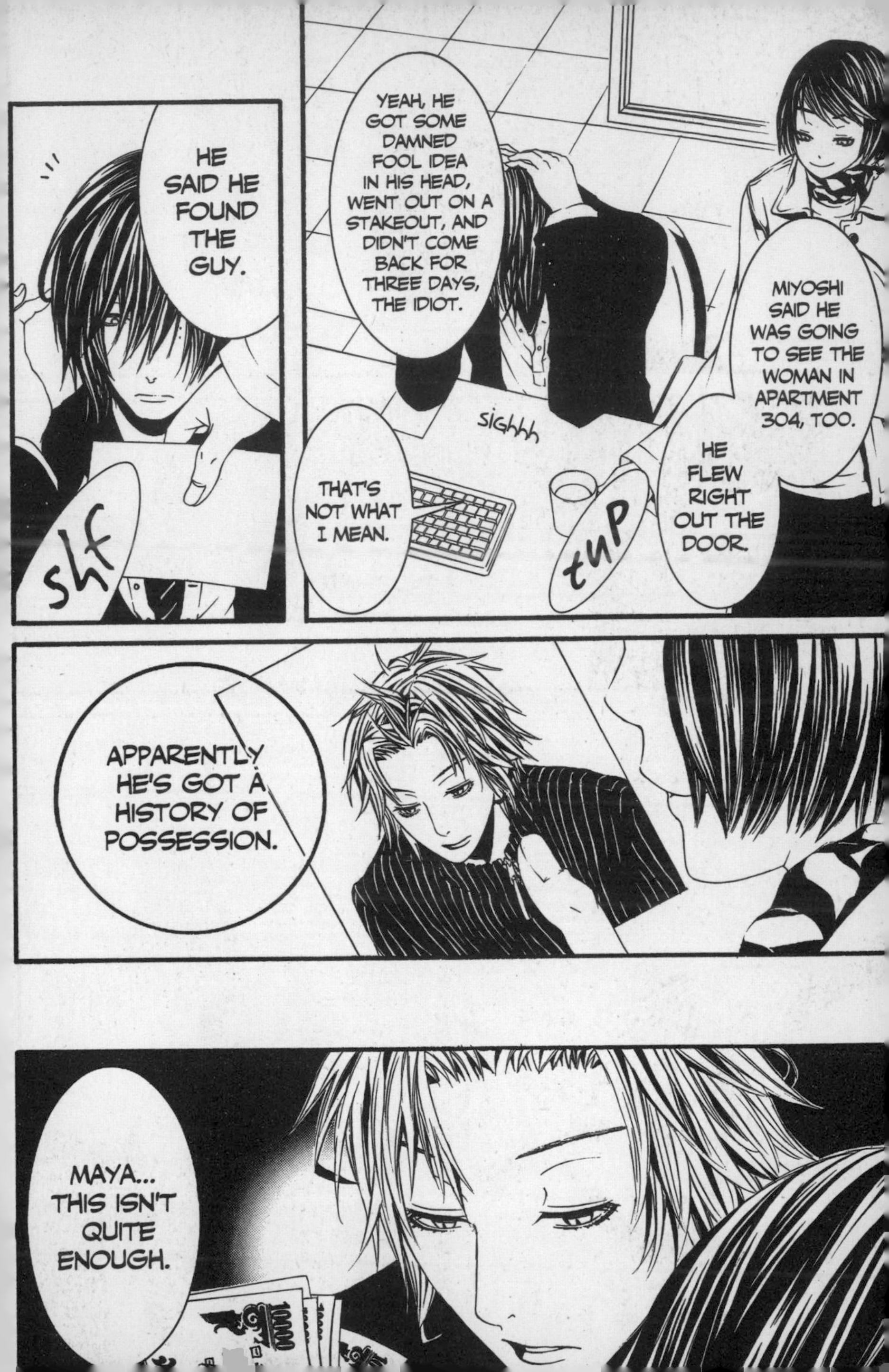
MIYOSHI SAID HE WAS GOING TO SEE THE WOMAN IN APARTMENT 304, TOO.
HE FLEW RIGHT OUT THE DOOR.
tup
YEAH, HE GOT SOME DAMNED FOOL IDEA IN HIS HEAD, WENT OUT ON A STAKEOUT, AND DIDN'T COME BACK FOR THREE DAYS, THE IDIOT.
sighhh
THAT'S NOT WHAT I MEAN.
HE SAID HE FOUND THE GUY.
shf
APPARENTLY HE'S GOT A HISTORY OF POSSESSION.
MAYA... THIS ISN'T QUITE ENOUGH.

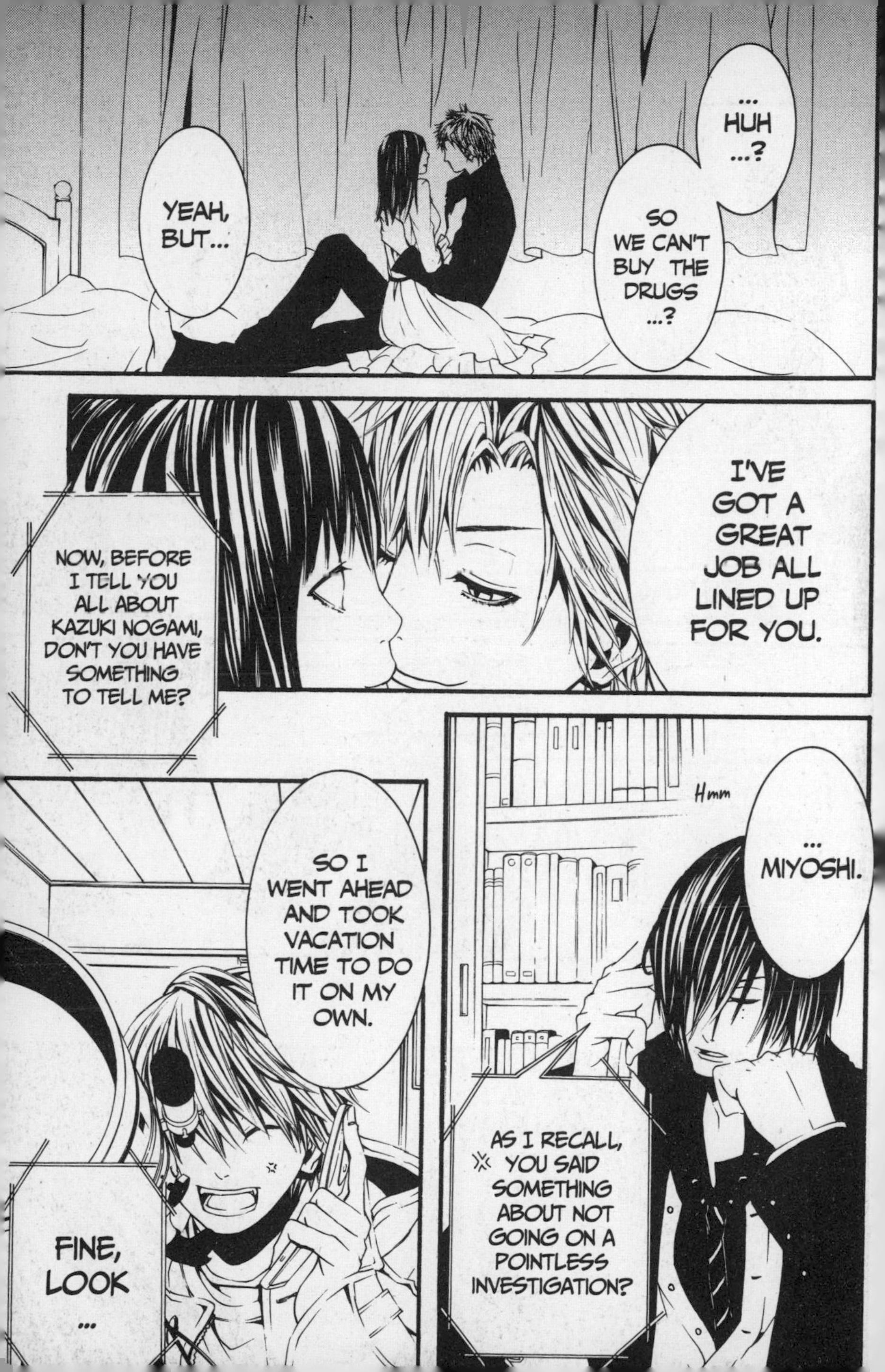
... HUH ...?
SO WE CAN'T BUY THE DRUGS ...?
YEAH, BUT...
I'VE GOT A GREAT JOB ALL LINED UP FOR YOU.
NOW, BEFORE I TELL YOU ALL ABOUT KAZUKI NOGAMI, DON'T YOU HAVE SOMETHING TO TELL ME?
Hmm
... MIYOSHI.
AS I RECALL, YOU SAID SOMETHING ABOUT NOT GOING ON A POINTLESS INVESTIGATION?
SO I WENT AHEAD AND TOOK VACATION TIME TO DO IT ON MY OWN.
FINE, LOOK ...

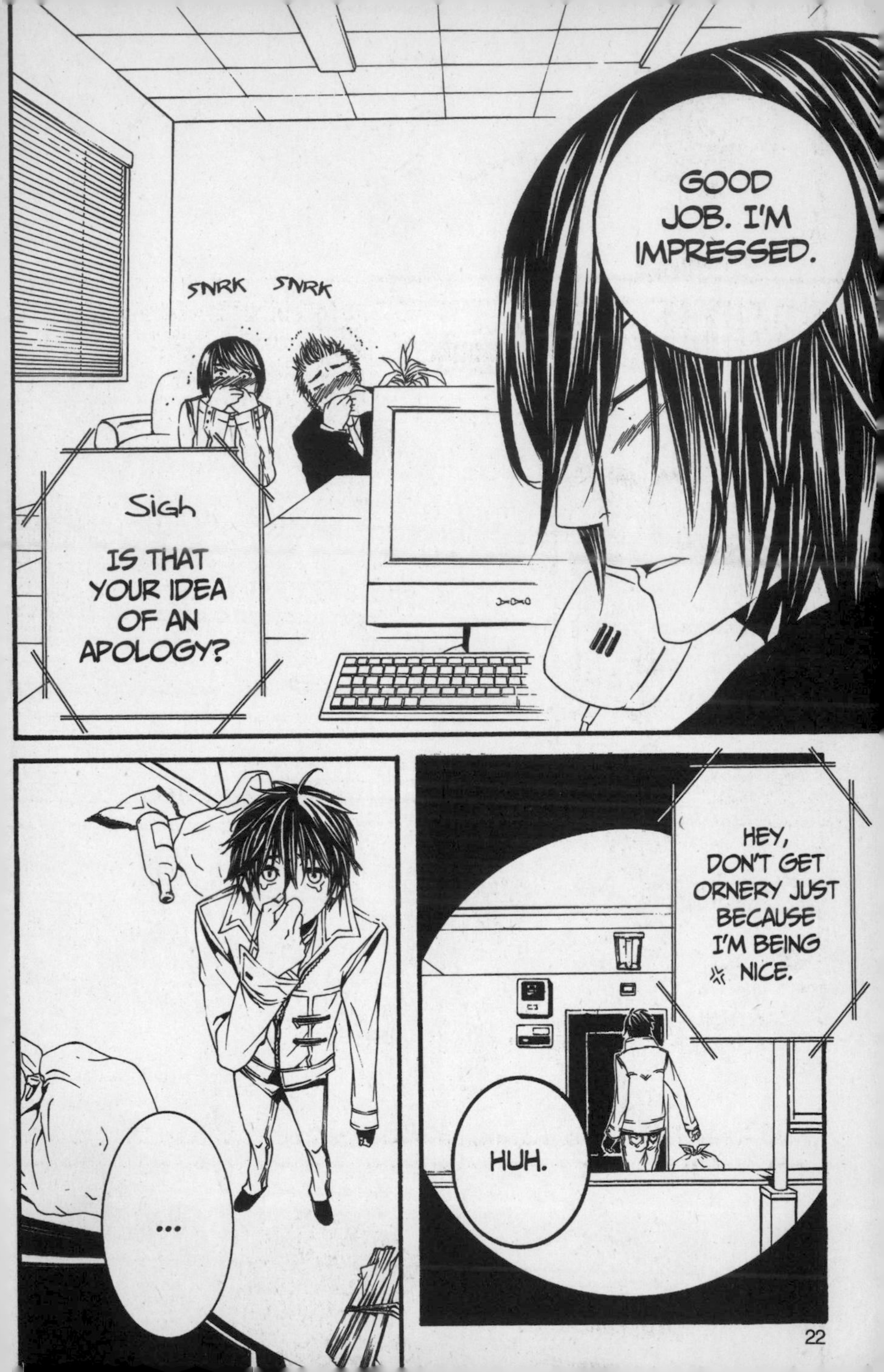
GOOD JOB. I'M IMPRESSED.
SNRK SNRK
Sigh
IS THAT YOUR IDEA OF AN APOLOGY?
HEY, DON'T GET ORNERY JUST BECAUSE I'M BEING NICE.
HUH.
...

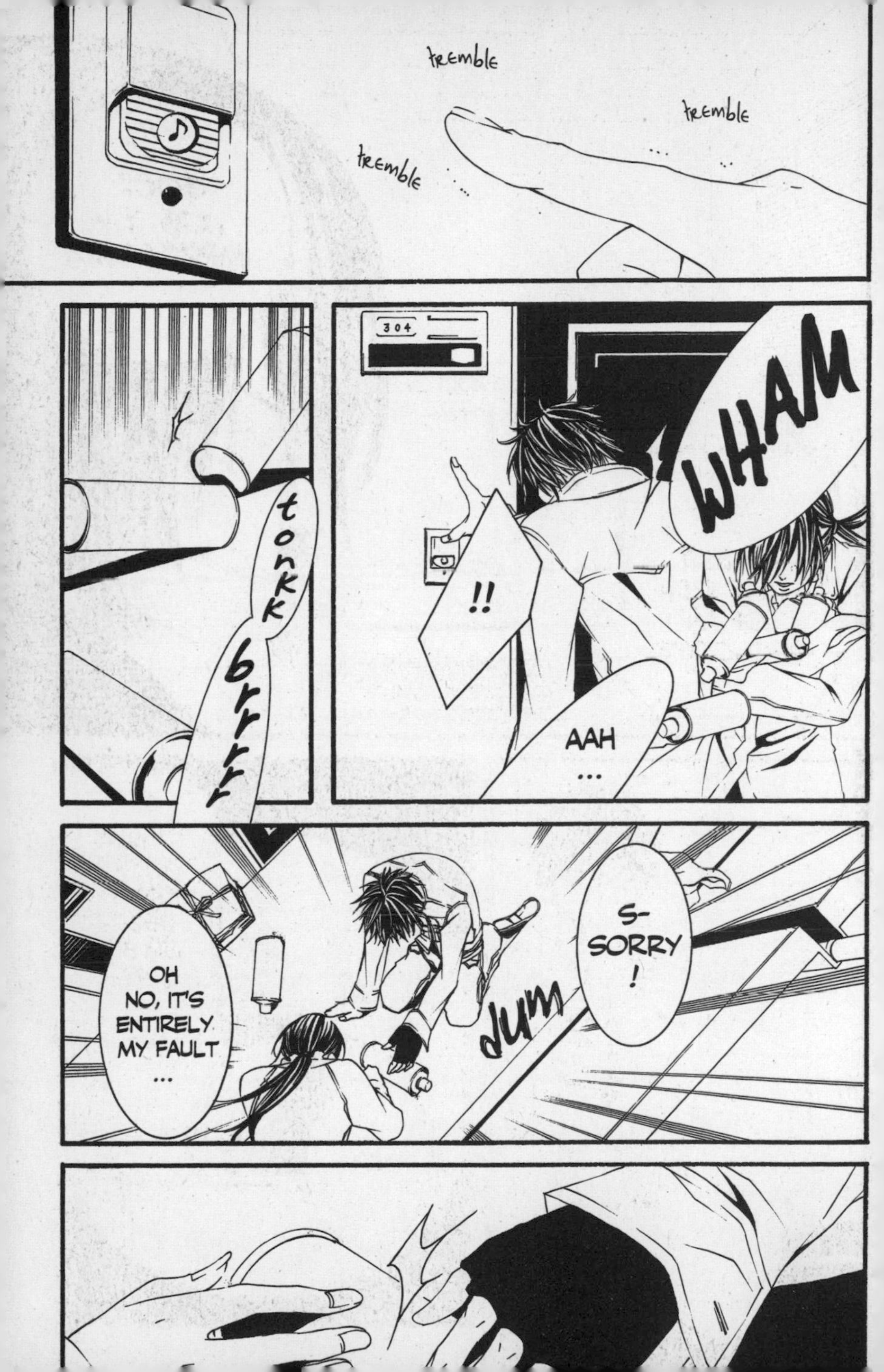
tremble
tremble
tremble
WHAM
!!
AAH ...
tonkk
brrrrr
S-SORRY!
dum
OH NO, IT'S ENTIRELY MY FAULT ...

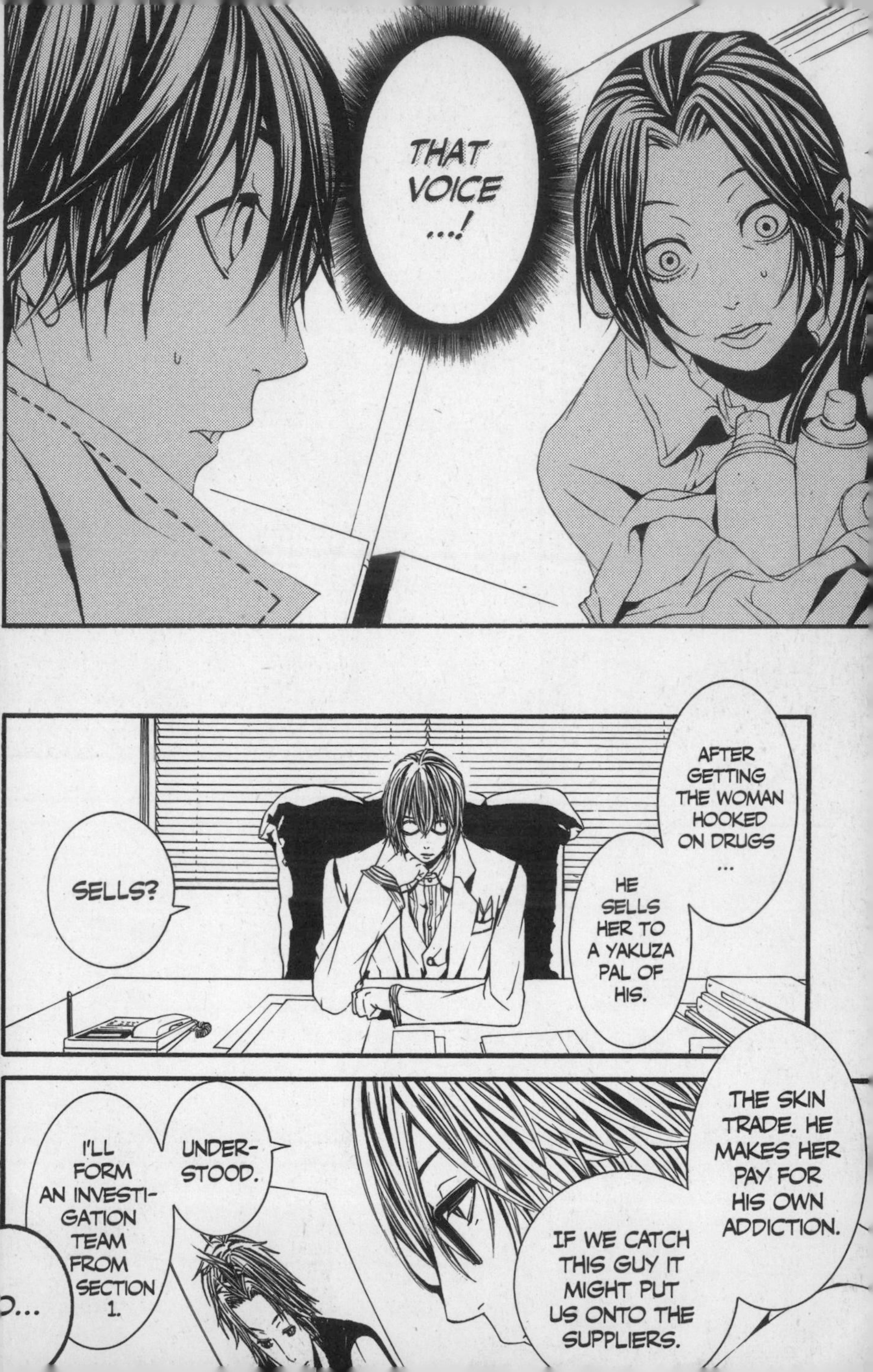
THAT VOICE ...!
AFTER GETTING THE WOMAN HOOKED ON DRUGS ...
HE SELLS HER TO A YAKUZA PAL OF HIS.
SELLS?
THE SKIN TRADE. HE MAKES HER PAY FOR HIS OWN ADDICTION.
IF WE CATCH THIS GUY IT MIGHT PUT US ONTO THE SUPPLIERS.
UNDERSTOOD.
I'LL FORM AN INVESTIGATION TEAM FROM SECTION 1.

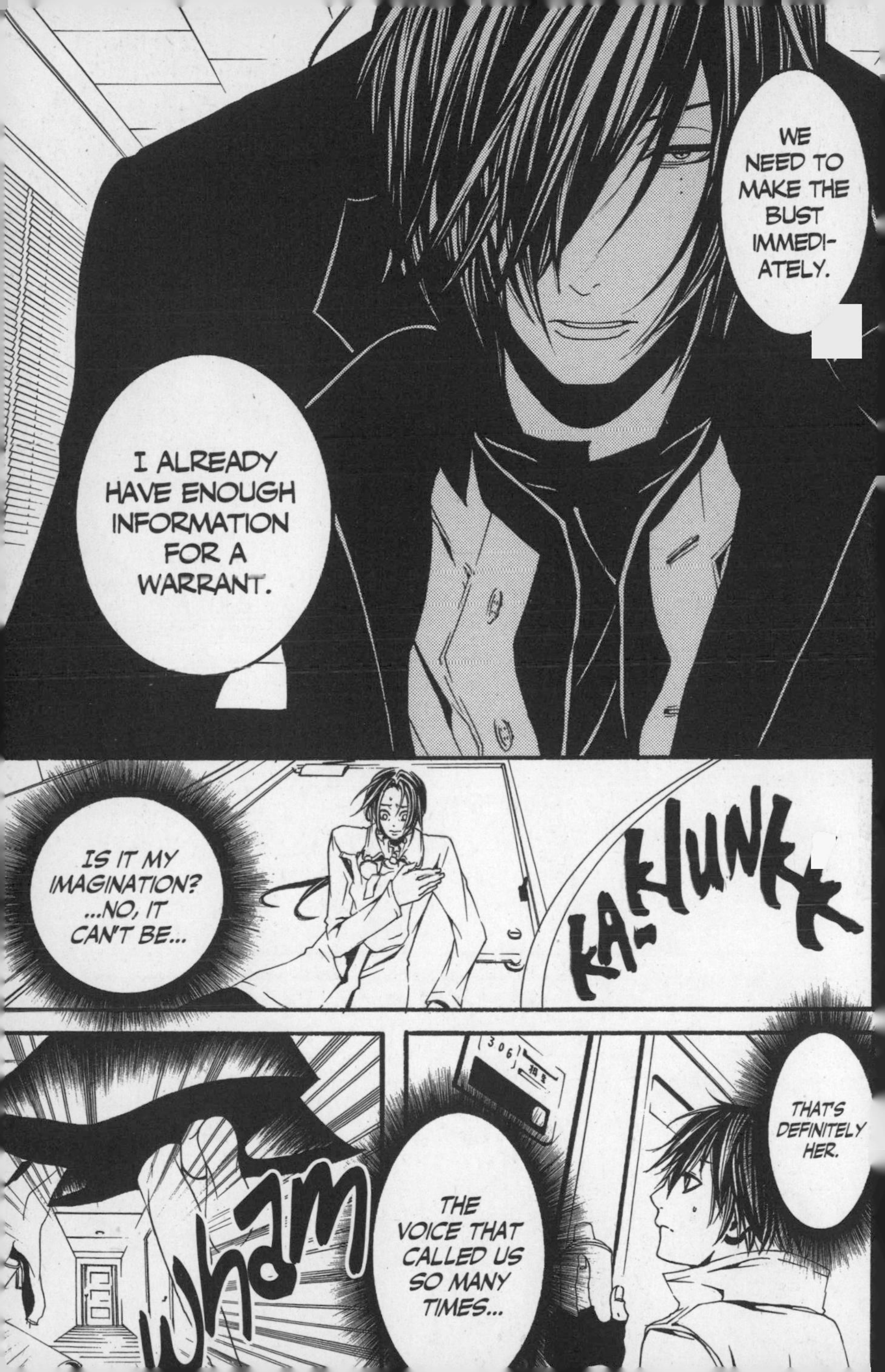
WE NEED TO MAKE THE BUST IMMEDI-ATELY.
I ALREADY HAVE ENOUGH INFORMATION FOR A WARRANT.
KA-KLUNK
IS IT MY IMAGINATION? ...NO, IT CAN'T BE...
306
THAT'S DEFINITELY HER.
THE VOICE THAT CALLED US SO MANY TIMES...
WHAM

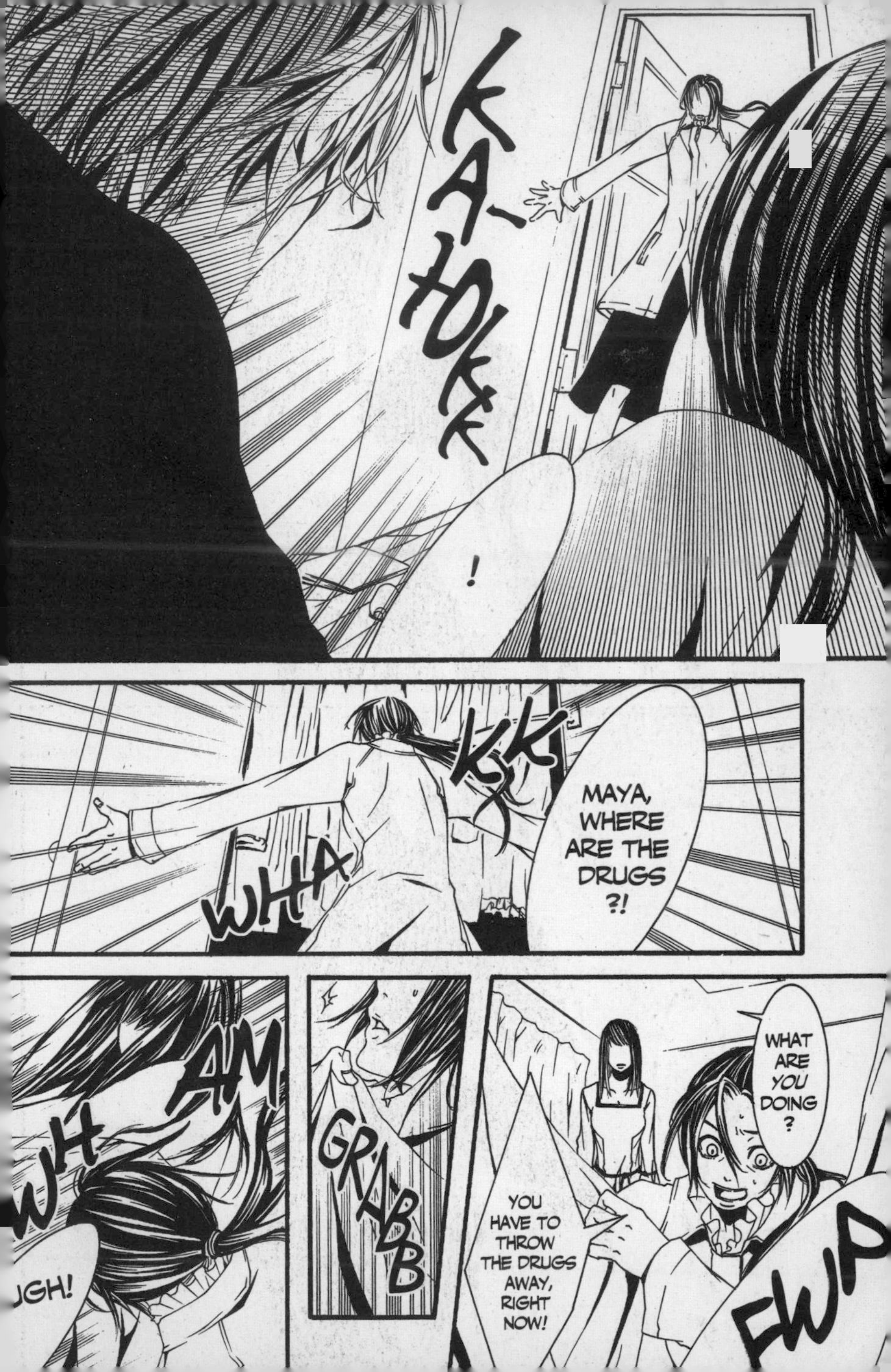
KA-THOKKK
!
MAYA, WHERE ARE THE DRUGS ?!
KK
WHA
WHAT ARE YOU DOING ?
YOU HAVE TO THROW THE DRUGS AWAY, RIGHT NOW!
FWA
GRABB
AM
WH
UGH!

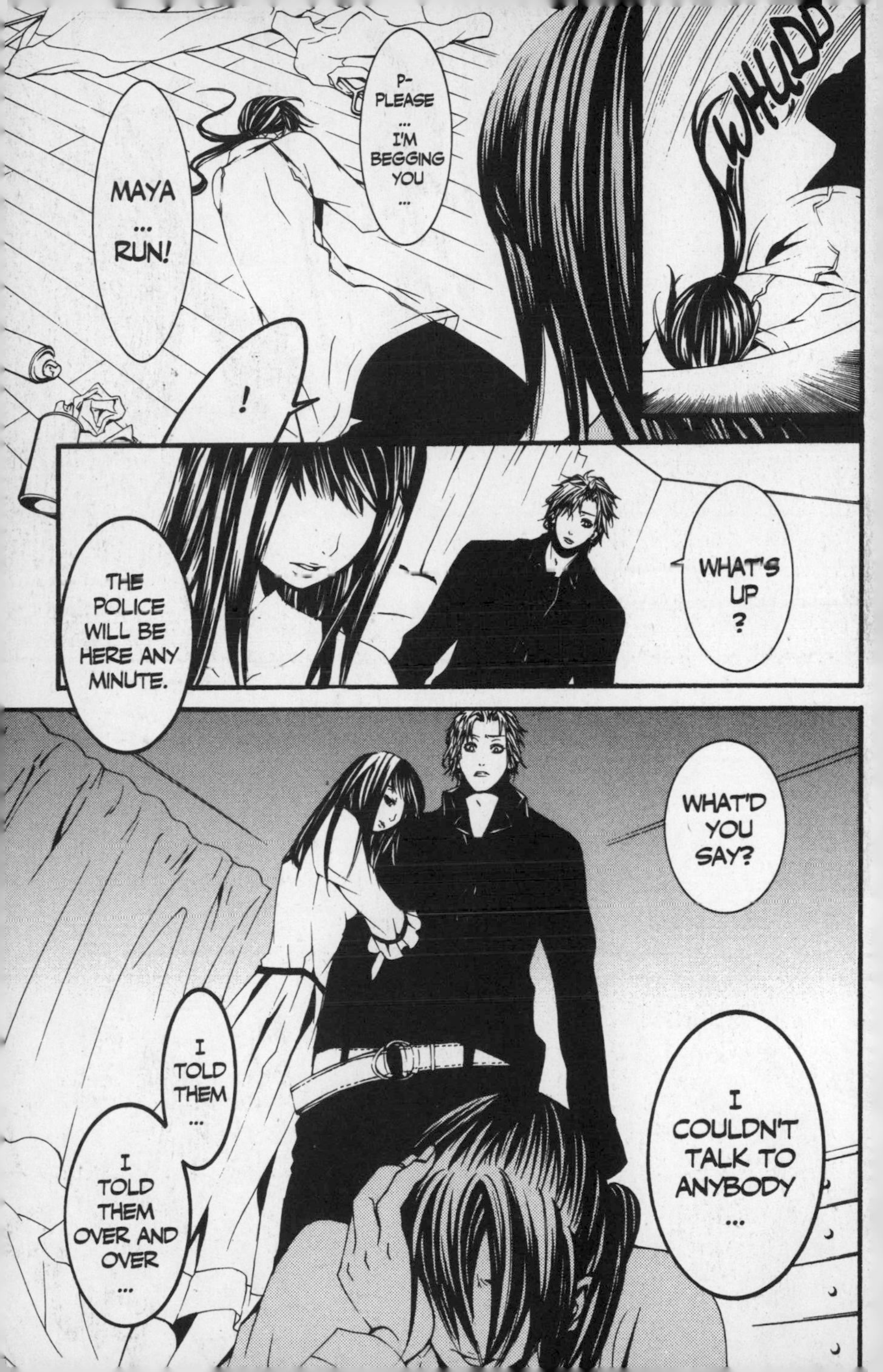
WHUDD
P-PLEASE ... I'M BEGGING YOU ...
MAYA ... RUN!
!
WHAT'S UP?
THE POLICE WILL BE HERE ANY MINUTE.
WHAT'D YOU SAY?
I COULDN'T TALK TO ANYBODY ...
I TOLD THEM ...
I TOLD THEM OVER AND OVER ...

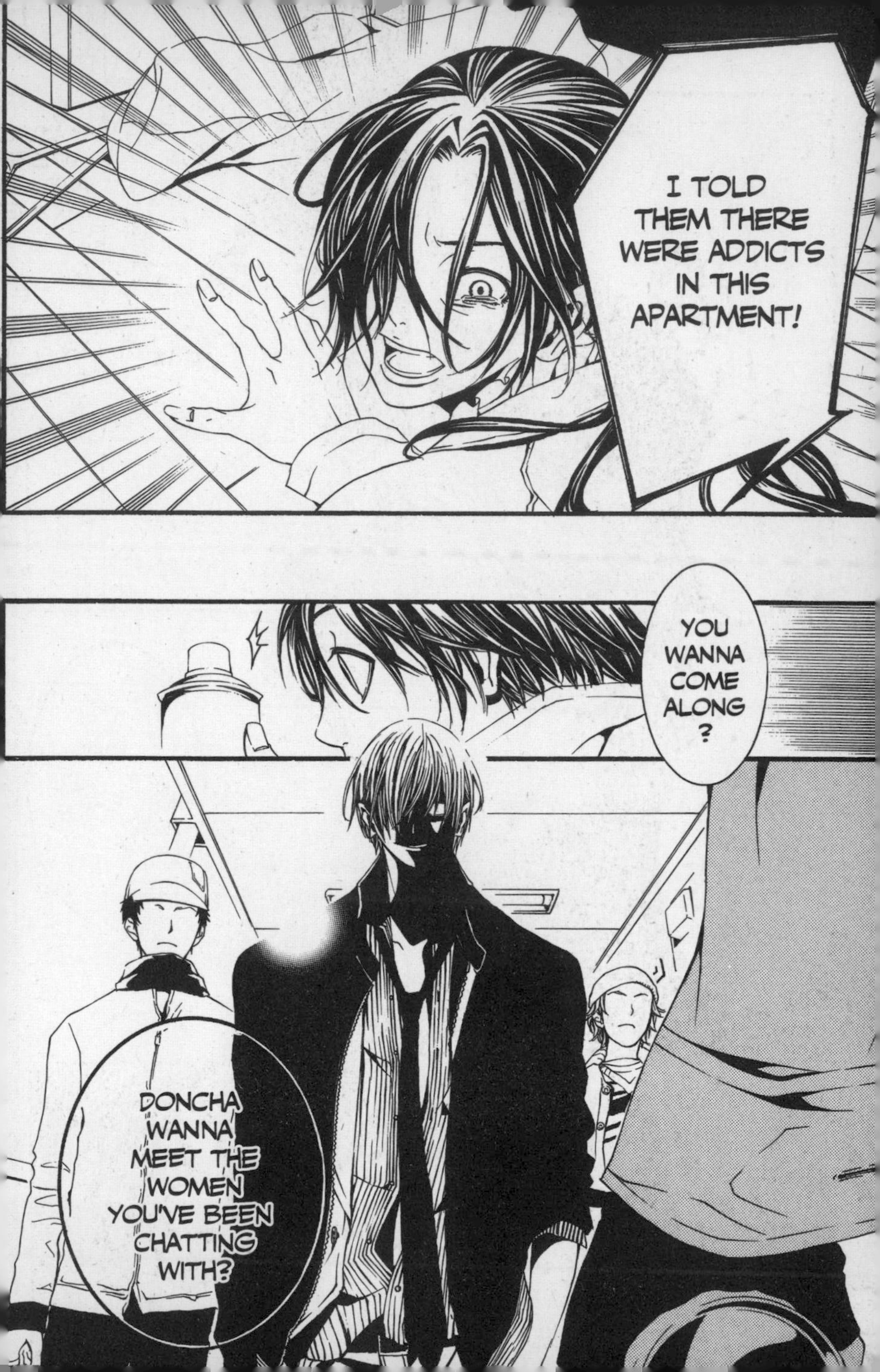
I TOLD THEM THERE WERE ADDICTS IN THIS APARTMENT!
YOU WANNA COME ALONG?
DONCHA WANNA MEET THE WOMEN YOU'VE BEEN CHATTING WITH?

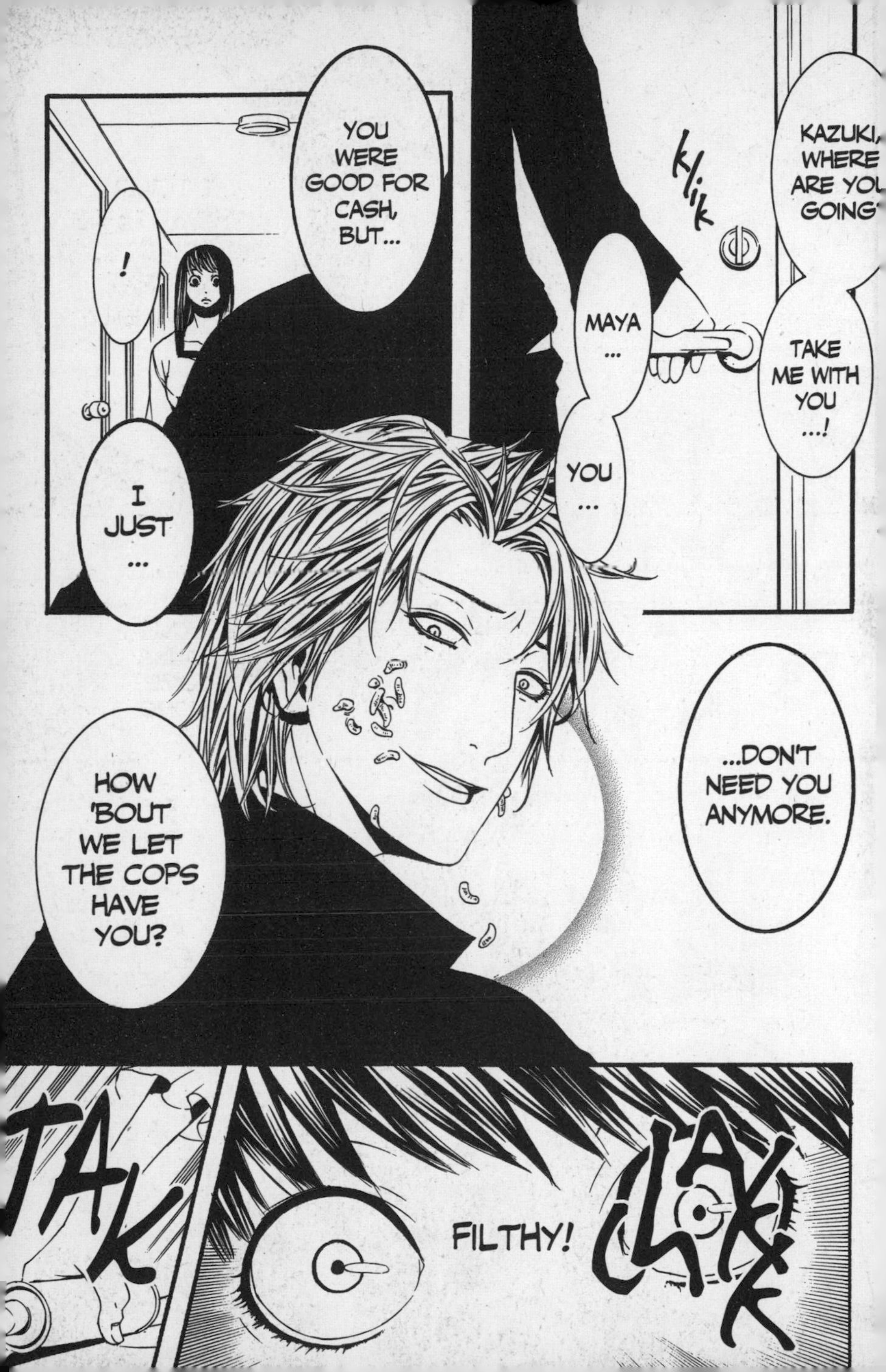
KAZUKI, WHERE ARE YOU GOING?
klik
TAKE ME WITH YOU ...!
MAYA ...
YOU ...
YOU WERE GOOD FOR CASH, BUT...
!
I JUST ...
...DON'T NEED YOU ANYMORE.
HOW 'BOUT WE LET THE COPS HAVE YOU?
CLAK
FILTHY!
TAK

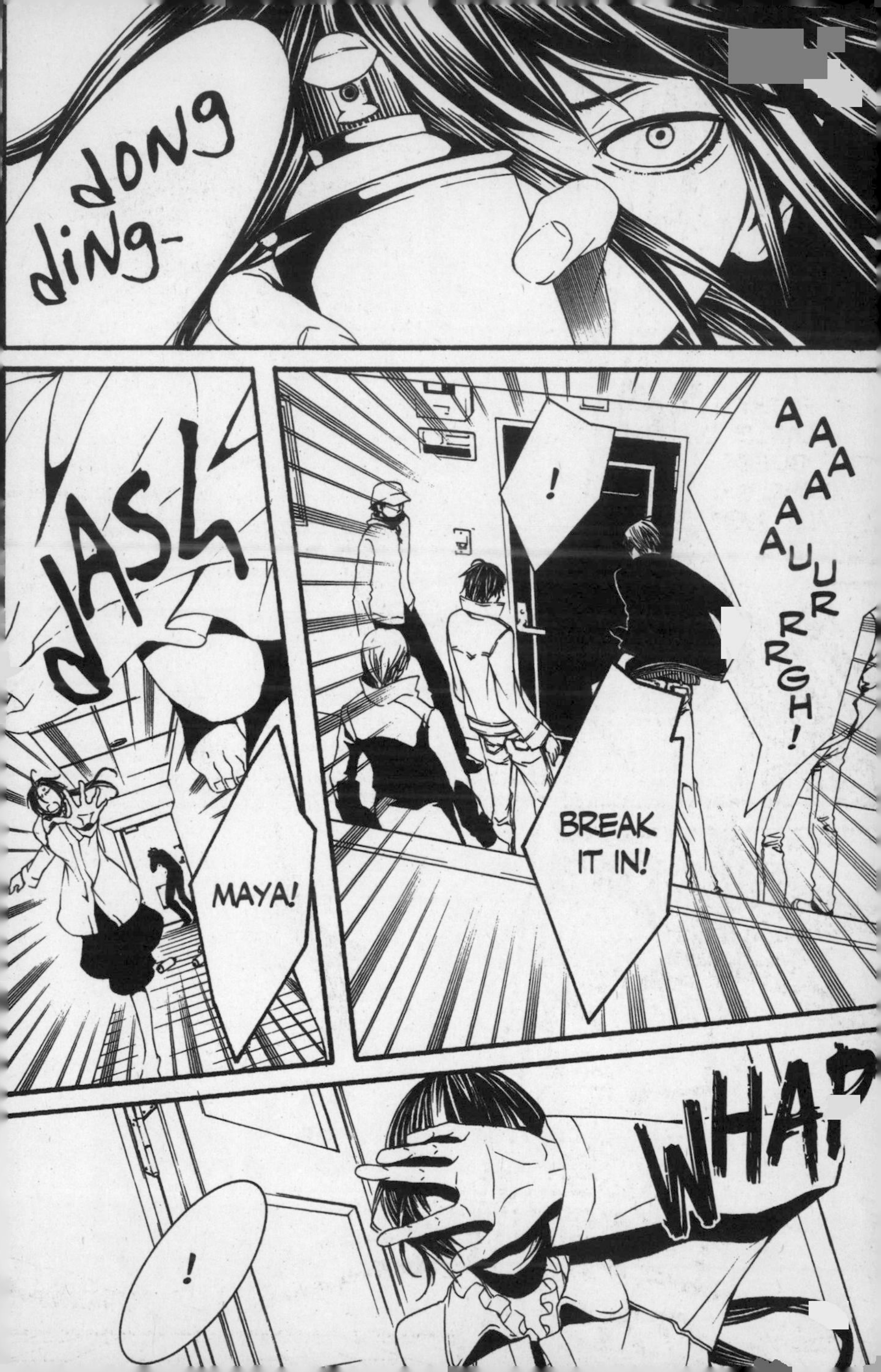
ding-dong
AAAAAAUURRRGH!
!
BREAK IT IN!
DASH
MAYA!
WHA?
!

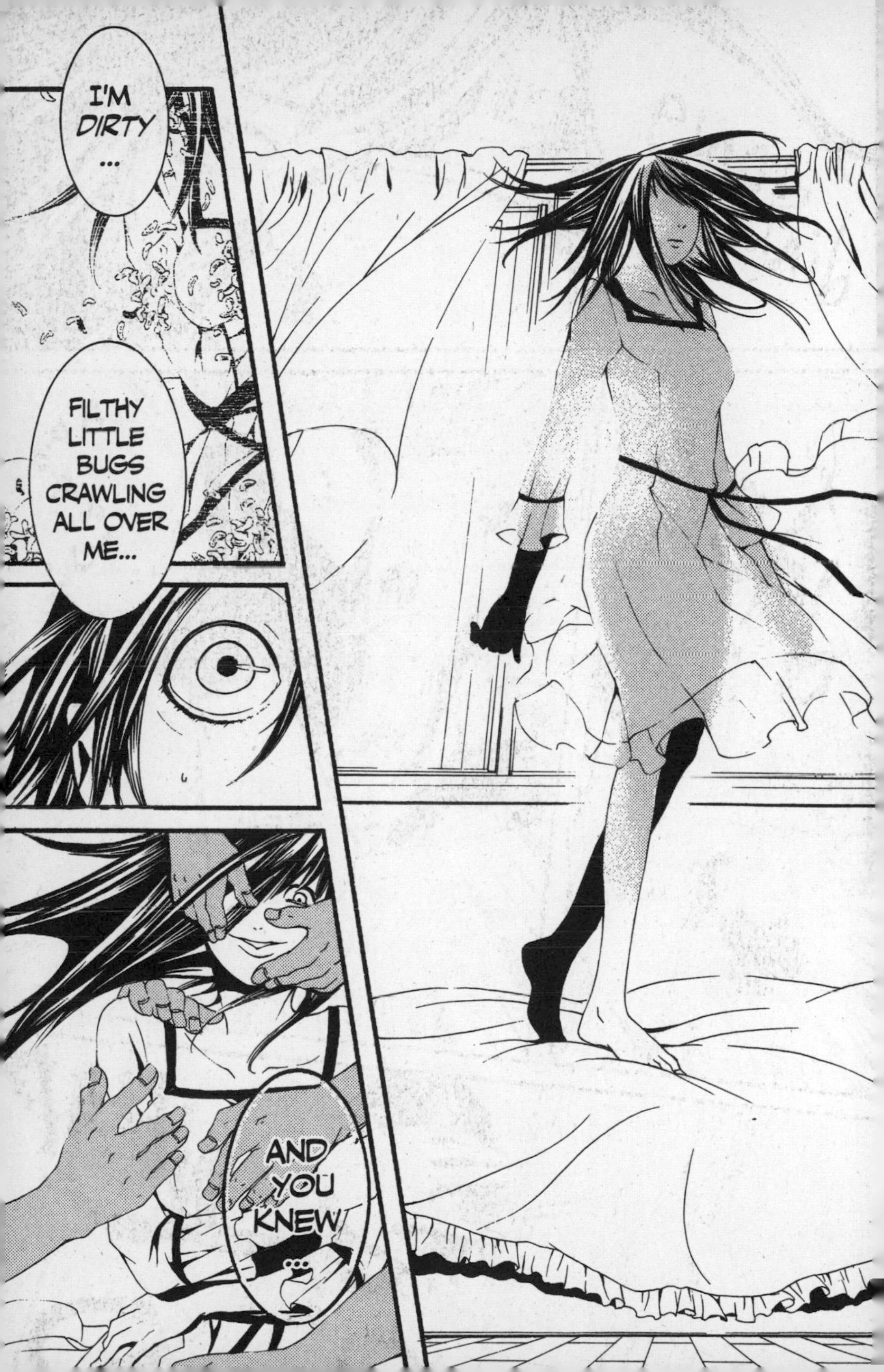
I'M *DIRTY* ...
FILTHY LITTLE BUGS CRAWLING ALL OVER ME...
AND YOU KNEW ...

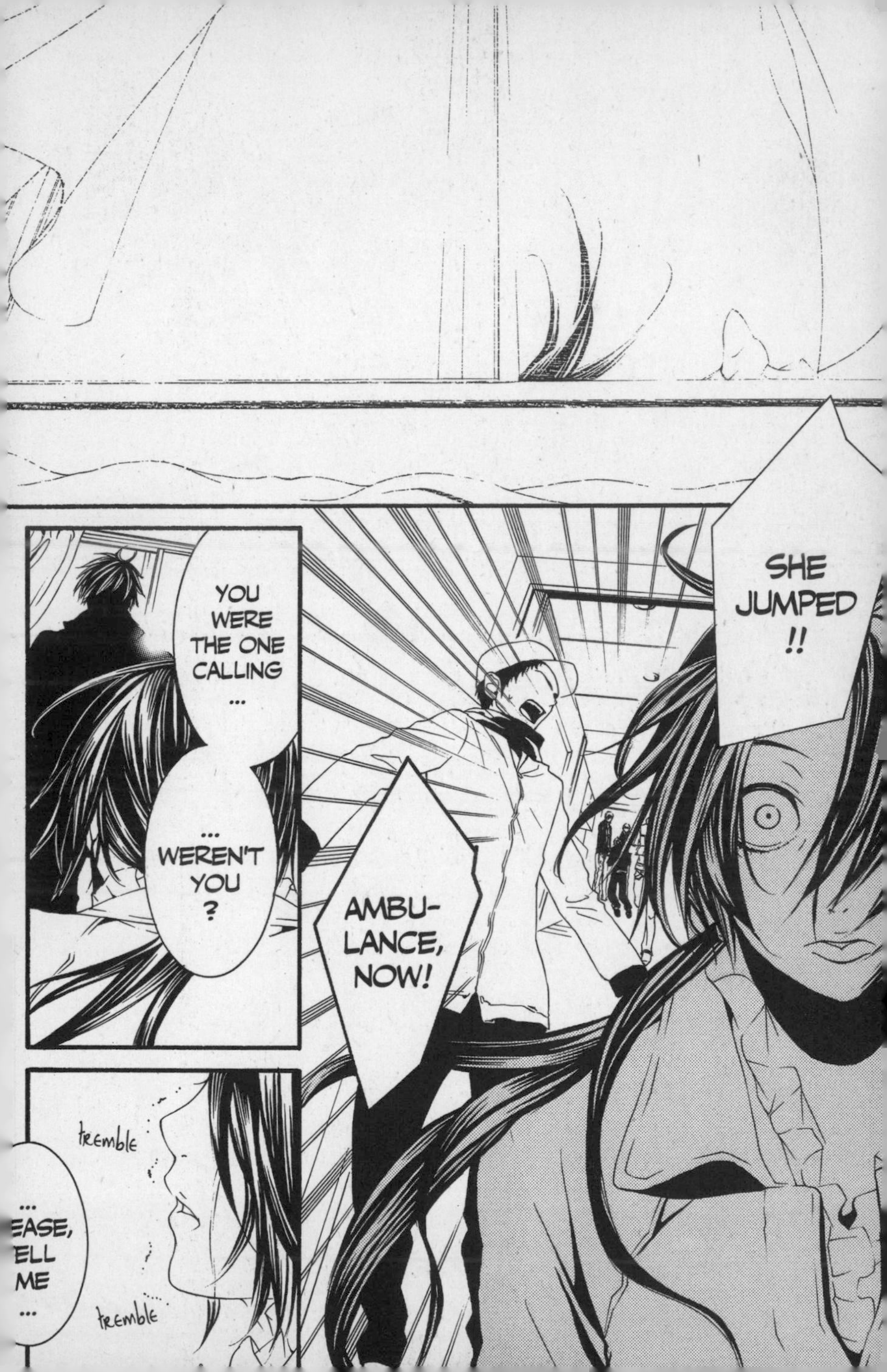
SHE JUMPED !!
AMBU-LANCE, NOW!
YOU WERE THE ONE CALLING ...
... WEREN'T YOU ?
tremble
... EASE, ELL ME ...
tremble

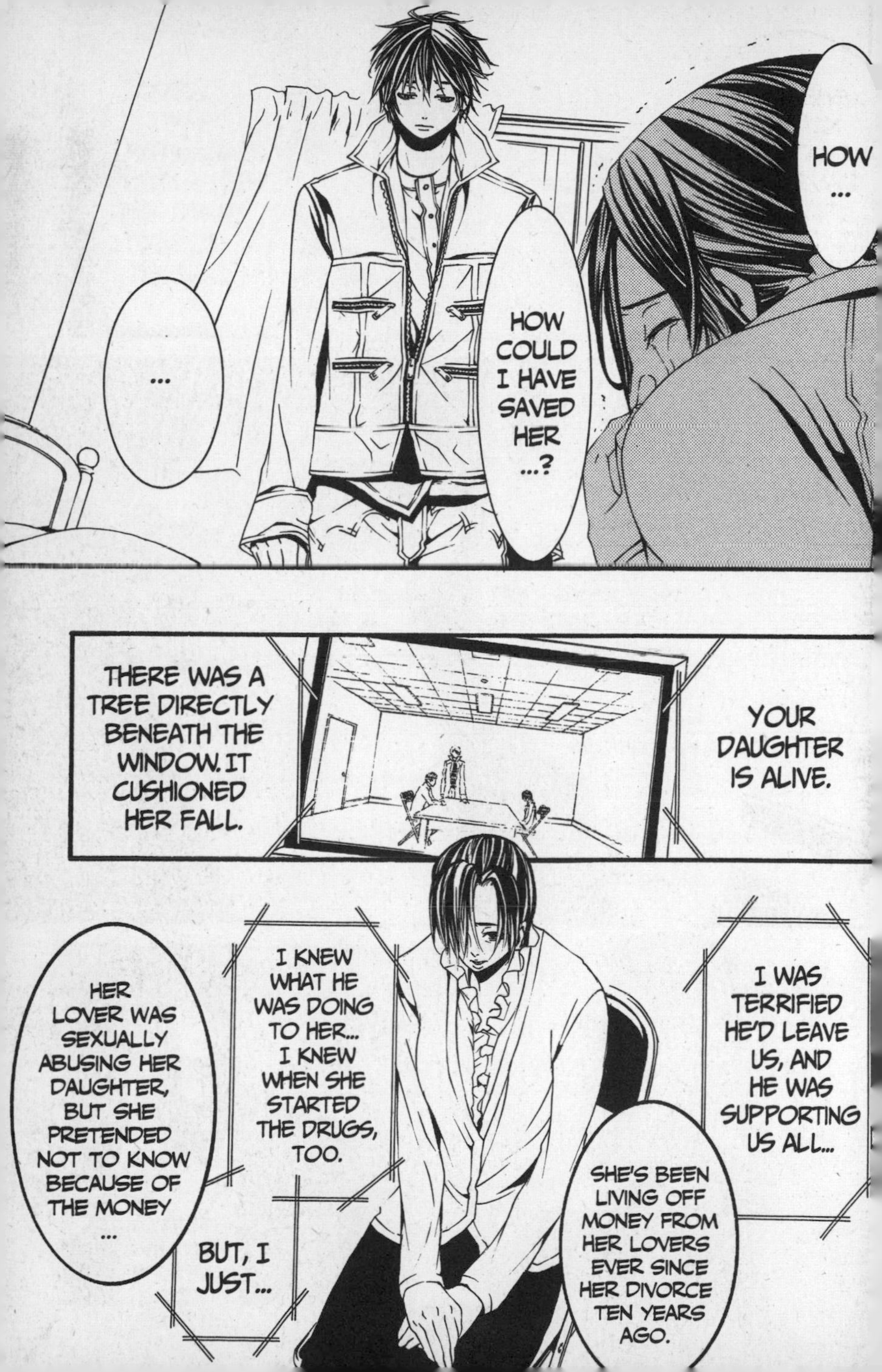
HOW ...
HOW COULD I HAVE SAVED HER ...?
...
YOUR DAUGHTER IS ALIVE.
THERE WAS A TREE DIRECTLY BENEATH THE WINDOW. IT CUSHIONED HER FALL.
I WAS TERRIFIED HE'D LEAVE US, AND HE WAS SUPPORTING US ALL...
SHE'S BEEN LIVING OFF MONEY FROM HER LOVERS EVER SINCE HER DIVORCE TEN YEARS AGO.
I KNEW WHAT HE WAS DOING TO HER... I KNEW WHEN SHE STARTED THE DRUGS, TOO.
BUT, I JUST...
HER LOVER WAS SEXUALLY ABUSING HER DAUGHTER, BUT SHE PRETENDED NOT TO KNOW BECAUSE OF THE MONEY ...

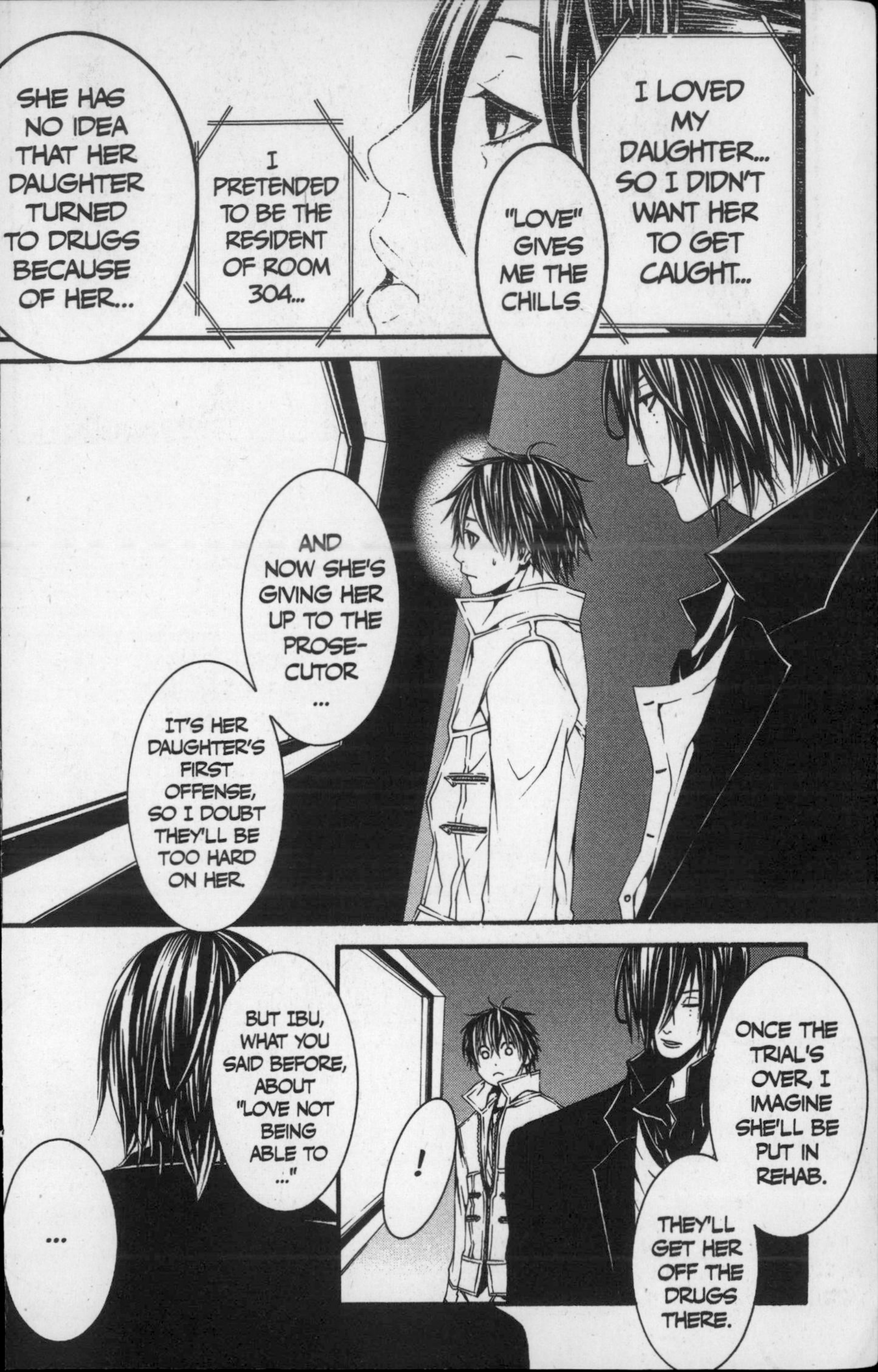
I LOVED MY DAUGHTER... SO I DIDN'T WANT HER TO GET CAUGHT...
"LOVE" GIVES ME THE CHILLS
I PRETENDED TO BE THE RESIDENT OF ROOM 304...
SHE HAS NO IDEA THAT HER DAUGHTER TURNED TO DRUGS BECAUSE OF HER...
AND NOW SHE'S GIVING HER UP TO THE PROSE-CUTOR ...
IT'S HER DAUGHTER'S FIRST OFFENSE, SO I DOUBT THEY'LL BE TOO HARD ON HER.
ONCE THE TRIAL'S OVER, I IMAGINE SHE'LL BE PUT IN REHAB.
THEY'LL GET HER OFF THE DRUGS THERE.
!
BUT IBU, WHAT YOU SAID BEFORE, ABOUT "LOVE NOT BEING ABLE TO ..."
...

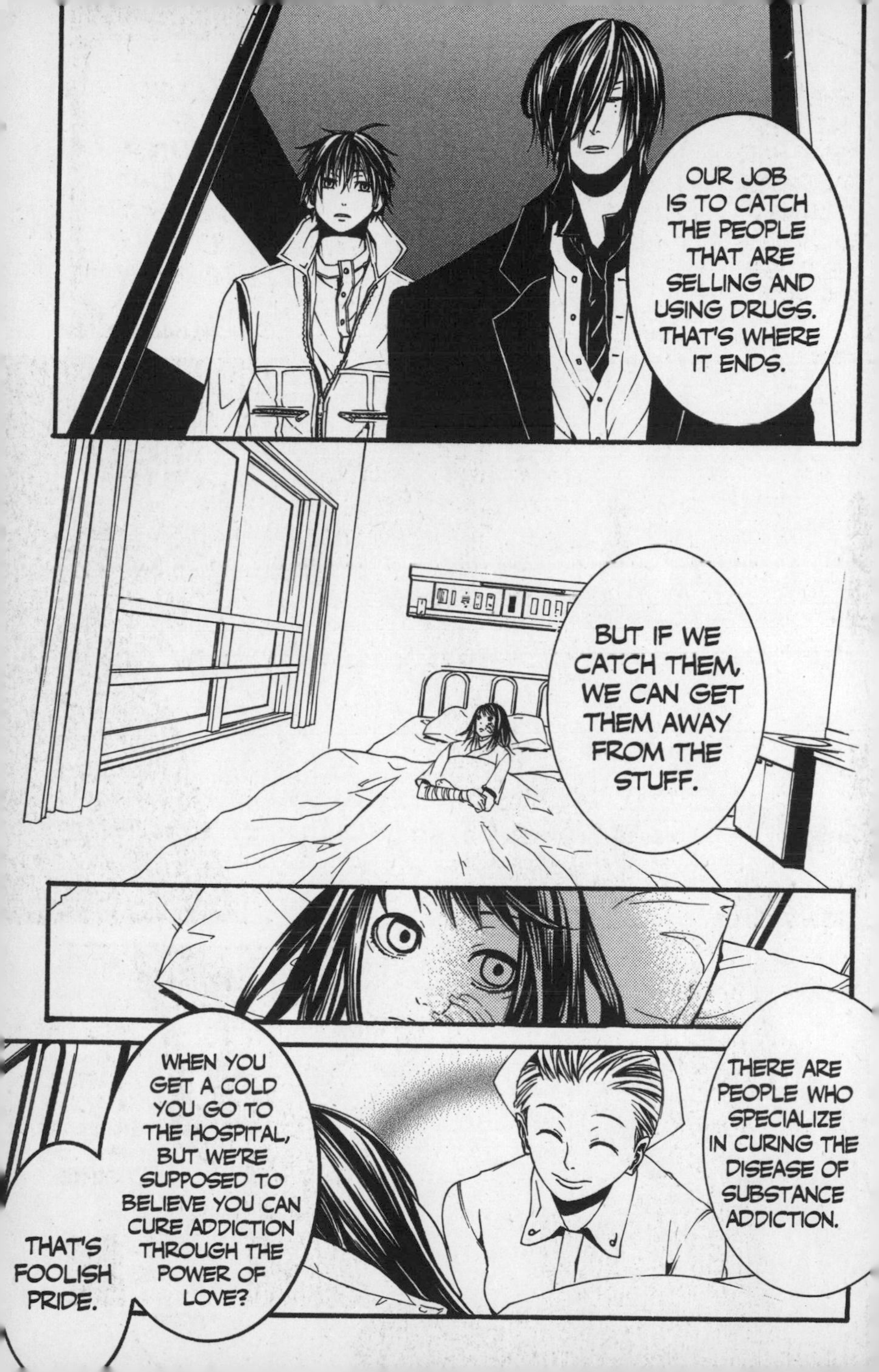
OUR JOB IS TO CATCH THE PEOPLE THAT ARE SELLING AND USING DRUGS. THAT'S WHERE IT ENDS.
BUT IF WE CATCH THEM, WE CAN GET THEM AWAY FROM THE STUFF.
THERE ARE PEOPLE WHO SPECIALIZE IN CURING THE DISEASE OF SUBSTANCE ADDICTION.
WHEN YOU GET A COLD YOU GO TO THE HOSPITAL, BUT WE'RE SUPPOSED TO BELIEVE YOU CAN CURE ADDICTION THROUGH THE POWER OF LOVE?
THAT'S FOOLISH PRIDE.

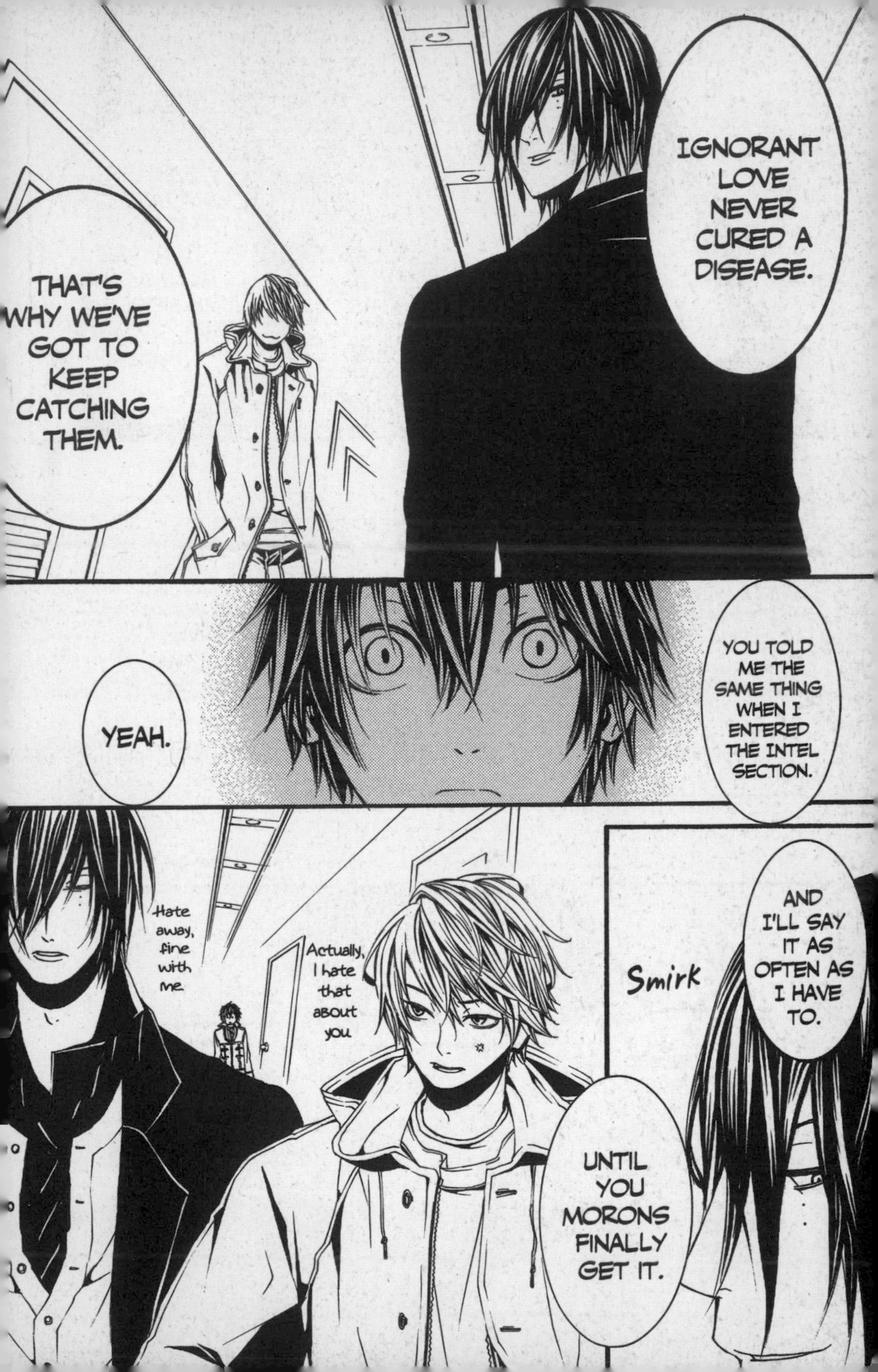
IGNORANT LOVE NEVER CURED A DISEASE.
THAT'S WHY WE'VE GOT TO KEEP CATCHING THEM.
YOU TOLD ME THE SAME THING WHEN I ENTERED THE INTEL SECTION.
YEAH.
AND I'LL SAY IT AS OFTEN AS I HAVE TO.
Smirk
UNTIL YOU MORONS FINALLY GET IT.
Actually, I hate that about you.
Hate away, fine with me.

[switch]

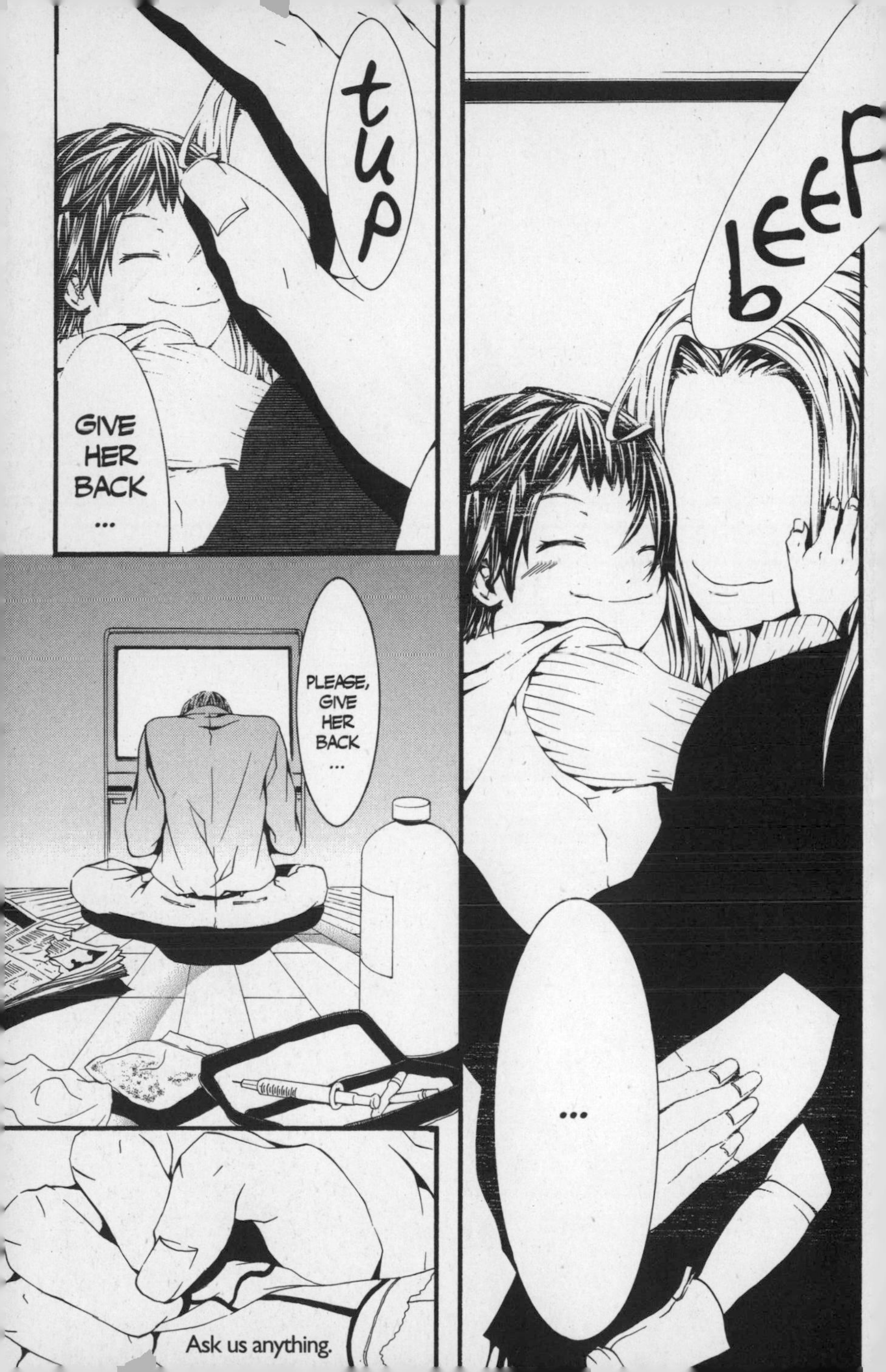
beep
...
tup
GIVE HER BACK ...
PLEASE, GIVE HER BACK ...
Ask us anything.

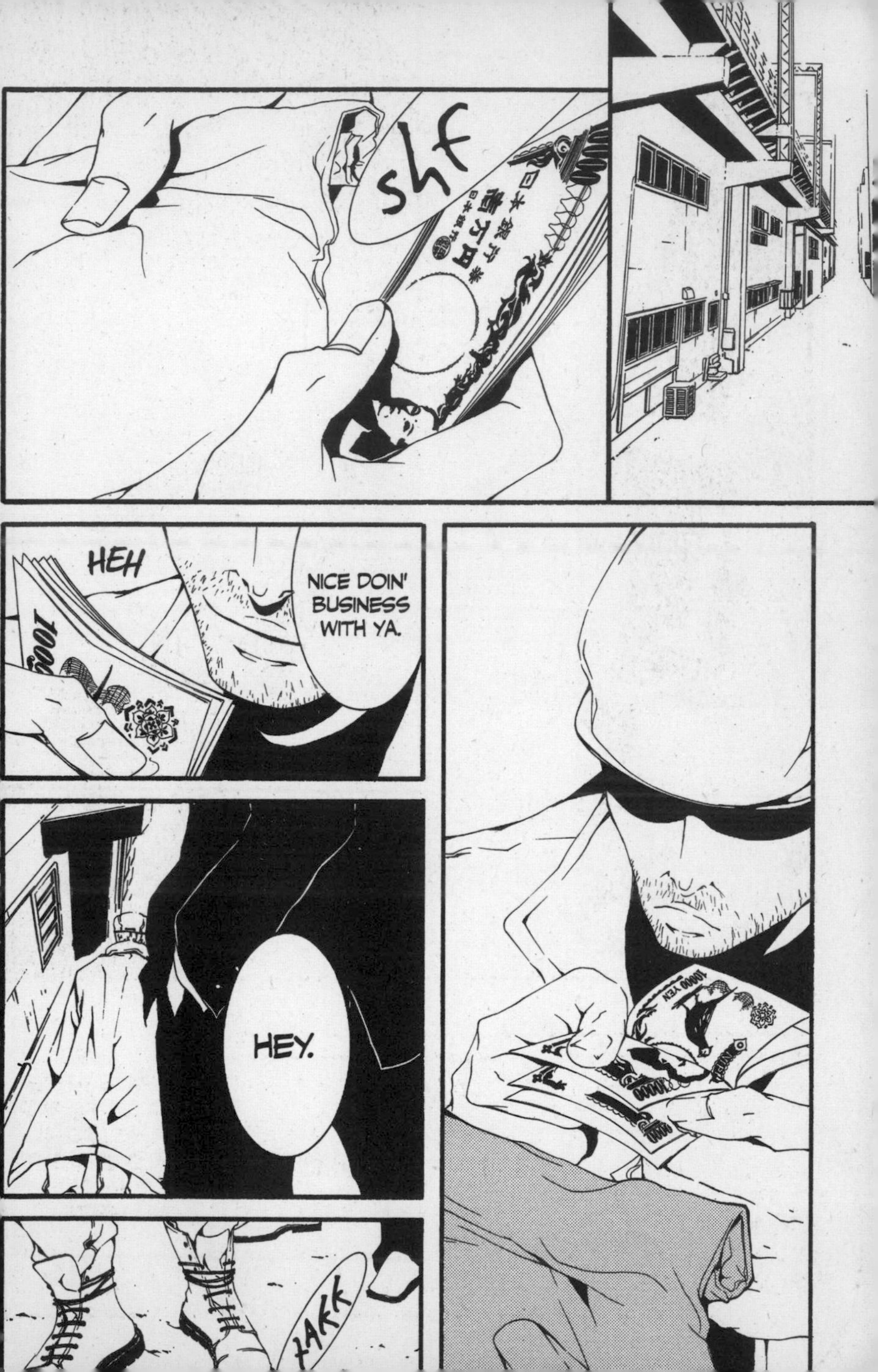
shf
NICE DOIN' BUSINESS WITH YA.
HEH
HEY.
TAKK

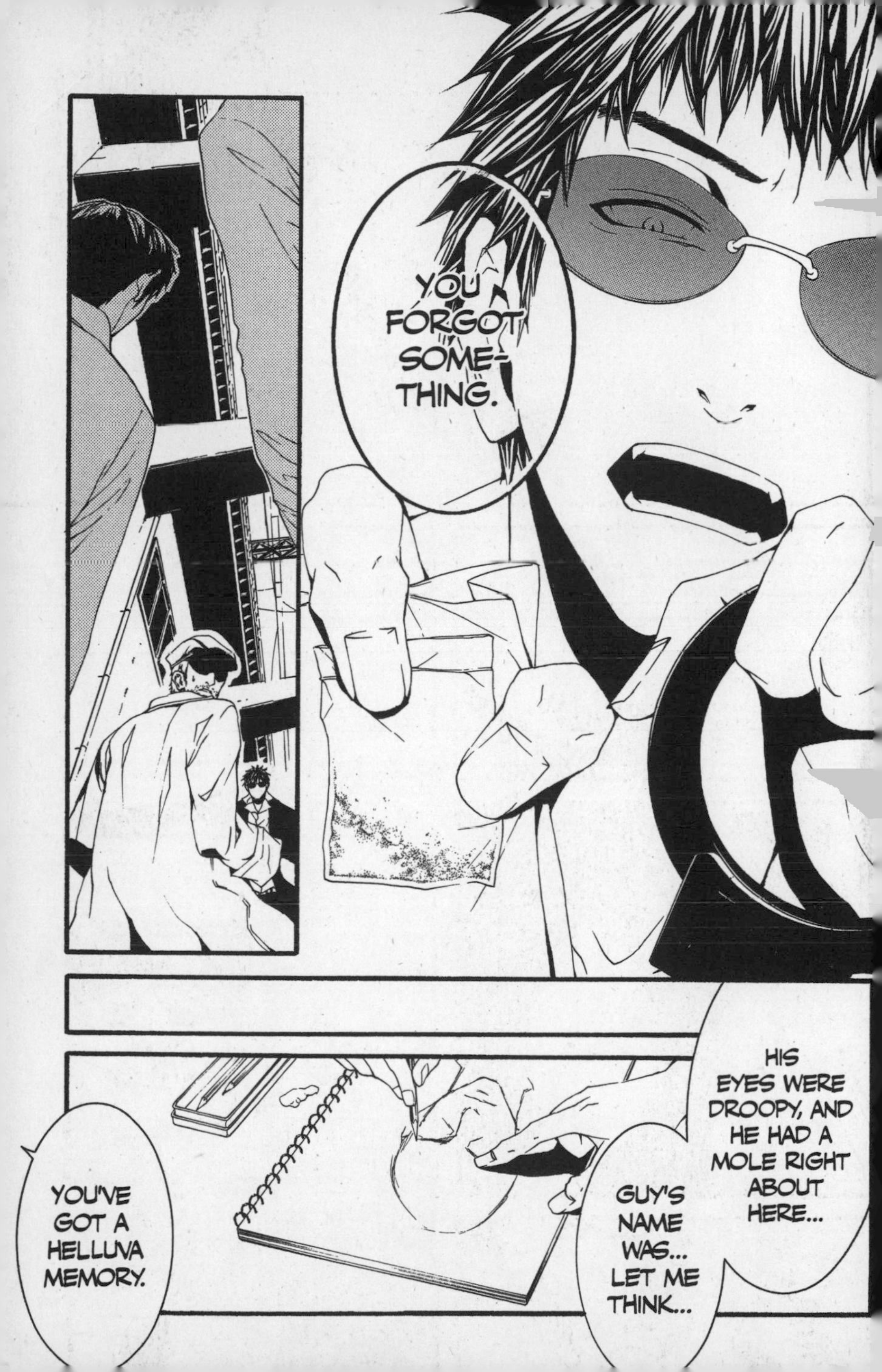
YOU FORGOT SOME-THING.
HIS EYES WERE DROOPY, AND HE HAD A MOLE RIGHT ABOUT HERE...
GUY'S NAME WAS... LET ME THINK...
YOU'VE GOT A HELLUVA MEMORY.

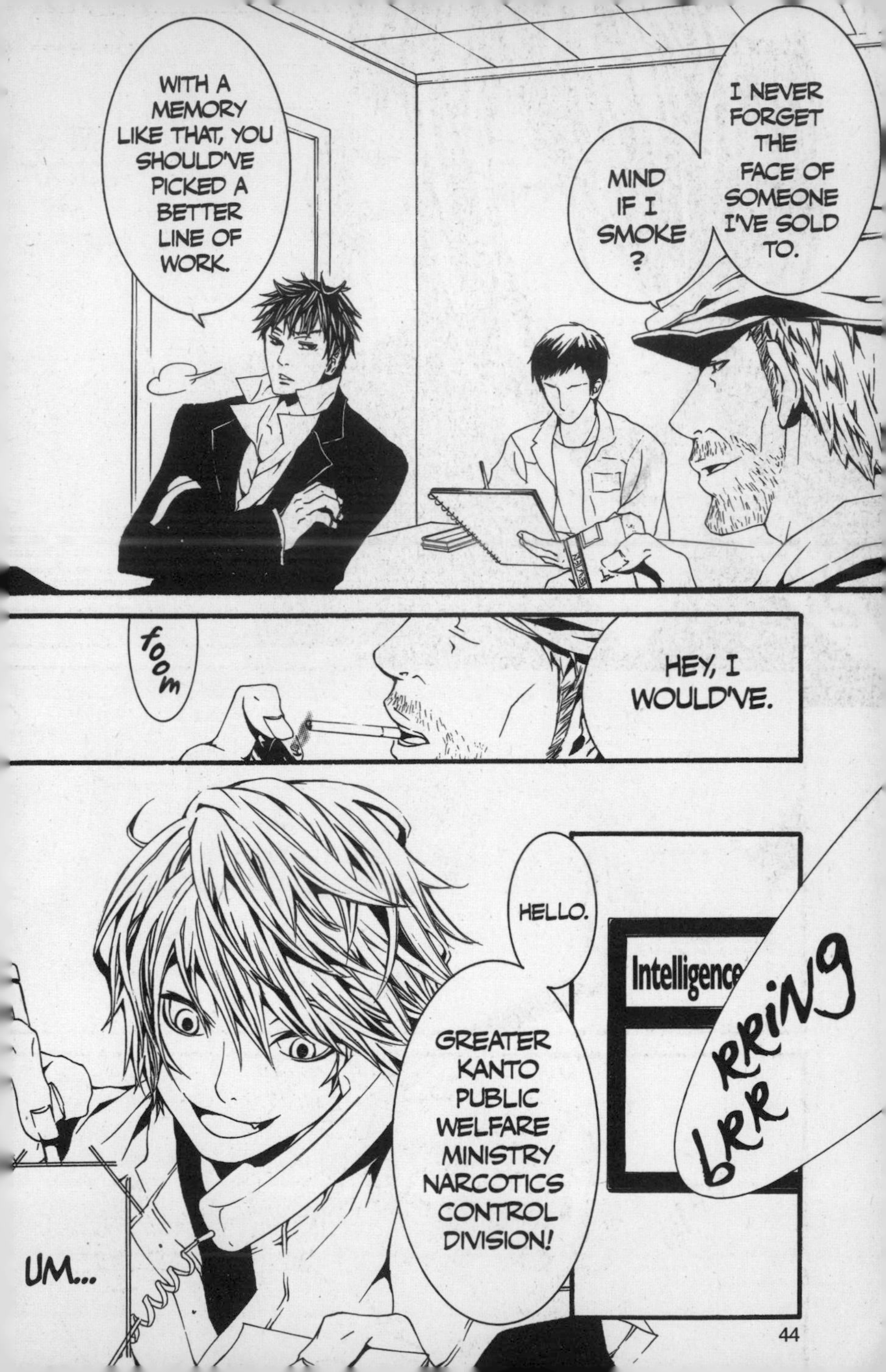
I NEVER FORGET THE FACE OF SOMEONE I'VE SOLD TO.
MIND IF I SMOKE?
WITH A MEMORY LIKE THAT, YOU SHOULD'VE PICKED A BETTER LINE OF WORK.
HEY, I WOULD'VE.
foom
RRING brr
HELLO.
Intelligence
GREATER KANTO PUBLIC WELFARE MINISTRY NARCOTICS CONTROL DIVISION!
UM...

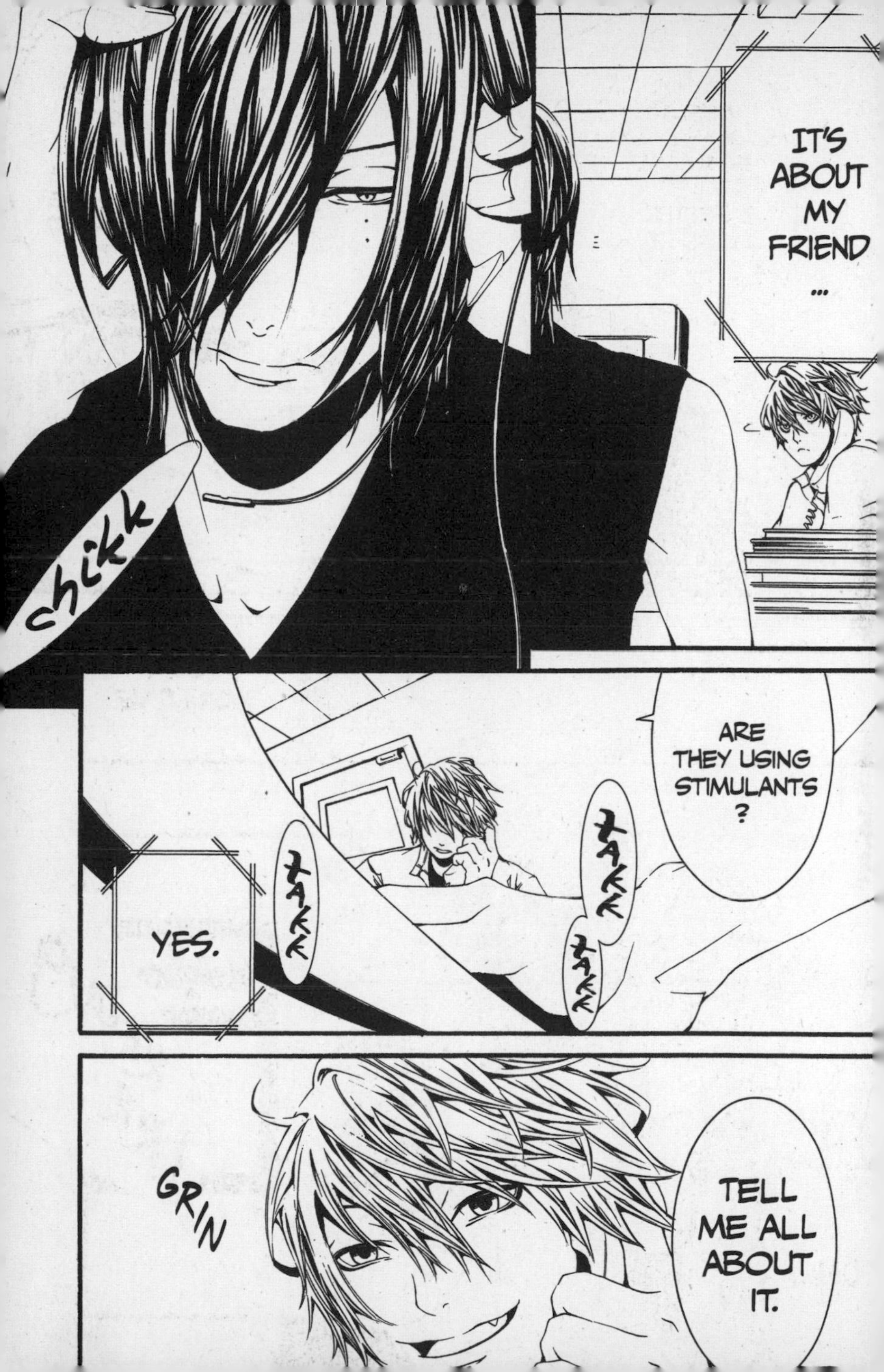
IT'S ABOUT MY FRIEND ...
CHIKK
ARE THEY USING STIMULANTS?
TAKK
TAKK
TAKK
YES.
TELL ME ALL ABOUT IT.
GRIN

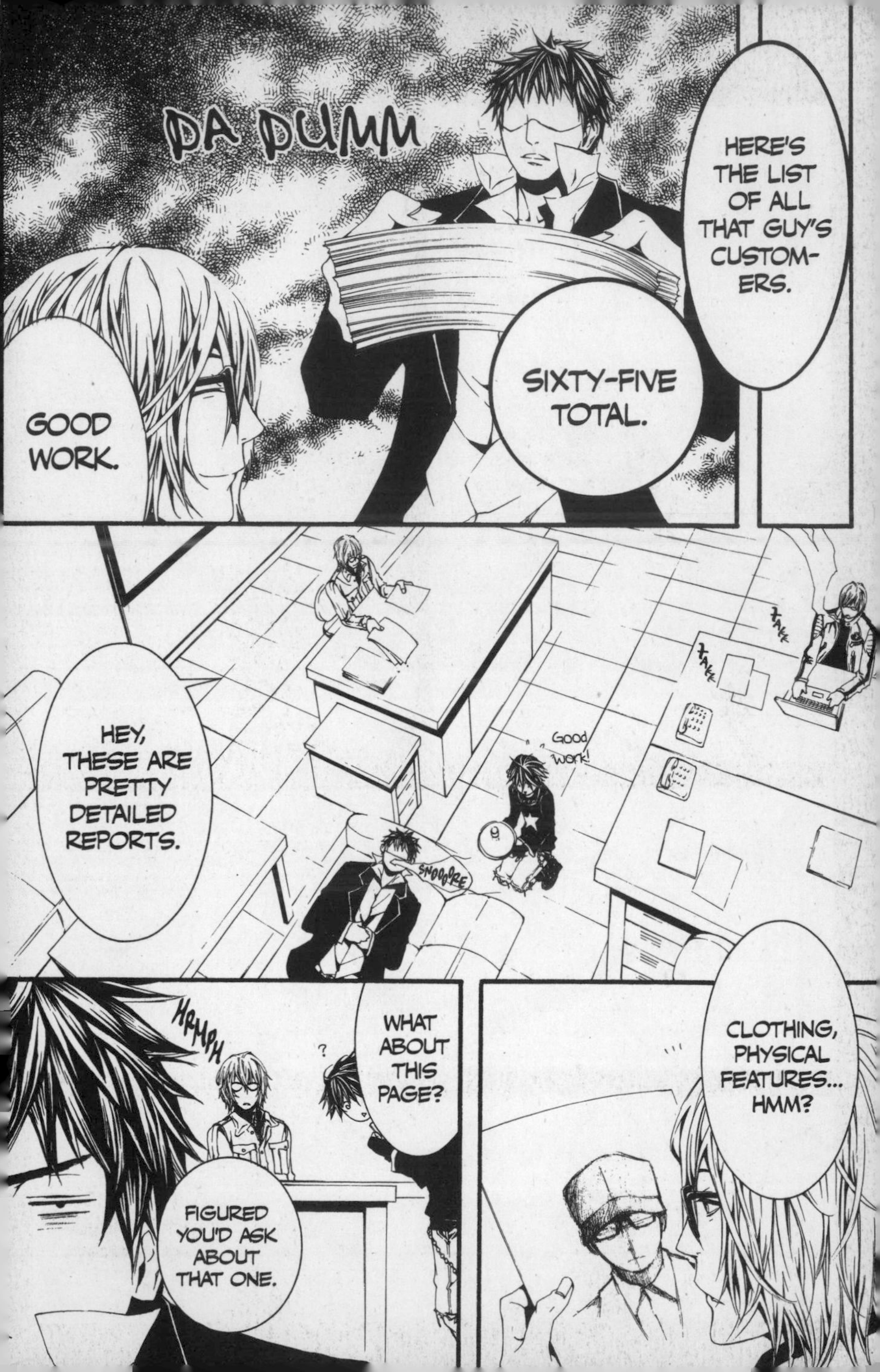
HERE'S THE LIST OF ALL THAT GUY'S CUSTOM-ERS.
SIXTY-FIVE TOTAL.
DA DUMM
GOOD WORK.
TAKE
TAKE
Good work!
SNOOORE
HEY, THESE ARE PRETTY DETAILED REPORTS.
CLOTHING, PHYSICAL FEATURES... HMM?
WHAT ABOUT THIS PAGE?
HRMPH
?
FIGURED YOU'D ASK ABOUT THAT ONE.

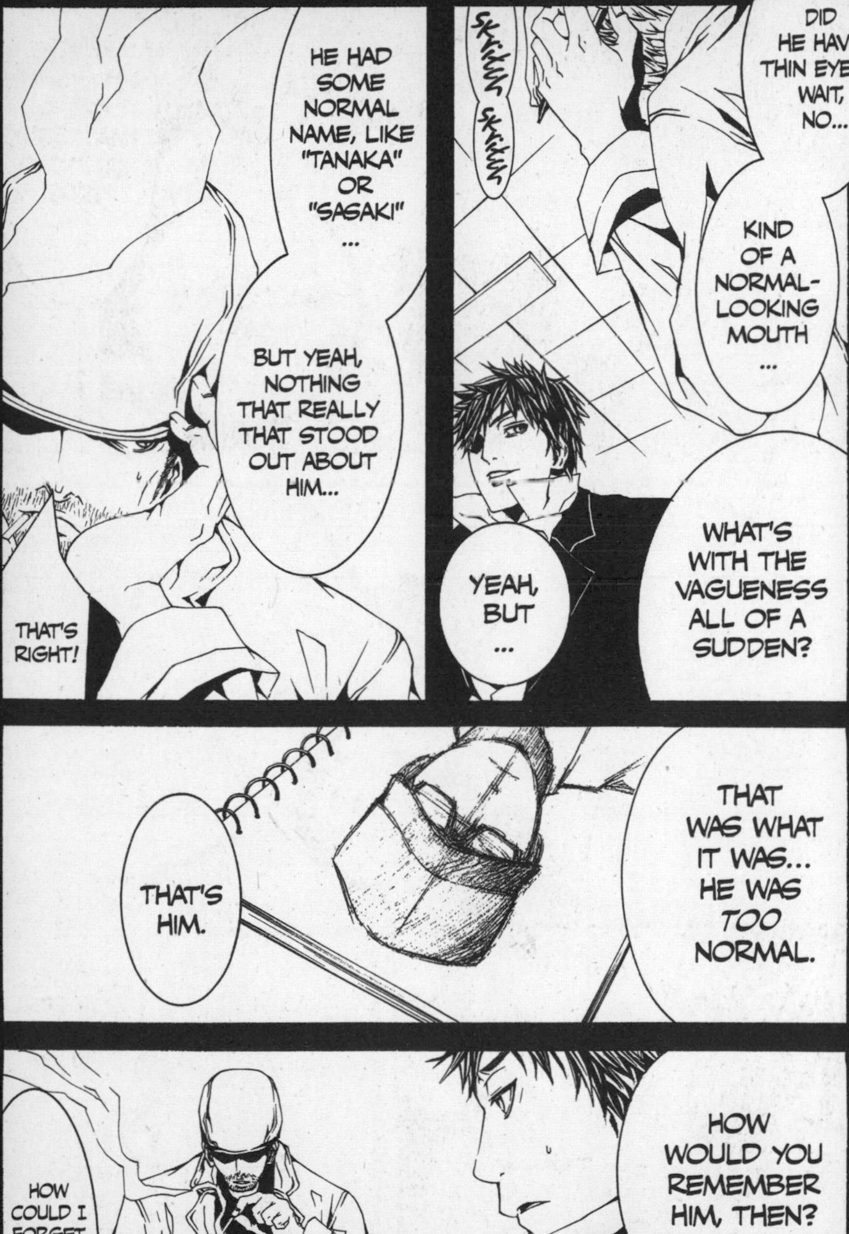
DID HE HAVE THIN EYES? WAIT, NO...
skritch skritch
KIND OF A NORMAL-LOOKING MOUTH ...
WHAT'S WITH THE VAGUENESS ALL OF A SUDDEN?
YEAH, BUT ...
HE HAD SOME NORMAL NAME, LIKE "TANAKA" OR "SASAKI" ...
BUT YEAH, NOTHING THAT REALLY THAT STOOD OUT ABOUT HIM...
THAT'S RIGHT!
THAT WAS WHAT IT WAS... HE WAS *TOO* NORMAL.
THAT'S HIM.
HOW WOULD YOU REMEMBER HIM, THEN?
HOW COULD I FORGET ?

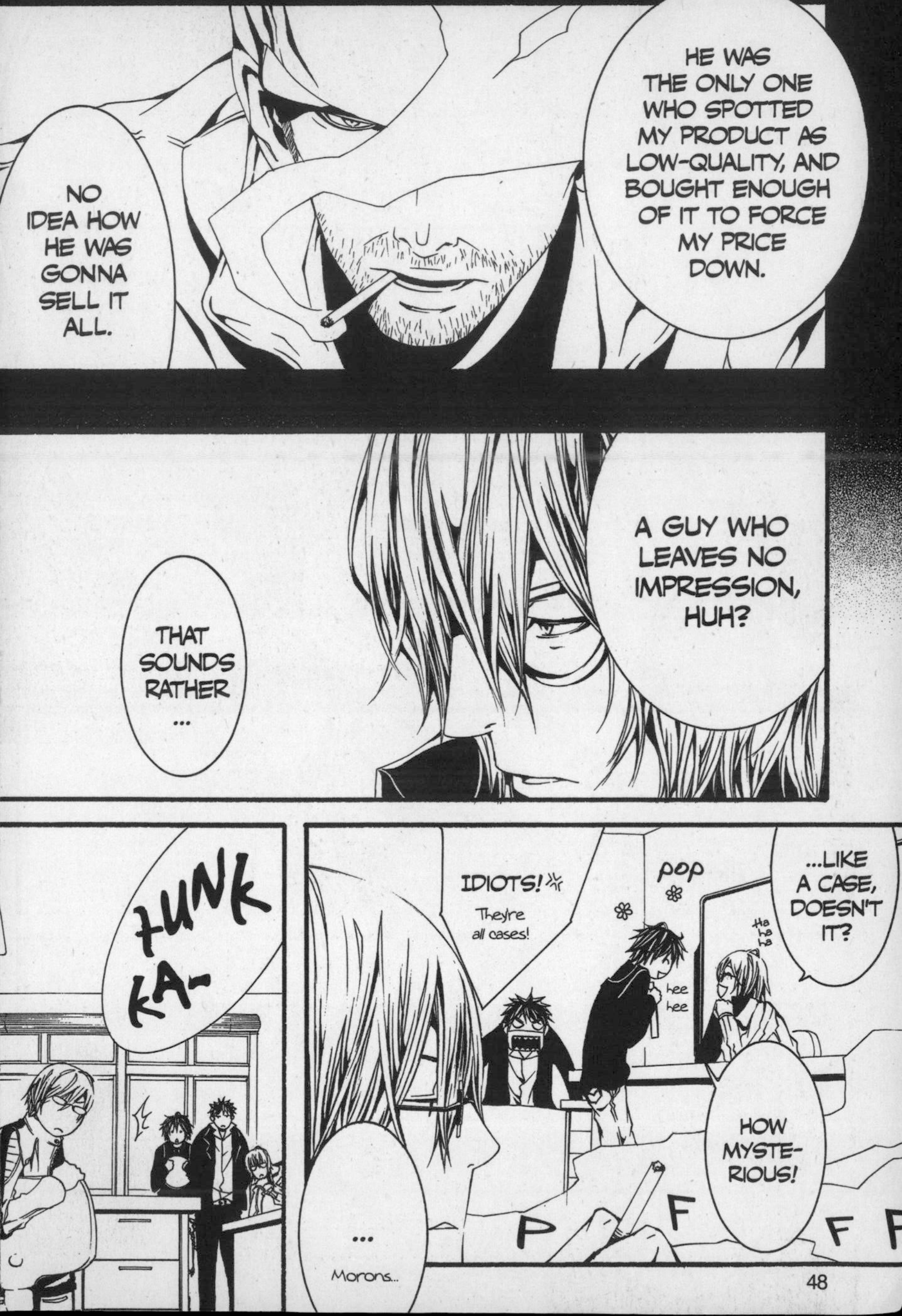
HE WAS THE ONLY ONE WHO SPOTTED MY PRODUCT AS LOW-QUALITY, AND BOUGHT ENOUGH OF IT TO FORCE MY PRICE DOWN.
NO IDEA HOW HE WAS GONNA SELL IT ALL.
A GUY WHO LEAVES NO IMPRESSION, HUH?
THAT SOUNDS RATHER ...
...LIKE A CASE, DOESN'T IT?
Ha ha ha
pop
hee hee
HOW MYSTE-RIOUS!
IDIOTS!
Theyre all cases!
P F F F
...
Morons...
ZUNK
KA-

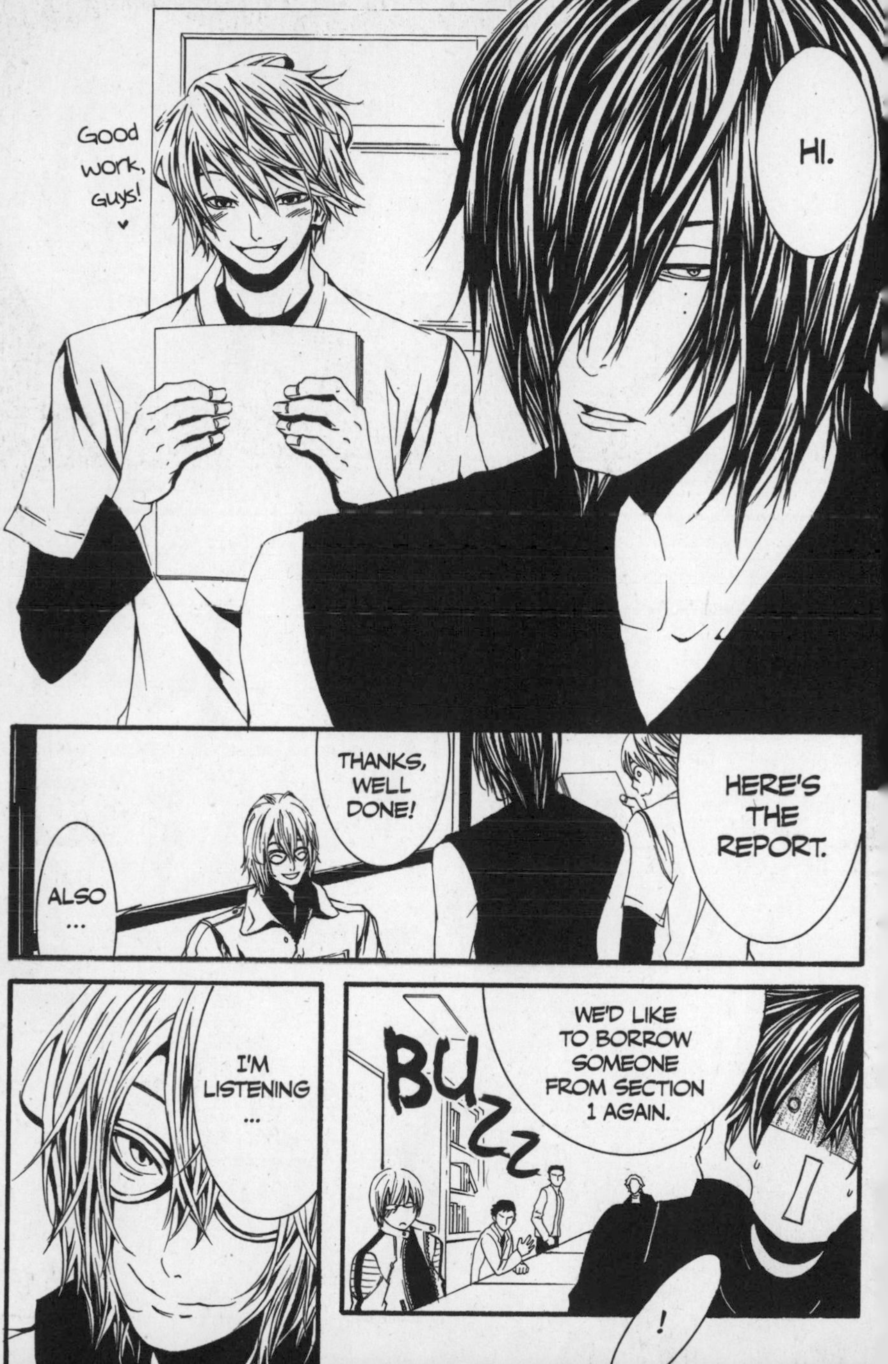
HI.
Good work, guys! ♥
HERE'S THE REPORT.
THANKS, WELL DONE!
ALSO ...
WE'D LIKE TO BORROW SOMEONE FROM SECTION 1 AGAIN.
BUZZ
!
I'M LISTENING ...

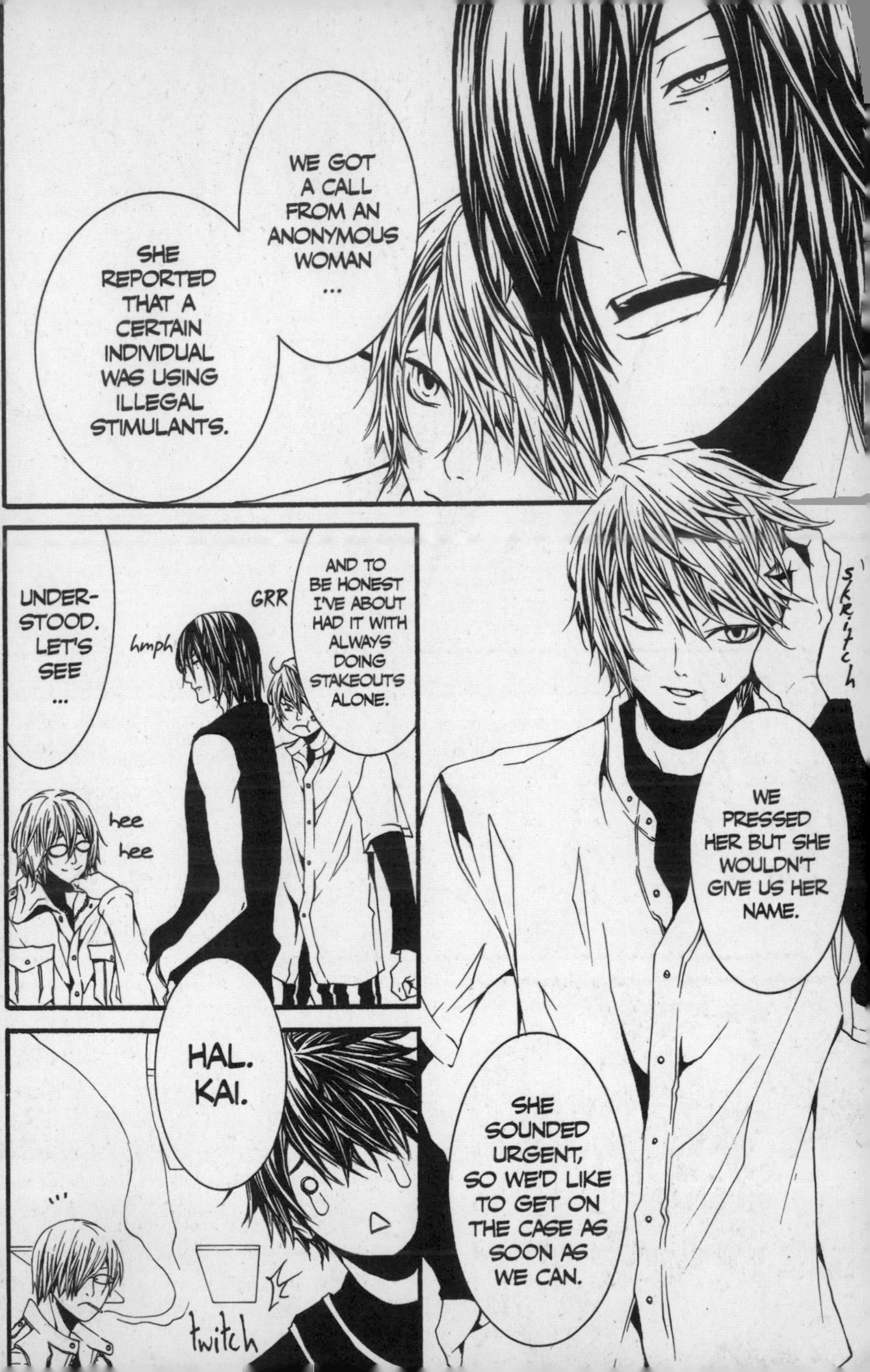
WE GOT A CALL FROM AN ANONYMOUS WOMAN ...
SHE REPORTED THAT A CERTAIN INDIVIDUAL WAS USING ILLEGAL STIMULANTS.
skritch
WE PRESSED HER BUT SHE WOULDN'T GIVE US HER NAME.
SHE SOUNDED URGENT, SO WE'D LIKE TO GET ON THE CASE AS SOON AS WE CAN.
AND TO BE HONEST I'VE ABOUT HAD IT WITH ALWAYS DOING STAKEOUTS ALONE.
GRR
hmph
UNDERSTOOD. LET'S SEE ...
hee hee
HAL. KAI.
...
twitch

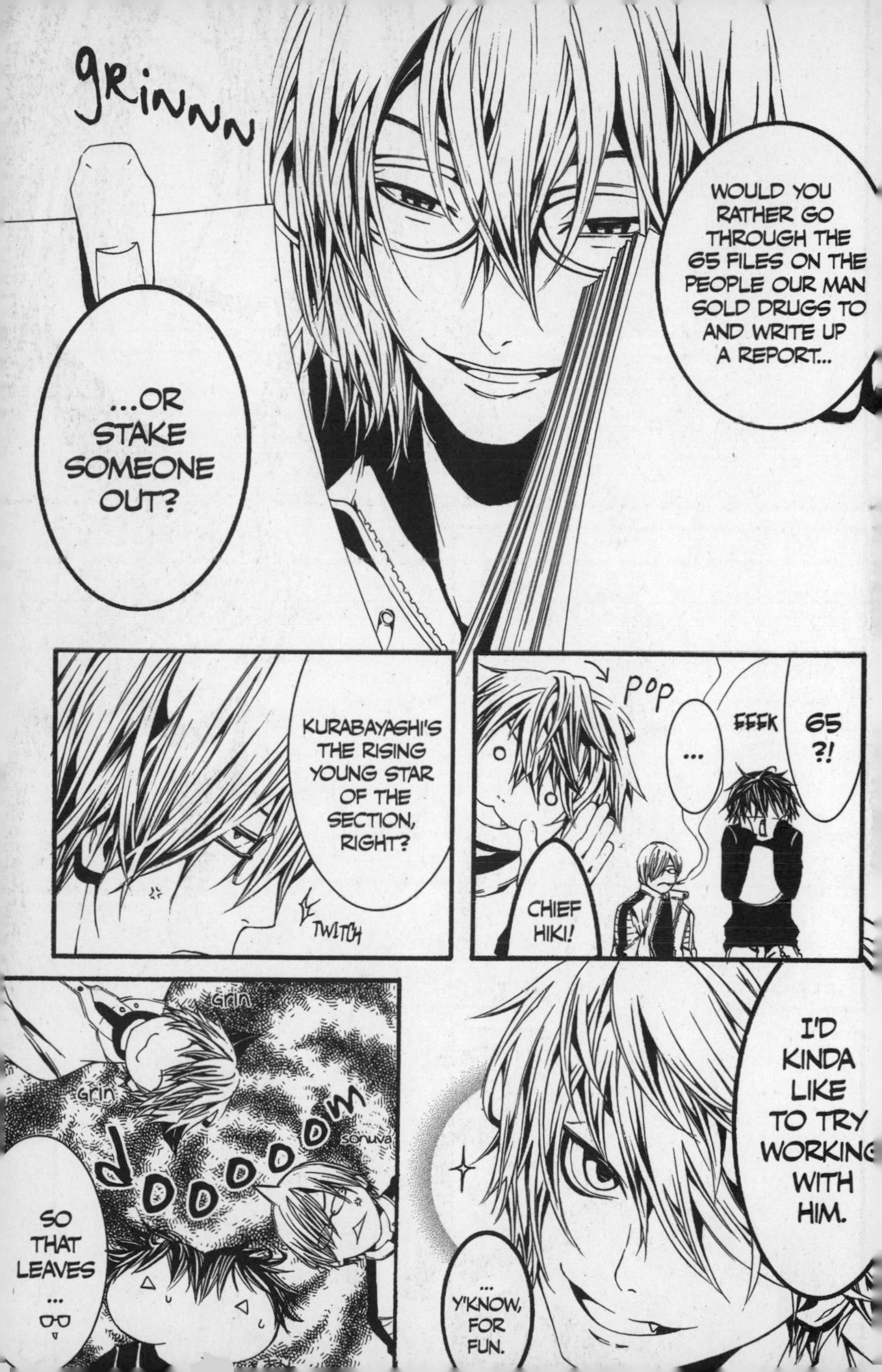
gRinnn
WOULD YOU RATHER GO THROUGH THE 65 FILES ON THE PEOPLE OUR MAN SOLD DRUGS TO AND WRITE UP A REPORT...
...OR STAKE SOMEONE OUT?
65 ?!
EEEK
...
pop
CHIEF HIKI!
KURABAYASHI'S THE RISING YOUNG STAR OF THE SECTION, RIGHT?
TWITCH
I'D KINDA LIKE TO TRY WORKING WITH HIM.
...Y'KNOW, FOR FUN.
grin
grin
dooooom
sonuva
SO THAT LEAVES ...

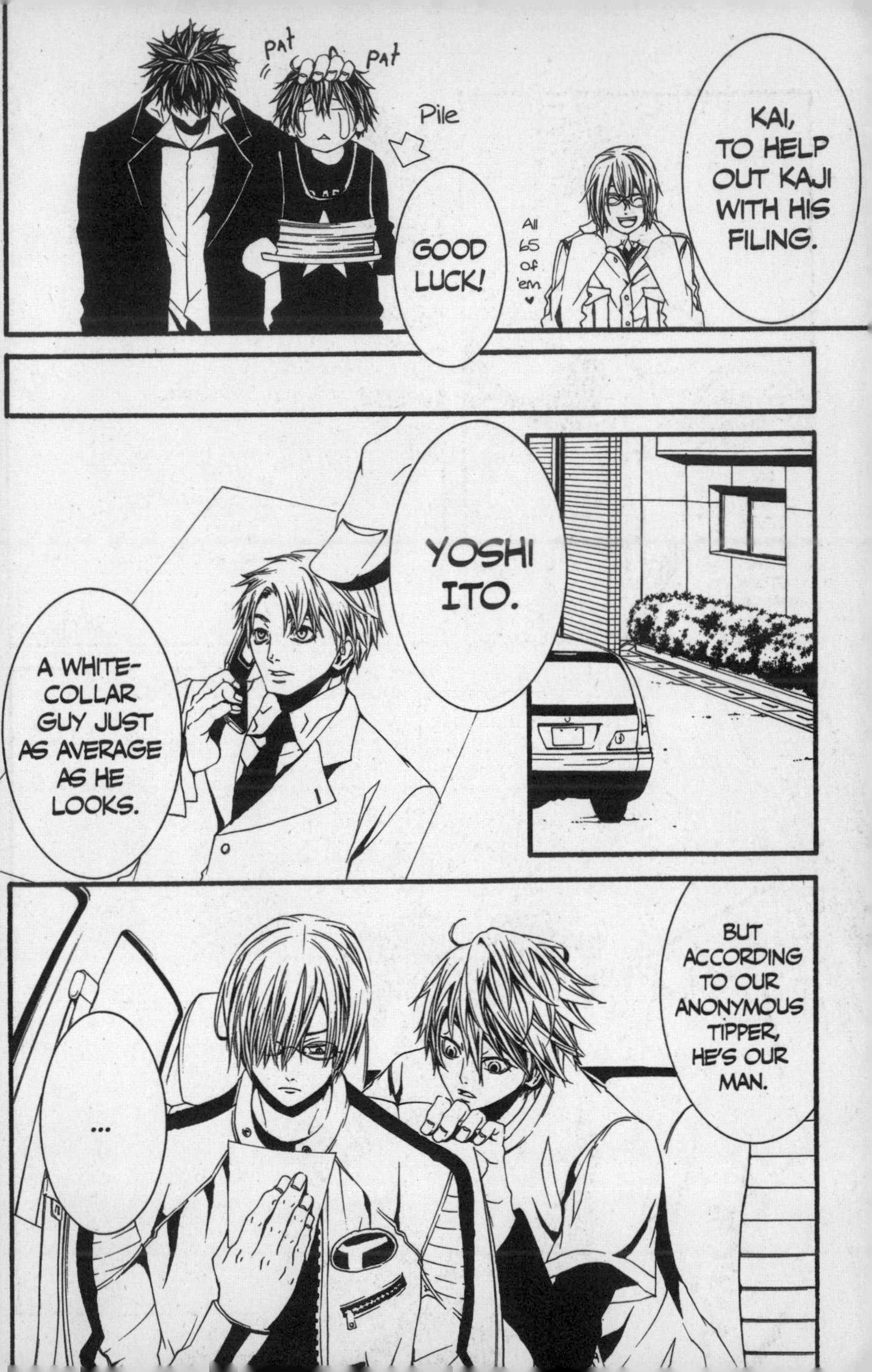
KAI, TO HELP OUT KAJI WITH HIS FILING.
All 65 of 'em ♥
GOOD LUCK!
Pile
pat pat
YOSHI ITO.
A WHITE-COLLAR GUY JUST AS AVERAGE AS HE LOOKS.
BUT ACCORDING TO OUR ANONYMOUS TIPPER, HE'S OUR MAN.
...

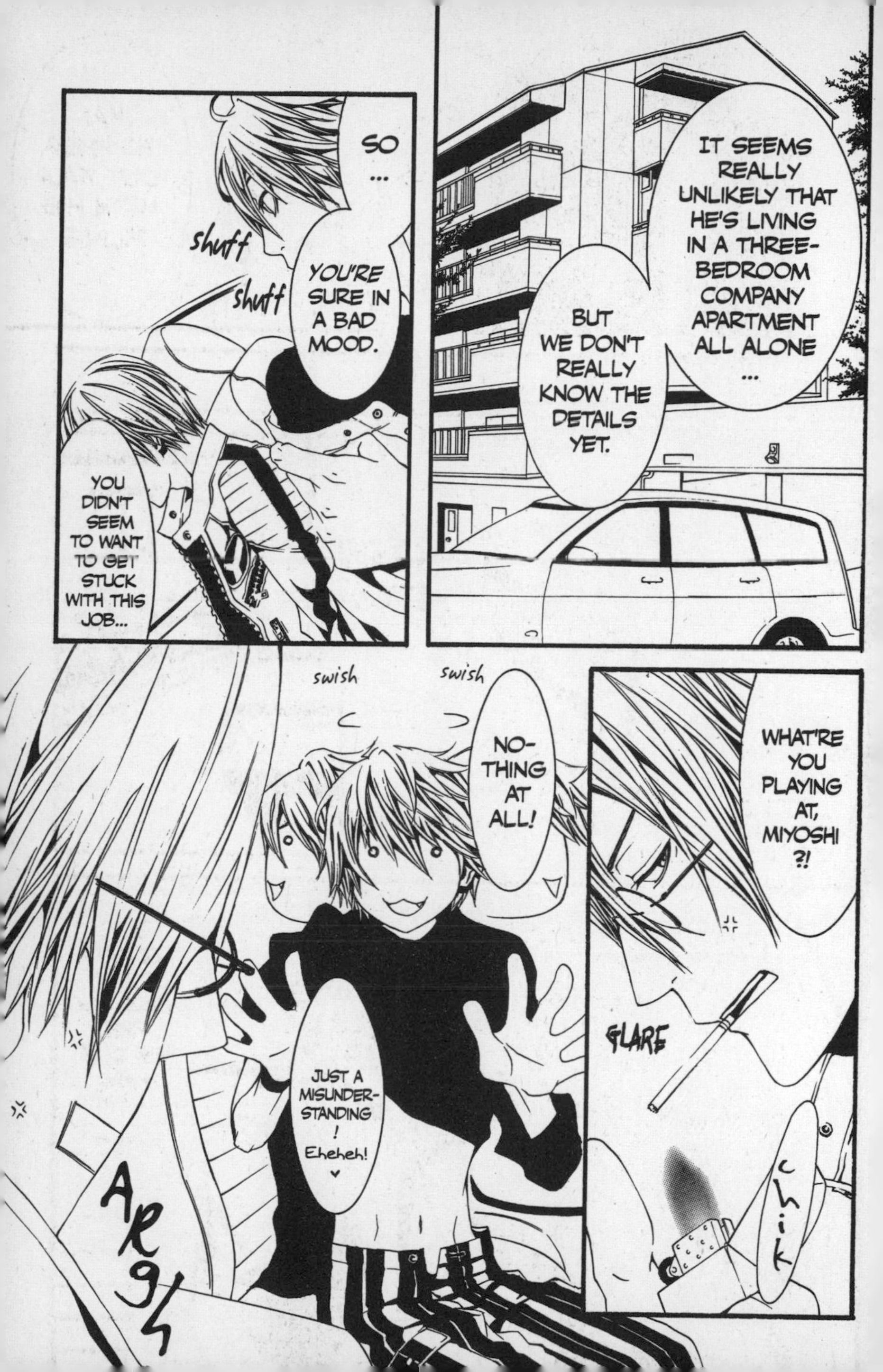
IT SEEMS REALLY UNLIKELY THAT HE'S LIVING IN A THREE-BEDROOM COMPANY APARTMENT ALL ALONE ...
BUT WE DON'T REALLY KNOW THE DETAILS YET.
SO ...
shuff
shuff
YOU'RE SURE IN A BAD MOOD.
YOU DIDN'T SEEM TO WANT TO GET STUCK WITH THIS JOB...
WHAT'RE YOU PLAYING AT, MIYOSHI ?!
GLARE
chik
swish
swish
NO-THING AT ALL!
JUST A MISUNDER-STANDING! Eheheh!
Argh

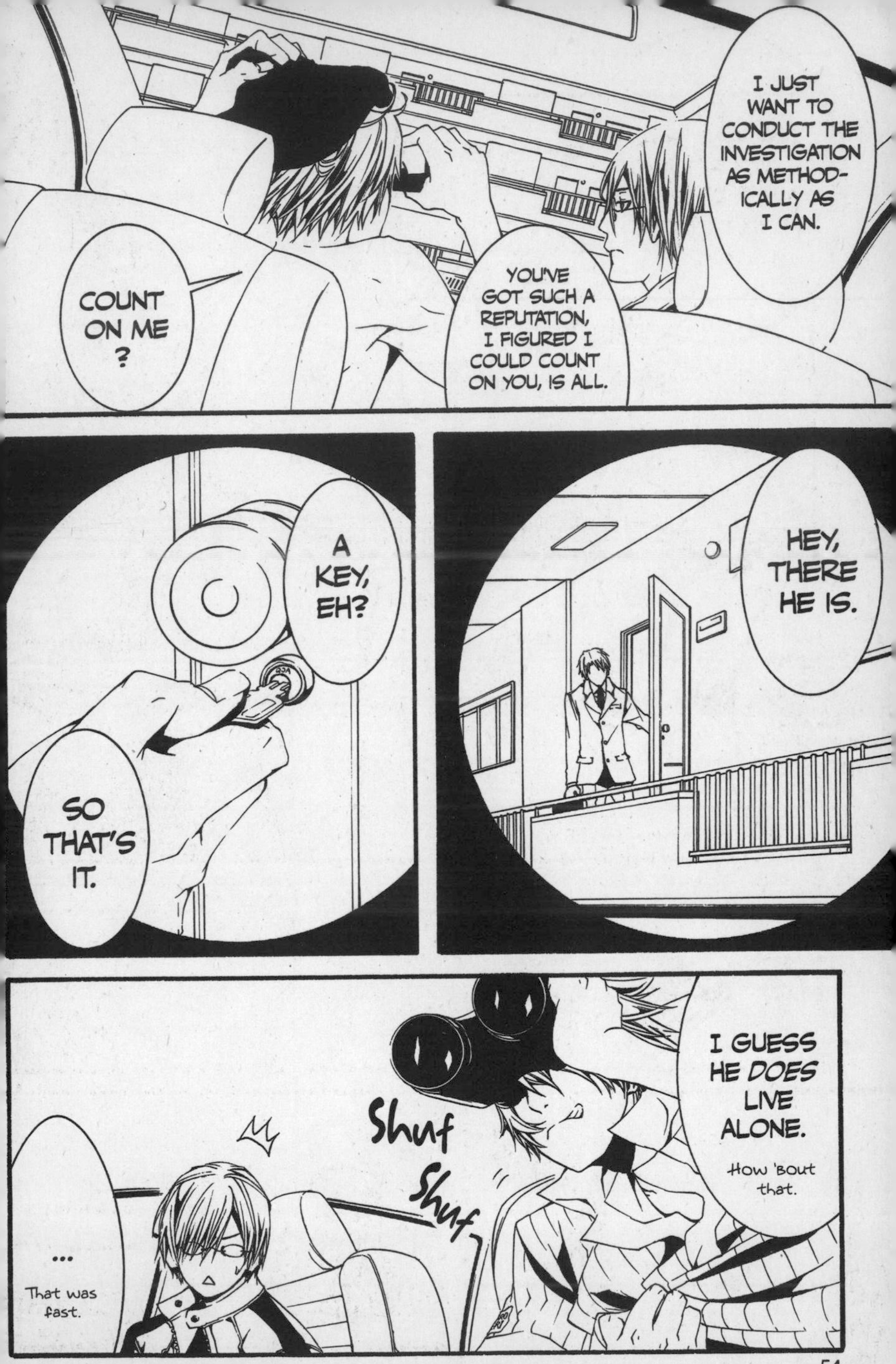
I JUST WANT TO CONDUCT THE INVESTIGATION AS METHOD-ICALLY AS I CAN.
YOU'VE GOT SUCH A REPUTATION, I FIGURED I COULD COUNT ON YOU, IS ALL.
COUNT ON ME ?
HEY, THERE HE IS.
A KEY, EH?
SO THAT'S IT.
I GUESS HE *DOES* LIVE ALONE.
How 'bout that.
Shuf
Shuf
...
That was fast.

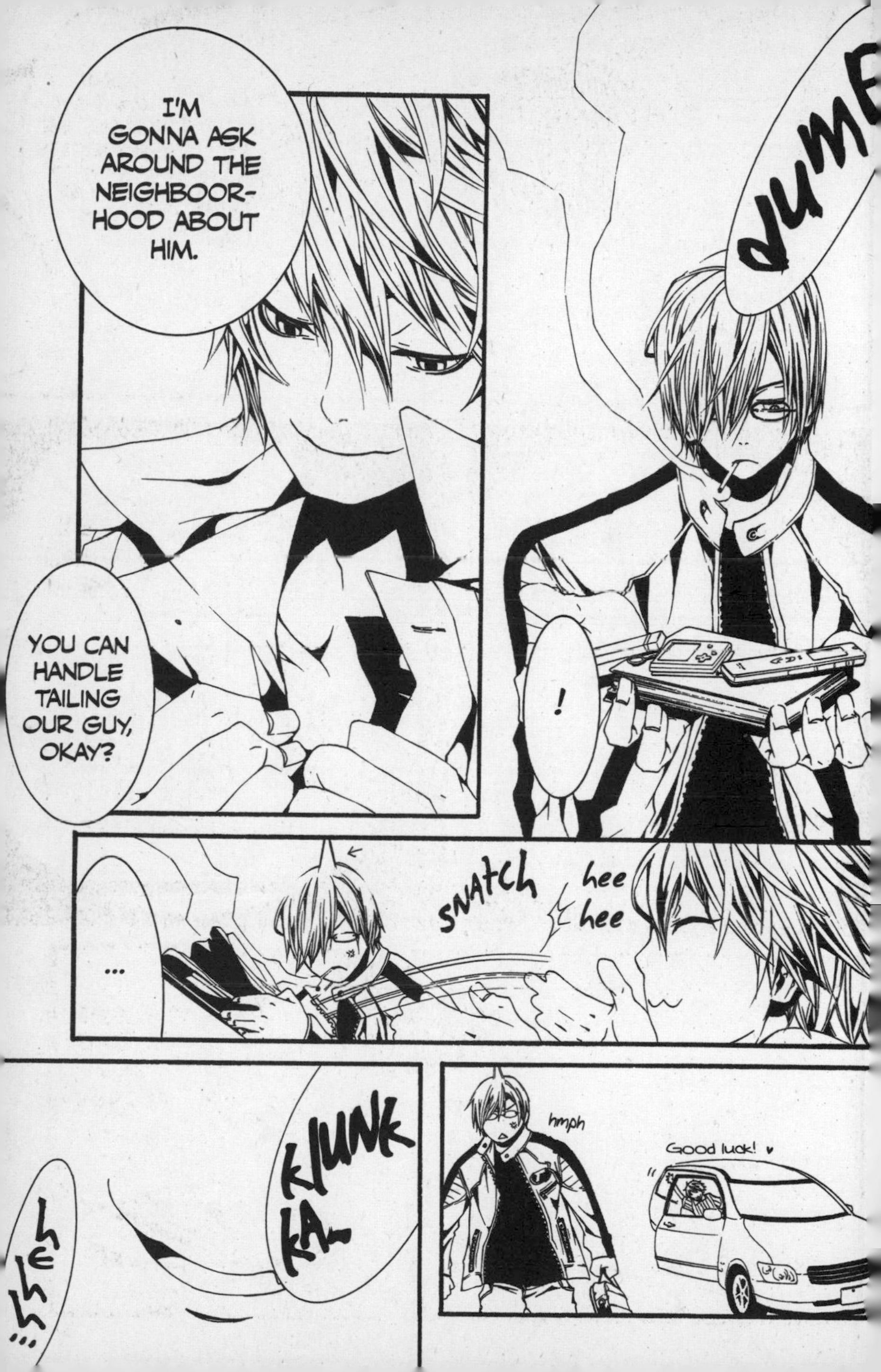
DUMP
!
I'M GONNA ASK AROUND THE NEIGHBOOR-HOOD ABOUT HIM.
YOU CAN HANDLE TAILING OUR GUY, OKAY?
hee hee
SNATCH
...
hmph
Good luck! ♥
KLUNK
KA
heh...

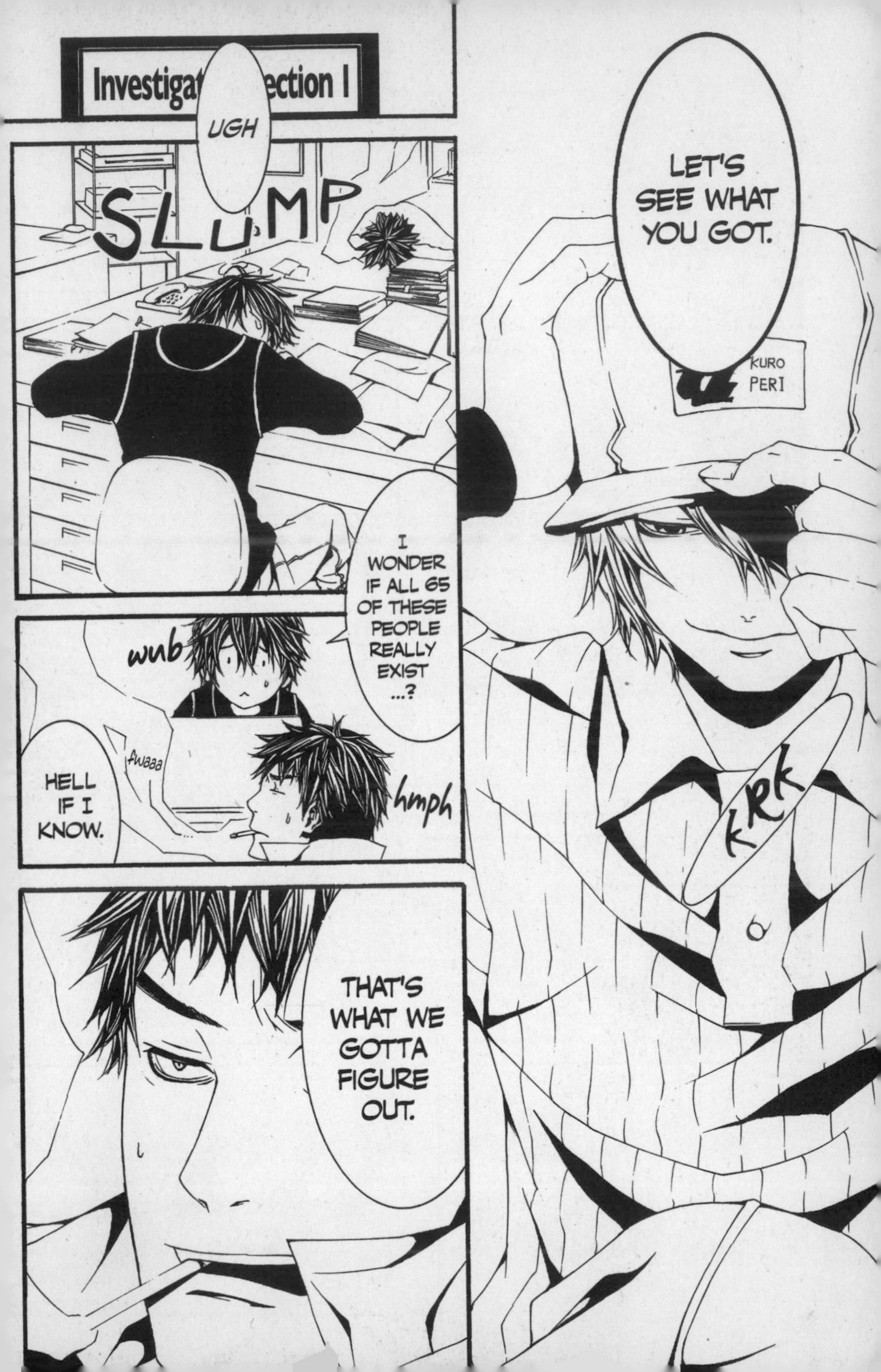
LET'S SEE WHAT YOU GOT.
KURO PERI
KRK
Investigat
ection I
UGH
SLUMP
I WONDER IF ALL 65 OF THESE PEOPLE REALLY EXIST ...?
wub
hmph
fwaaa
HELL IF I KNOW.
THAT'S WHAT WE GOTTA FIGURE OUT.

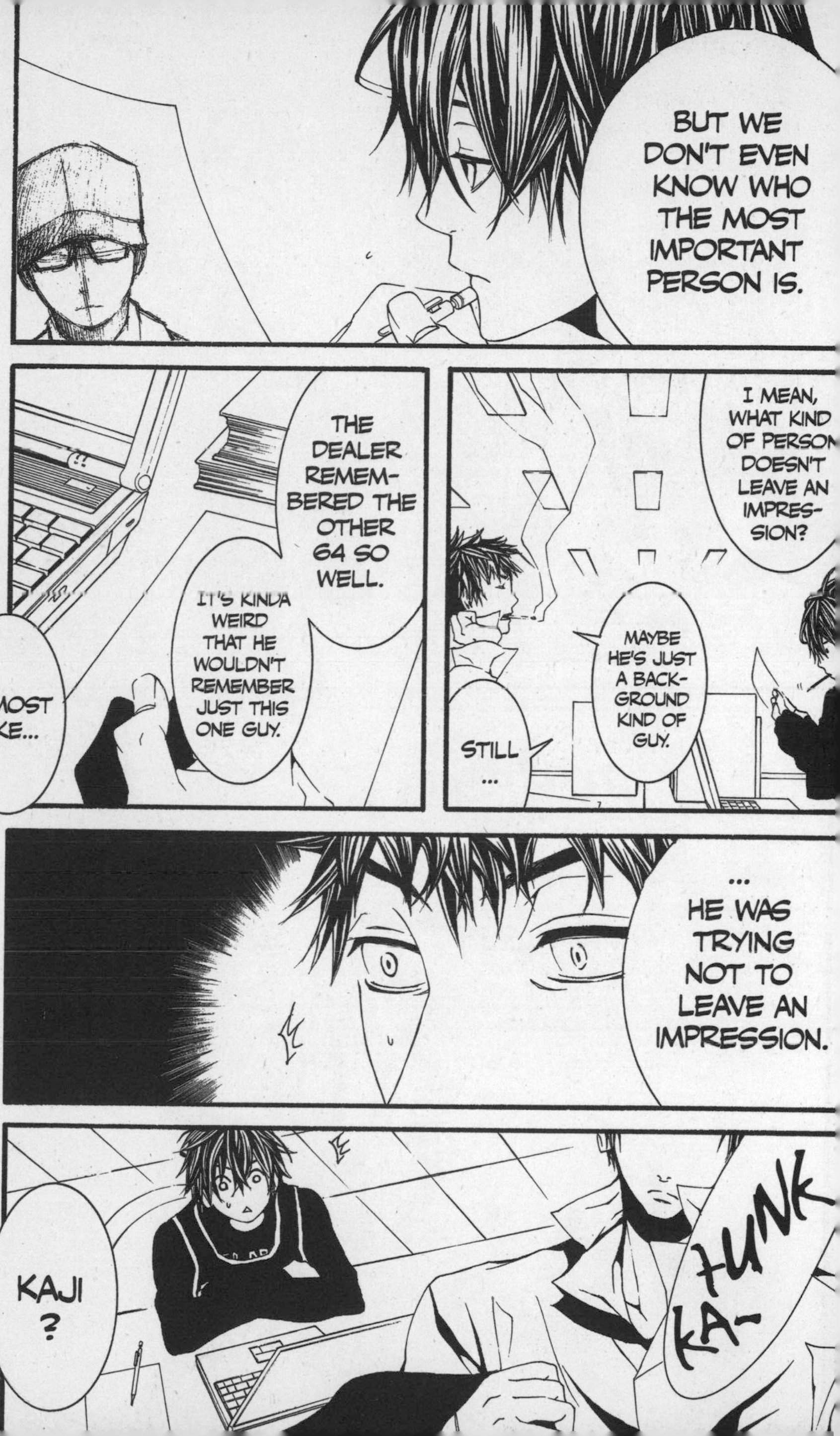
BUT WE DON'T EVEN KNOW WHO THE MOST IMPORTANT PERSON IS.
I MEAN, WHAT KIND OF PERSON DOESN'T LEAVE AN IMPRESSION?
MAYBE HE'S JUST A BACKGROUND KIND OF GUY.
STILL ...
THE DEALER REMEMBERED THE OTHER 64 SO WELL.
IT'S KINDA WEIRD THAT HE WOULDN'T REMEMBER JUST THIS ONE GUY.
ALMOST LIKE...
... HE WAS TRYING NOT TO LEAVE AN IMPRESSION.
KA-TUNK
KAJI ?

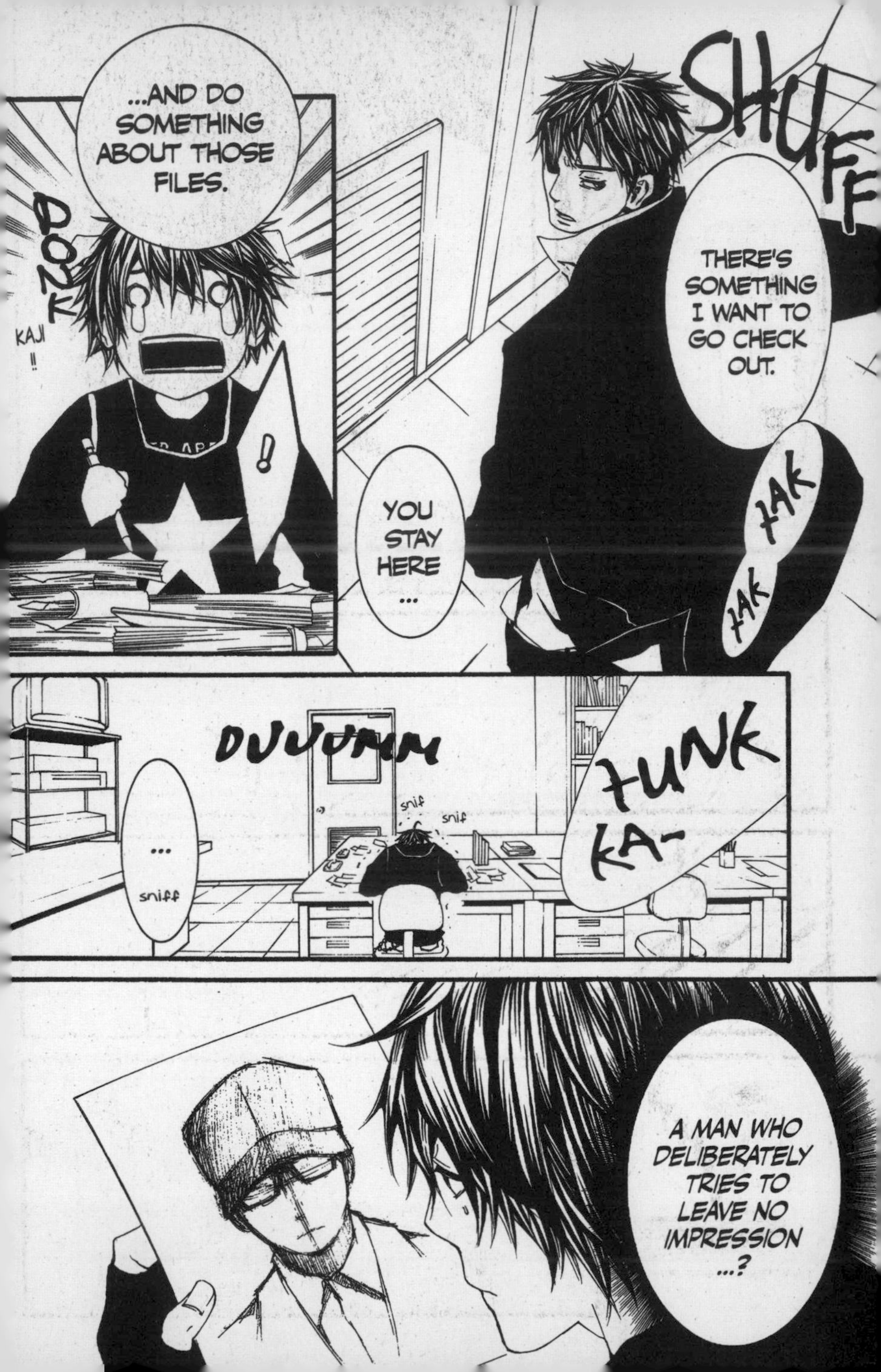
SHUFF
THERE'S SOMETHING I WANT TO GO CHECK OUT.
YOU STAY HERE ...
TAK TAK
...AND DO SOMETHING ABOUT THOSE FILES.
DONK
KAJI !!
!
KA-TUNK
DUUUMM
snif snif
... sniff
A MAN WHO DELIBERATELY TRIES TO LEAVE NO IMPRESSION ...?

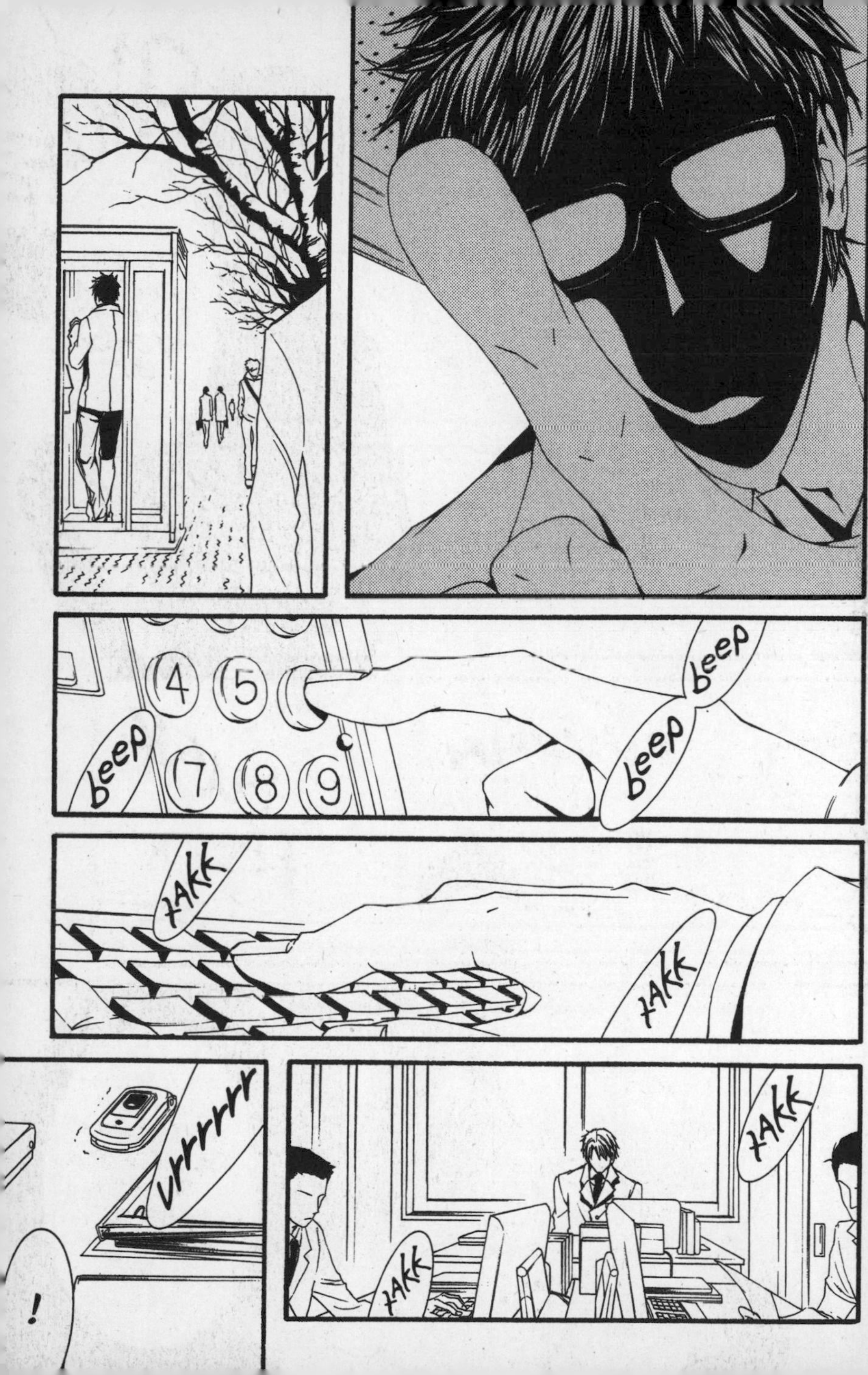
beep
beep
beep
takk
takk
takk
takk
vrrrrrr
!

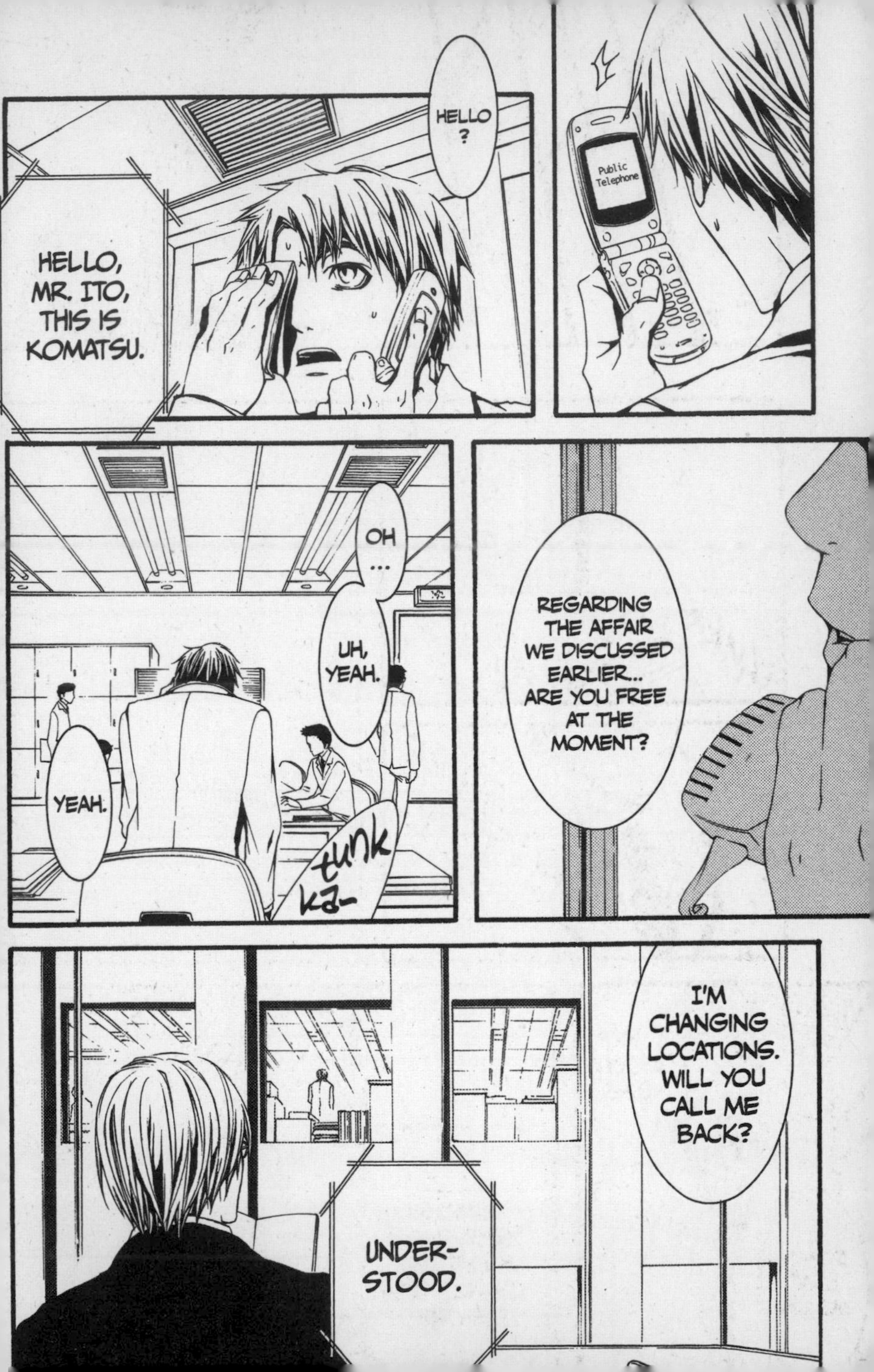
Public Telephone
HELLO ?
HELLO, MR. ITO, THIS IS KOMATSU.
REGARDING THE AFFAIR WE DISCUSSED EARLIER... ARE YOU FREE AT THE MOMENT?
OH ...
UH, YEAH.
YEAH.
tunk ka-
I'M CHANGING LOCATIONS. WILL YOU CALL ME BACK?
UNDER-STOOD.

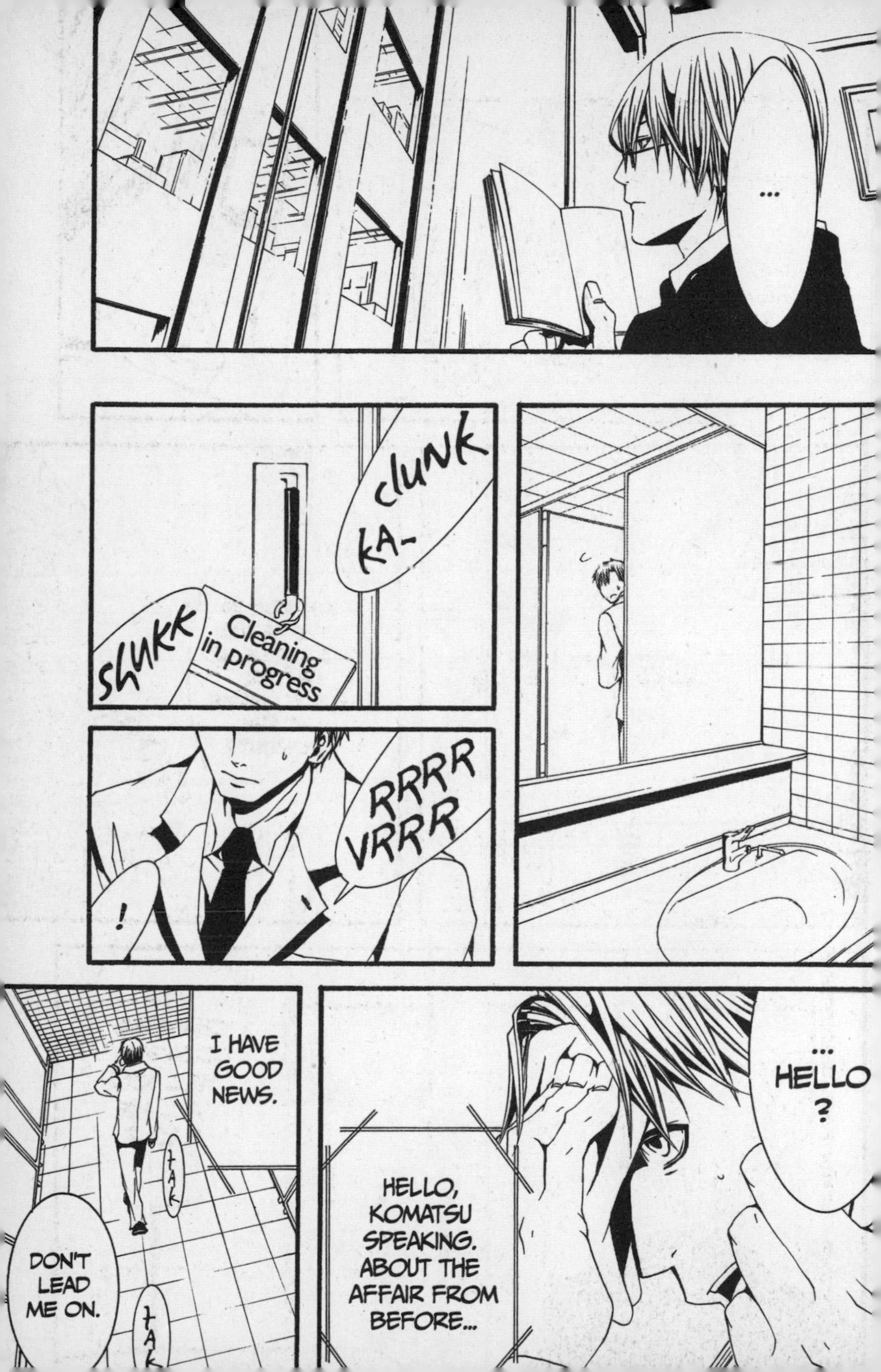
...
KA-
clunk
Cleaning in progress
SHUKK
RRRR VRRR
!
... HELLO ?
HELLO, KOMATSU SPEAKING. ABOUT THE AFFAIR FROM BEFORE...
I HAVE GOOD NEWS.
TAK
DON'T LEAD ME ON.
TAK

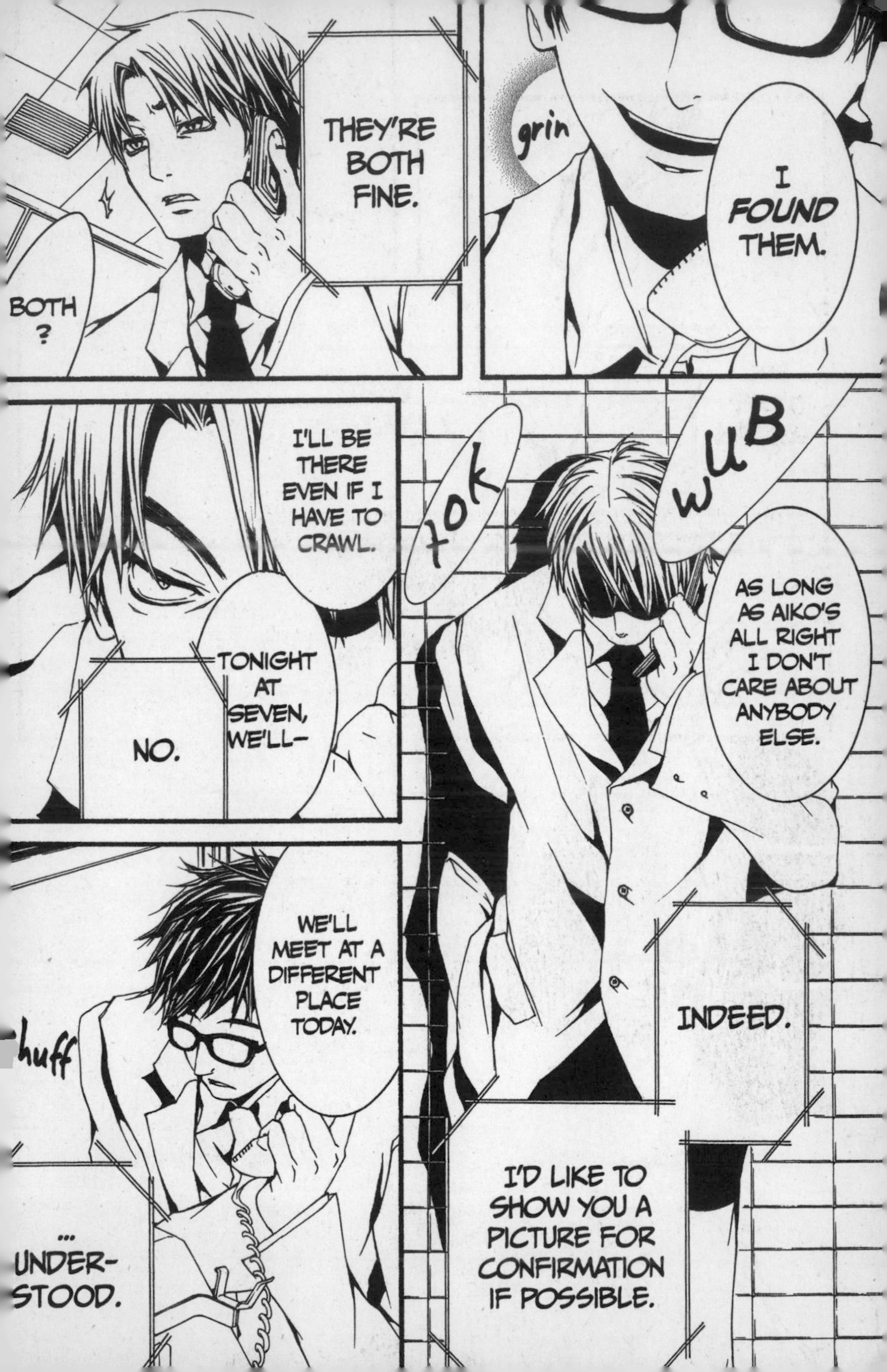
I FOUND THEM.
grin
THEY'RE BOTH FINE.
BOTH?
wUB
tok
AS LONG AS AIKO'S ALL RIGHT I DON'T CARE ABOUT ANYBODY ELSE.
INDEED.
I'D LIKE TO SHOW YOU A PICTURE FOR CONFIRMATION IF POSSIBLE.
I'LL BE THERE EVEN IF I HAVE TO CRAWL.
TONIGHT AT SEVEN, WE'LL-
NO.
WE'LL MEET AT A DIFFERENT PLACE TODAY.
huff
...UNDER-STOOD.

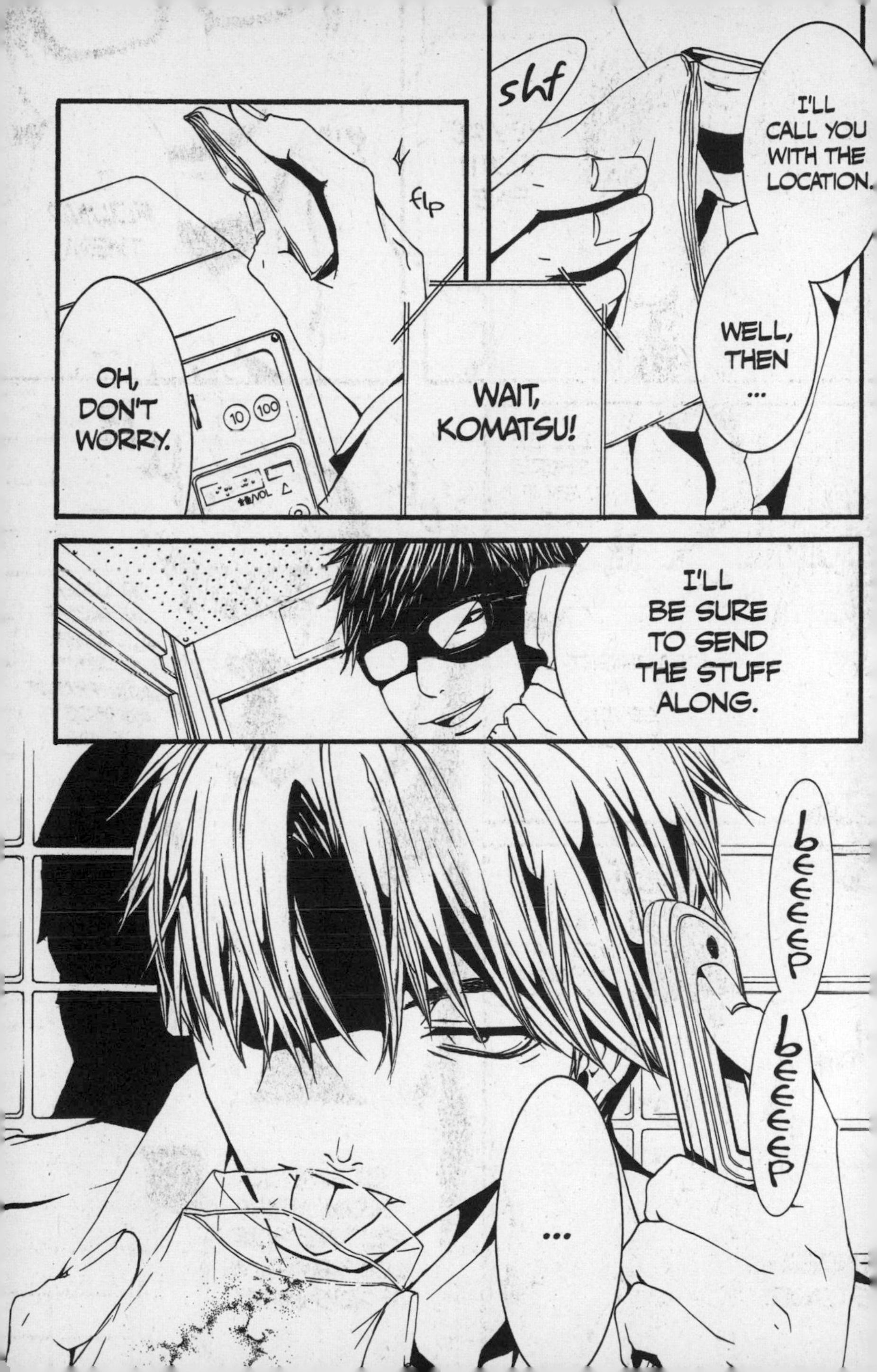
shf
I'LL CALL YOU WITH THE LOCATION.
WELL, THEN ...
WAIT, KOMATSU!
flp
OH, DON'T WORRY.
I'LL BE SURE TO SEND THE STUFF ALONG.
beeeep
beeeep
...

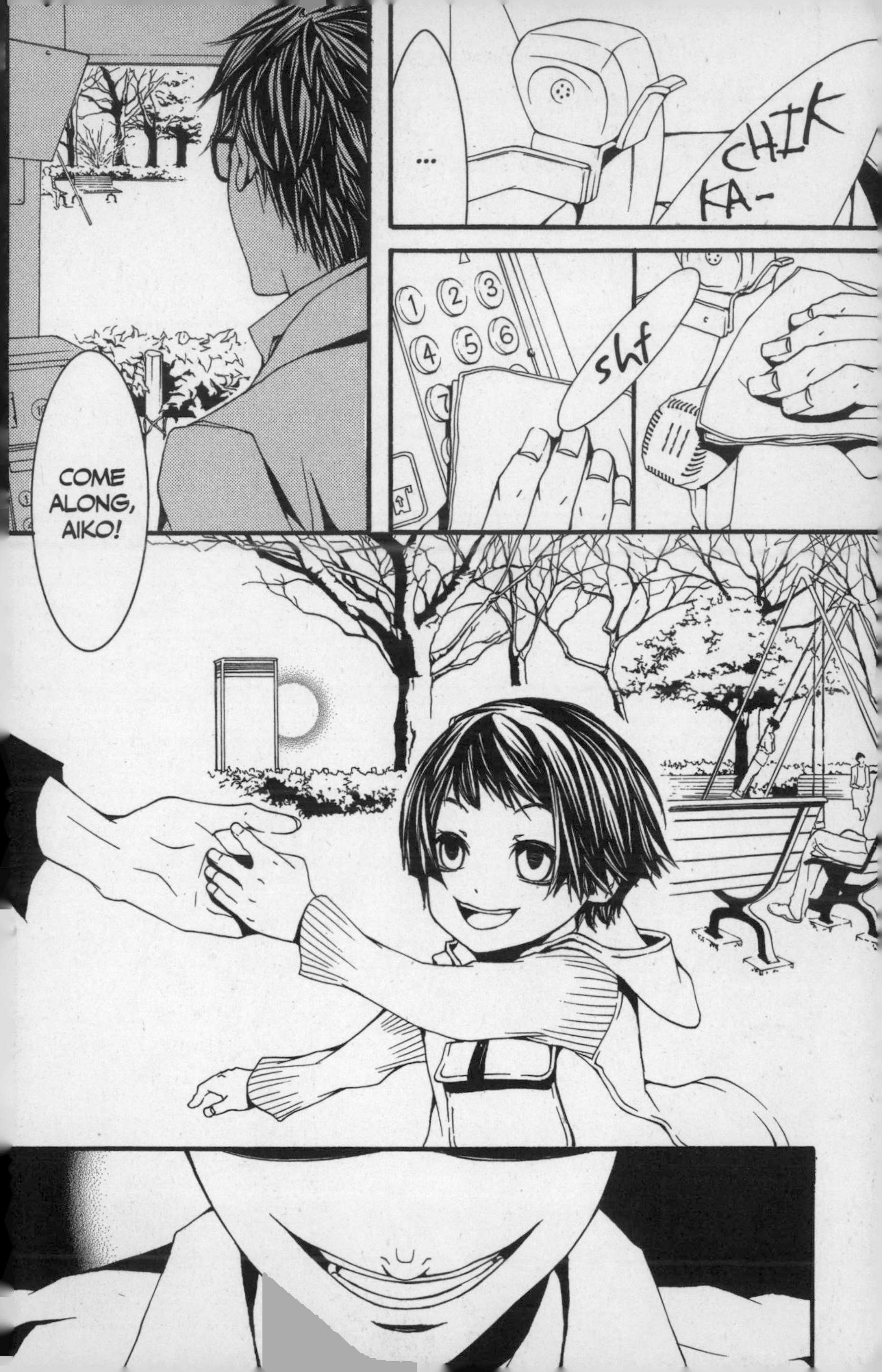
KA-CHIK
...
shf
COME ALONG, AIKO!

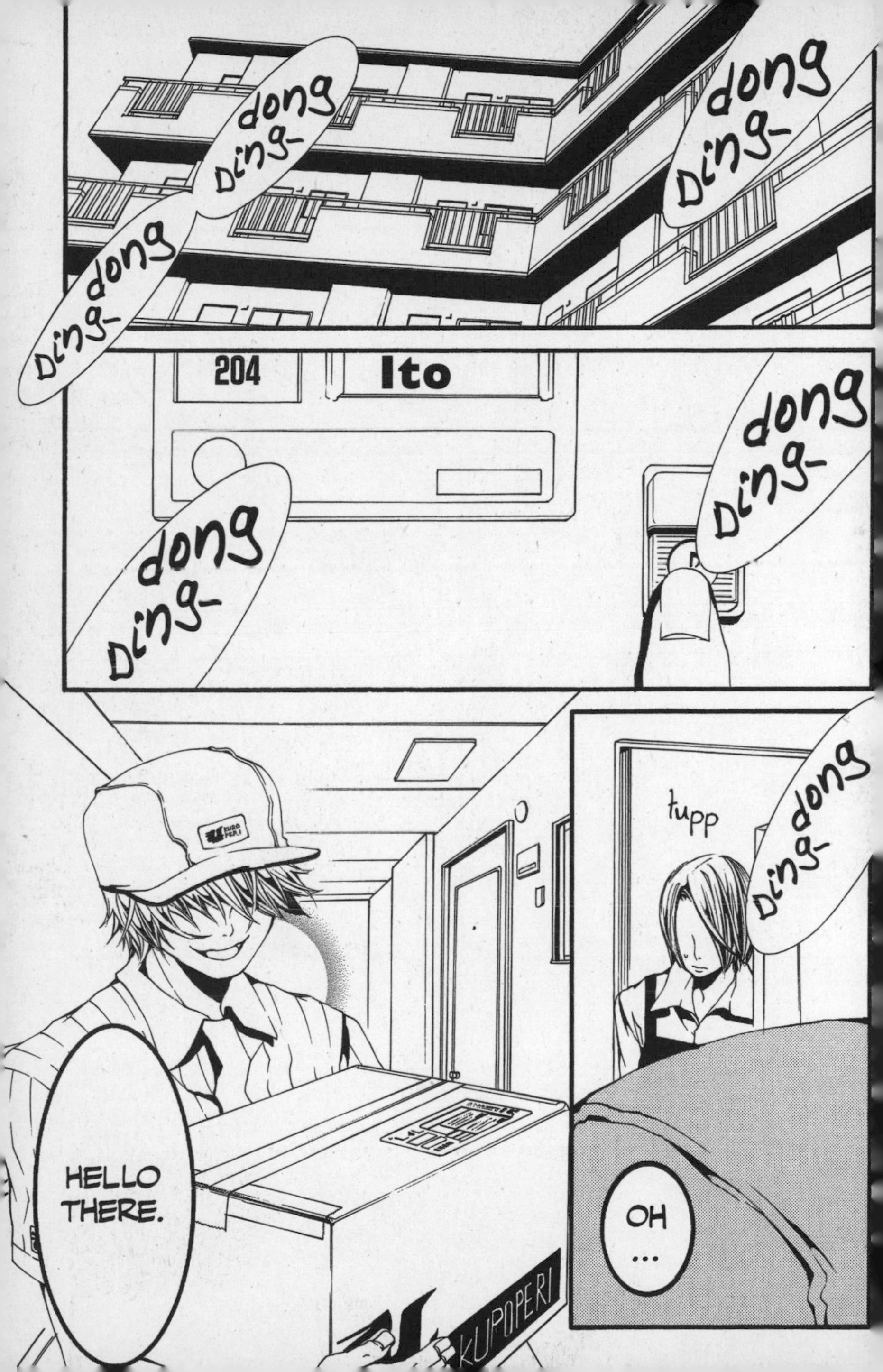

Ding-dong
Ding-dong
Ding-dong
Ito
204
Ding-dong
Ding-dong
Ding-dong
tupp
OH ...
HELLO THERE.
EURO PERI
KUPOPERI

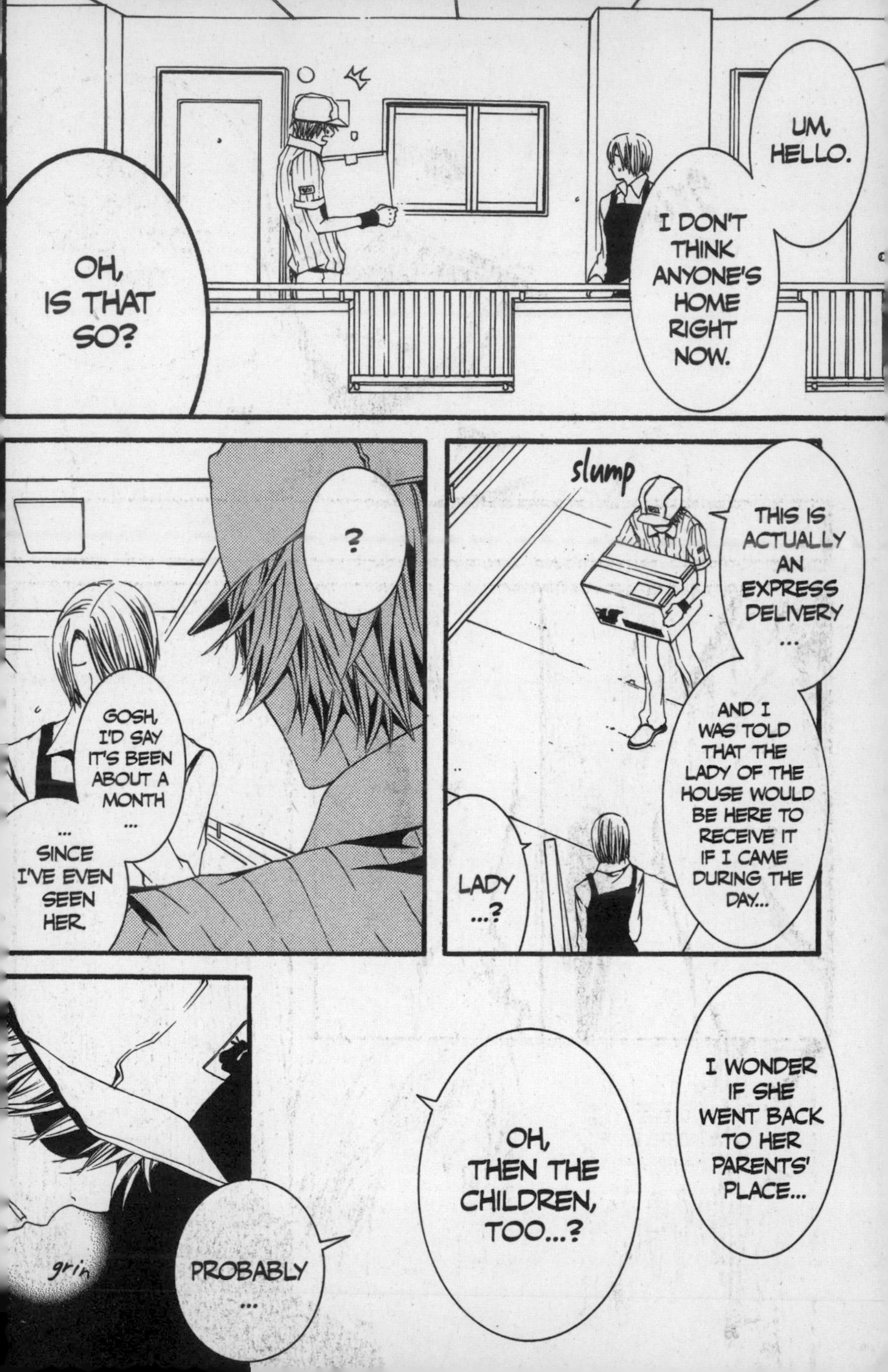
UM, HELLO.
I DON'T THINK ANYONE'S HOME RIGHT NOW.
OH, IS THAT SO?
slump
THIS IS ACTUALLY AN EXPRESS DELIVERY ...
AND I WAS TOLD THAT THE LADY OF THE HOUSE WOULD BE HERE TO RECEIVE IT IF I CAME DURING THE DAY...
LADY ...?
?
GOSH, I'D SAY IT'S BEEN ABOUT A MONTH ...
... SINCE I'VE EVEN SEEN HER.
I WONDER IF SHE WENT BACK TO HER PARENTS' PLACE...
OH, THEN THE CHILDREN, TOO...?
PROBABLY ...
grin

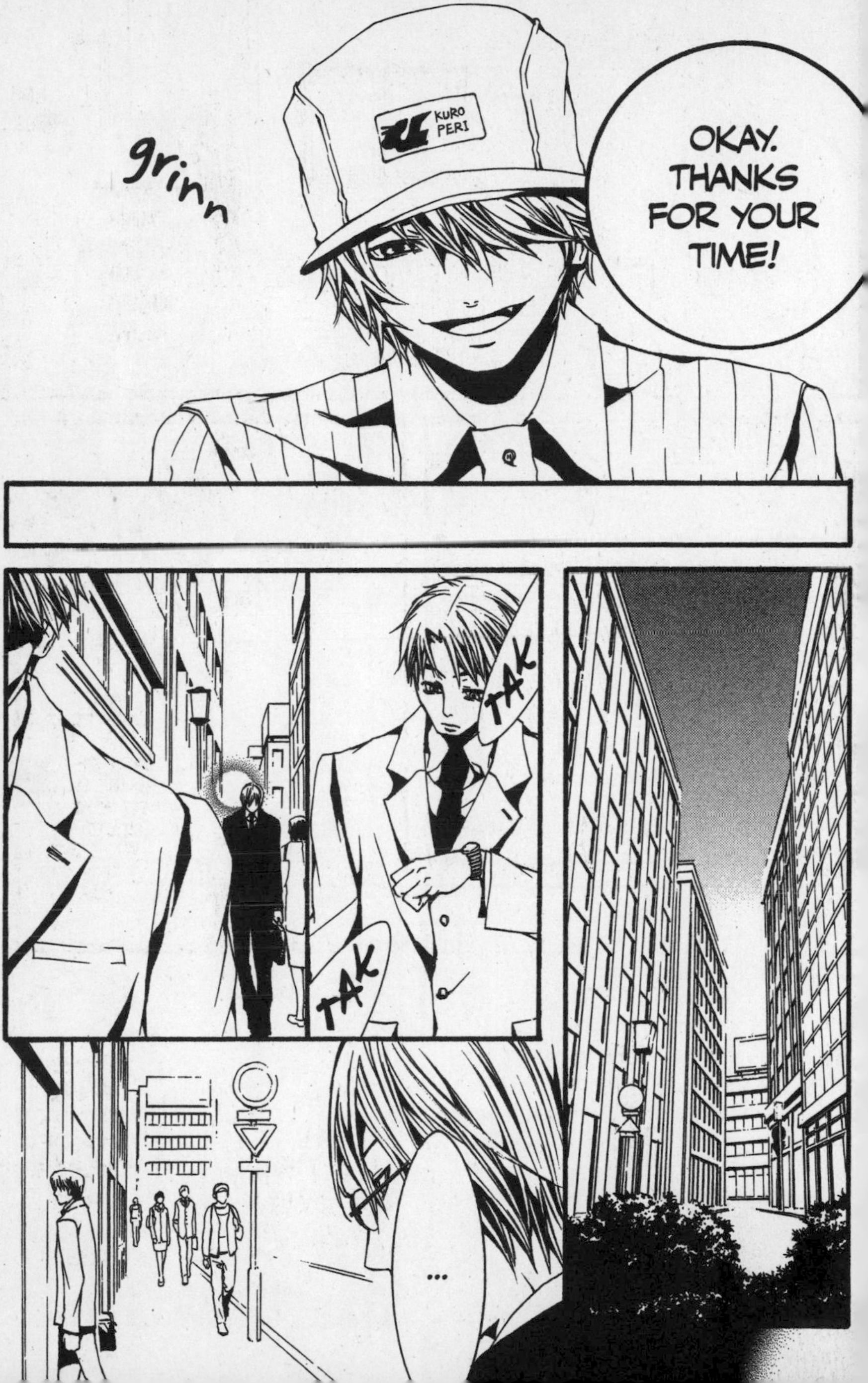
OKAY. THANKS FOR YOUR TIME!
KURO PERI
grinn
TAK
TAK
...

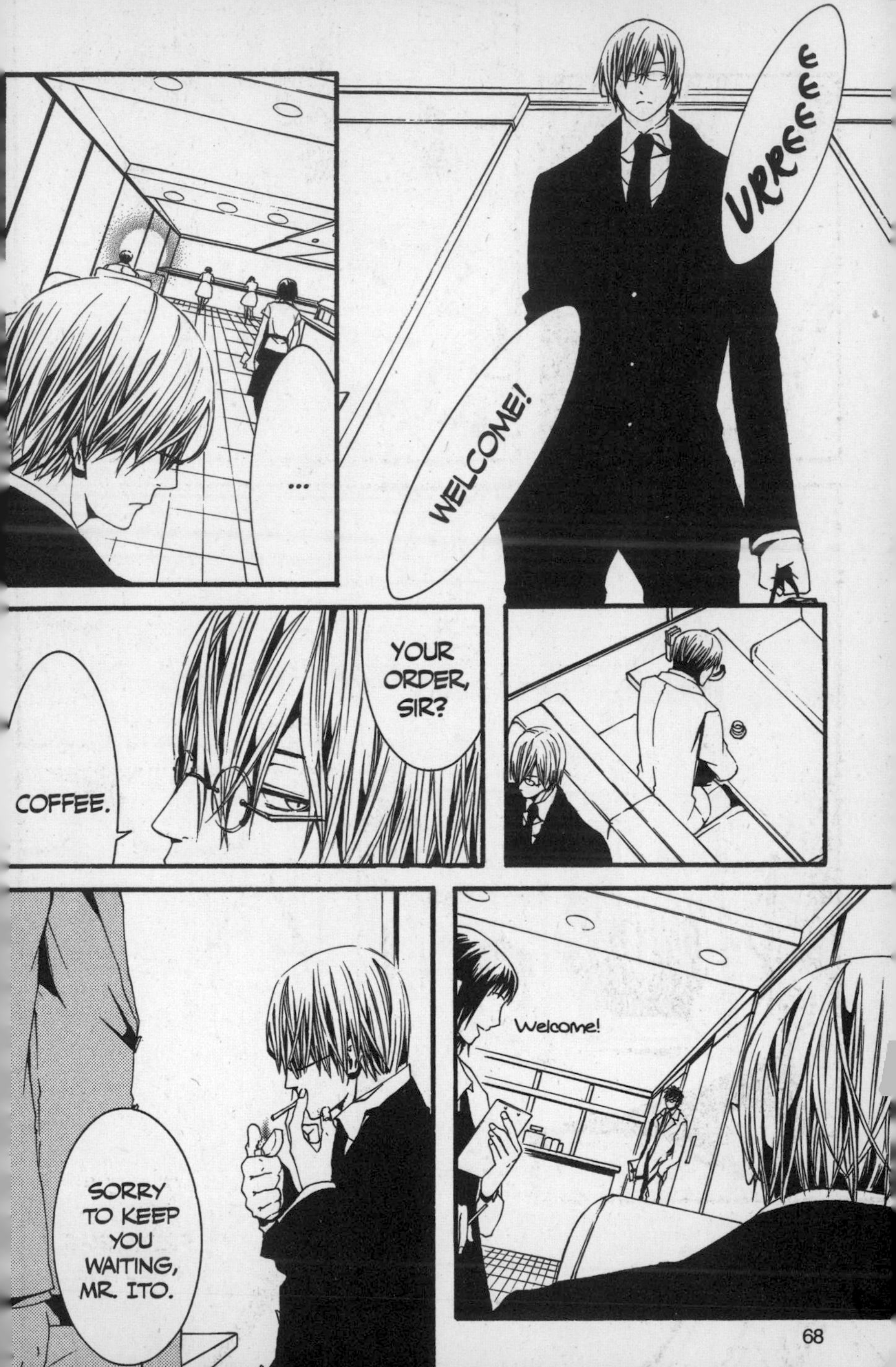
URREEEE
WELCOME!
...
YOUR ORDER, SIR?
COFFEE.
Welcome!
SORRY TO KEEP YOU WAITING, MR. ITO.

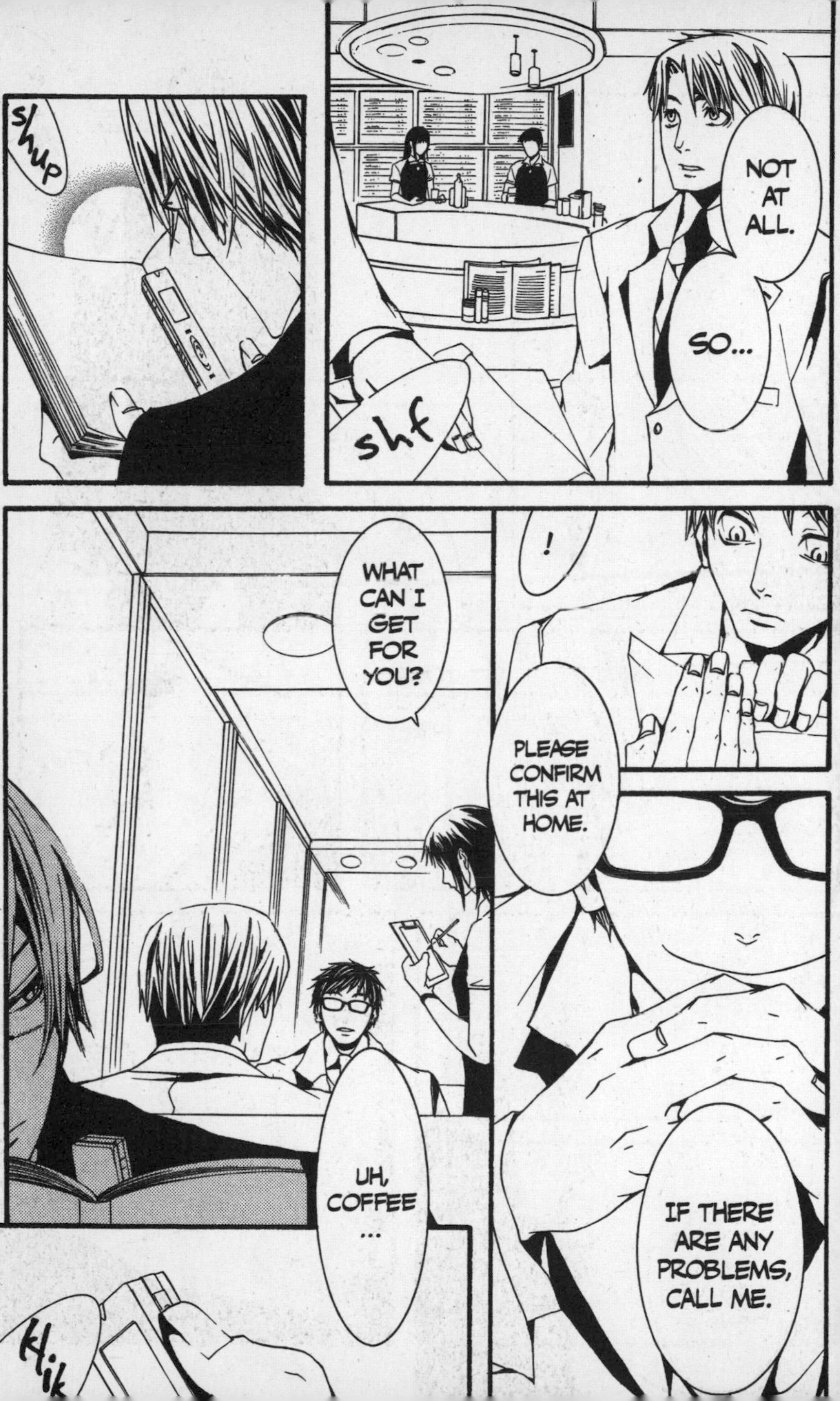
NOT AT ALL.
SO...
shf
shup
!
PLEASE CONFIRM THIS AT HOME.
IF THERE ARE ANY PROBLEMS, CALL ME.
WHAT CAN I GET FOR YOU?
UH, COFFEE ...
klik

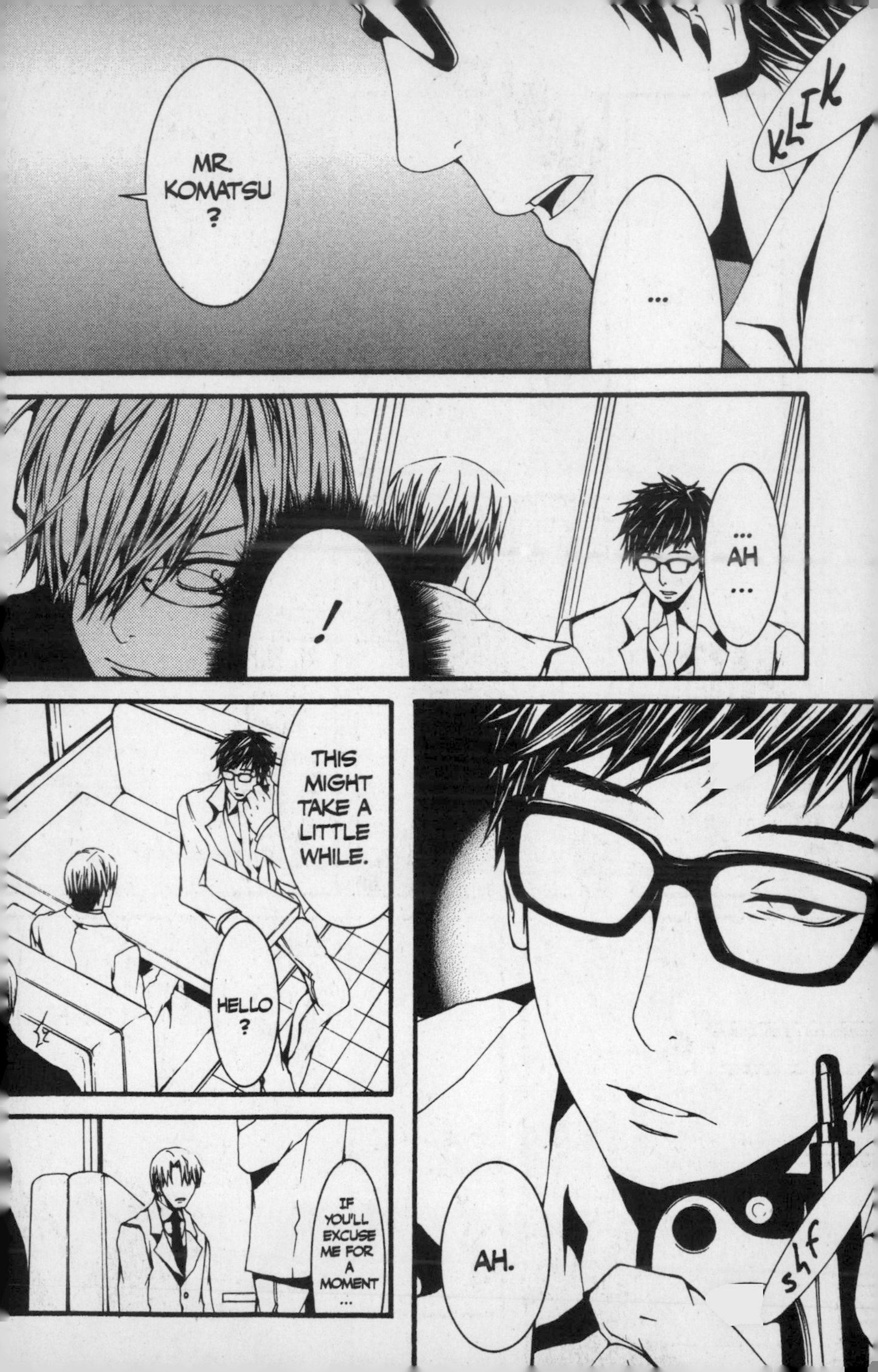
KLIK
...
MR. KOMATSU ?
... AH ...
!
shf
AH.
THIS MIGHT TAKE A LITTLE WHILE.
HELLO ?
IF YOU'LL EXCUSE ME FOR A MOMENT ...

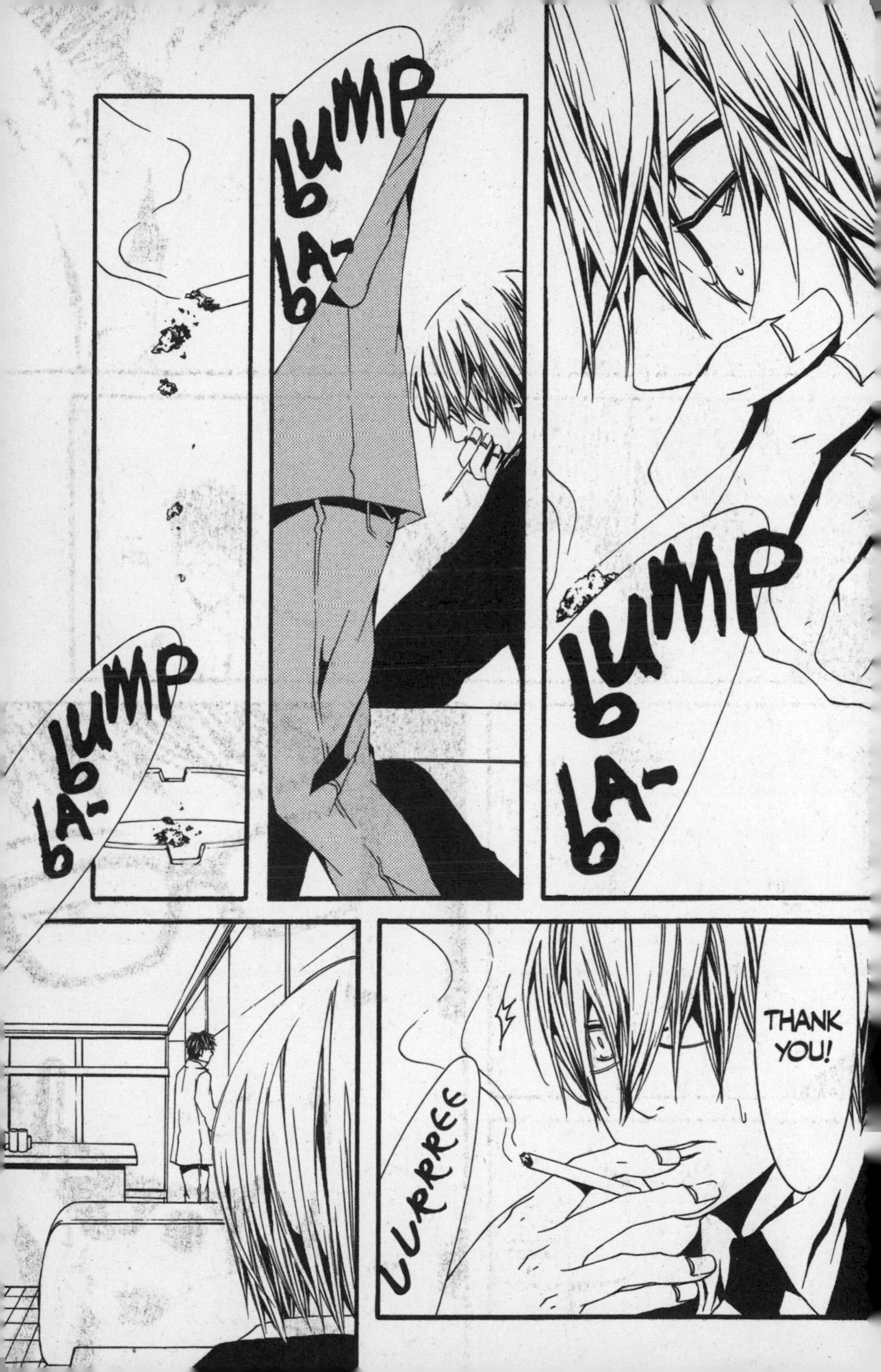
ba-bump
ba-bump
ba-bump
THANK YOU!
UURRREE

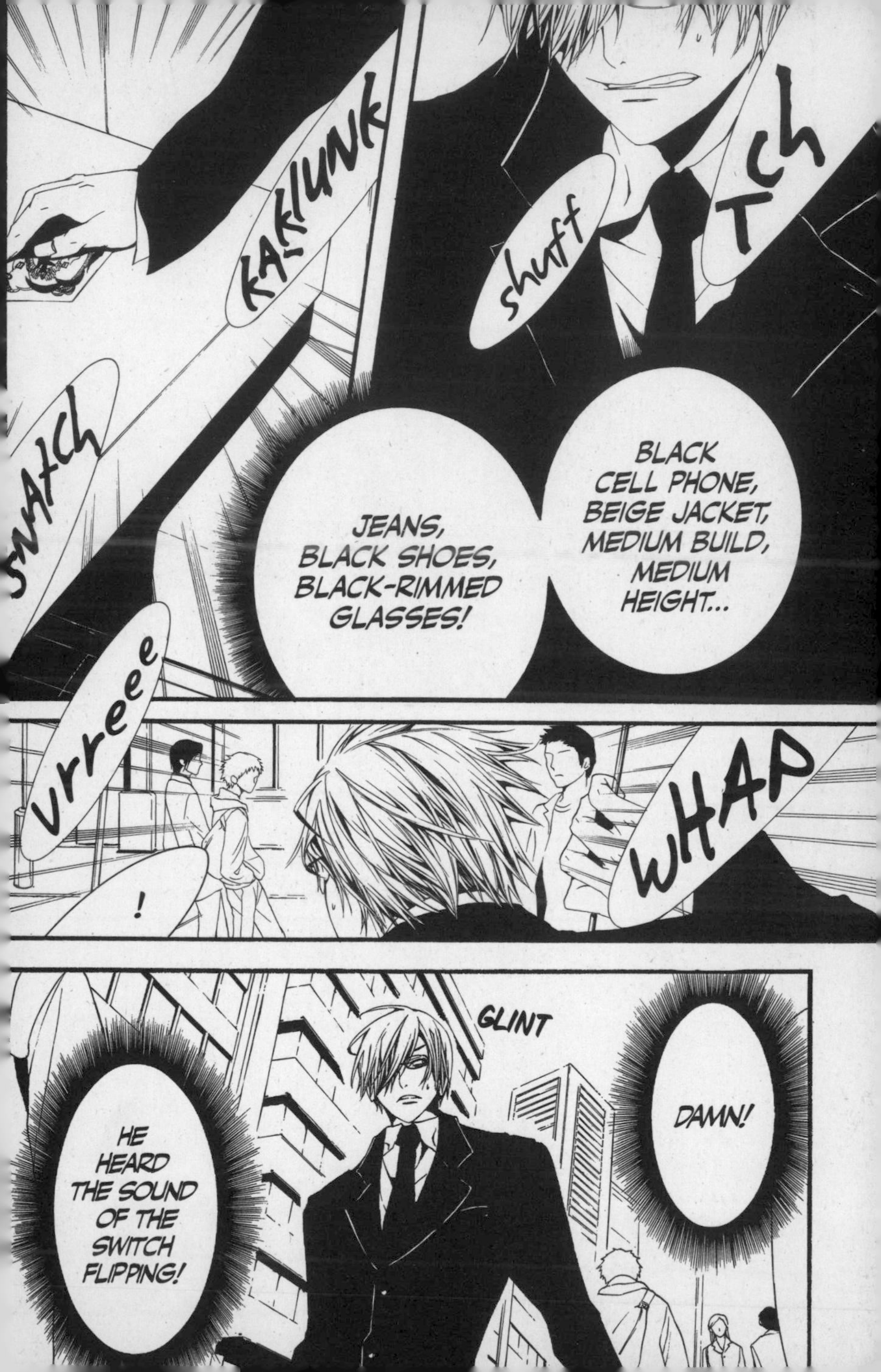
TCH
shuff
KA-KLUNK
SWATCH
BLACK CELL PHONE, BEIGE JACKET, MEDIUM BUILD, MEDIUM HEIGHT...
JEANS, BLACK SHOES, BLACK-RIMMED GLASSES!
WHAP
vrreee
!
DAMN!
GLINT
HE HEARD THE SOUND OF THE SWITCH FLIPPING!

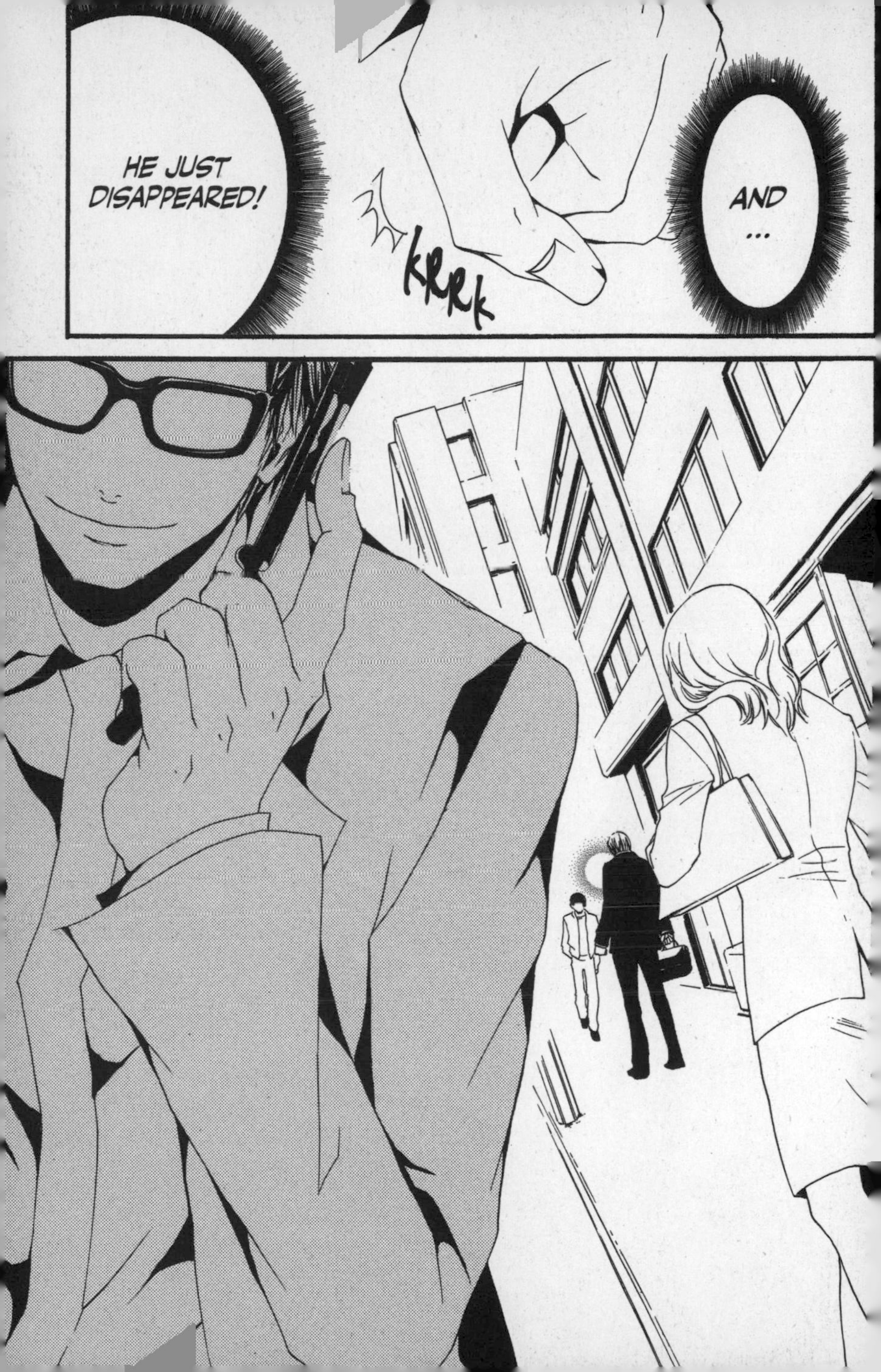
AND ...
KRRK
HE JUST DISAPPEARED!

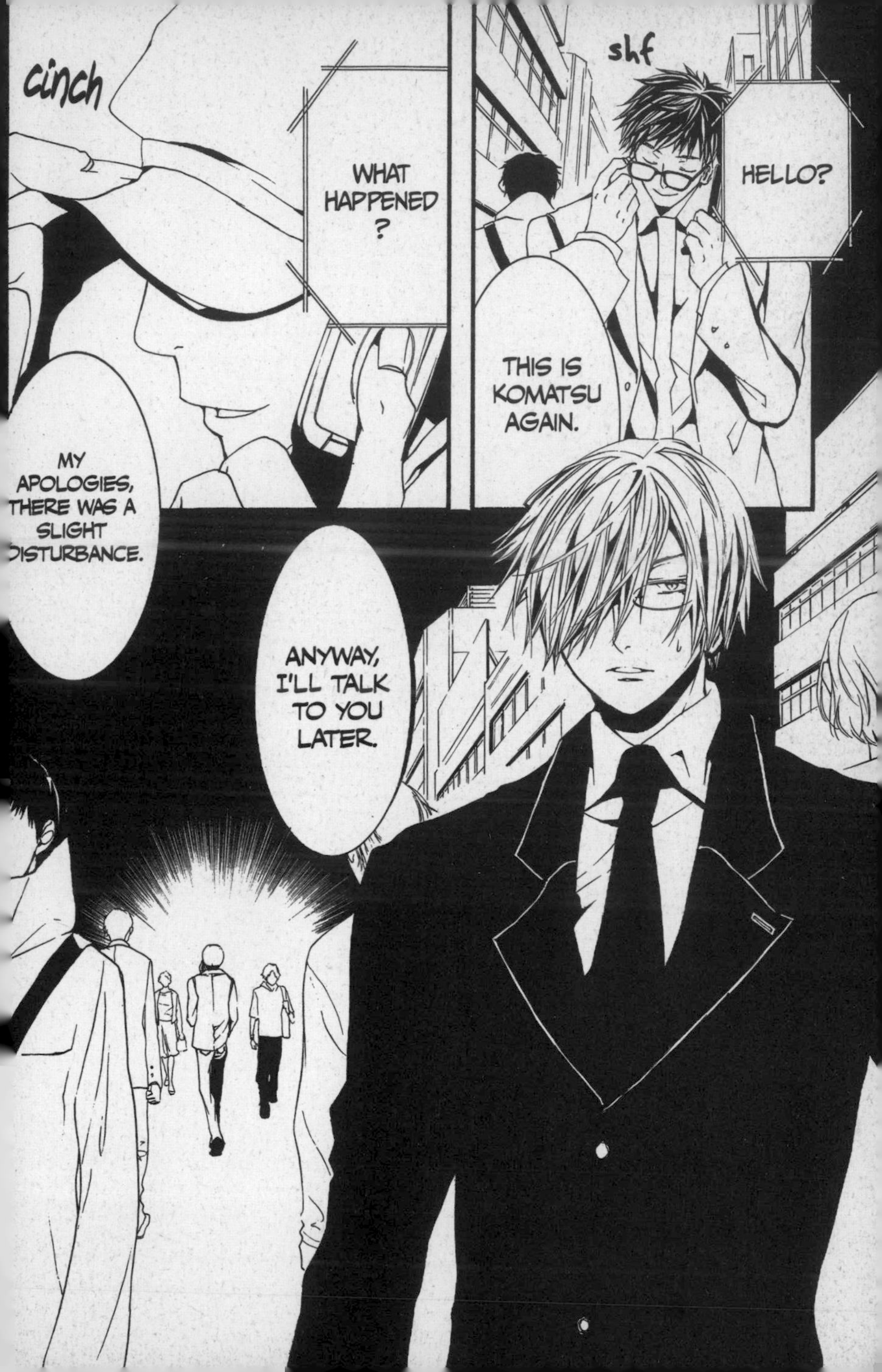
shf
HELLO?
THIS IS KOMATSU AGAIN.
cinch
WHAT HAPPENED?
MY APOLOGIES, THERE WAS A SLIGHT DISTURBANCE.
ANYWAY, I'LL TALK TO YOU LATER.

[switch]

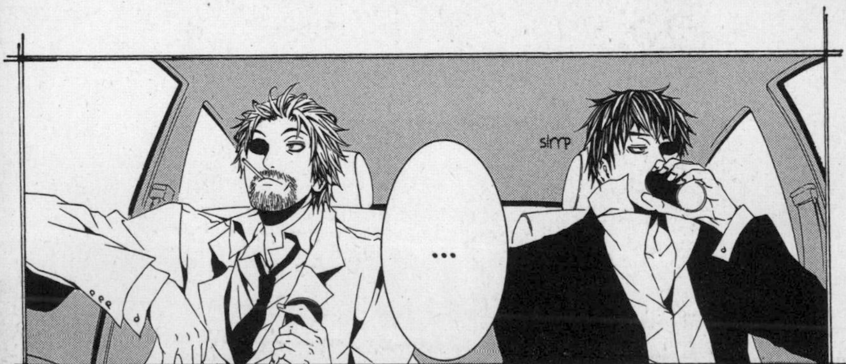
sirrp
...

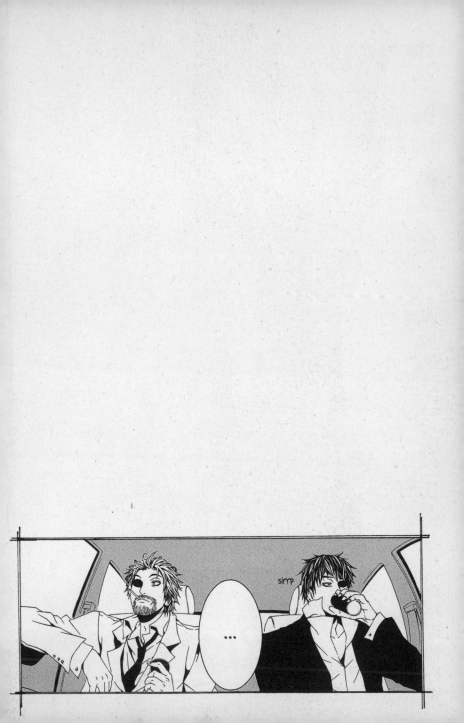

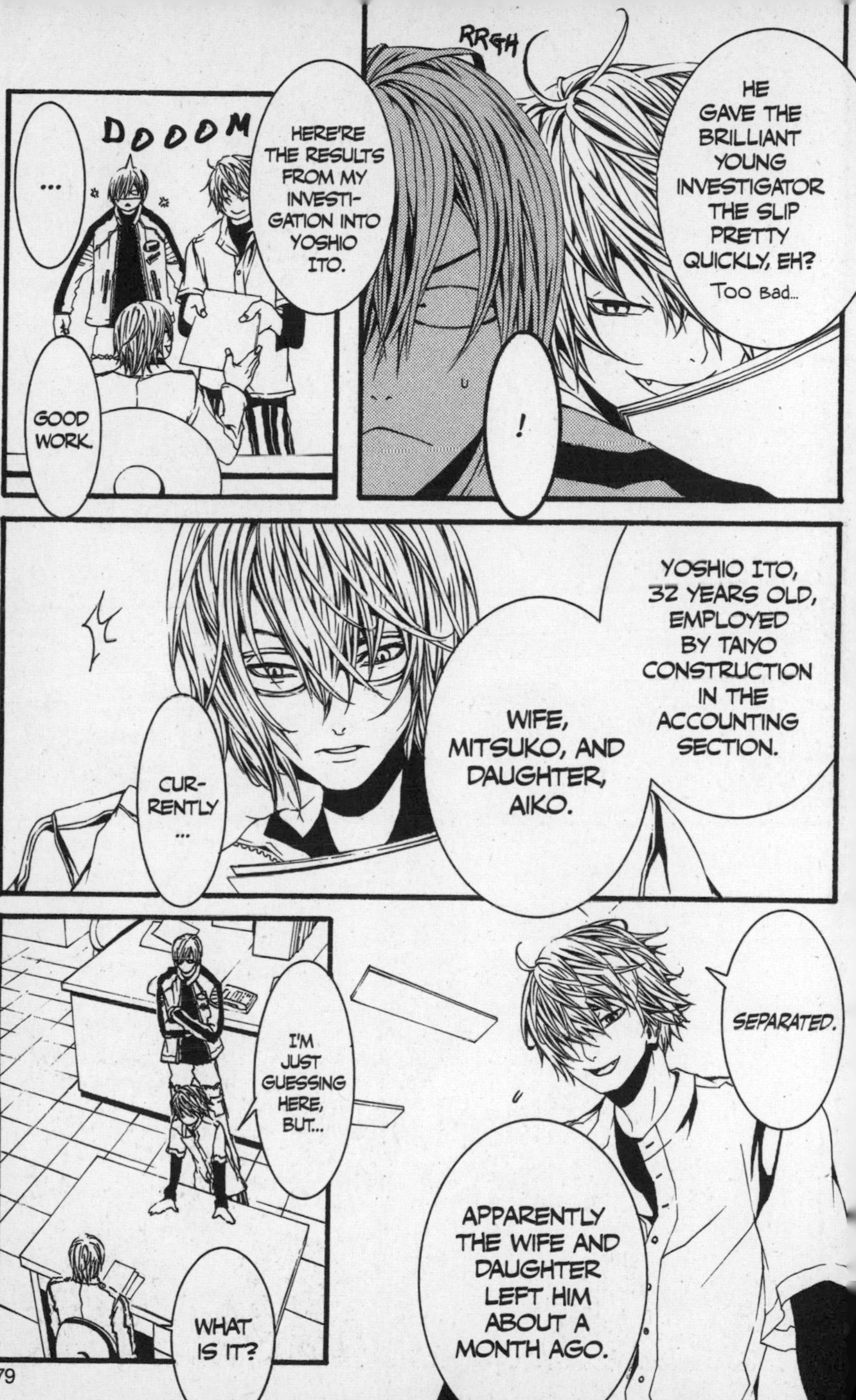
RRGH
HE GAVE THE BRILLIANT YOUNG INVESTIGATOR THE SLIP PRETTY QUICKLY, EH? Too bad...
!
HERE'RE THE RESULTS FROM MY INVESTI-GATION INTO YOSHIO ITO.
DOOOM
...
GOOD WORK.
YOSHIO ITO, 32 YEARS OLD, EMPLOYED BY TAIYO CONSTRUCTION IN THE ACCOUNTING SECTION.
WIFE, MITSUKO, AND DAUGHTER, AIKO.
CUR-RENTLY...
SEPARATED.
APPARENTLY THE WIFE AND DAUGHTER LEFT HIM ABOUT A MONTH AGO.
I'M JUST GUESSING HERE, BUT...
WHAT IS IT?

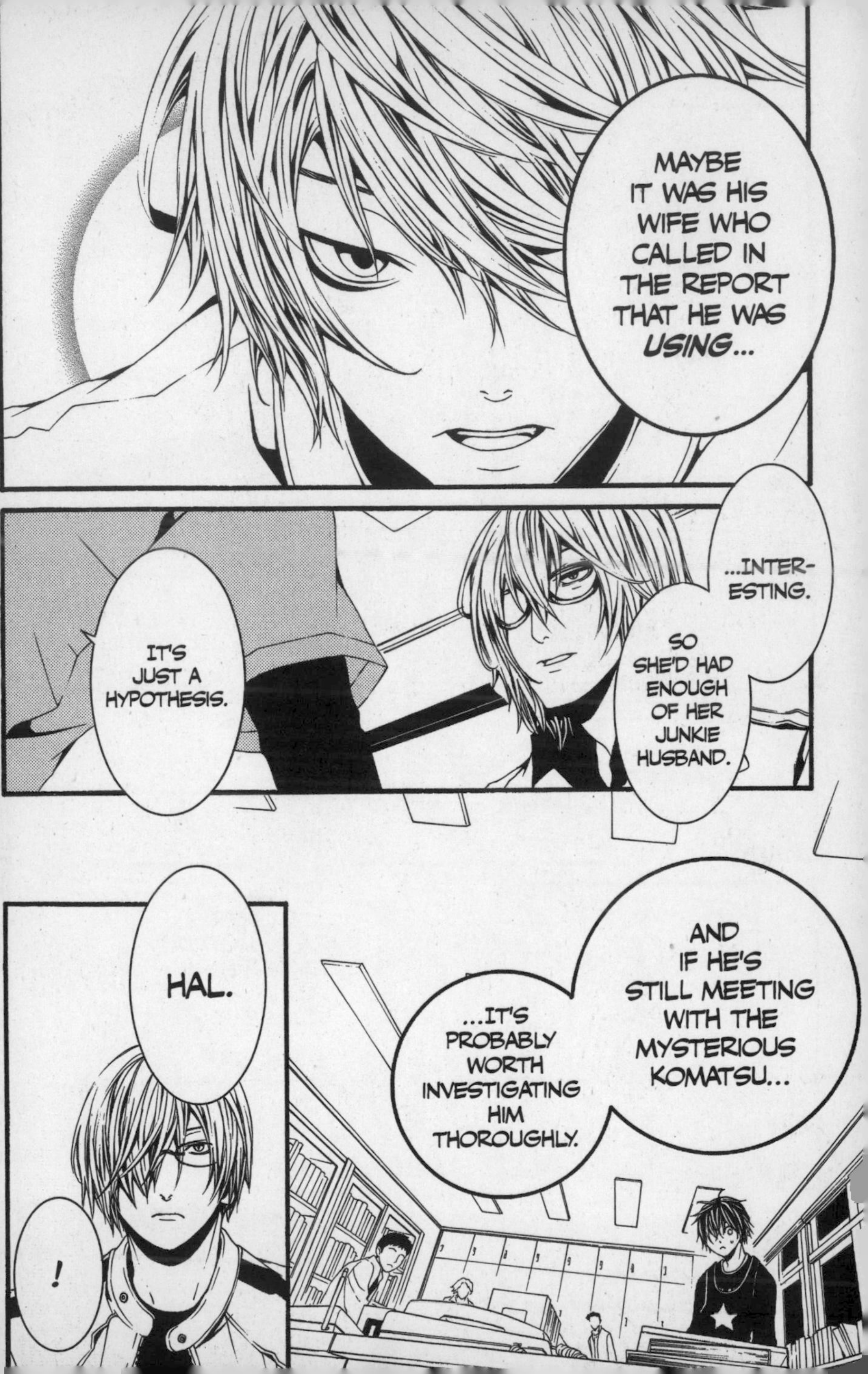
MAYBE IT WAS HIS WIFE WHO CALLED IN THE REPORT THAT HE WAS *USING*...
...INTER-ESTING.
SO SHE'D HAD ENOUGH OF HER JUNKIE HUSBAND.
IT'S JUST A HYPOTHESIS.
AND IF HE'S STILL MEETING WITH THE MYSTERIOUS KOMATSU...
...IT'S PROBABLY WORTH INVESTIGATING HIM THOROUGHLY.
HAL.
!

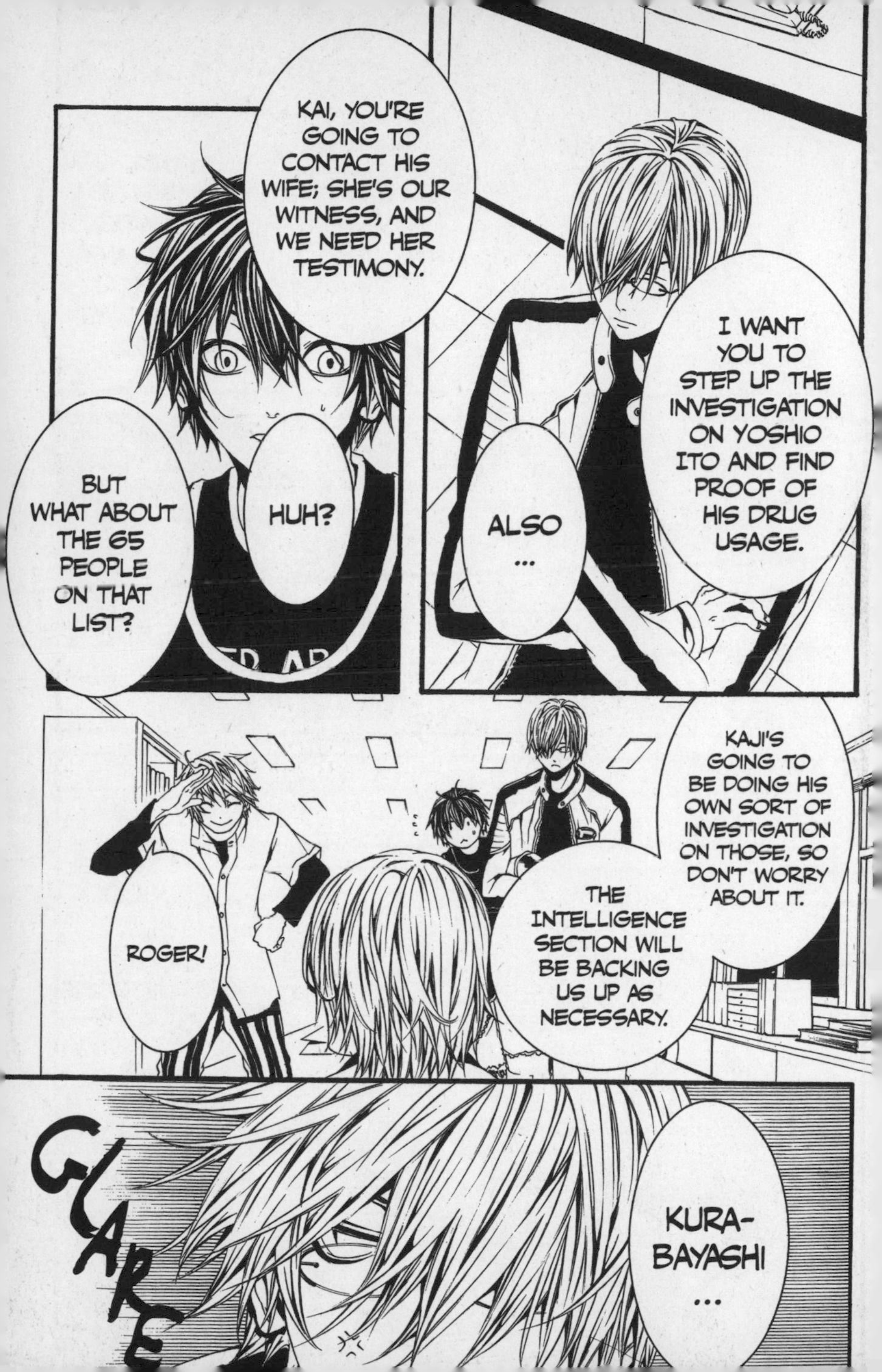
KAI, YOU'RE GOING TO CONTACT HIS WIFE; SHE'S OUR WITNESS, AND WE NEED HER TESTIMONY.
ALSO ...
I WANT YOU TO STEP UP THE INVESTIGATION ON YOSHIO ITO AND FIND PROOF OF HIS DRUG USAGE.
HUH?
BUT WHAT ABOUT THE 65 PEOPLE ON THAT LIST?
KAJI'S GOING TO BE DOING HIS OWN SORT OF INVESTIGATION ON THOSE, SO DON'T WORRY ABOUT IT.
THE INTELLIGENCE SECTION WILL BE BACKING US UP AS NECESSARY.
ROGER!
KURA-BAYASHI ...
GLARE

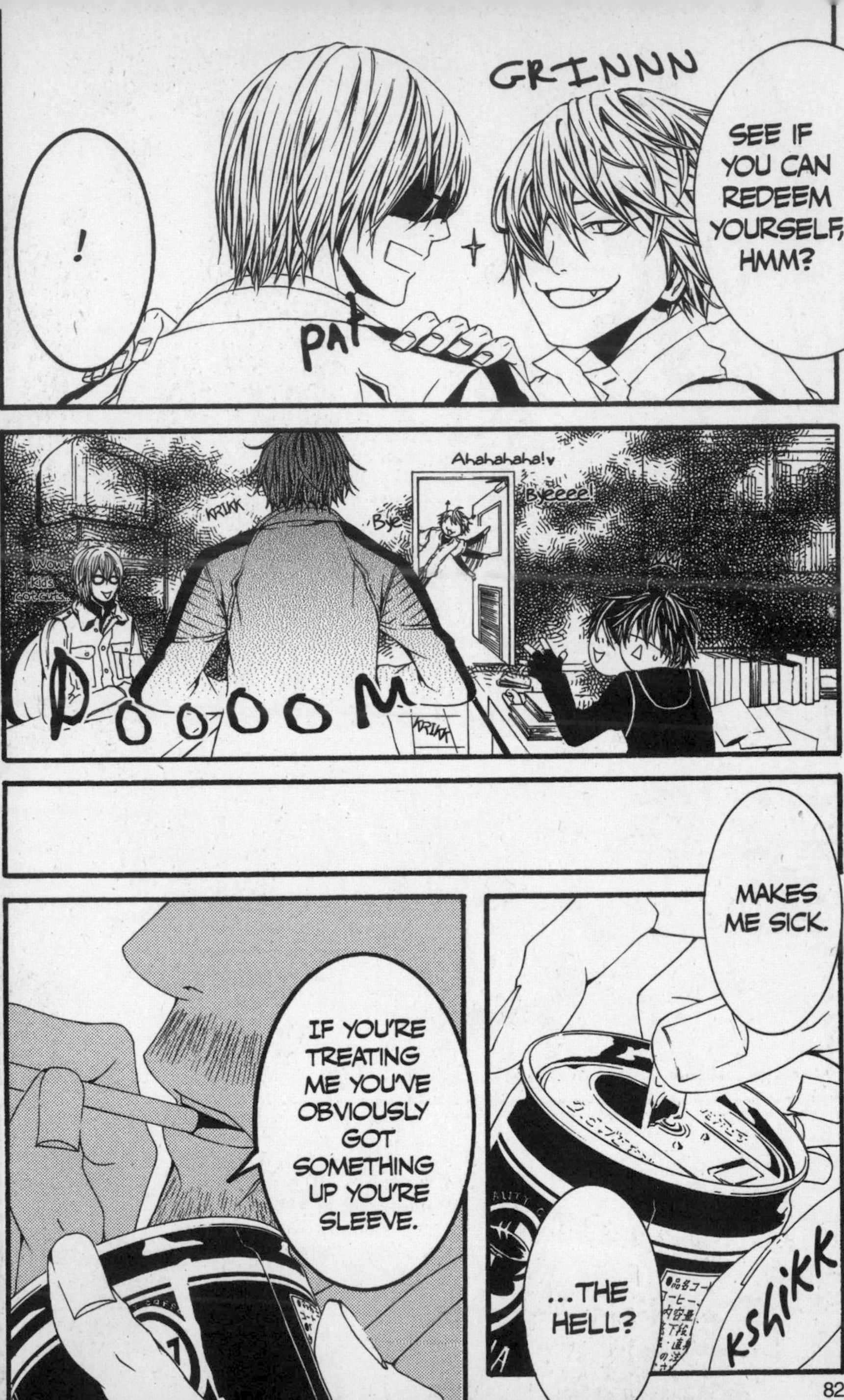
SEE IF YOU CAN REDEEM YOURSELF, HMM?
GRINNN
PAT
!
Ahahahaha!♥
Byeeee!
Bye
KRIKK
Wow. Kids got guts...
DOOOOM
KRIKK
MAKES ME SICK.
KSHIKK
...THE HELL?
IF YOU'RE TREATING ME YOU'VE OBVIOUSLY GOT SOMETHING UP YOU'RE SLEEVE.

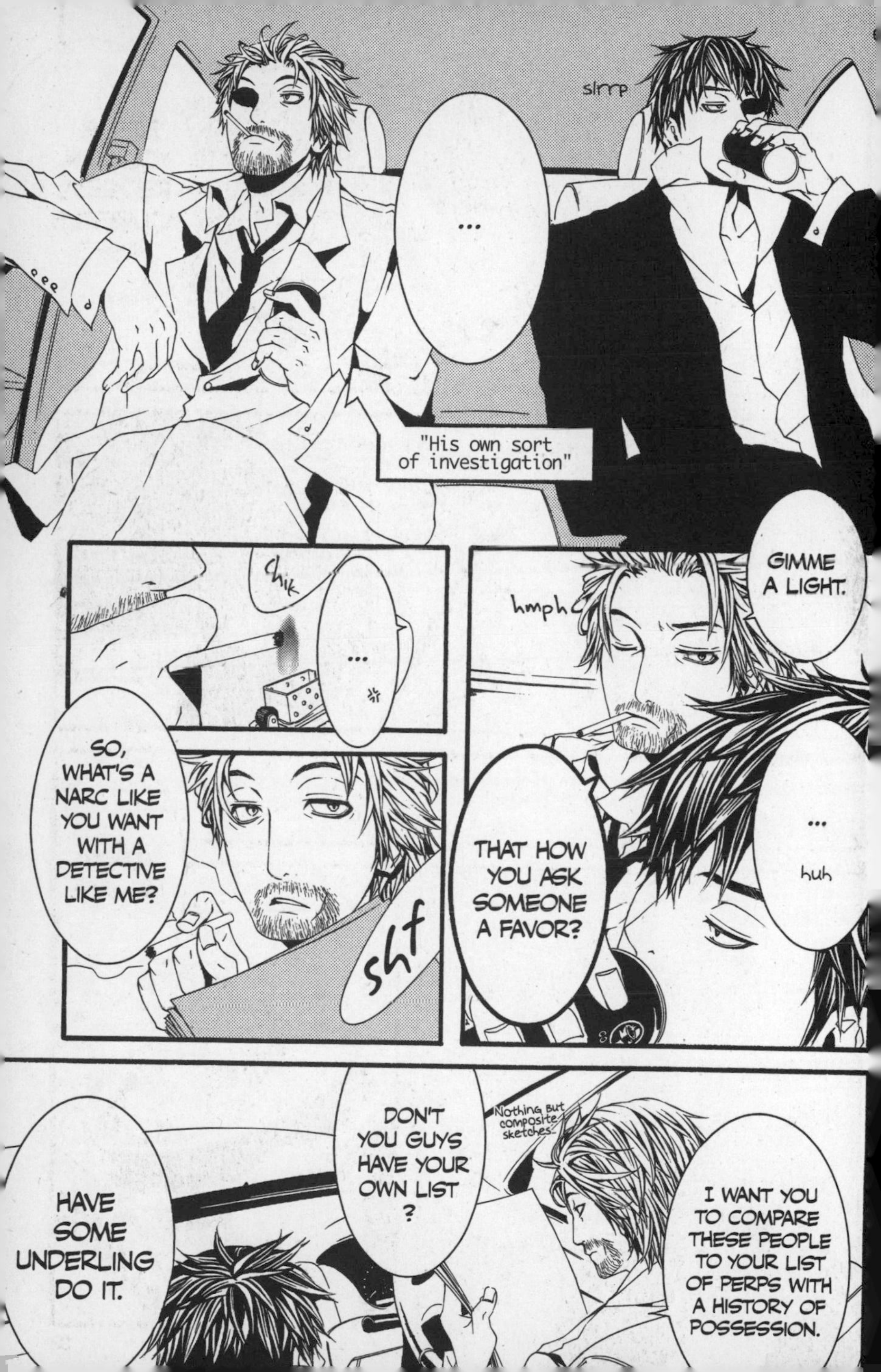
slrrp
...
"His own sort of investigation"
GIMME A LIGHT.
hmph
...
huh
THAT HOW YOU ASK SOMEONE A FAVOR?
chik
...
SO, WHAT'S A NARC LIKE YOU WANT WITH A DETECTIVE LIKE ME?
shf
I WANT YOU TO COMPARE THESE PEOPLE TO YOUR LIST OF PERPS WITH A HISTORY OF POSSESSION.
Nothing but composite sketches
DON'T YOU GUYS HAVE YOUR OWN LIST ?
HAVE SOME UNDERLING DO IT.

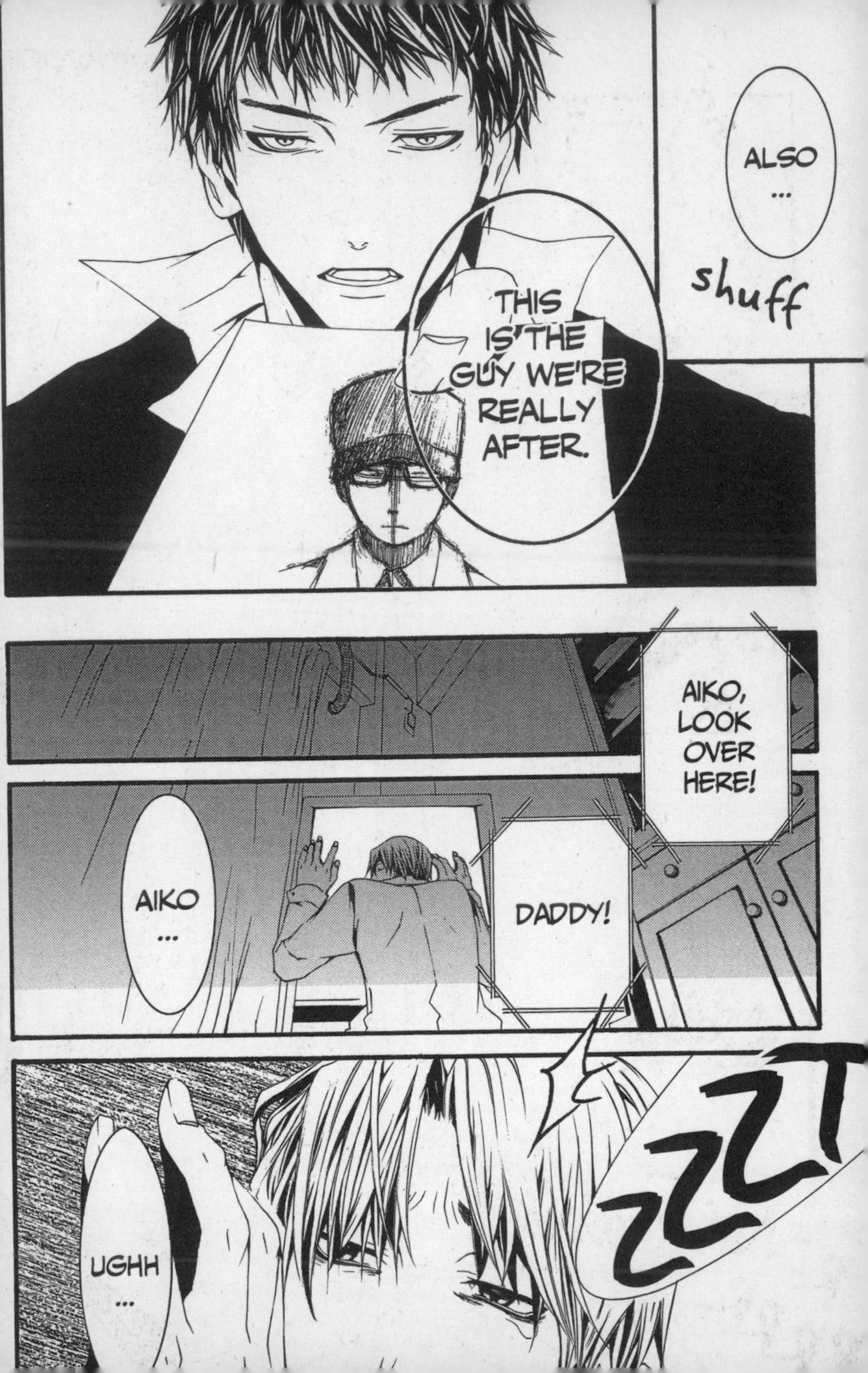
ALSO ...
shuff
THIS IS THE GUY WE'RE REALLY AFTER.
AIKO, LOOK OVER HERE!
DADDY!
AIKO ...
ZZZT
UGHH ...

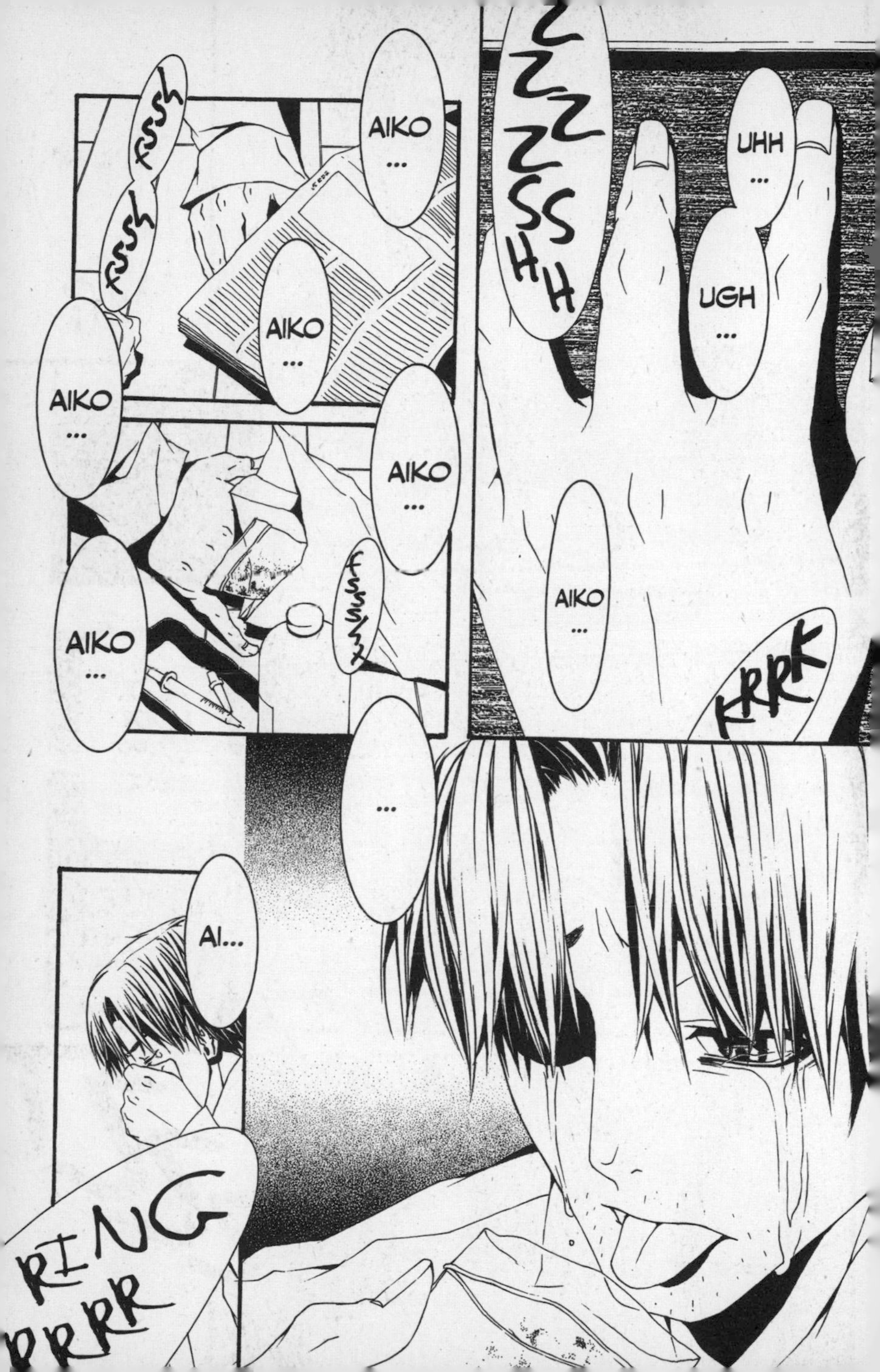
ZZZZSSHH
UHH...
UGH...
AIKO...
KRRK
AIKO...
fssh
fssh
AIKO...
AIKO...
AIKO...
fssssh
AIKO...
...
AI...
RING
RRRR

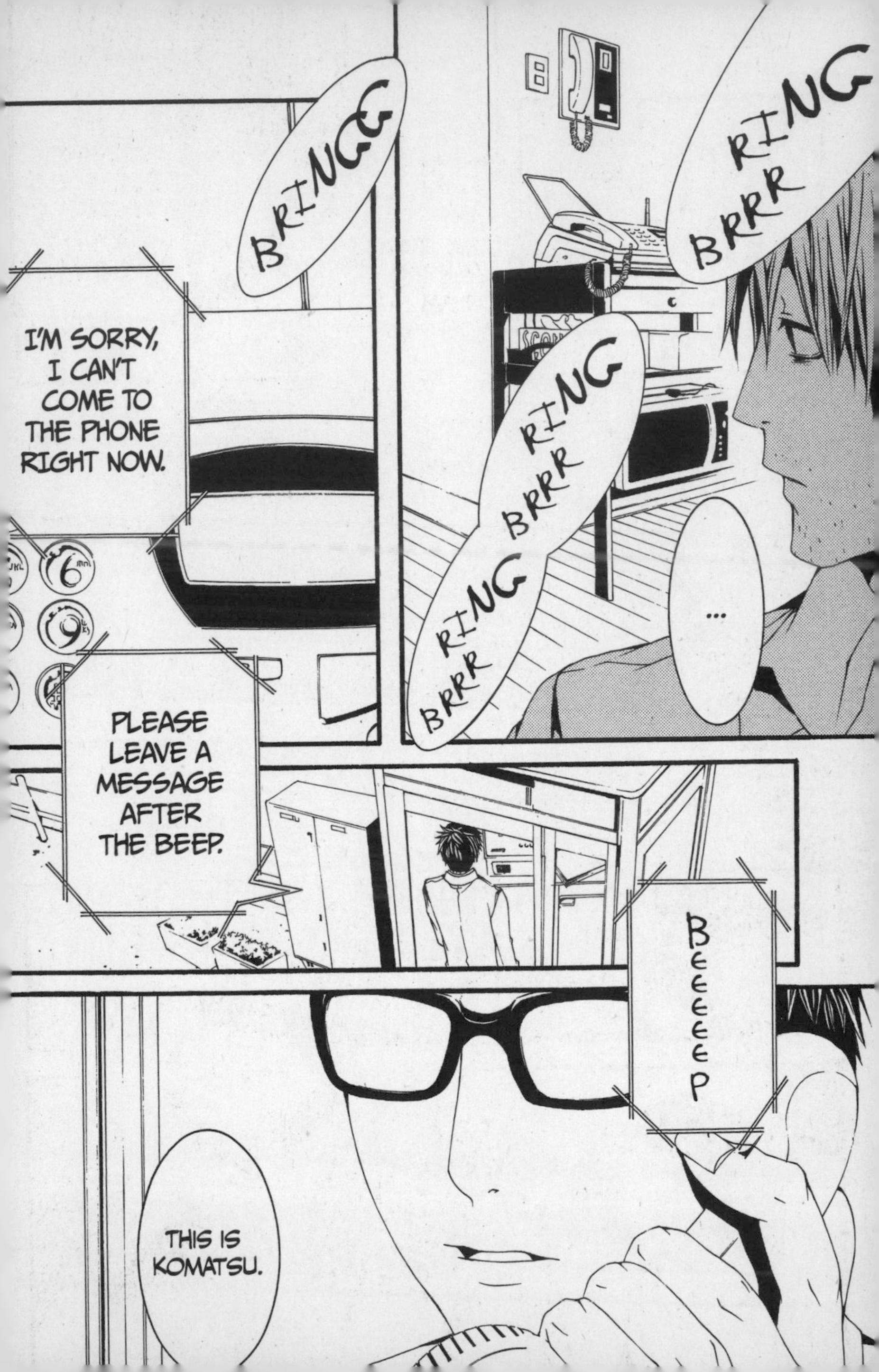
RING BRRR
RING BRRR
RING BRRR
...
BRINGG
I'M SORRY, I CAN'T COME TO THE PHONE RIGHT NOW.
PLEASE LEAVE A MESSAGE AFTER THE BEEP.
Beeeeep
THIS IS KOMATSU.

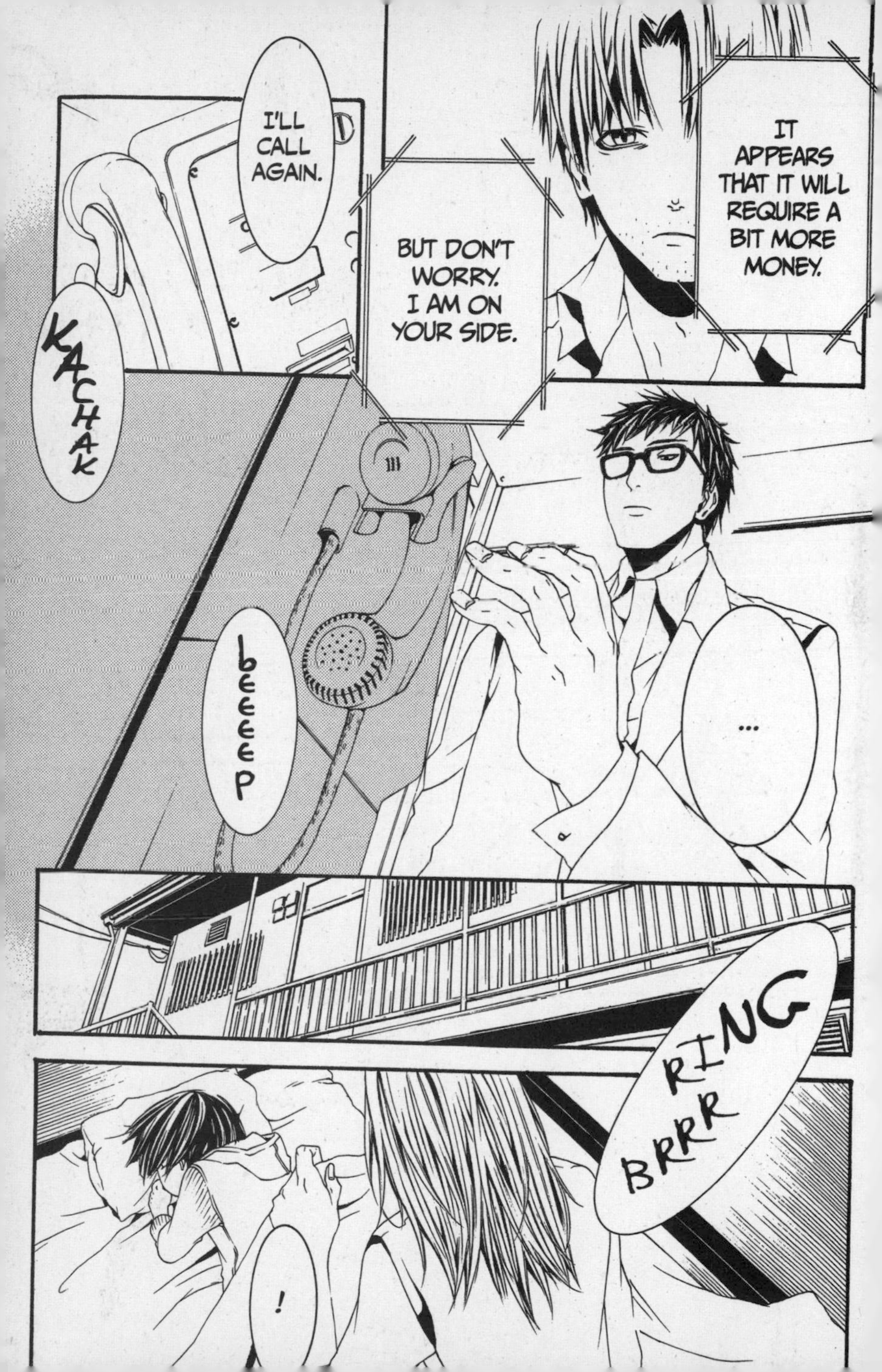
IT APPEARS THAT IT WILL REQUIRE A BIT MORE MONEY.
BUT DON'T WORRY. I AM ON YOUR SIDE.
I'LL CALL AGAIN.
KACHAK
...
beeeep
RING BRRR
!

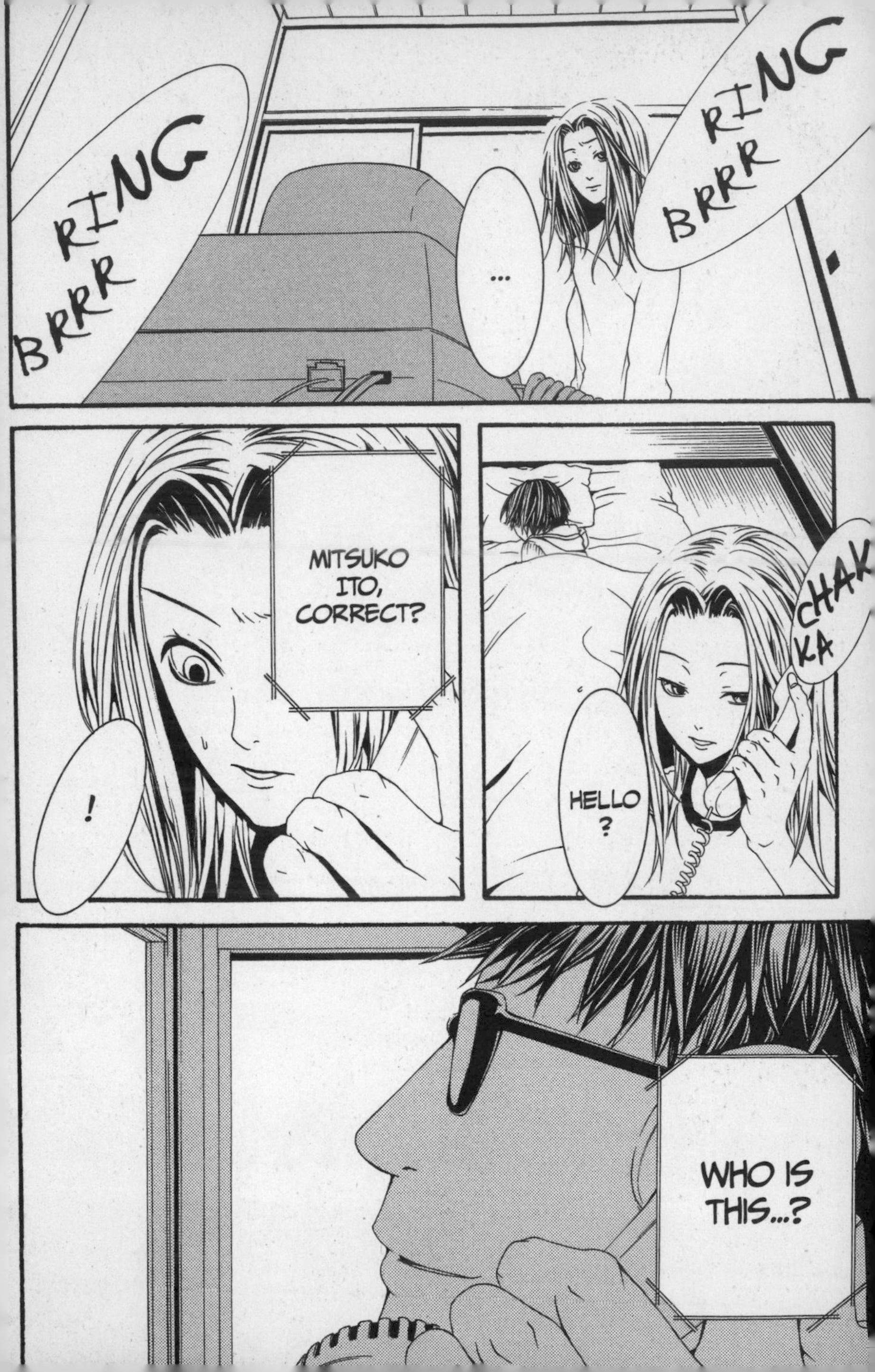
RING BRRR
...
RING BRRR
CHAKA
HELLO?
MITSUKO ITO, CORRECT?
!
WHO IS THIS...?

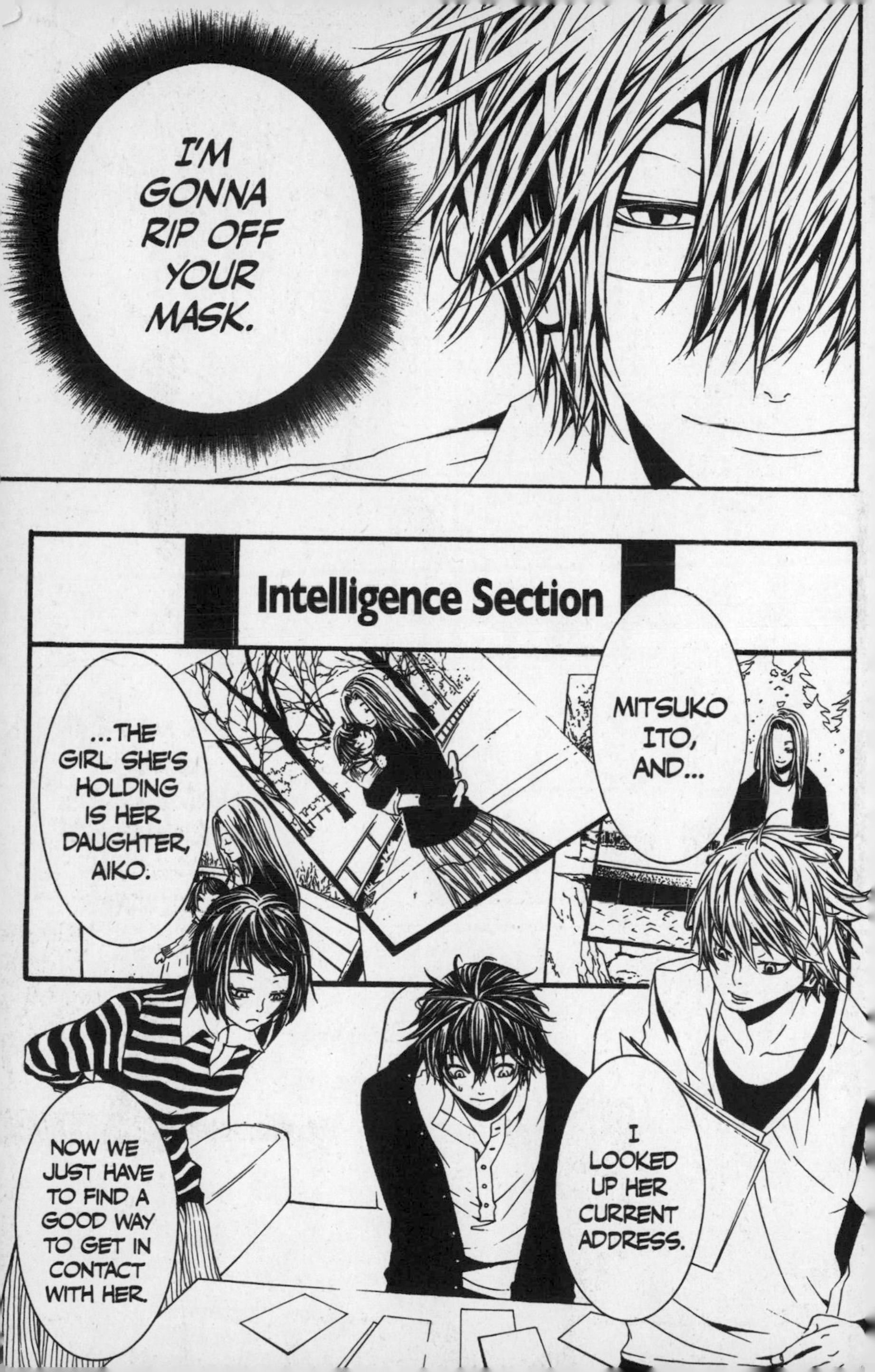
I'M GONNA RIP OFF YOUR MASK.
Intelligence Section
MITSUKO ITO, AND...
...THE GIRL SHE'S HOLDING IS HER DAUGHTER, AIKO.
I LOOKED UP HER CURRENT ADDRESS.
NOW WE JUST HAVE TO FIND A GOOD WAY TO GET IN CONTACT WITH HER.

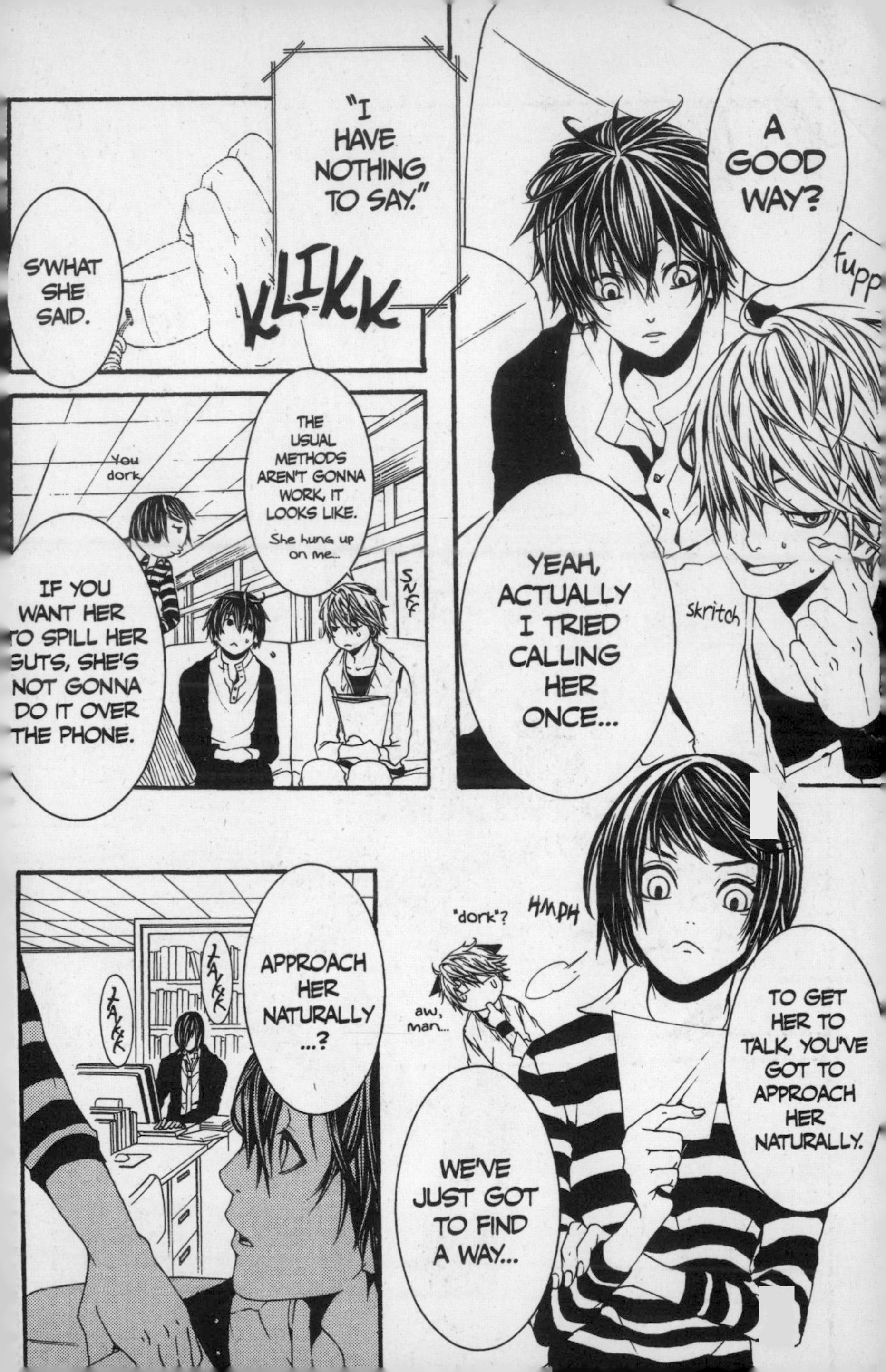
A GOOD WAY?
fupp
YEAH, ACTUALLY I TRIED CALLING HER ONCE...
skritch
"I HAVE NOTHING TO SAY."
KLIKK
S'WHAT SHE SAID.
THE USUAL METHODS AREN'T GONNA WORK, IT LOOKS LIKE.
She hung up on me...
SNFF
You dork
IF YOU WANT HER TO SPILL HER GUTS, SHE'S NOT GONNA DO IT OVER THE PHONE.
TO GET HER TO TALK, YOU'VE GOT TO APPROACH HER NATURALLY.
HMPH
"dork"?
aw, man...
WE'VE JUST GOT TO FIND A WAY...
APPROACH HER NATURALLY ...?
TAKK
TAKK

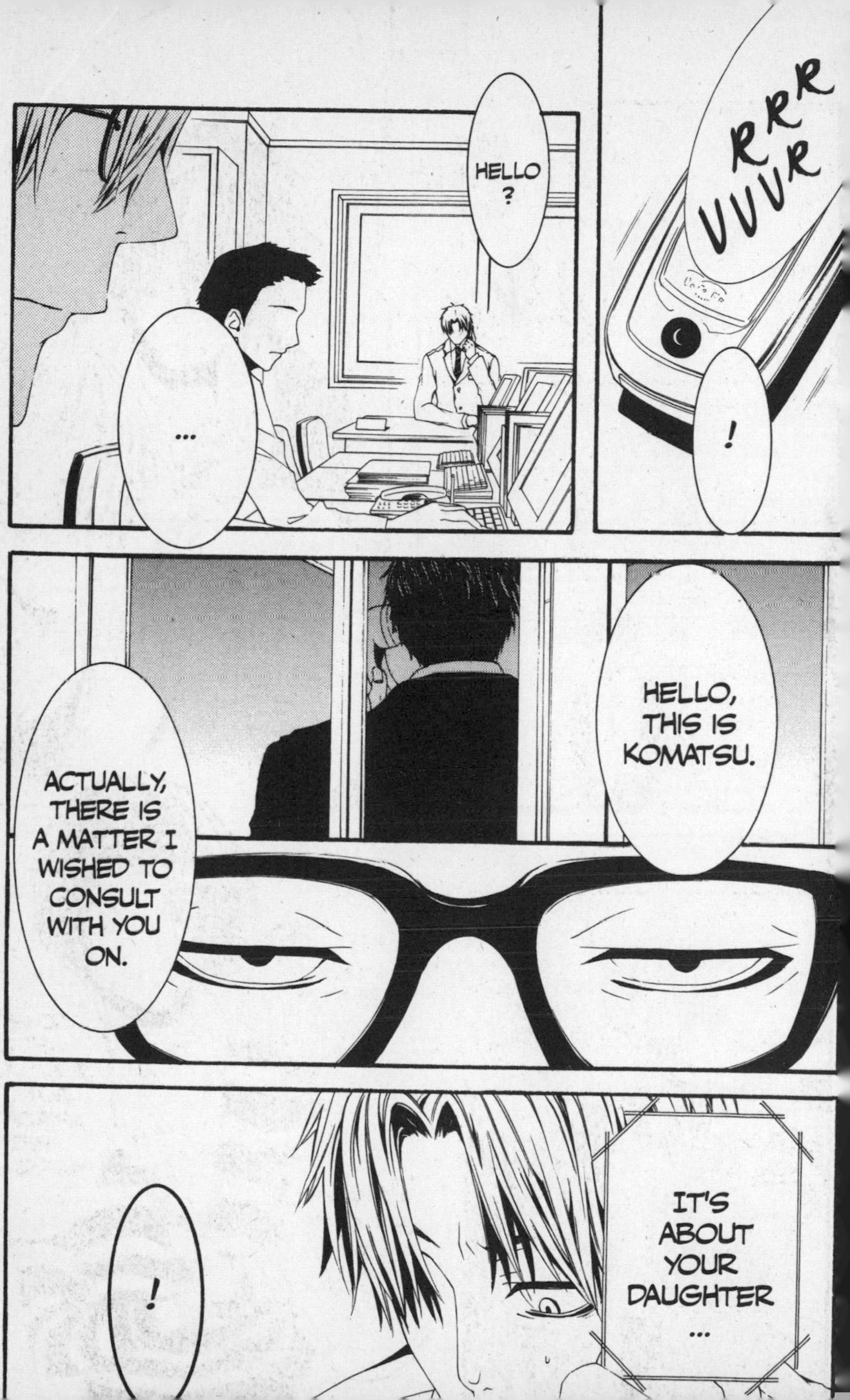
RRR VUUR
!
HELLO ?
...
HELLO, THIS IS KOMATSU.
ACTUALLY, THERE IS A MATTER I WISHED TO CONSULT WITH YOU ON.
IT'S ABOUT YOUR DAUGHTER ...
!

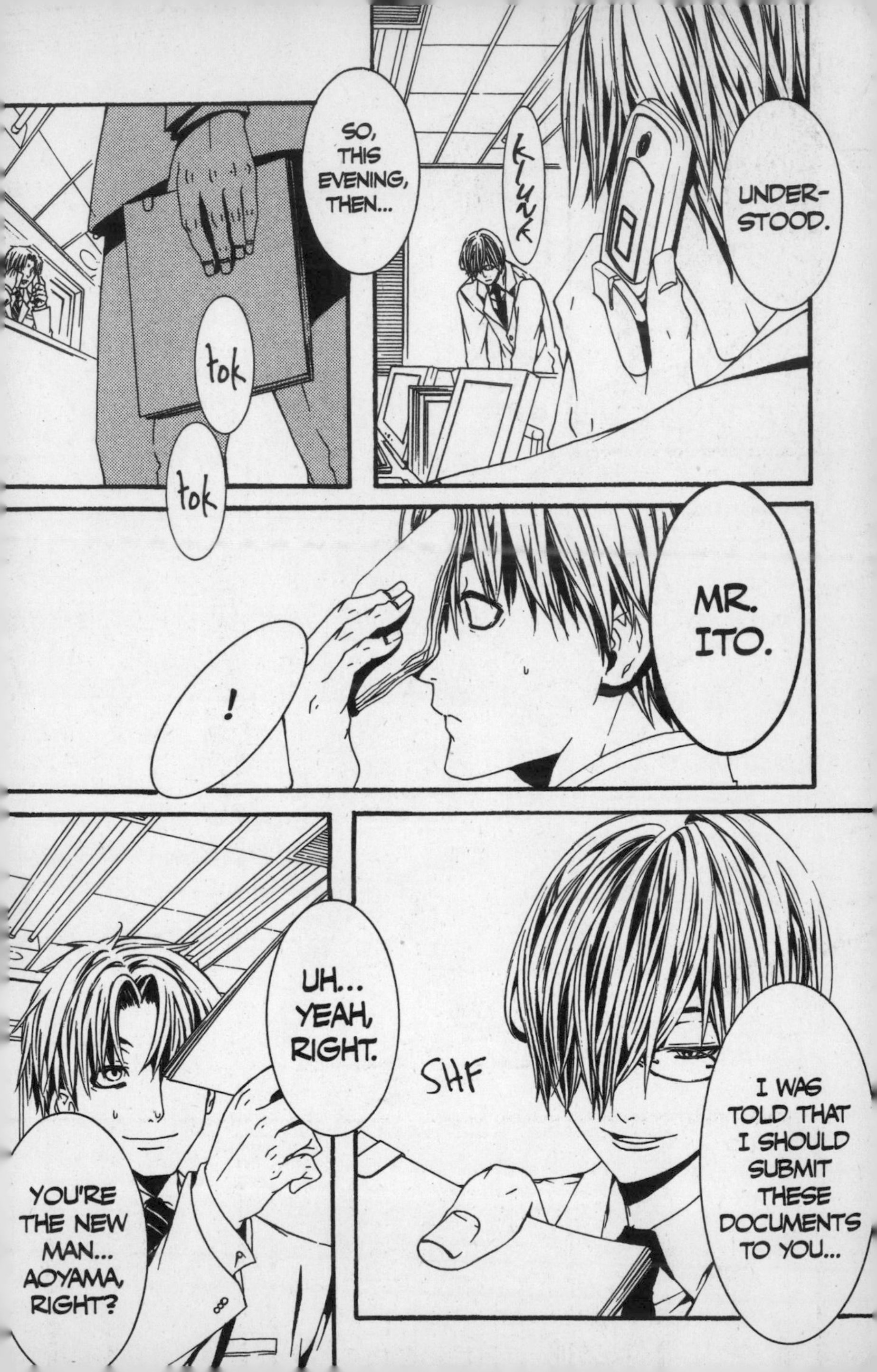
UNDER-STOOD.
KLUNK
SO, THIS EVENING, THEN...
tok
tok
MR. ITO.
!
I WAS TOLD THAT I SHOULD SUBMIT THESE DOCUMENTS TO YOU...
SHF
UH... YEAH, RIGHT.
YOU'RE THE NEW MAN... AOYAMA, RIGHT?

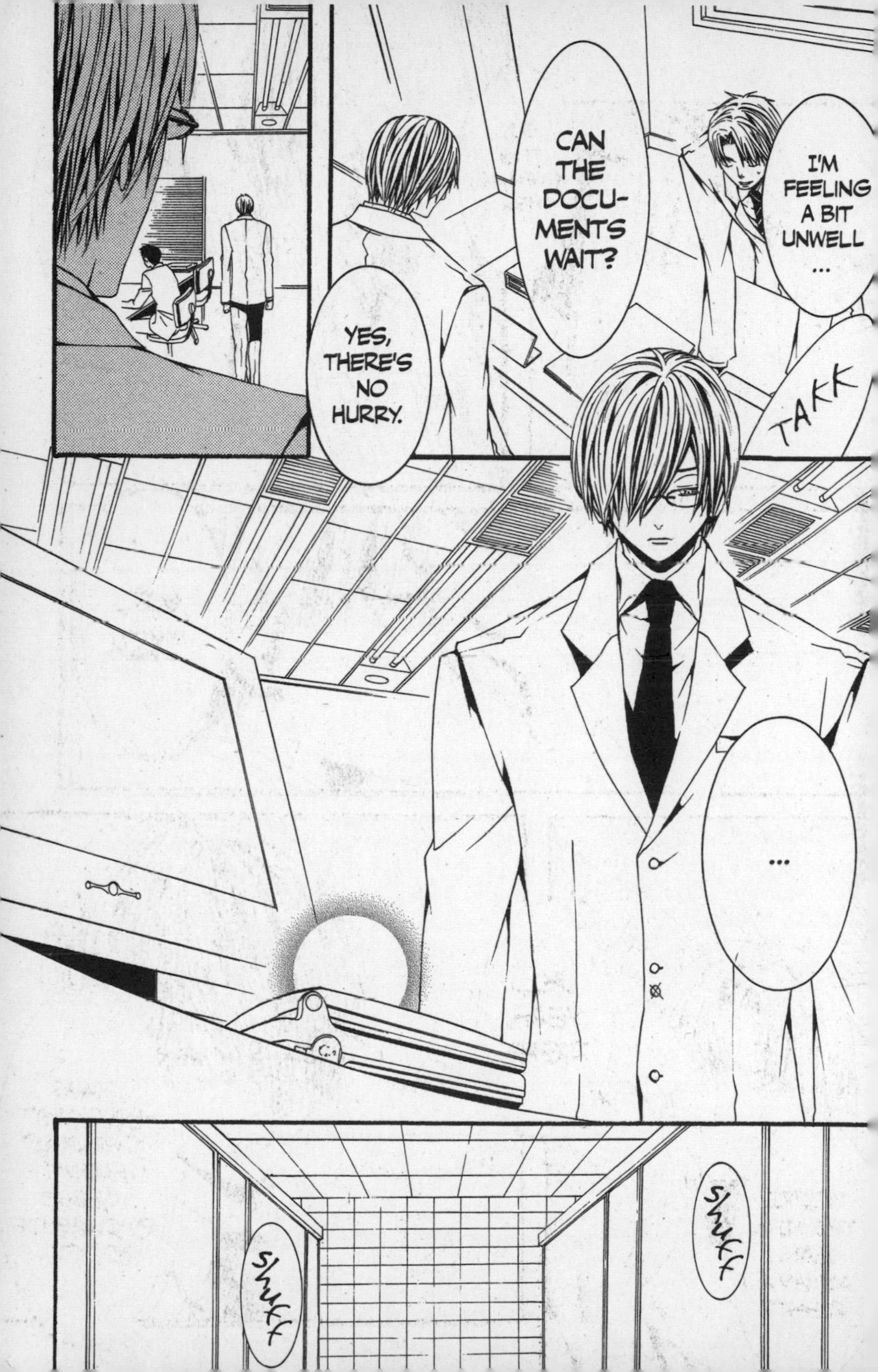
I'M FEELING A BIT UNWELL ...
CAN THE DOCUMENTS WAIT?
YES, THERE'S NO HURRY.
TAKK
...
SHUFF
SHUFF

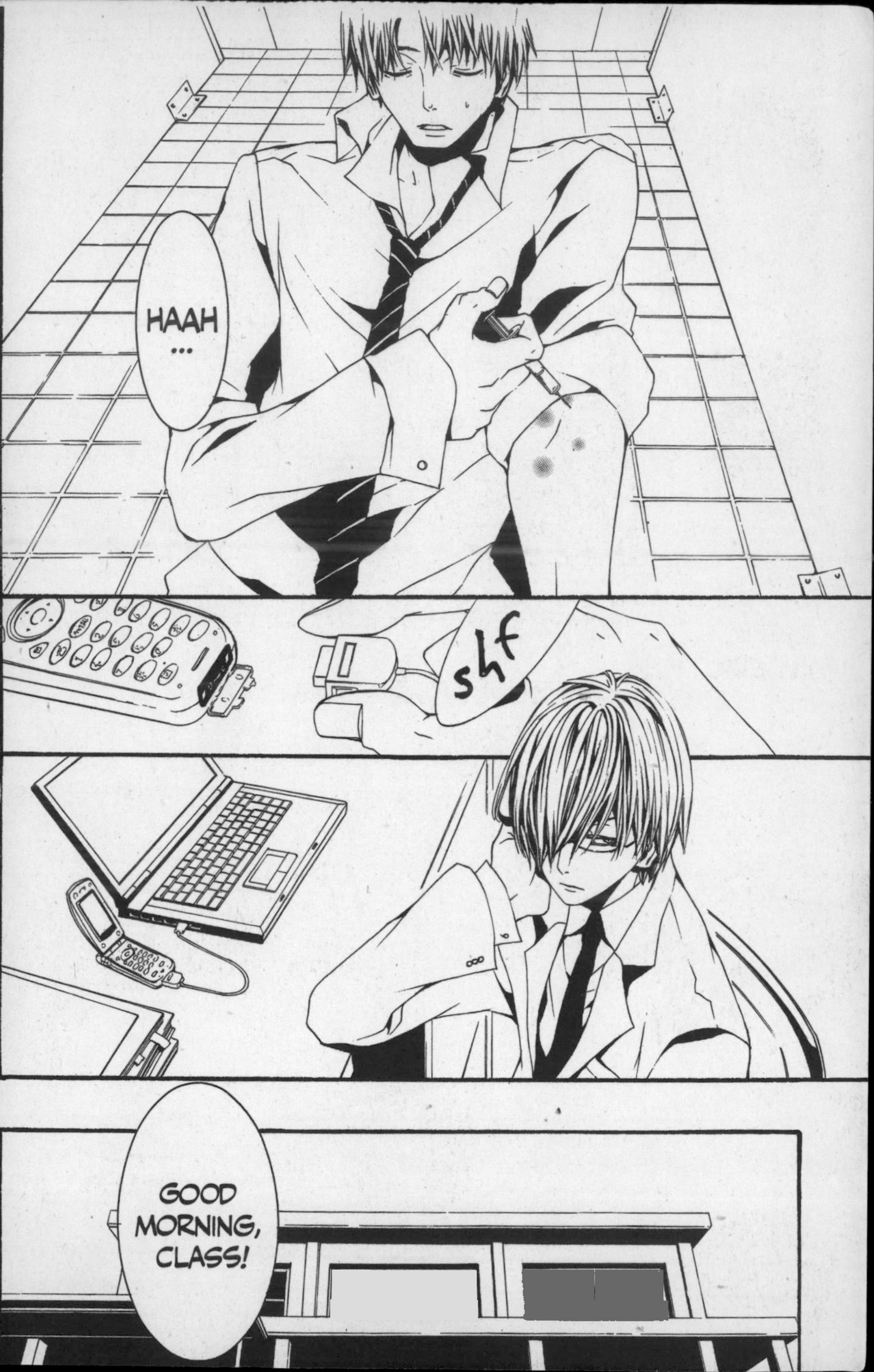
HAAH...
shf
GOOD MORNING, CLASS!

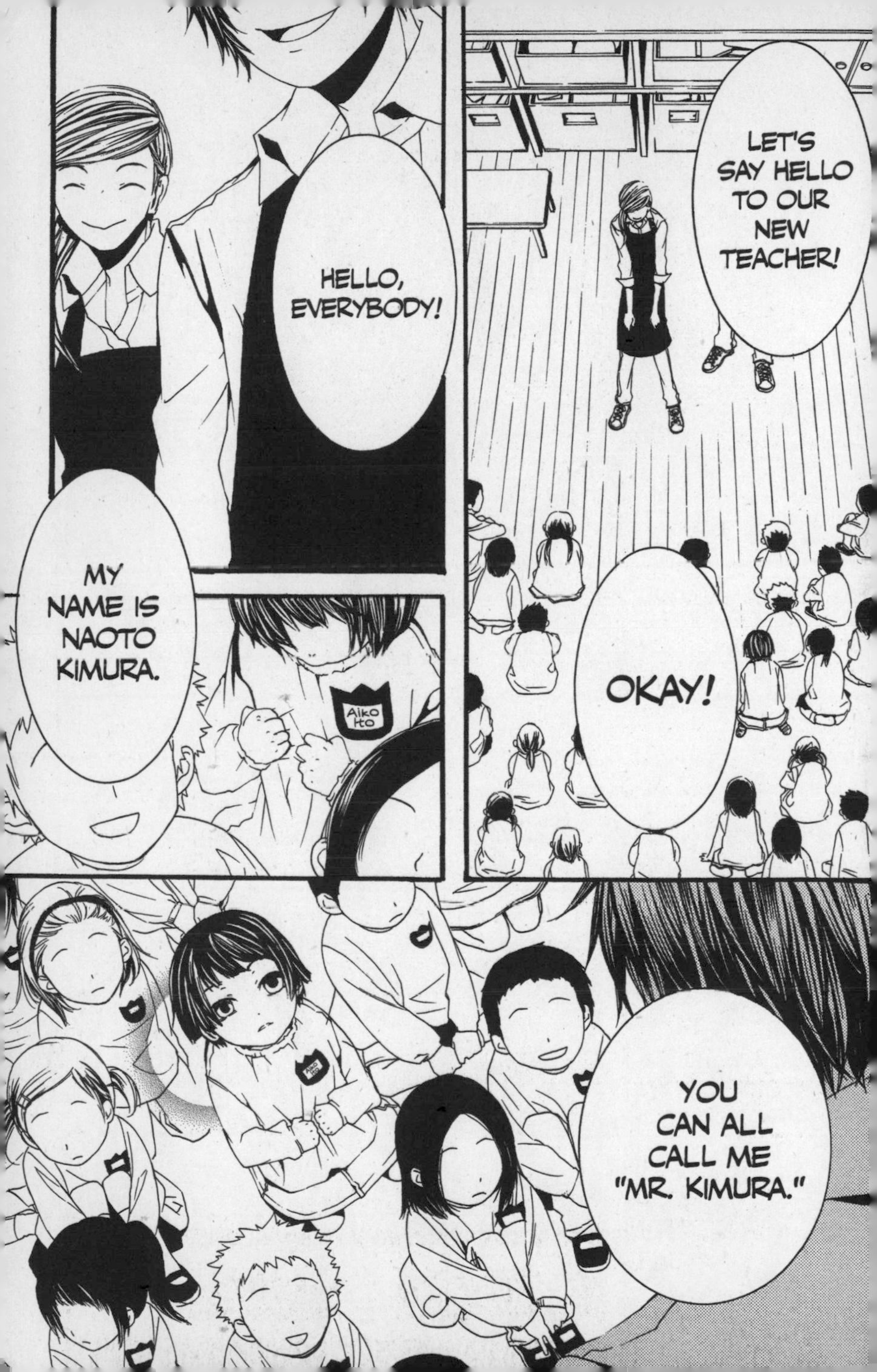
LET'S SAY HELLO TO OUR NEW TEACHER!
OKAY!
HELLO, EVERYBODY!
MY NAME IS NAOTO KIMURA.
Aiko Ito
YOU CAN ALL CALL ME "MR. KIMURA."

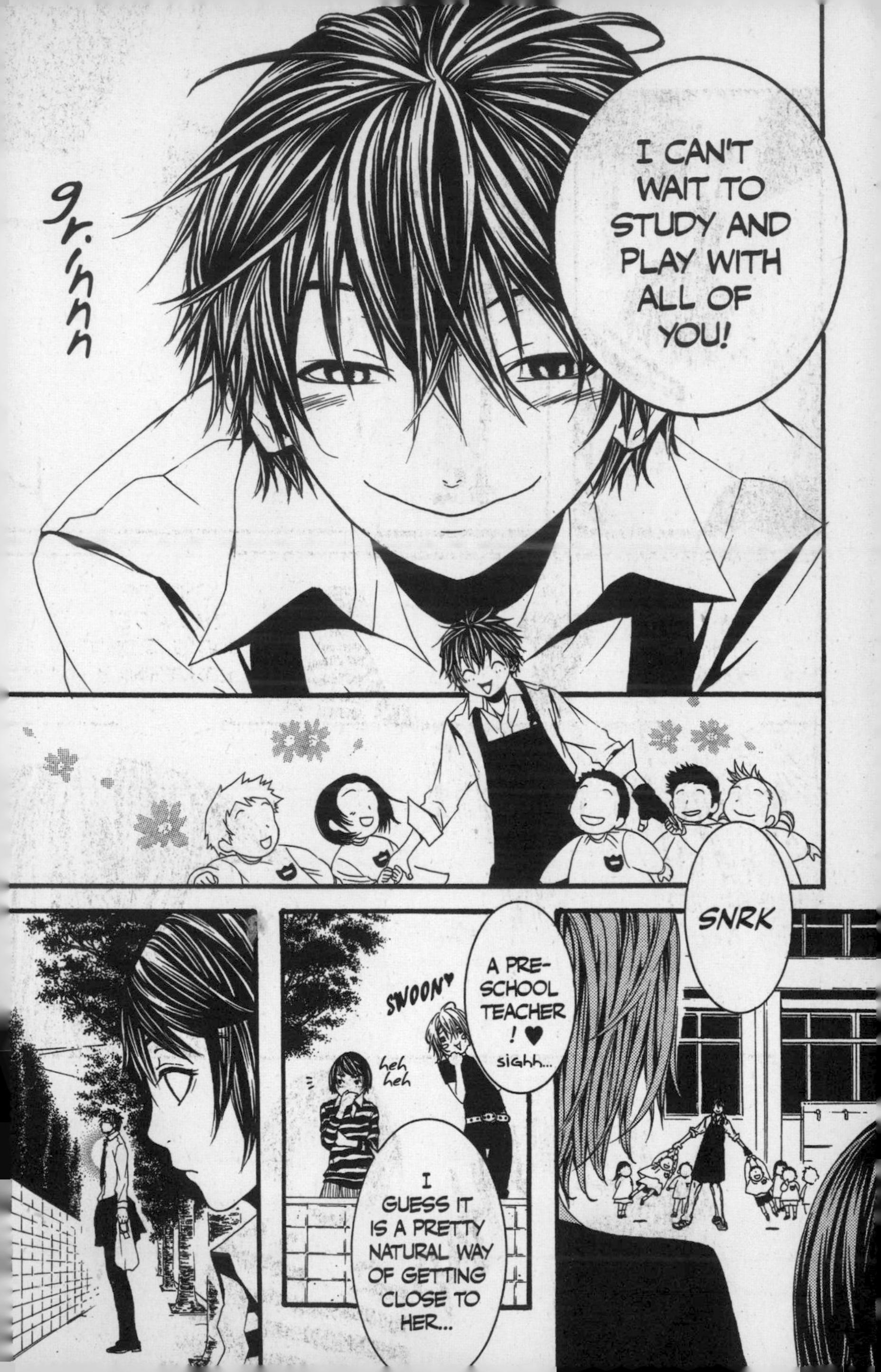
I CAN'T WAIT TO STUDY AND PLAY WITH ALL OF YOU!
grinnn
SNRK
A PRE-SCHOOL TEACHER! ♥
sighh...
SWOON♥
heh heh
I GUESS IT IS A PRETTY NATURAL WAY OF GETTING CLOSE TO HER...

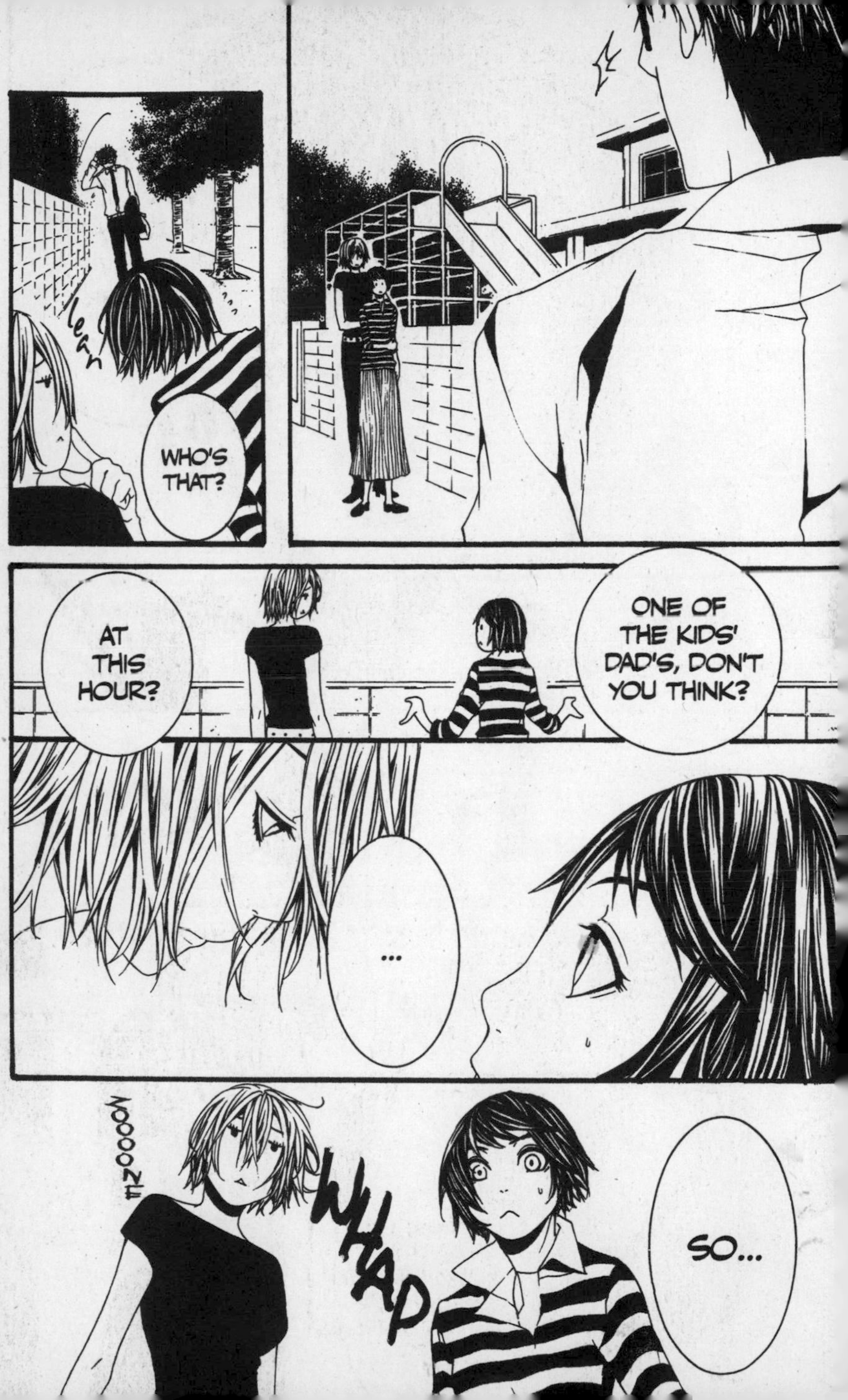
lean
WHO'S THAT?
ONE OF THE KIDS' DAD'S, DON'T YOU THINK?
AT THIS HOUR?
...
SO...
WHAP
ZOOOONE

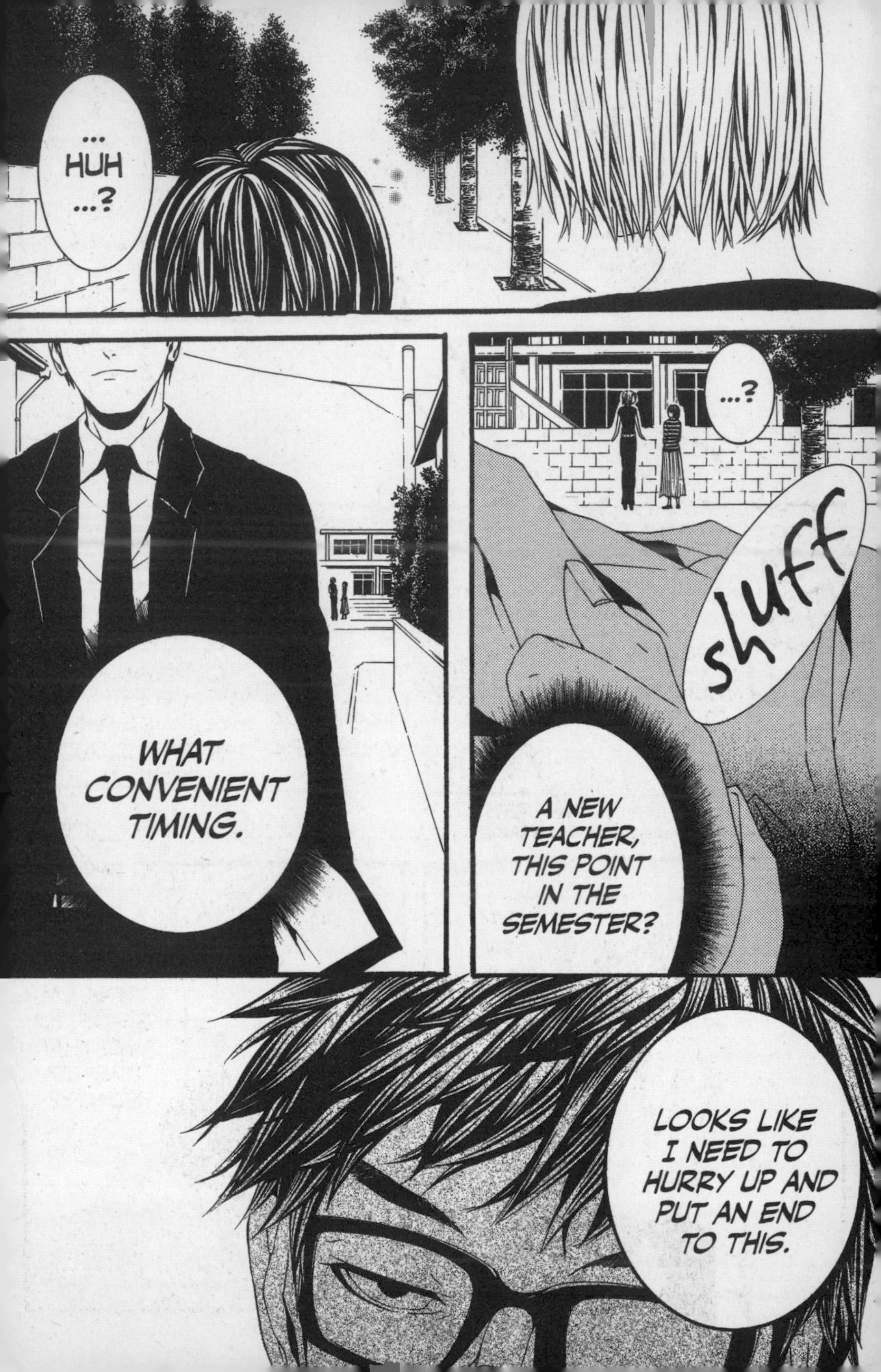
... HUH ...?
...?
shuff
A NEW TEACHER, THIS POINT IN THE SEMESTER?
WHAT CONVENIENT TIMING.
LOOKS LIKE I NEED TO HURRY UP AND PUT AN END TO THIS.

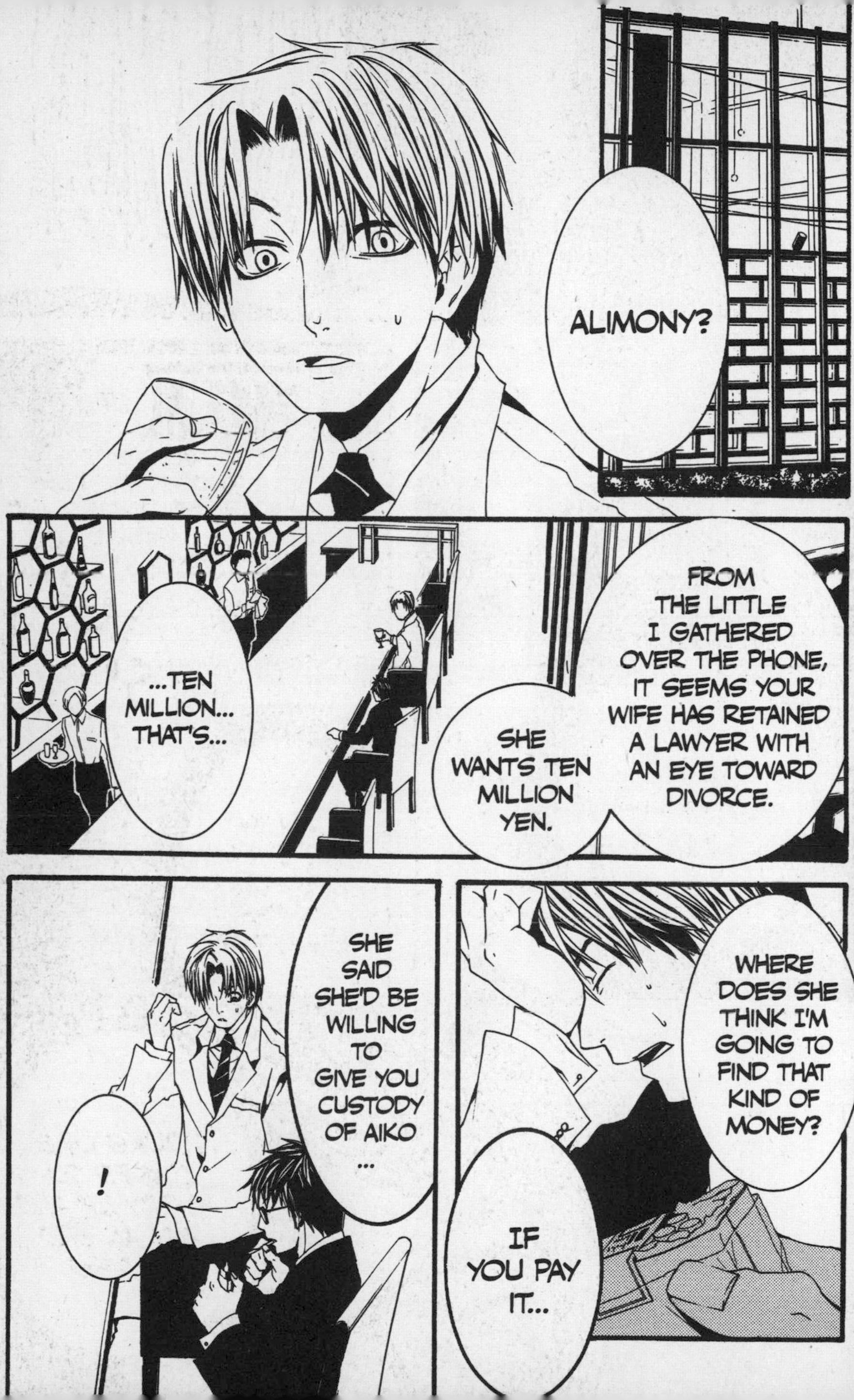
ALIMONY?
FROM THE LITTLE I GATHERED OVER THE PHONE, IT SEEMS YOUR WIFE HAS RETAINED A LAWYER WITH AN EYE TOWARD DIVORCE.
SHE WANTS TEN MILLION YEN.
...TEN MILLION... THAT'S...
WHERE DOES SHE THINK I'M GOING TO FIND THAT KIND OF MONEY?
IF YOU PAY IT...
SHE SAID SHE'D BE WILLING TO GIVE YOU CUSTODY OF AIKO ...
!

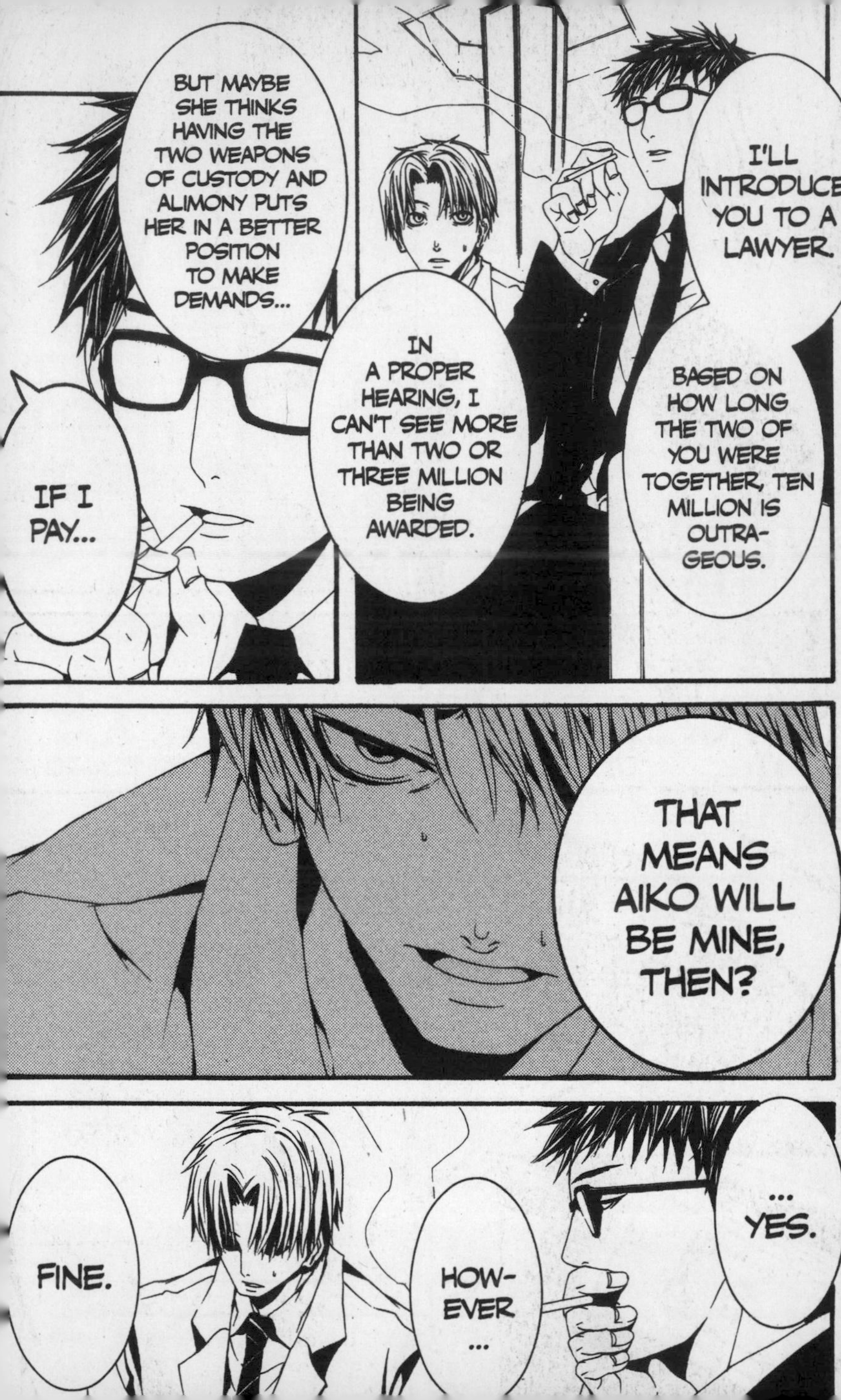
I'LL INTRODUCE YOU TO A LAWYER.
BASED ON HOW LONG THE TWO OF YOU WERE TOGETHER, TEN MILLION IS OUTRA-GEOUS.
IN A PROPER HEARING, I CAN'T SEE MORE THAN TWO OR THREE MILLION BEING AWARDED.
BUT MAYBE SHE THINKS HAVING THE TWO WEAPONS OF CUSTODY AND ALIMONY PUTS HER IN A BETTER POSITION TO MAKE DEMANDS...
IF I PAY...
THAT MEANS AIKO WILL BE MINE, THEN?
... YES.
HOW-EVER ...
FINE.

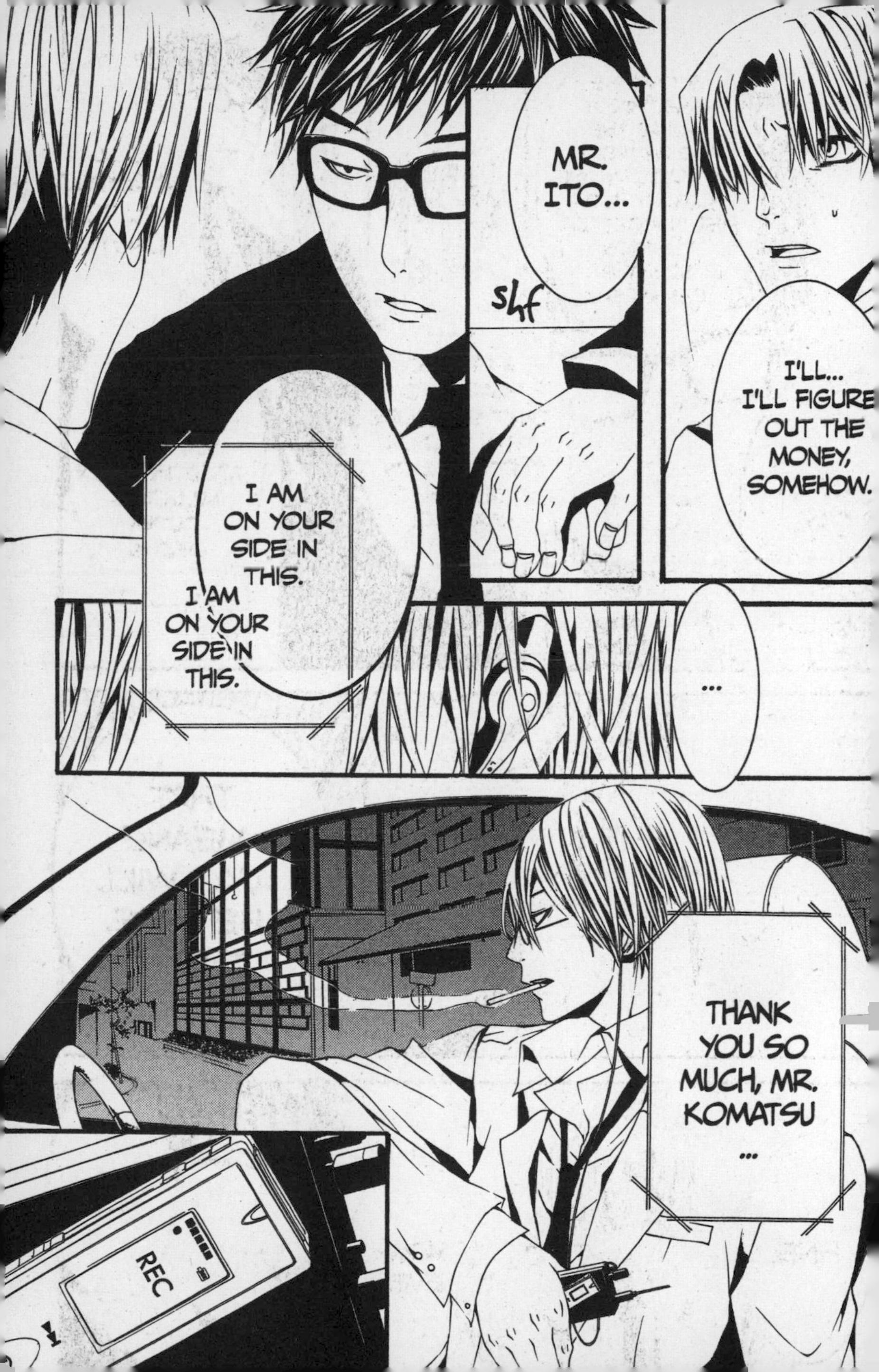
I'LL... I'LL FIGURE OUT THE MONEY, SOMEHOW.
MR. ITO...
shf
I AM ON YOUR SIDE IN THIS.
...
I AM ON YOUR SIDE IN THIS.
THANK YOU SO MUCH, MR. KOMATSU ...
REC

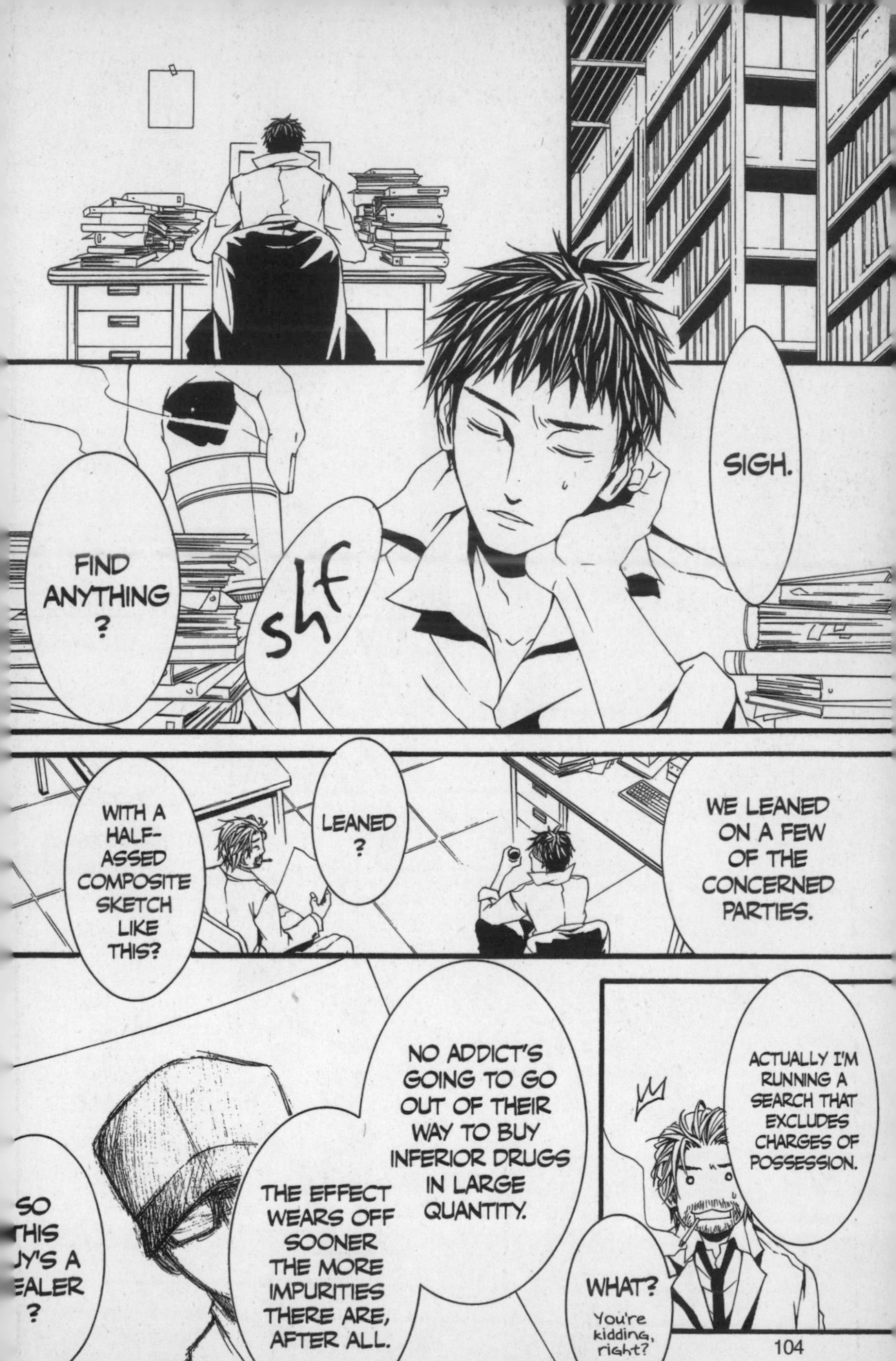
SIGH.
shf
FIND ANYTHING?
WE LEANED ON A FEW OF THE CONCERNED PARTIES.
LEANED?
WITH A HALF-ASSED COMPOSITE SKETCH LIKE THIS?
ACTUALLY I'M RUNNING A SEARCH THAT EXCLUDES CHARGES OF POSSESSION.
WHAT?
You're kidding, right?
NO ADDICT'S GOING TO GO OUT OF THEIR WAY TO BUY INFERIOR DRUGS IN LARGE QUANTITY.
THE EFFECT WEARS OFF SOONER THE MORE IMPURITIES THERE ARE, AFTER ALL.
SO THIS UY'S A EALER?

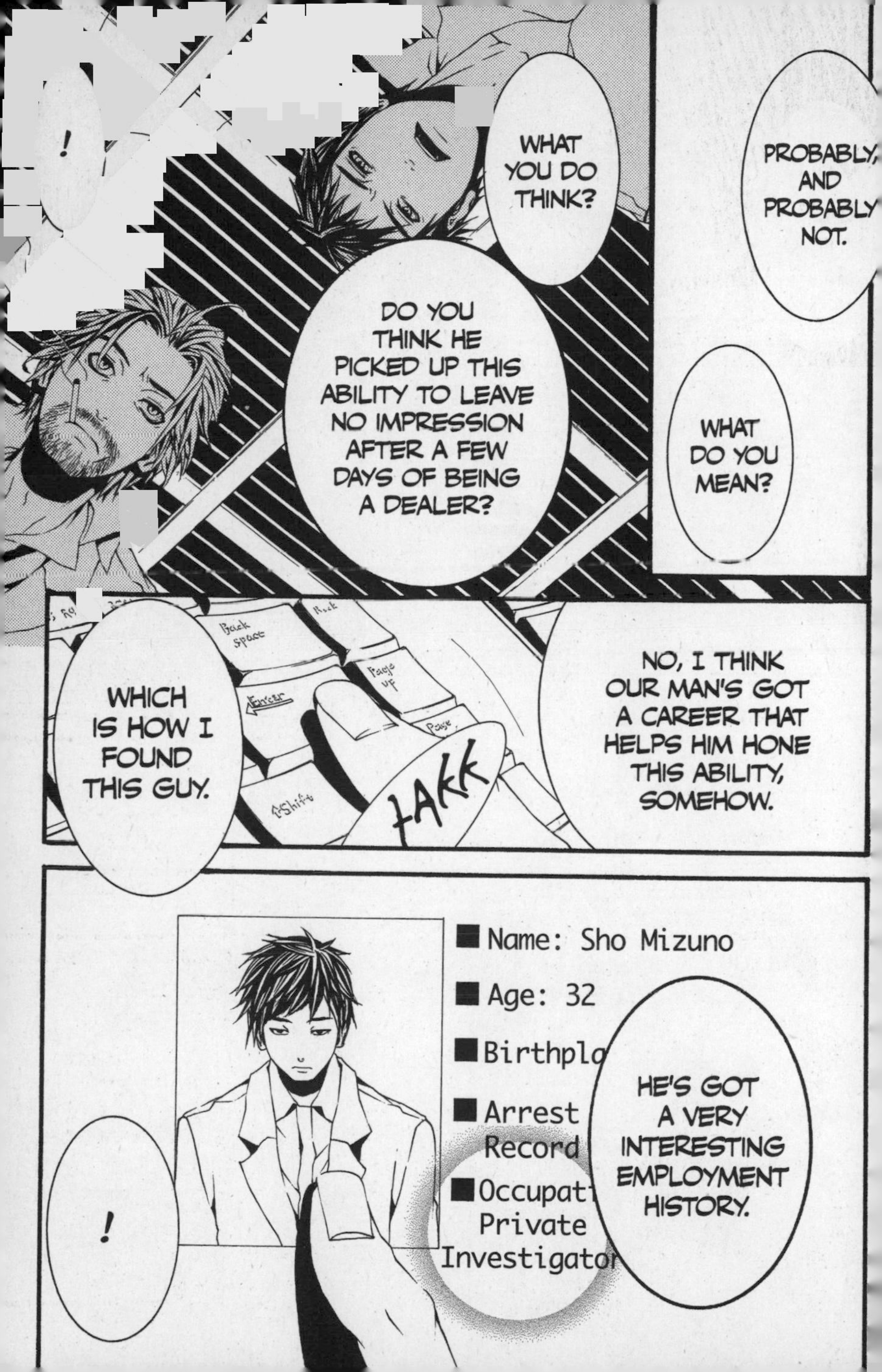
PROBABLY, AND PROBABLY NOT.
WHAT DO YOU MEAN?
WHAT YOU DO THINK?
DO YOU THINK HE PICKED UP THIS ABILITY TO LEAVE NO IMPRESSION AFTER A FEW DAYS OF BEING A DEALER?
!
NO, I THINK OUR MAN'S GOT A CAREER THAT HELPS HIM HONE THIS ABILITY, SOMEHOW.
TAKK
WHICH IS HOW I FOUND THIS GUY.
HE'S GOT A VERY INTERESTING EMPLOYMENT HISTORY.
■Name: Sho Mizuno
■Age: 32
■Birthpl
■Arrest Record
■Occupat
Private Investigator
!

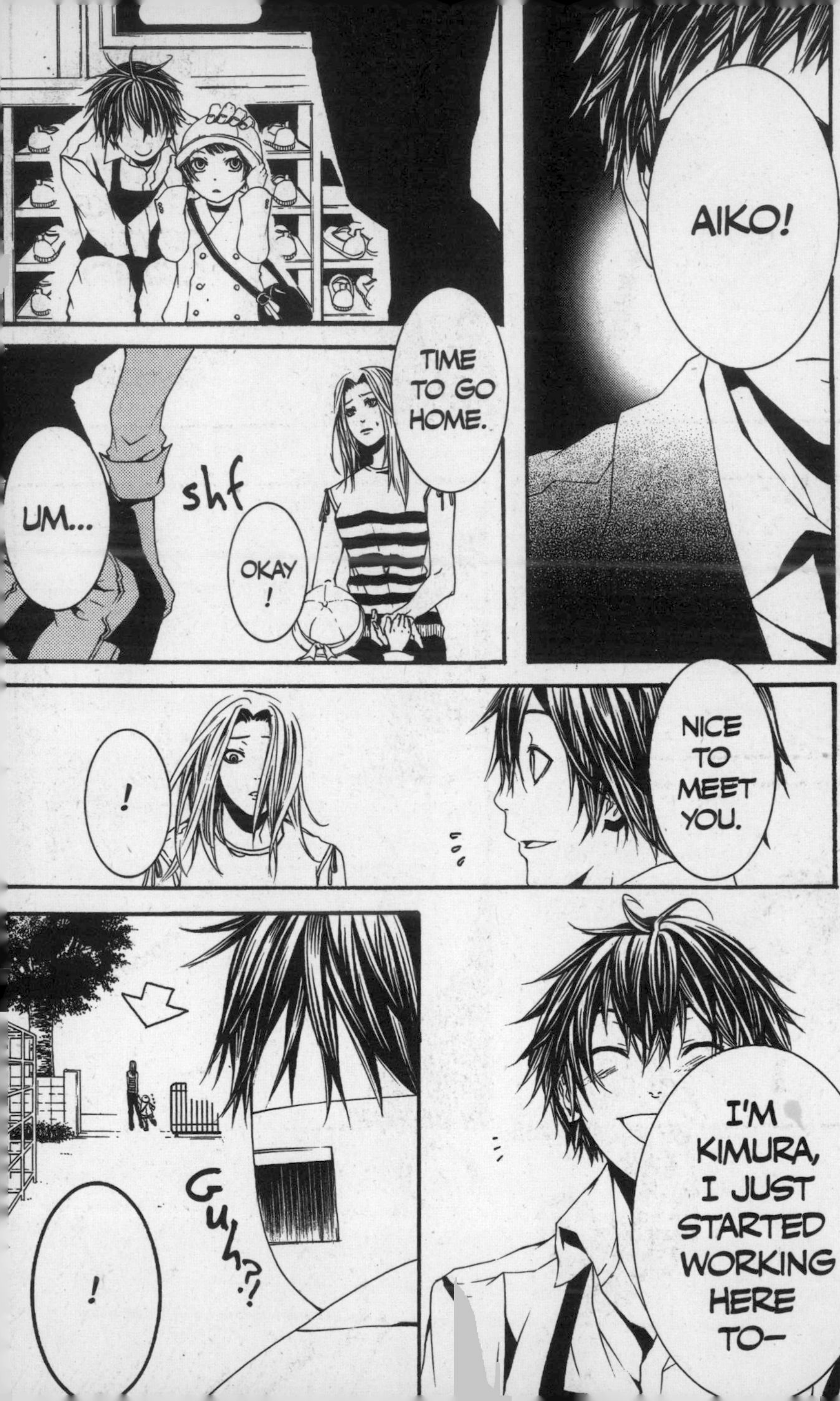
AIKO!
TIME TO GO HOME.
shf
OKAY!
UM...
NICE TO MEET YOU.
!
I'M KIMURA, I JUST STARTED WORKING HERE TO—
Guh?!
!

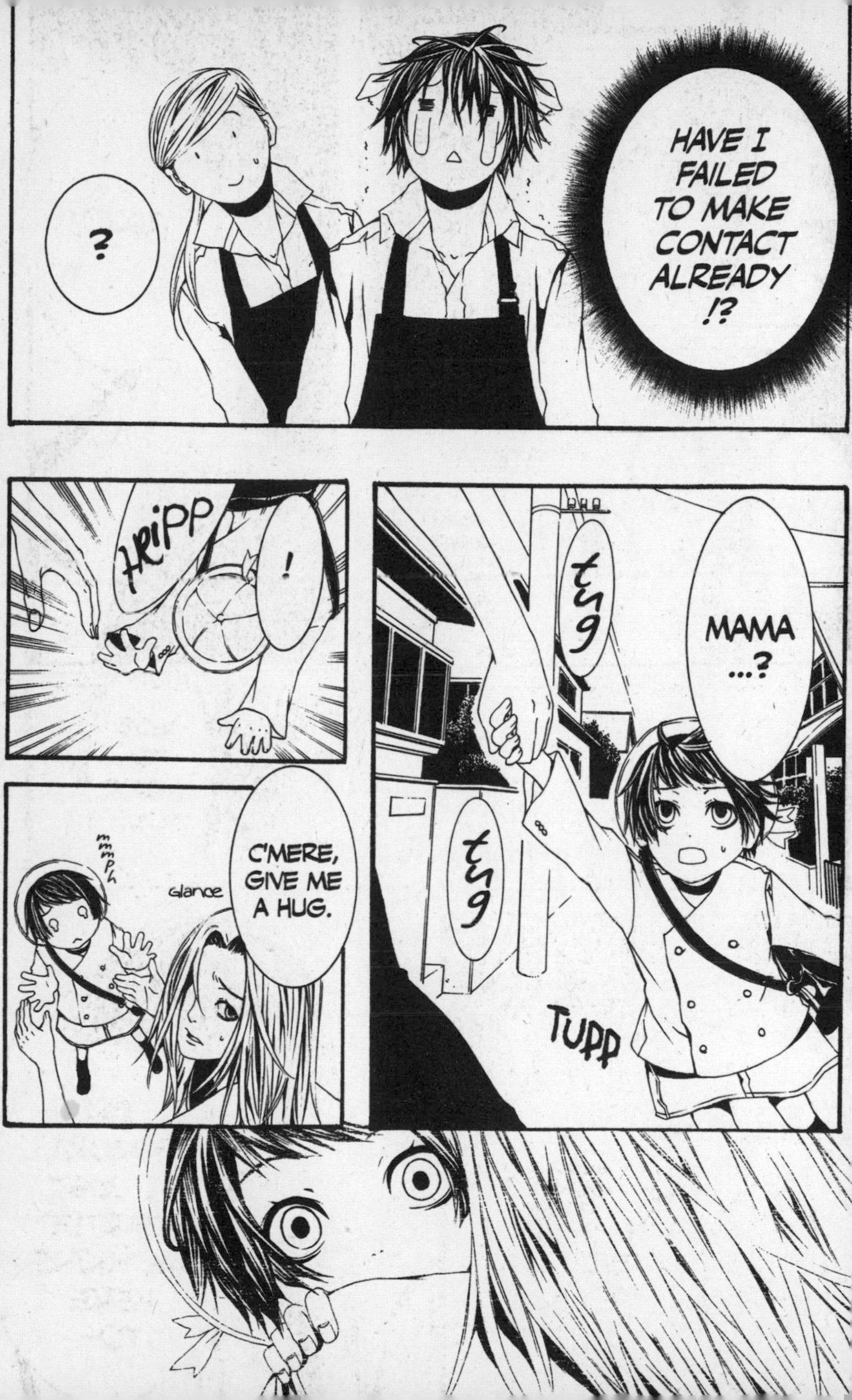
HAVE I FAILED TO MAKE CONTACT ALREADY !?
?
MAMA ...?
tug
tug
TUPP
!
HRIPP
C'MERE, GIVE ME A HUG.
Glance
mmmph

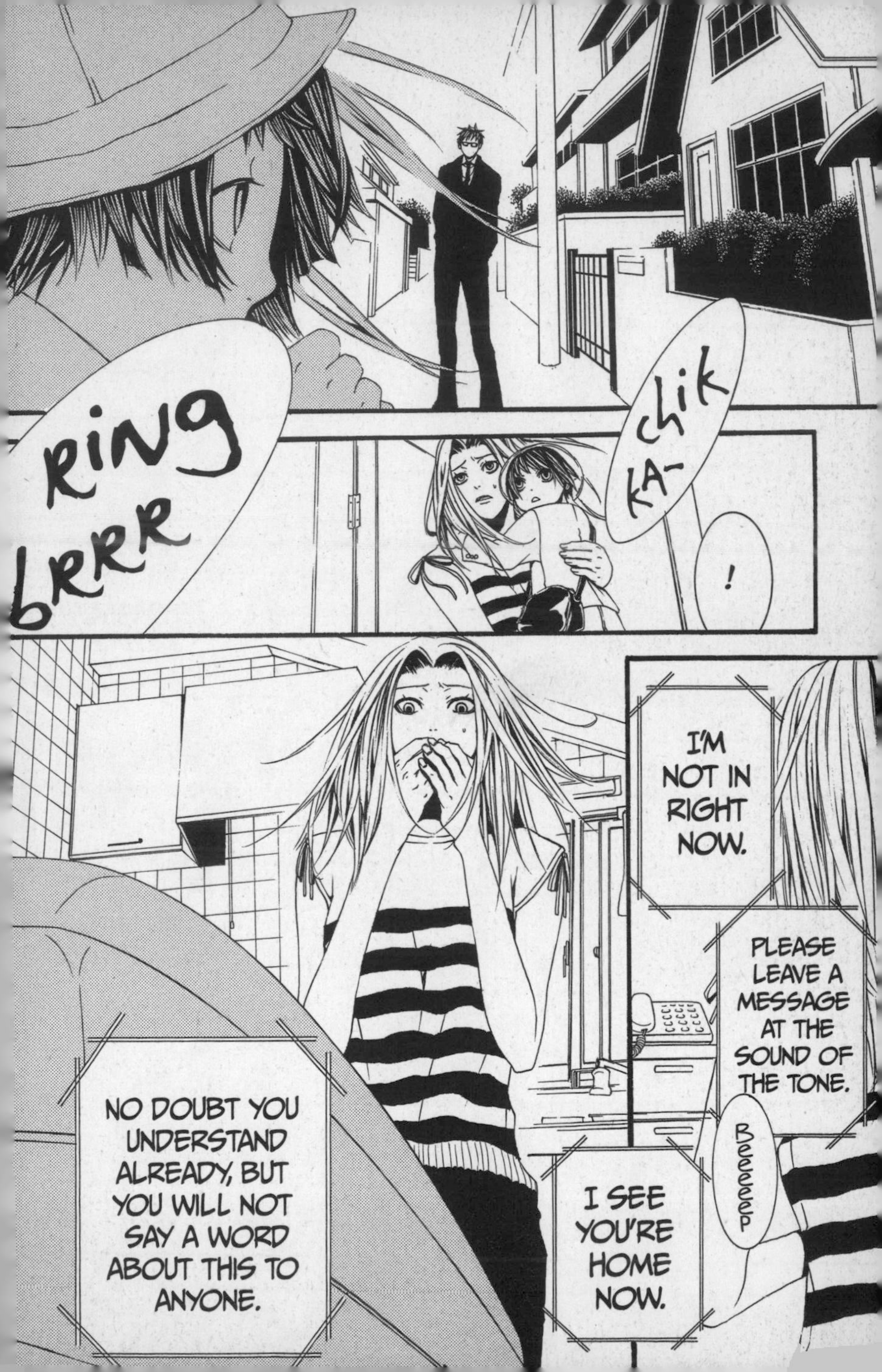
KA-chik
!
RING brrr
I'M NOT IN RIGHT NOW.
PLEASE LEAVE A MESSAGE AT THE SOUND OF THE TONE.
Beeeeep
I SEE YOU'RE HOME NOW.
NO DOUBT YOU UNDERSTAND ALREADY, BUT YOU WILL NOT SAY A WORD ABOUT THIS TO ANYONE.

[switch]
スイッチ

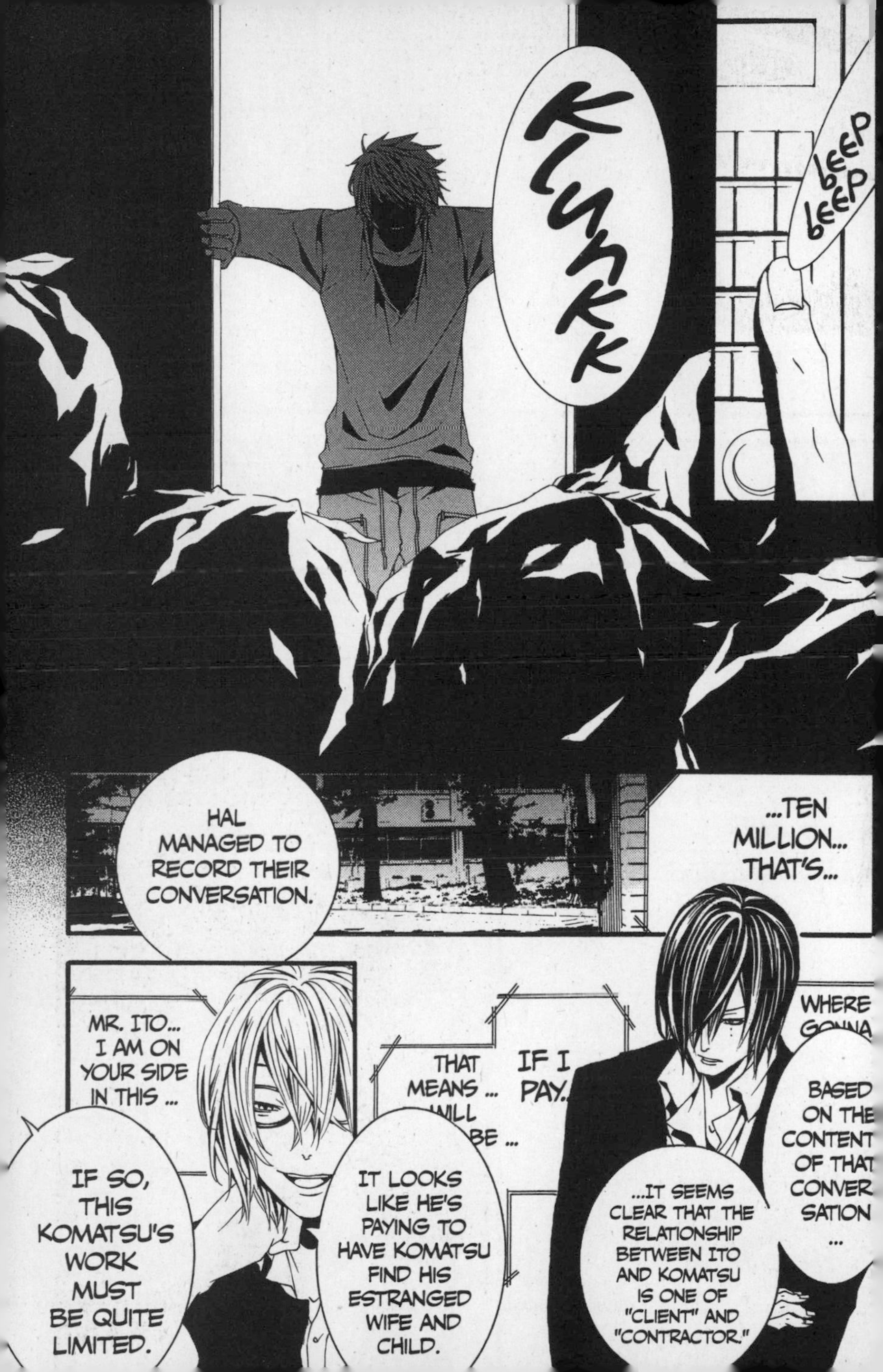
beep beep
KLUNKK
...TEN MILLION... THAT'S...
HAL MANAGED TO RECORD THEIR CONVERSATION.
WHERE
BASED ON THE CONTENT OF THAT CONVERSATION ...
...IT SEEMS CLEAR THAT THE RELATIONSHIP BETWEEN ITO AND KOMATSU IS ONE OF "CLIENT" AND "CONTRACTOR."
IF I PAY..
THAT MEANS ... WILL BE ...
MR. ITO... I AM ON YOUR SIDE IN THIS ...
IT LOOKS LIKE HE'S PAYING TO HAVE KOMATSU FIND HIS ESTRANGED WIFE AND CHILD.
IF SO, THIS KOMATSU'S WORK MUST BE QUITE LIMITED.

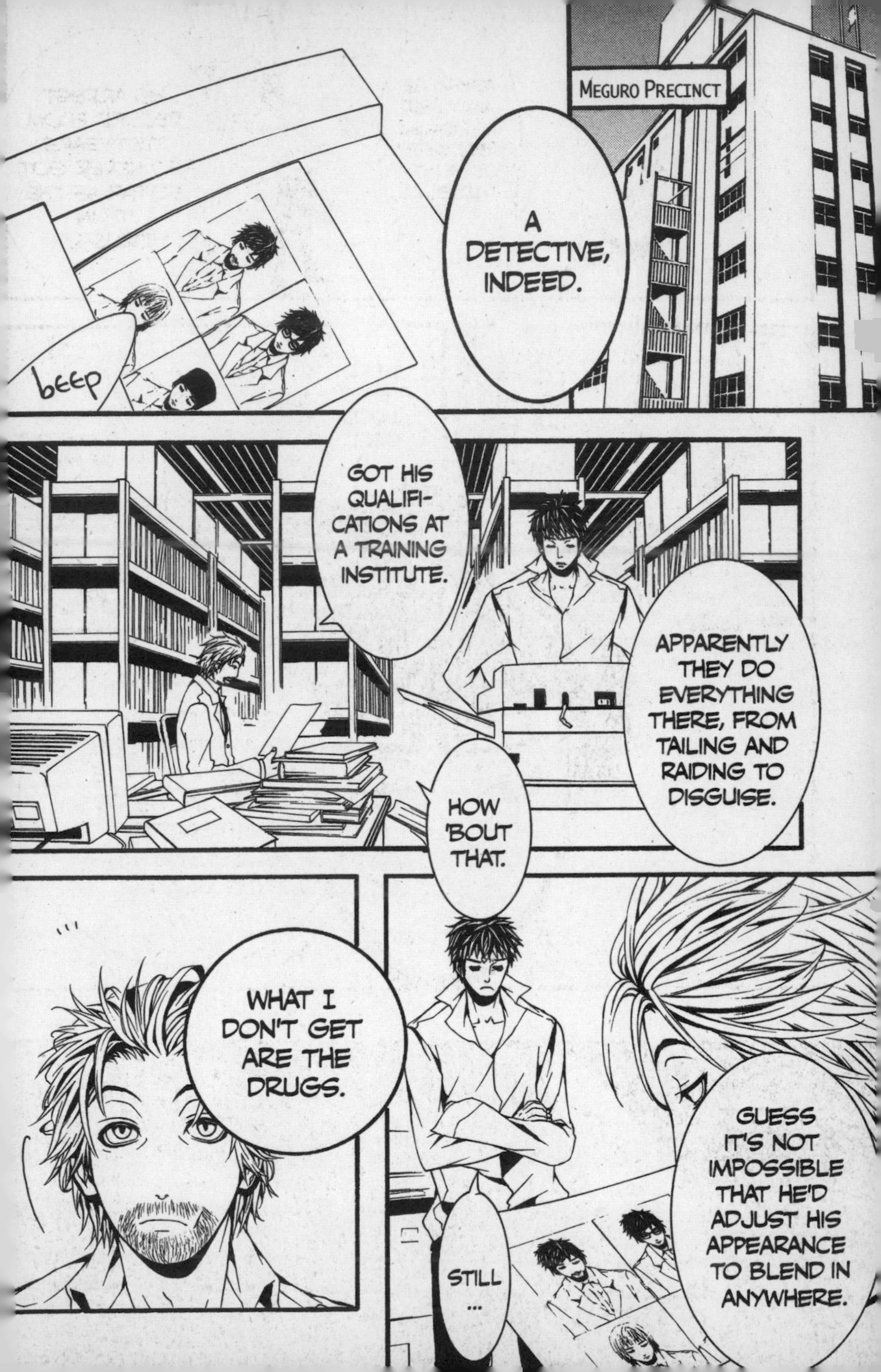
MEGURO PRECINCT
A DETECTIVE, INDEED.
beep
GOT HIS QUALIFI-CATIONS AT A TRAINING INSTITUTE.
APPARENTLY THEY DO EVERYTHING THERE, FROM TAILING AND RAIDING TO DISGUISE.
HOW 'BOUT THAT.
GUESS IT'S NOT IMPOSSIBLE THAT HE'D ADJUST HIS APPEARANCE TO BLEND IN ANYWHERE.
STILL ...
WHAT I DON'T GET ARE THE DRUGS.

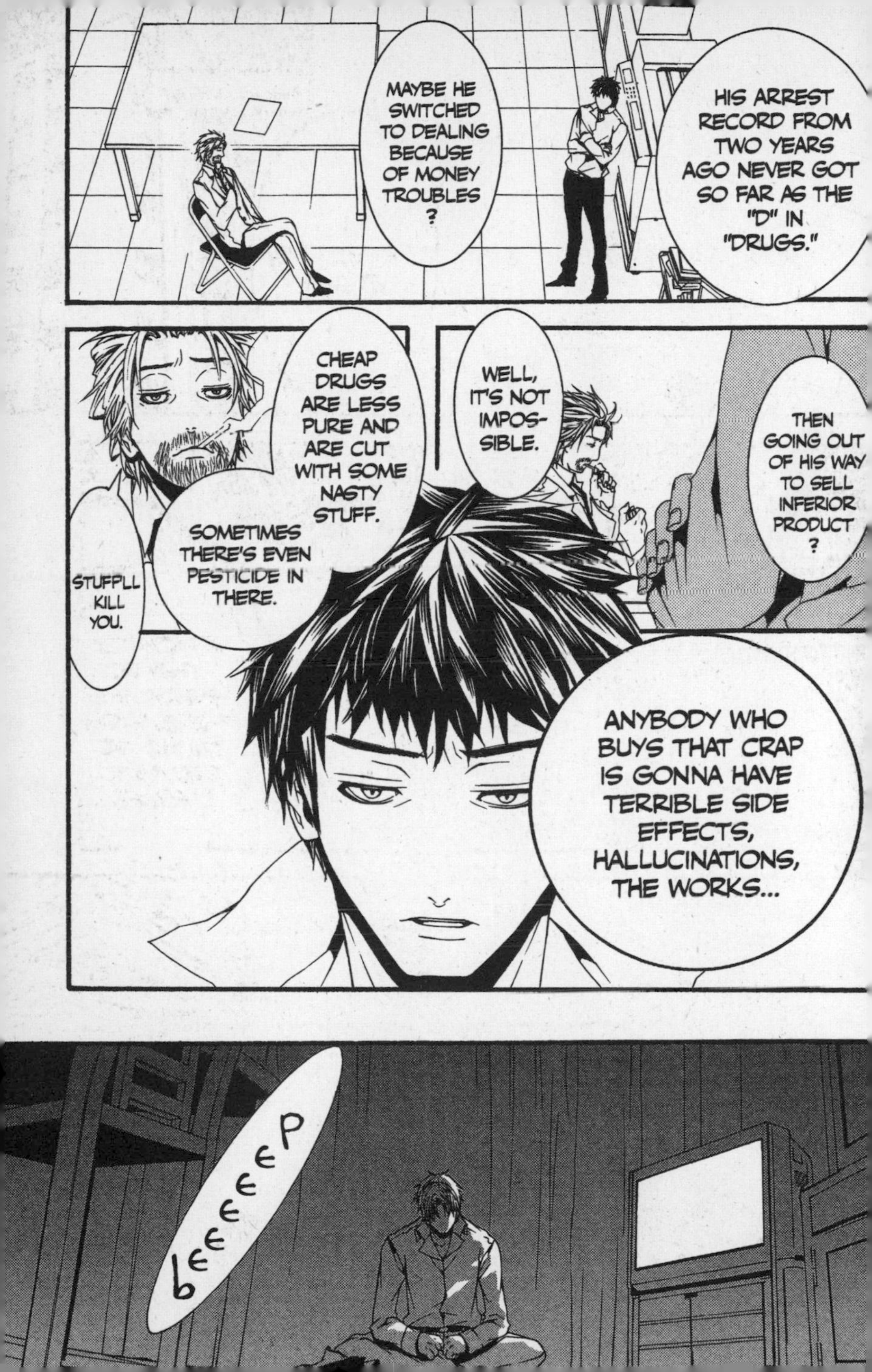
HIS ARREST RECORD FROM TWO YEARS AGO NEVER GOT SO FAR AS THE "D" IN "DRUGS."
MAYBE HE SWITCHED TO DEALING BECAUSE OF MONEY TROUBLES ?
THEN GOING OUT OF HIS WAY TO SELL INFERIOR PRODUCT ?
WELL, IT'S NOT IMPOS-SIBLE.
CHEAP DRUGS ARE LESS PURE AND ARE CUT WITH SOME NASTY STUFF.
SOMETIMES THERE'S EVEN PESTICIDE IN THERE.
STUFFLL KILL YOU.
ANYBODY WHO BUYS THAT CRAP IS GONNA HAVE TERRIBLE SIDE EFFECTS, HALLUCINATIONS, THE WORKS...
beeeeep

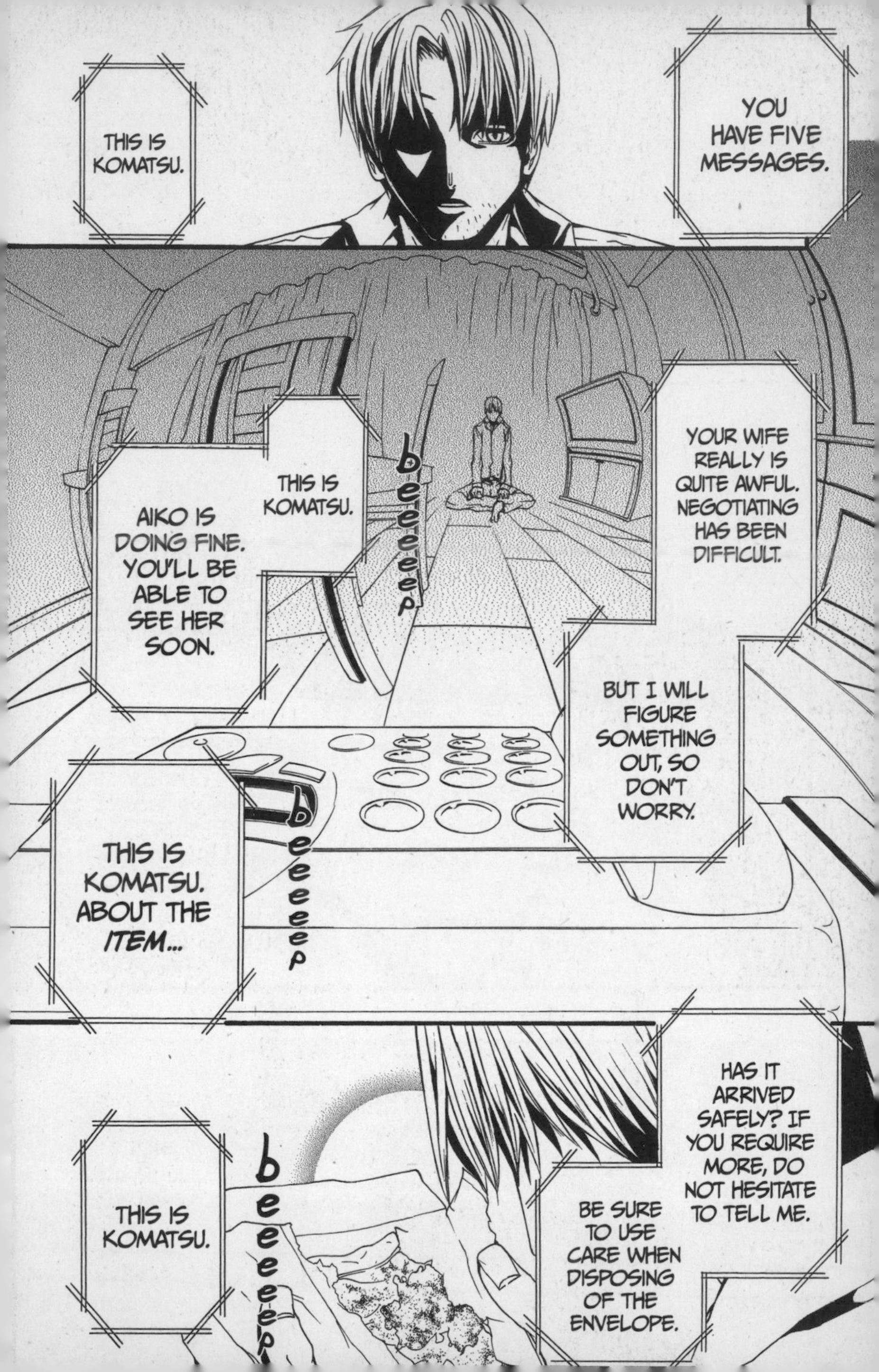
YOU HAVE FIVE MESSAGES.
THIS IS KOMATSU.
YOUR WIFE REALLY IS QUITE AWFUL. NEGOTIATING HAS BEEN DIFFICULT.
BUT I WILL FIGURE SOMETHING OUT, SO DON'T WORRY.
beeeeep
THIS IS KOMATSU.
AIKO IS DOING FINE. YOU'LL BE ABLE TO SEE HER SOON.
beeeeep
THIS IS KOMATSU. ABOUT THE *ITEM*...
HAS IT ARRIVED SAFELY? IF YOU REQUIRE MORE, DO NOT HESITATE TO TELL ME.
BE SURE TO USE CARE WHEN DISPOSING OF THE ENVELOPE.
beeeeep
THIS IS KOMATSU.

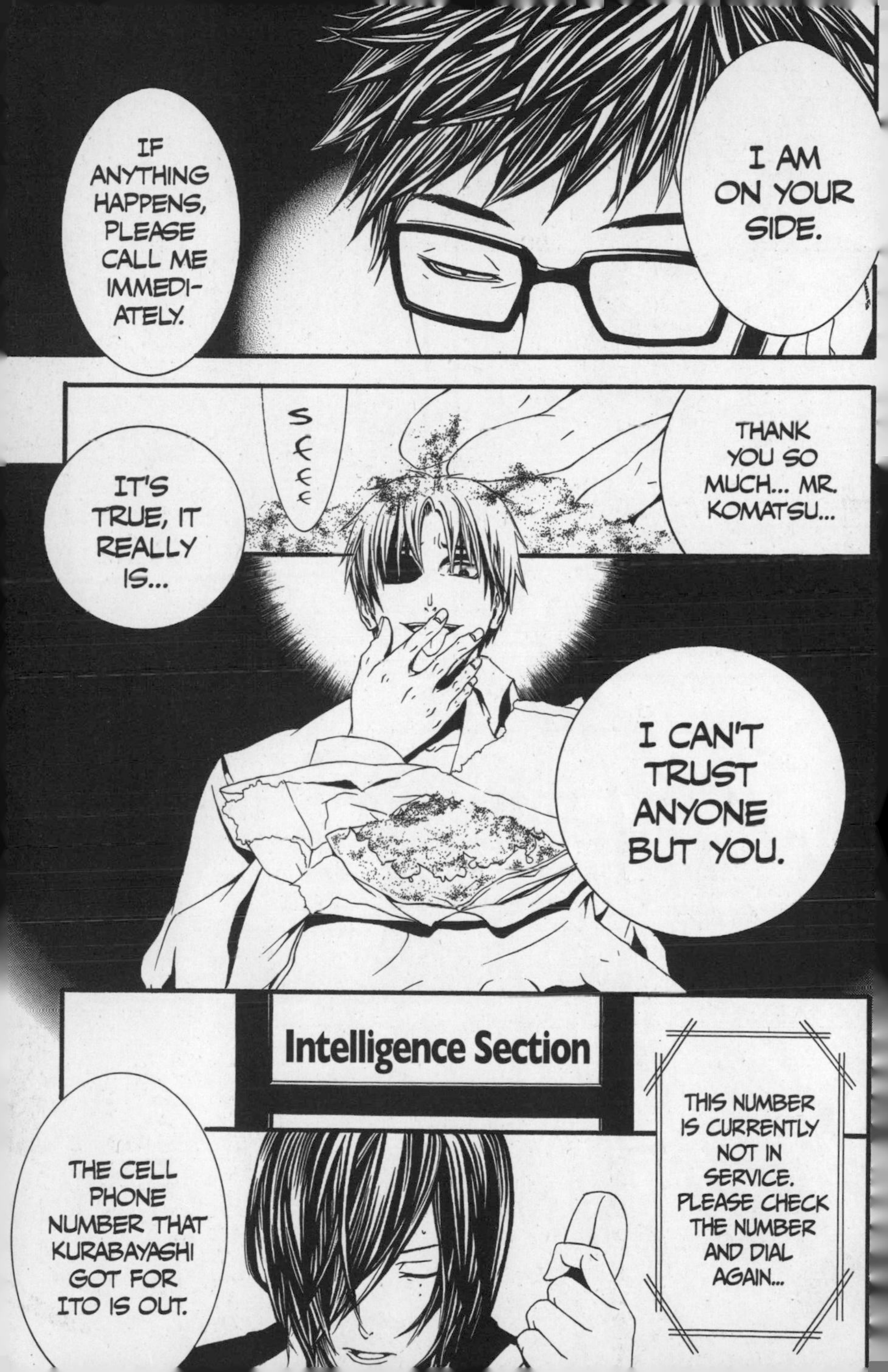
I AM ON YOUR SIDE.
IF ANYTHING HAPPENS, PLEASE CALL ME IMMEDIATELY.
THANK YOU SO MUCH... MR. KOMATSU...
IT'S TRUE, IT REALLY IS...
I CAN'T TRUST ANYONE BUT YOU.
Intelligence Section
THIS NUMBER IS CURRENTLY NOT IN SERVICE. PLEASE CHECK THE NUMBER AND DIAL AGAIN...
THE CELL PHONE NUMBER THAT KURABAYASHI GOT FOR ITO IS OUT.

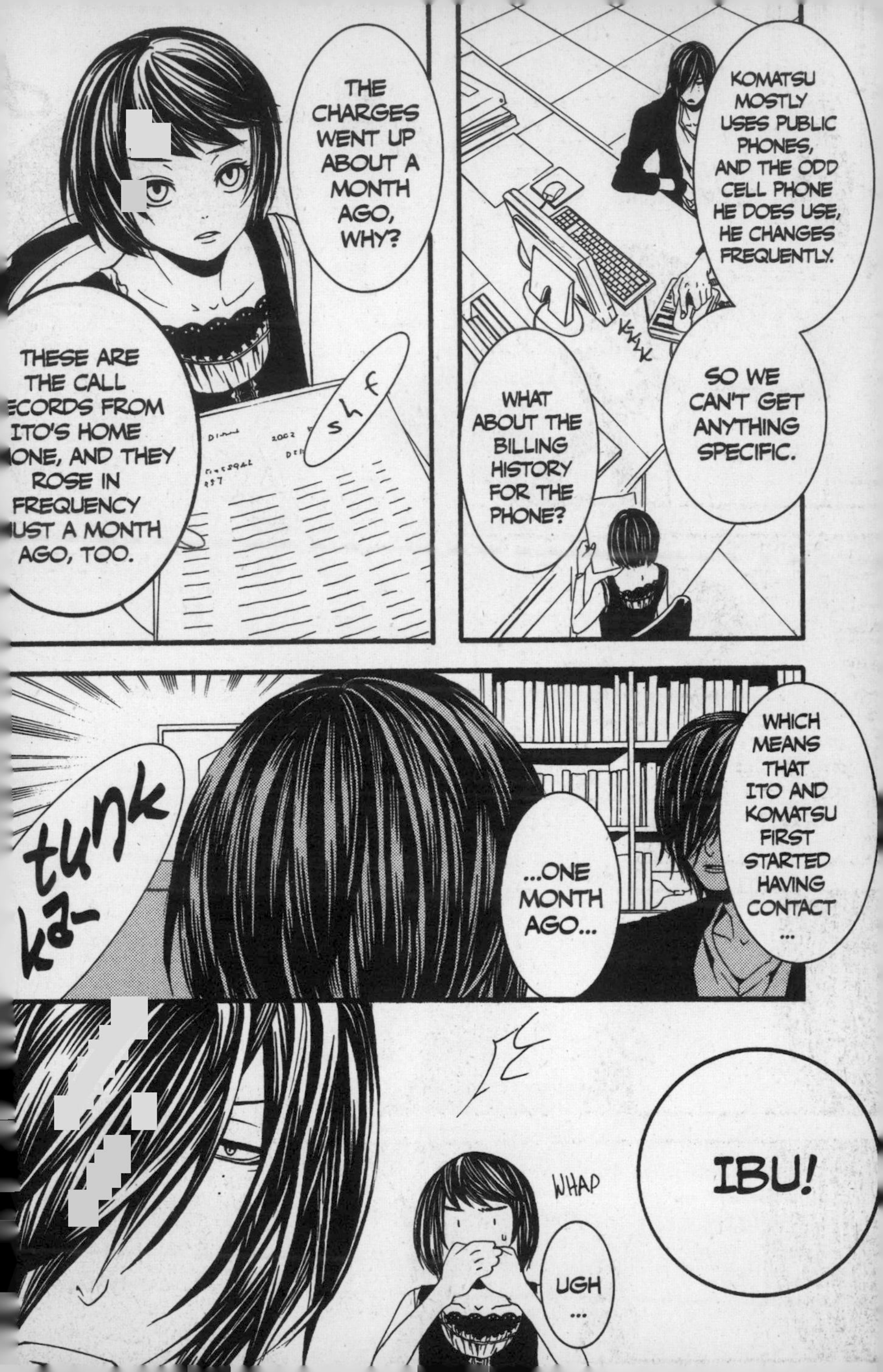
KOMATSU MOSTLY USES PUBLIC PHONES, AND THE ODD CELL PHONE HE DOES USE, HE CHANGES FREQUENTLY.
KVKK
SO WE CAN'T GET ANYTHING SPECIFIC.
WHAT ABOUT THE BILLING HISTORY FOR THE PHONE?
THE CHARGES WENT UP ABOUT A MONTH AGO, WHY?
shf
THESE ARE THE CALL ECORDS FROM ITO'S HOME IONE, AND THEY ROSE IN FREQUENCY IUST A MONTH AGO, TOO.
WHICH MEANS THAT ITO AND KOMATSU FIRST STARTED HAVING CONTACT ...
...ONE MONTH AGO...
ka-tunk
IBU!
WHAP
UGH ...

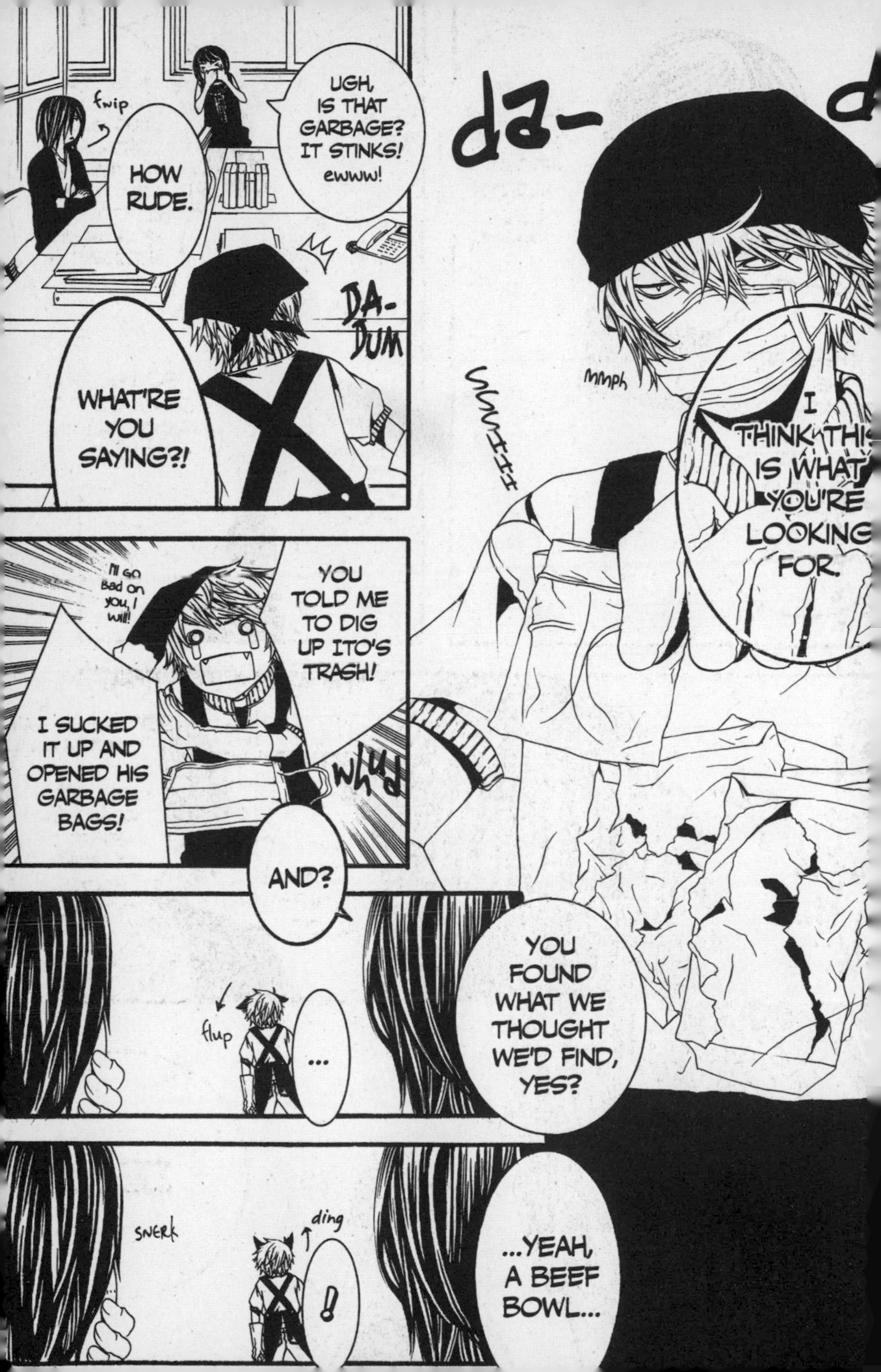
da- d
mmph
uuuurrrr
I THINK THIS IS WHAT YOU'RE LOOKING FOR.
UGH, IS THAT GARBAGE? IT STINKS! ewww!
fwip
HOW RUDE.
DA-DUM
WHAT'RE YOU SAYING?!
YOU TOLD ME TO DIG UP ITO'S TRASH!
I'll go bad on you, I will!
I SUCKED IT UP AND OPENED HIS GARBAGE BAGS!
whup
AND?
YOU FOUND WHAT WE THOUGHT WE'D FIND, YES?
flup
...
...YEAH, A BEEF BOWL...
ding
!
snerk

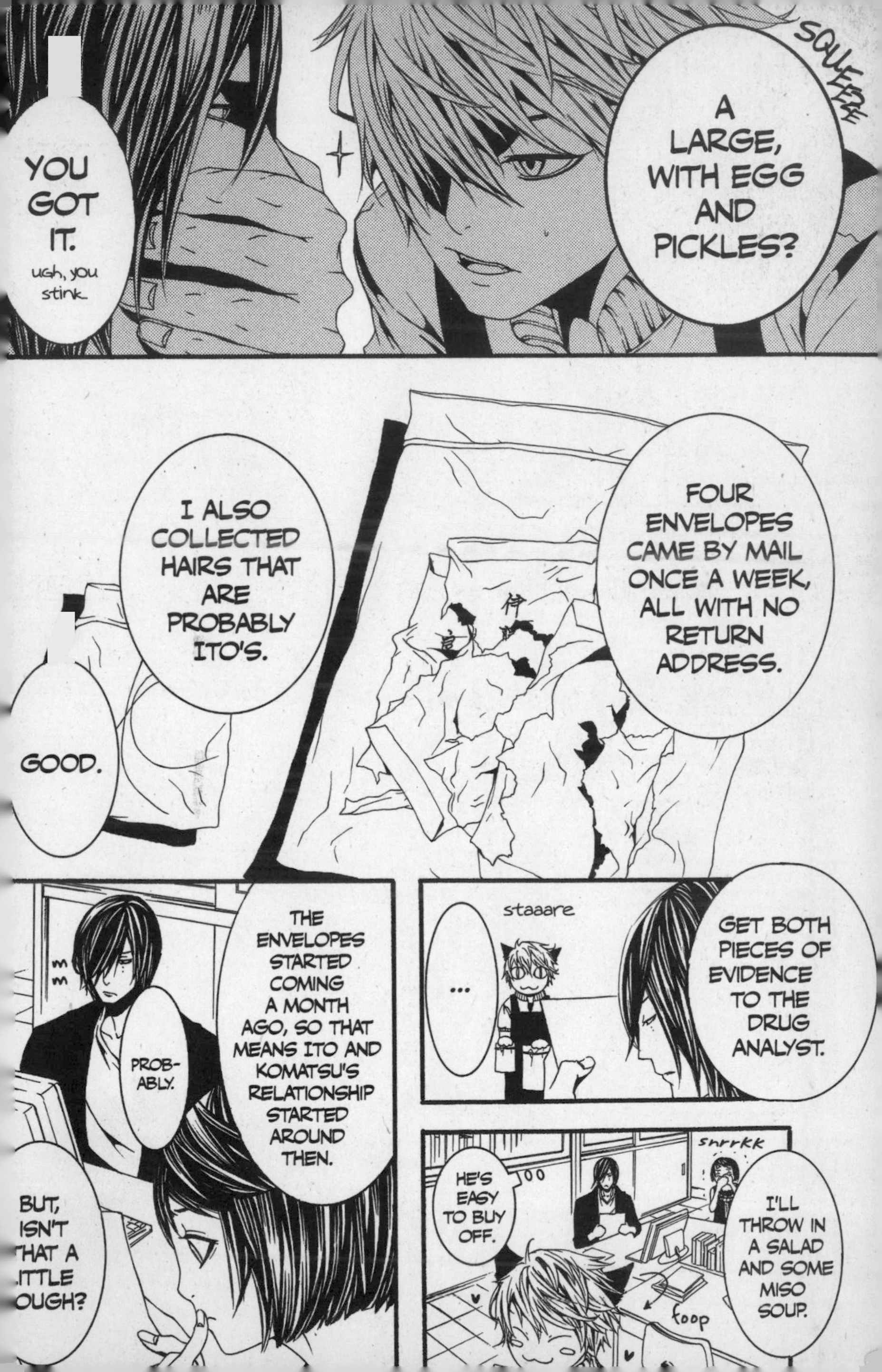
SQUEEEZE
A LARGE, WITH EGG AND PICKLES?
YOU GOT IT.
ugh, you stink
FOUR ENVELOPES CAME BY MAIL ONCE A WEEK, ALL WITH NO RETURN ADDRESS.
I ALSO COLLECTED HAIRS THAT ARE PROBABLY ITO'S.
GOOD.
GET BOTH PIECES OF EVIDENCE TO THE DRUG ANALYST.
staaare
...
I'LL THROW IN A SALAD AND SOME MISO SOUP.
snrrkk
HE'S EASY TO BUY OFF.
foop
THE ENVELOPES STARTED COMING A MONTH AGO, SO THAT MEANS ITO AND KOMATSU'S RELATIONSHIP STARTED AROUND THEN.
mm
PROB-ABLY.
BUT, ISN'T HAT A ITTLE OUGH?

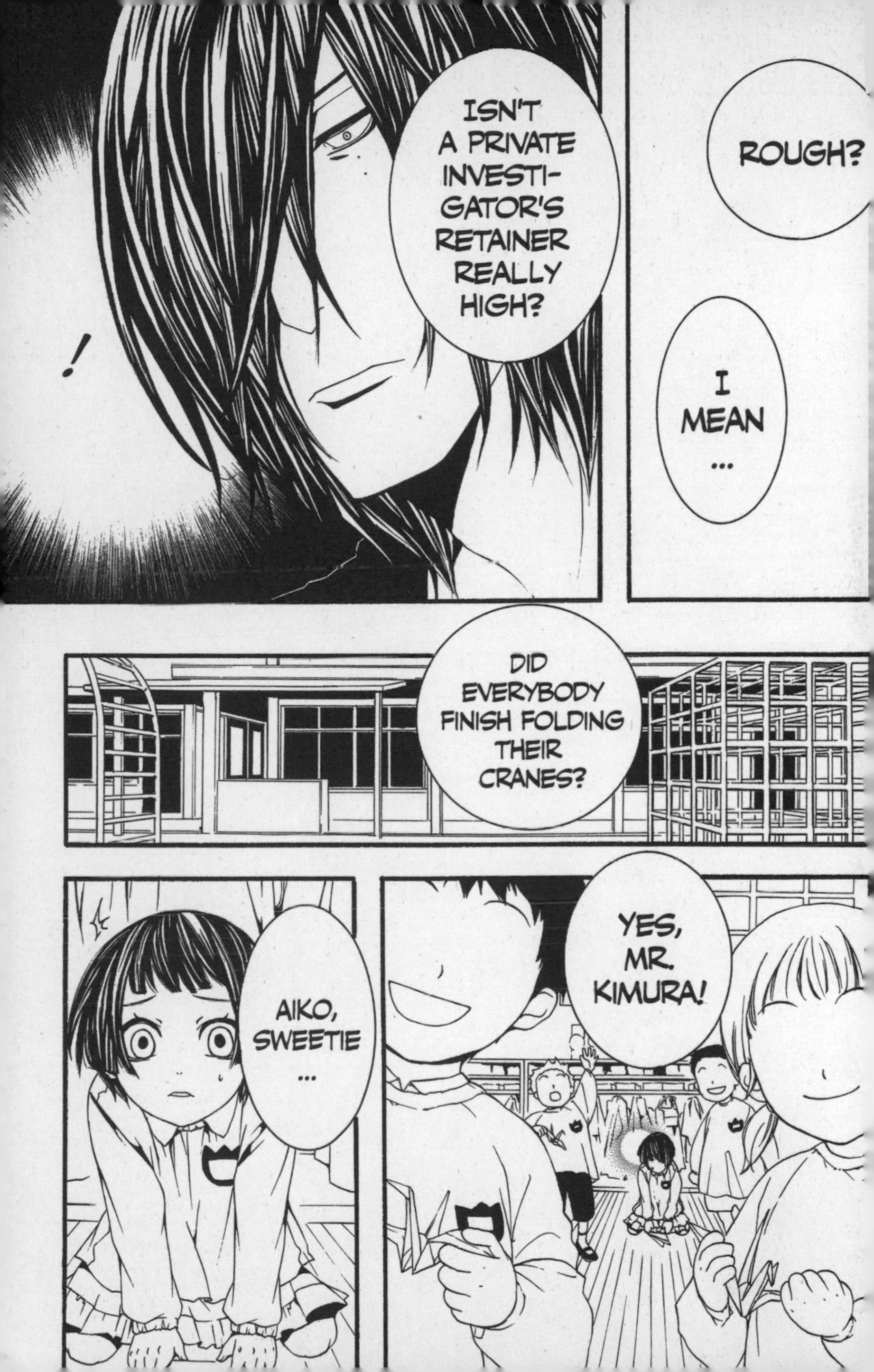
ROUGH?
I MEAN ...
ISN'T A PRIVATE INVESTI- GATOR'S RETAINER REALLY HIGH?
!
DID EVERYBODY FINISH FOLDING THEIR CRANES?
YES, MR. KIMURA!
AIKO, SWEETIE ...

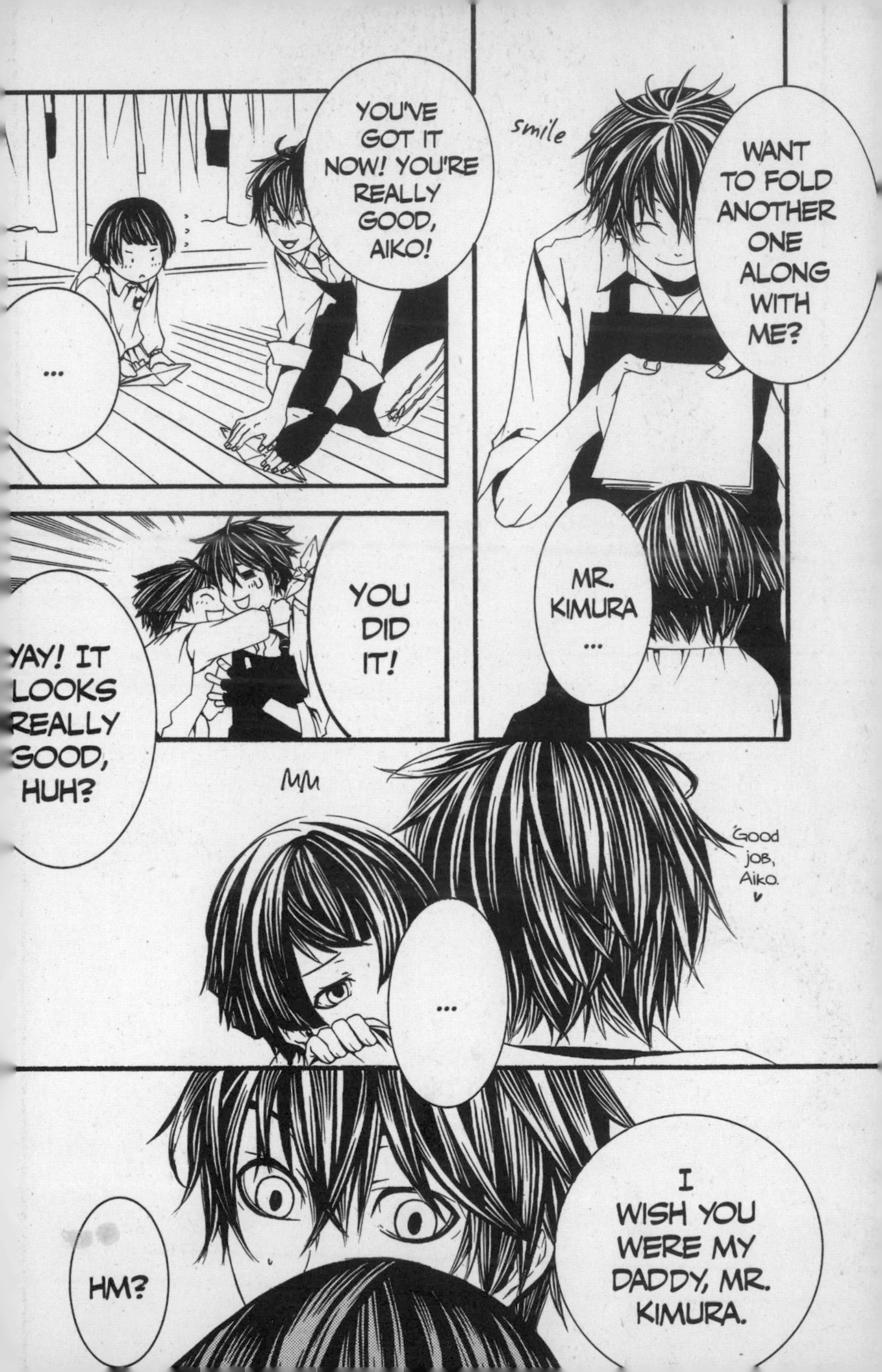
smile
WANT TO FOLD ANOTHER ONE ALONG WITH ME?
MR. KIMURA ...
YOU'VE GOT IT NOW! YOU'RE REALLY GOOD, AIKO!
...
YOU DID IT!
YAY! IT LOOKS REALLY GOOD, HUH?
MM
Good job, Aiko.
...
I WISH YOU WERE MY DADDY, MR. KIMURA.
HM?

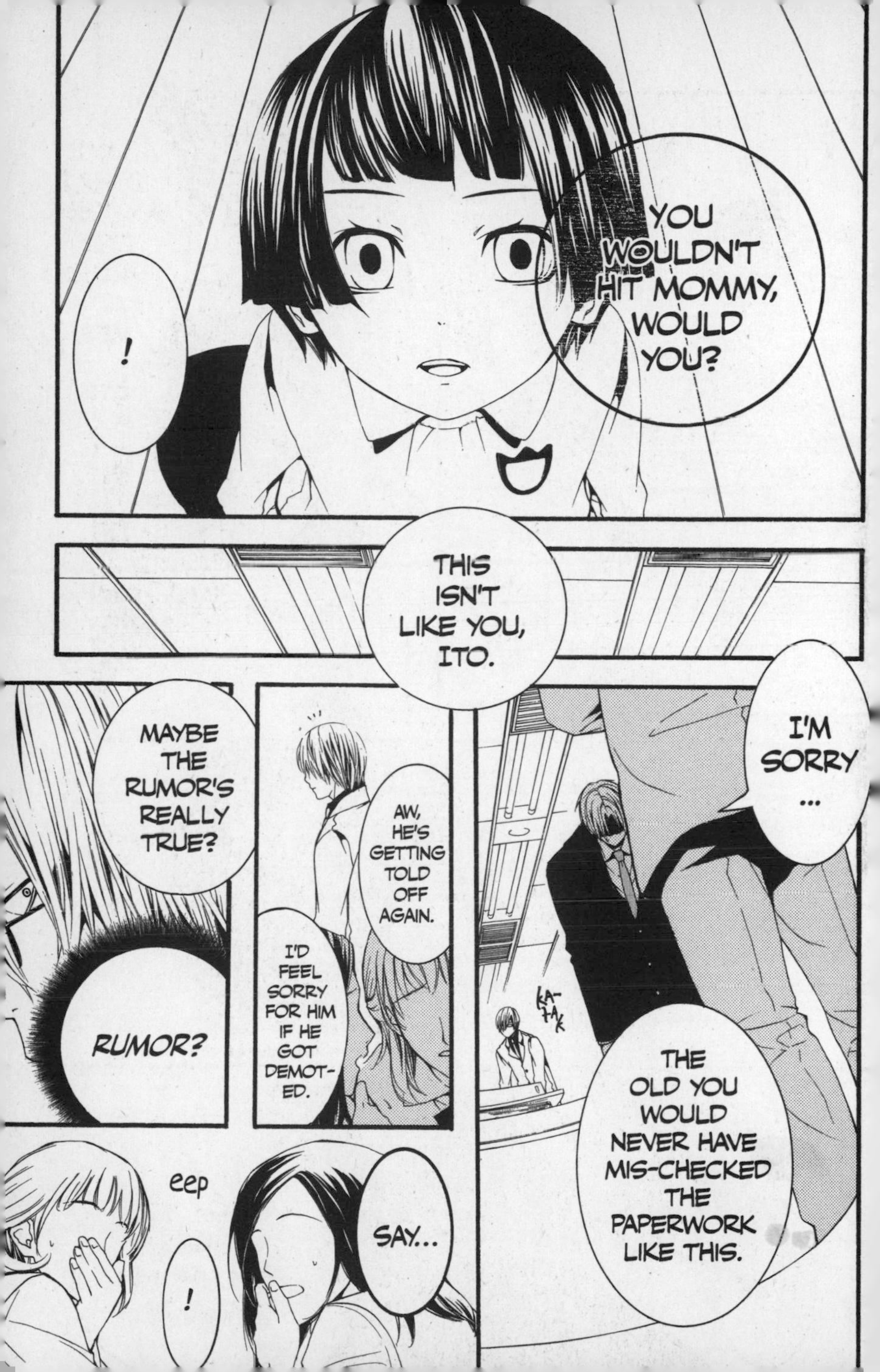
YOU WOULDN'T HIT MOMMY, WOULD YOU?
!
THIS ISN'T LIKE YOU, ITO.
I'M SORRY ...
KA-TAK
THE OLD YOU WOULD NEVER HAVE MIS-CHECKED THE PAPERWORK LIKE THIS.
AW, HE'S GETTING TOLD OFF AGAIN.
I'D FEEL SORRY FOR HIM IF HE GOT DEMOT-ED.
MAYBE THE RUMOR'S REALLY TRUE?
RUMOR?
SAY...
!
eep

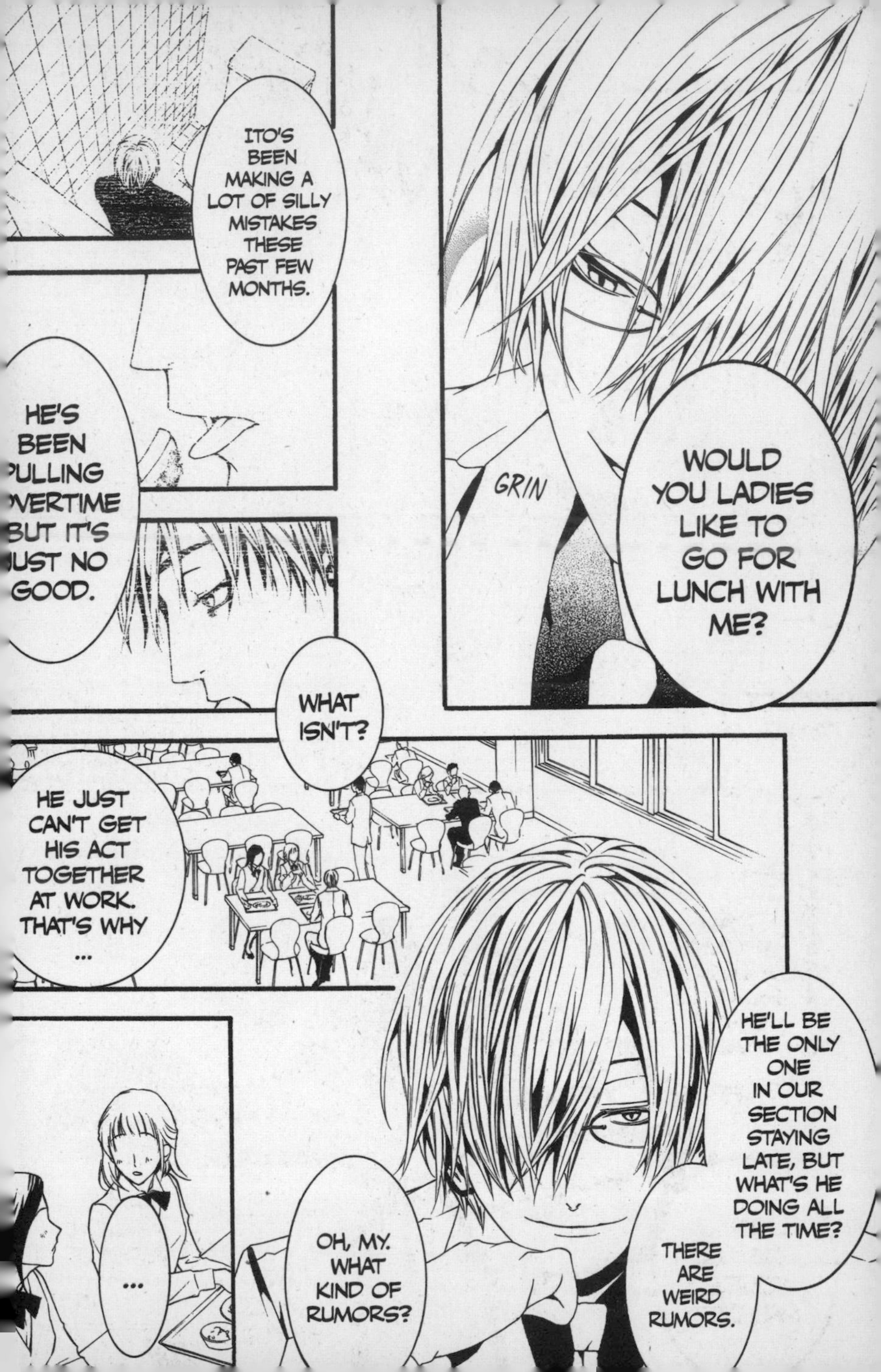
WOULD YOU LADIES LIKE TO GO FOR LUNCH WITH ME?
GRIN
ITO'S BEEN MAKING A LOT OF SILLY MISTAKES THESE PAST FEW MONTHS.
HE'S BEEN PULLING OVERTIME BUT IT'S JUST NO GOOD.
WHAT ISN'T?
HE JUST CAN'T GET HIS ACT TOGETHER AT WORK. THAT'S WHY ...
HE'LL BE THE ONLY ONE IN OUR SECTION STAYING LATE, BUT WHAT'S HE DOING ALL THE TIME?
THERE ARE WEIRD RUMORS.
OH, MY. WHAT KIND OF RUMORS?
...

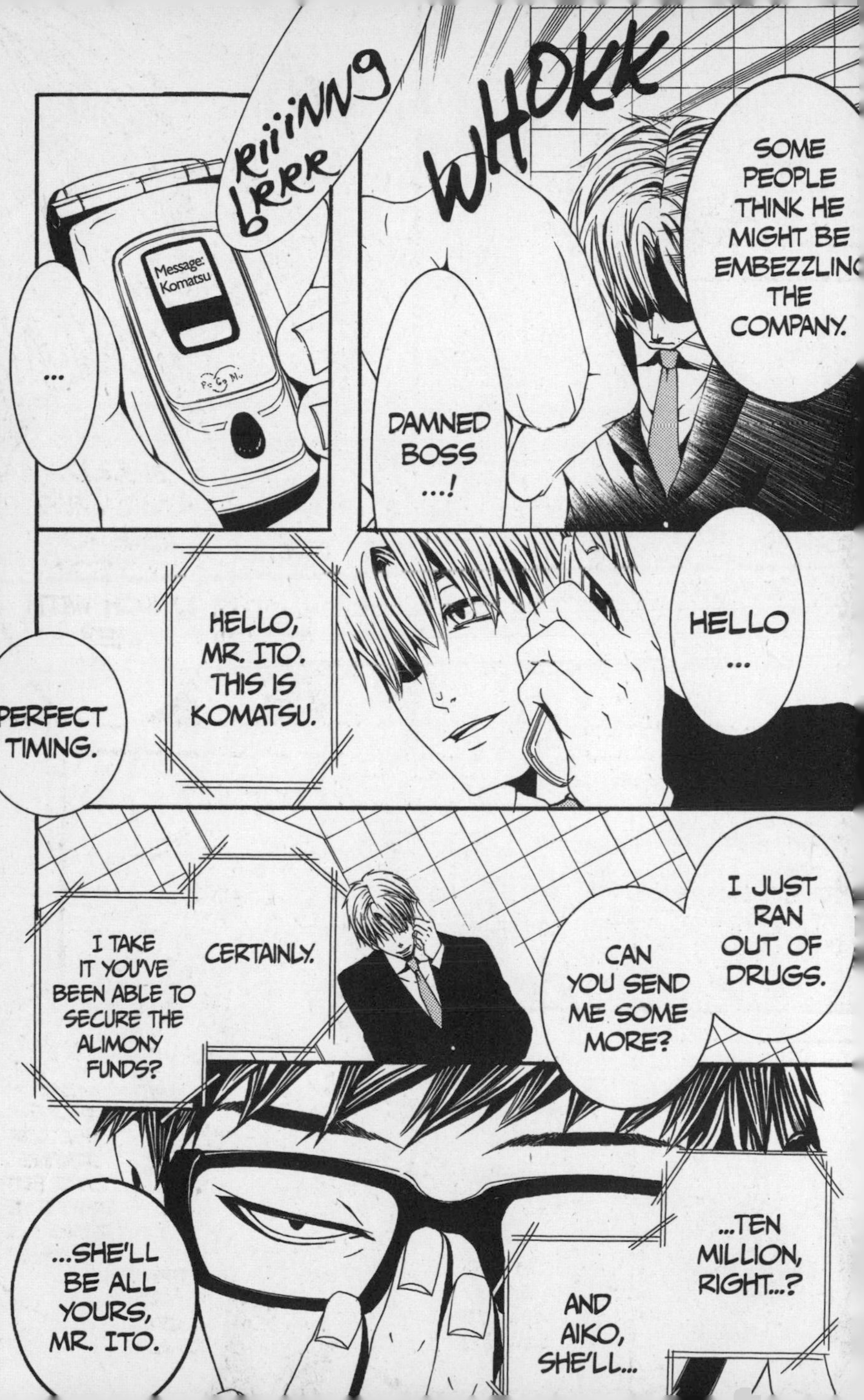
SOME PEOPLE THINK HE MIGHT BE EMBEZZLING THE COMPANY.
WHOKK
DAMNED BOSS ...!
RiiiiNNg bRRR
Message: Komatsu
...
HELLO ...
HELLO, MR. ITO. THIS IS KOMATSU.
PERFECT TIMING.
I JUST RAN OUT OF DRUGS.
CAN YOU SEND ME SOME MORE?
CERTAINLY.
I TAKE IT YOU'VE BEEN ABLE TO SECURE THE ALIMONY FUNDS?
...TEN MILLION, RIGHT...?
AND AIKO, SHE'LL...
...SHE'LL BE ALL YOURS, MR. ITO.

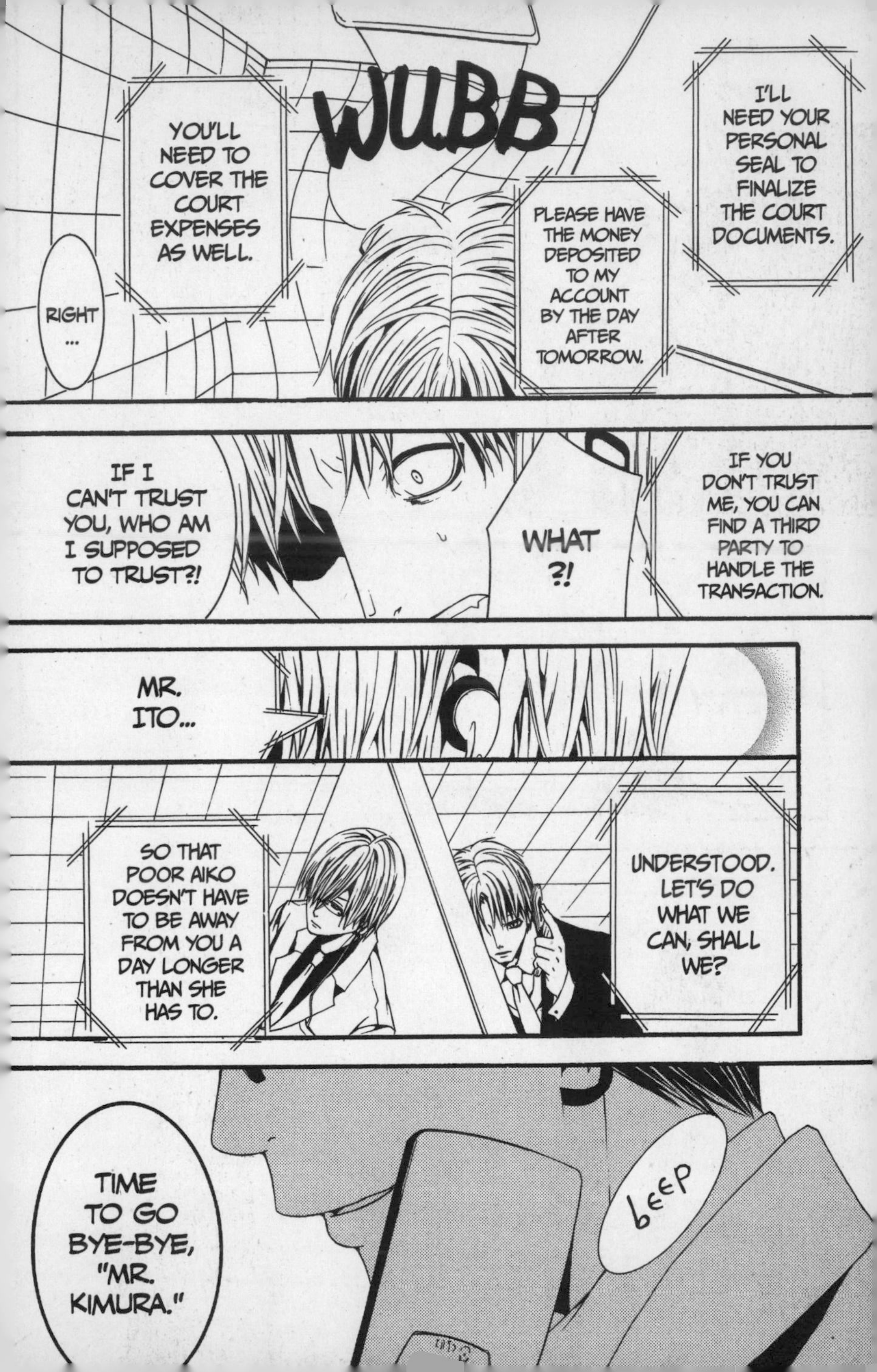
I'LL NEED YOUR PERSONAL SEAL TO FINALIZE THE COURT DOCUMENTS.
PLEASE HAVE THE MONEY DEPOSITED TO MY ACCOUNT BY THE DAY AFTER TOMORROW.
WUBB
YOU'LL NEED TO COVER THE COURT EXPENSES AS WELL.
RIGHT ...
IF YOU DON'T TRUST ME, YOU CAN FIND A THIRD PARTY TO HANDLE THE TRANSACTION.
WHAT ?!
IF I CAN'T TRUST YOU, WHO AM I SUPPOSED TO TRUST?!
MR. ITO...
UNDERSTOOD. LET'S DO WHAT WE CAN, SHALL WE?
SO THAT POOR AIKO DOESN'T HAVE TO BE AWAY FROM YOU A DAY LONGER THAN SHE HAS TO.
beep
TIME TO GO BYE-BYE, "MR. KIMURA."

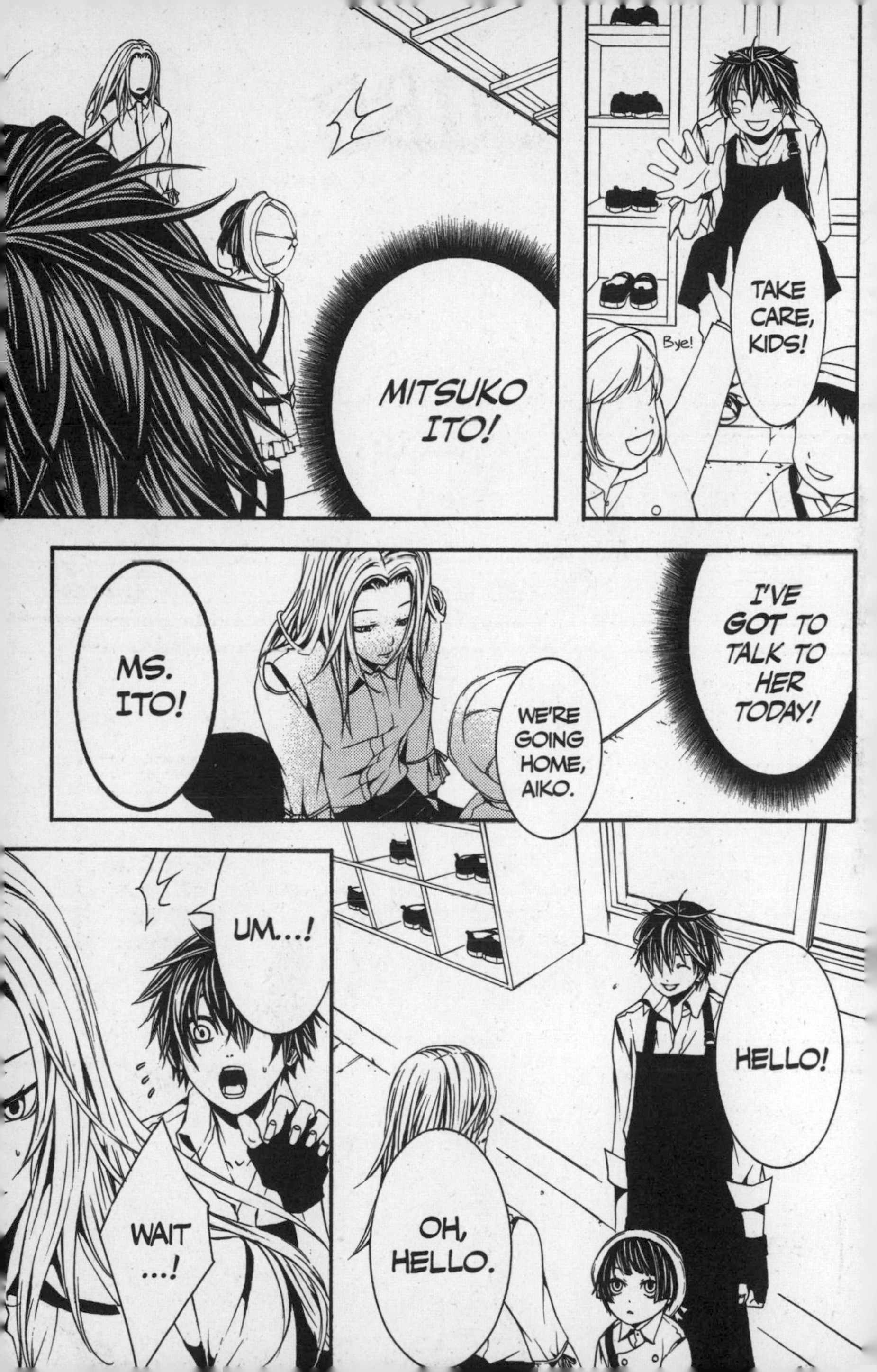
TAKE CARE, KIDS!
Bye!
MITSUKO ITO!
I'VE GOT TO TALK TO HER TODAY!
WE'RE GOING HOME, AIKO.
MS. ITO!
HELLO!
OH, HELLO.
UM...!
WAIT ...!

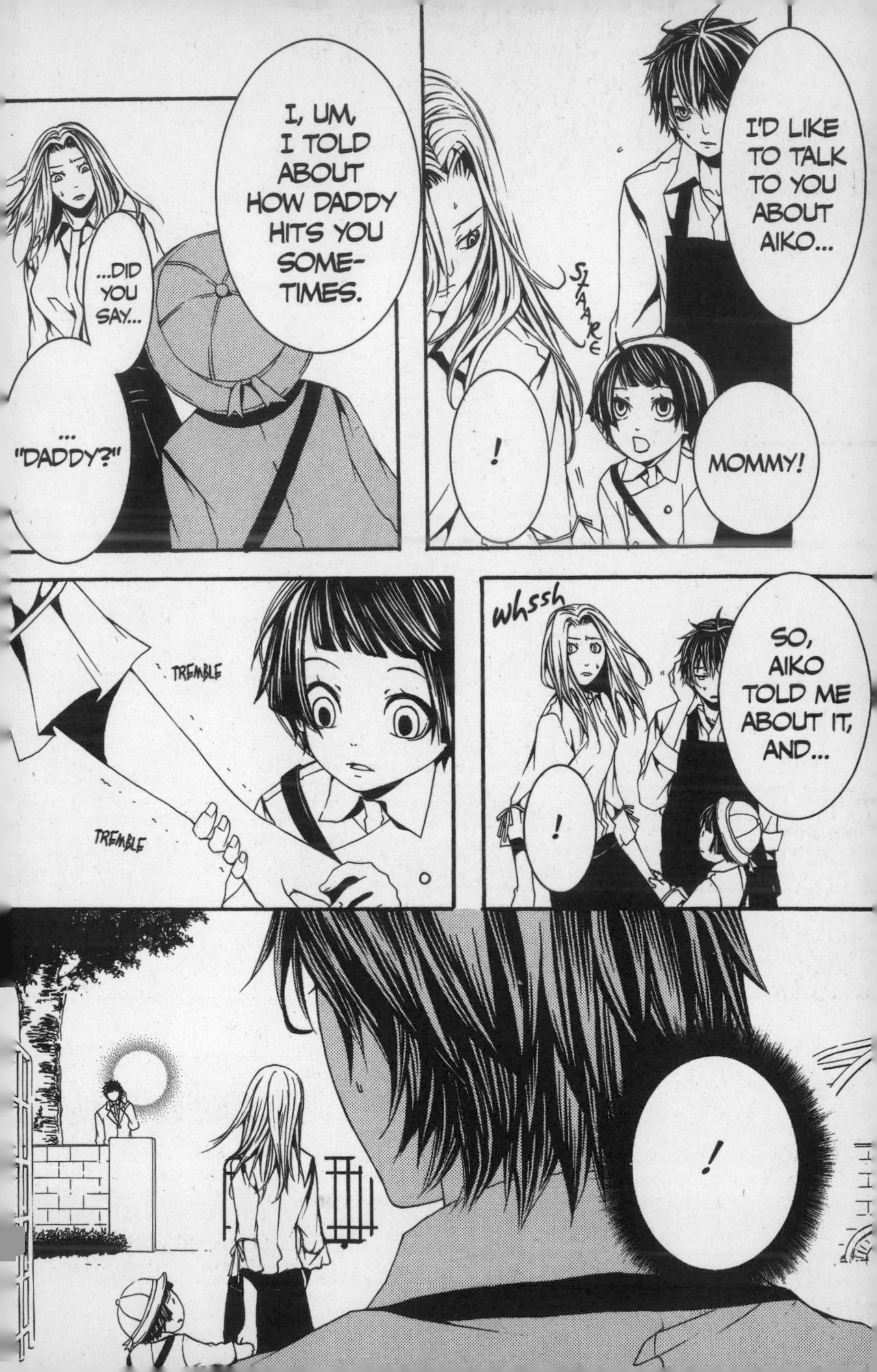

I'D LIKE TO TALK TO YOU ABOUT AIKO...
STAAARE
MOMMY!
!
I, UM, I TOLD ABOUT HOW DADDY HITS YOU SOME-TIMES.
...DID YOU SAY...
... "DADDY?"
whssh
SO, AIKO TOLD ME ABOUT IT, AND...
!
TREMBLE
TREMBLE
!

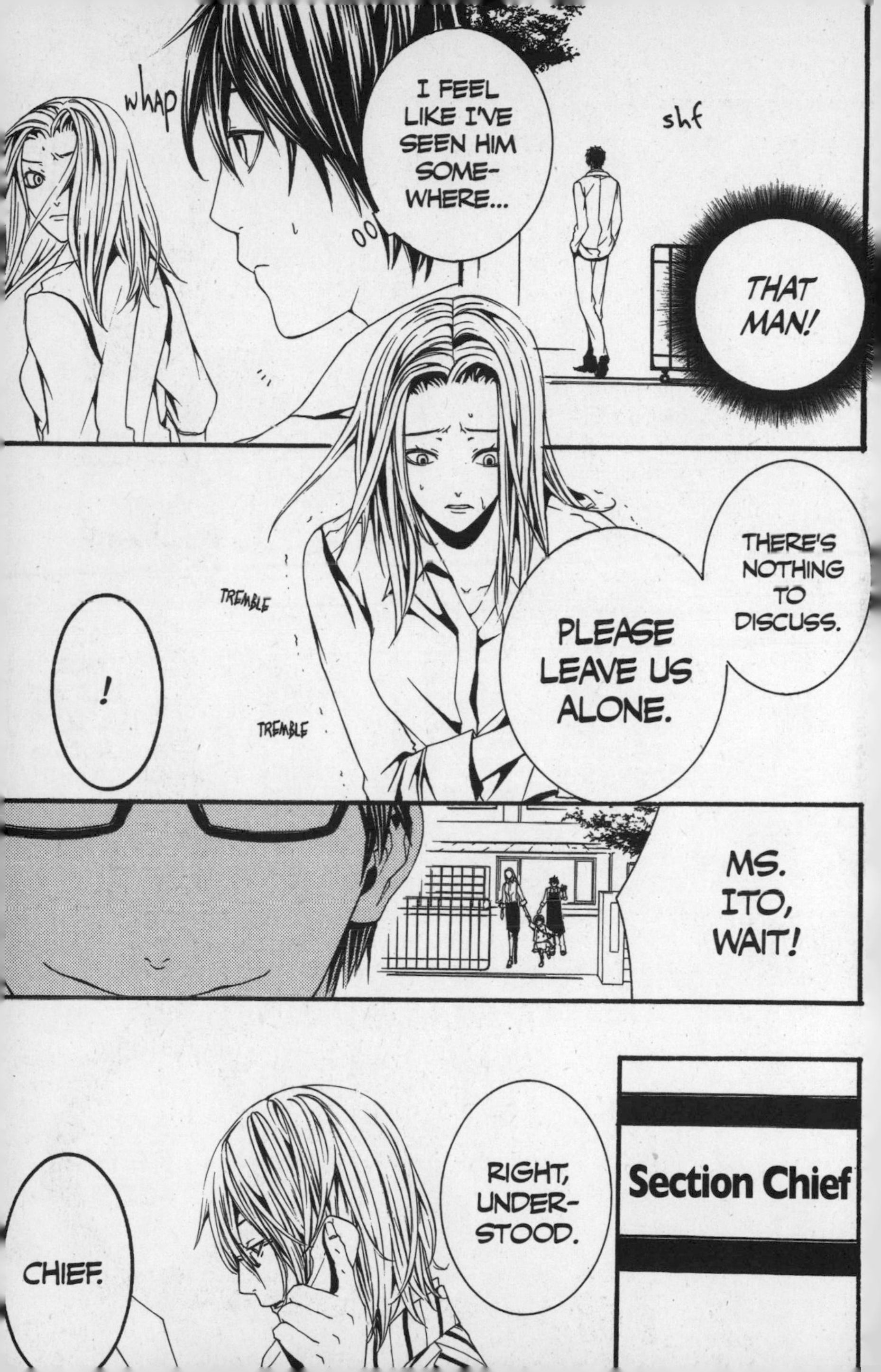
THAT MAN!
shf
I FEEL LIKE I'VE SEEN HIM SOME-WHERE...
whap
THERE'S NOTHING TO DISCUSS.
PLEASE LEAVE US ALONE.
TREMBLE
TREMBLE
!
MS. ITO, WAIT!
Section Chief
RIGHT, UNDER-STOOD.
CHIEF.

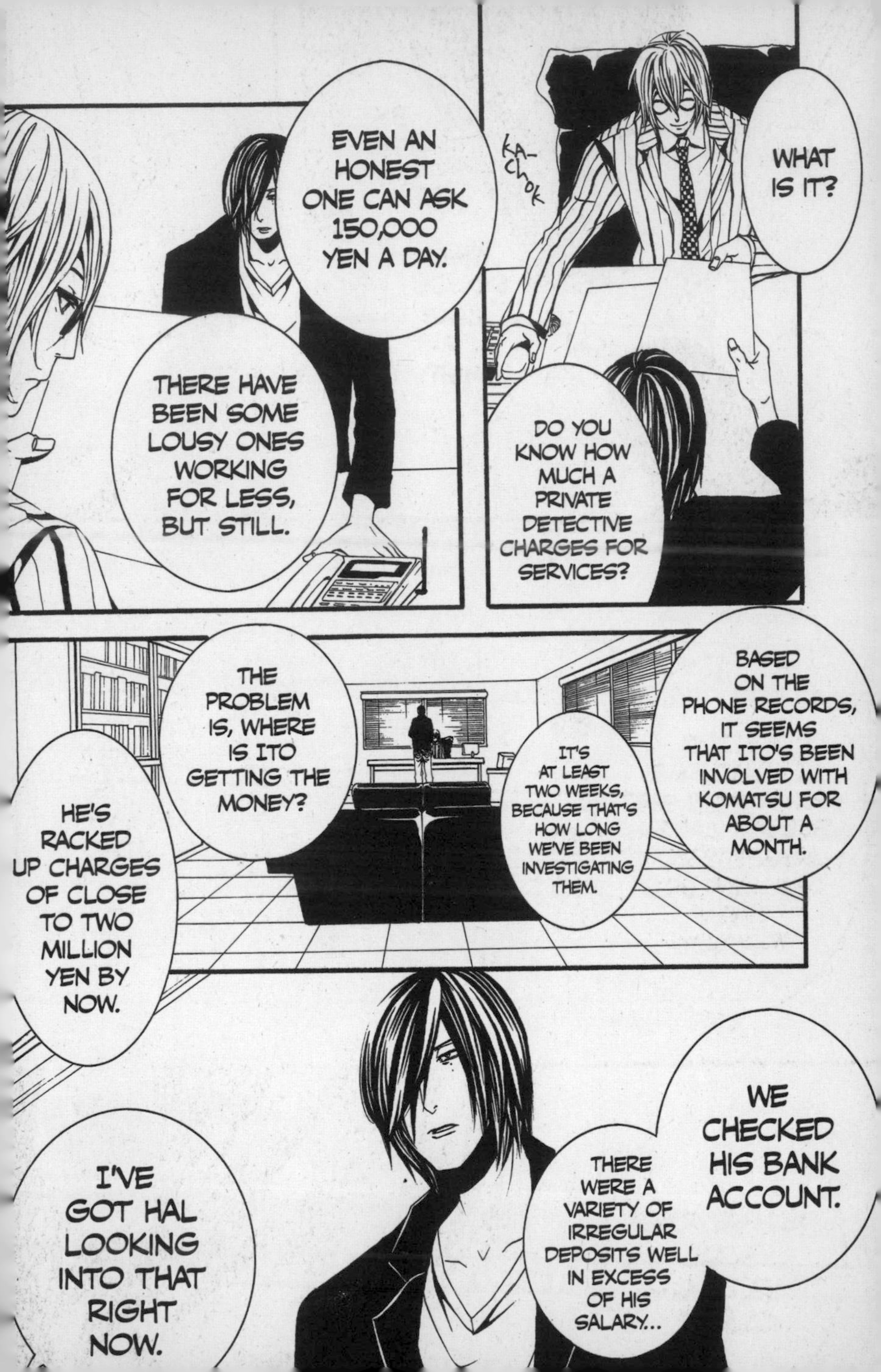
WHAT IS IT?
KA-CHOK
DO YOU KNOW HOW MUCH A PRIVATE DETECTIVE CHARGES FOR SERVICES?
EVEN AN HONEST ONE CAN ASK 150,000 YEN A DAY.
THERE HAVE BEEN SOME LOUSY ONES WORKING FOR LESS, BUT STILL.
BASED ON THE PHONE RECORDS, IT SEEMS THAT ITO'S BEEN INVOLVED WITH KOMATSU FOR ABOUT A MONTH.
IT'S AT LEAST TWO WEEKS, BECAUSE THAT'S HOW LONG WE'VE BEEN INVESTIGATING THEM.
THE PROBLEM IS, WHERE IS ITO GETTING THE MONEY?
HE'S RACKED UP CHARGES OF CLOSE TO TWO MILLION YEN BY NOW.
WE CHECKED HIS BANK ACCOUNT.
THERE WERE A VARIETY OF IRREGULAR DEPOSITS WELL IN EXCESS OF HIS SALARY...
I'VE GOT HAL LOOKING INTO THAT RIGHT NOW.

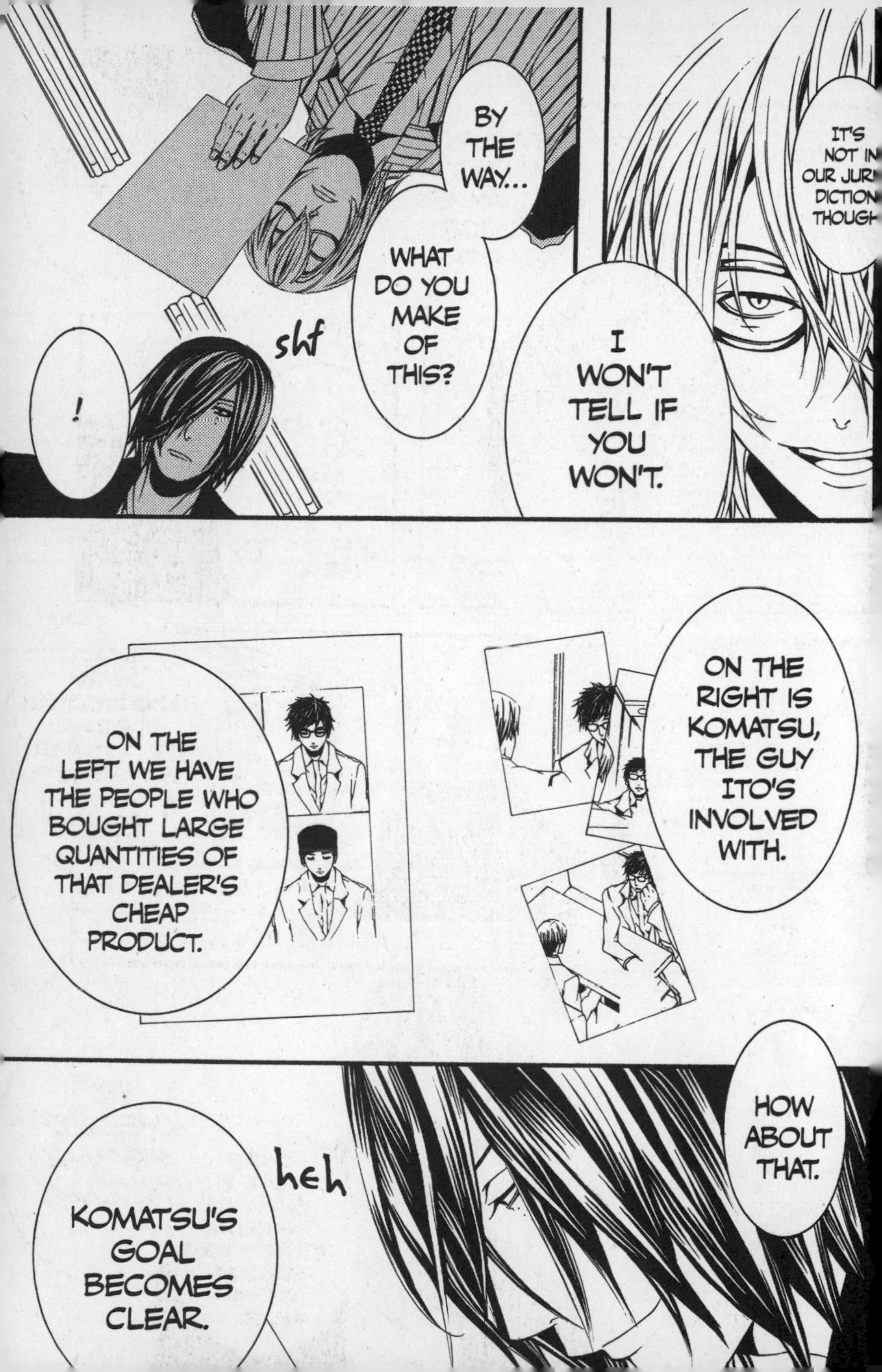
IT'S NOT IN OUR JURI DICTION THOUGH
I WON'T TELL IF YOU WON'T.
BY THE WAY...
WHAT DO YOU MAKE OF THIS?
shf
!
ON THE RIGHT IS KOMATSU, THE GUY ITO'S INVOLVED WITH.
ON THE LEFT WE HAVE THE PEOPLE WHO BOUGHT LARGE QUANTITIES OF THAT DEALER'S CHEAP PRODUCT.
HOW ABOUT THAT.
heh
KOMATSU'S GOAL BECOMES CLEAR.

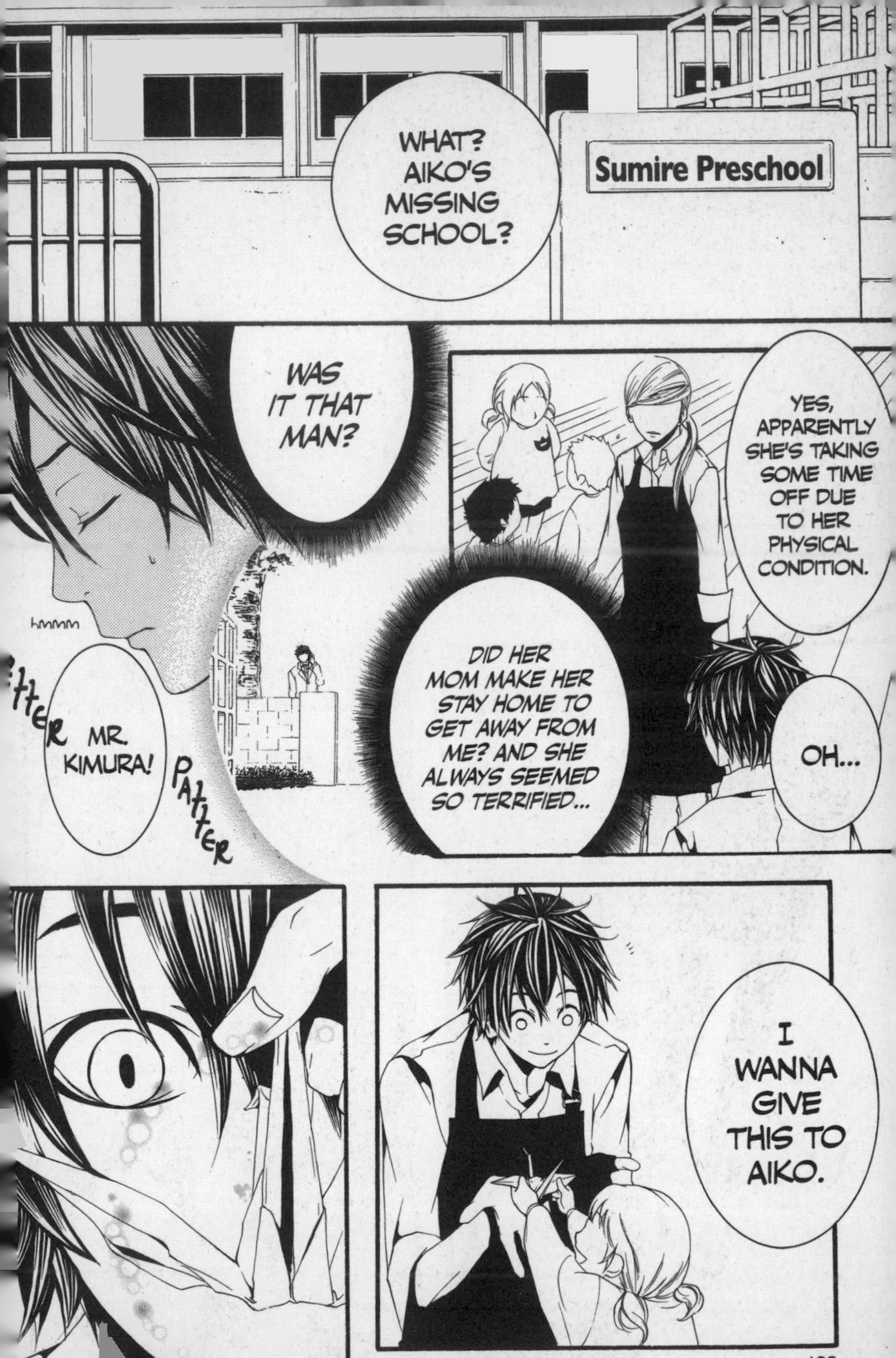
Sumire Preschool
WHAT? AIKO'S MISSING SCHOOL?
YES, APPARENTLY SHE'S TAKING SOME TIME OFF DUE TO HER PHYSICAL CONDITION.
OH...
DID HER MOM MAKE HER STAY HOME TO GET AWAY FROM ME? AND SHE ALWAYS SEEMED SO TERRIFIED...
WAS IT THAT MAN?
hmmm
MR. KIMURA!
PATTER
I WANNA GIVE THIS TO AIKO.

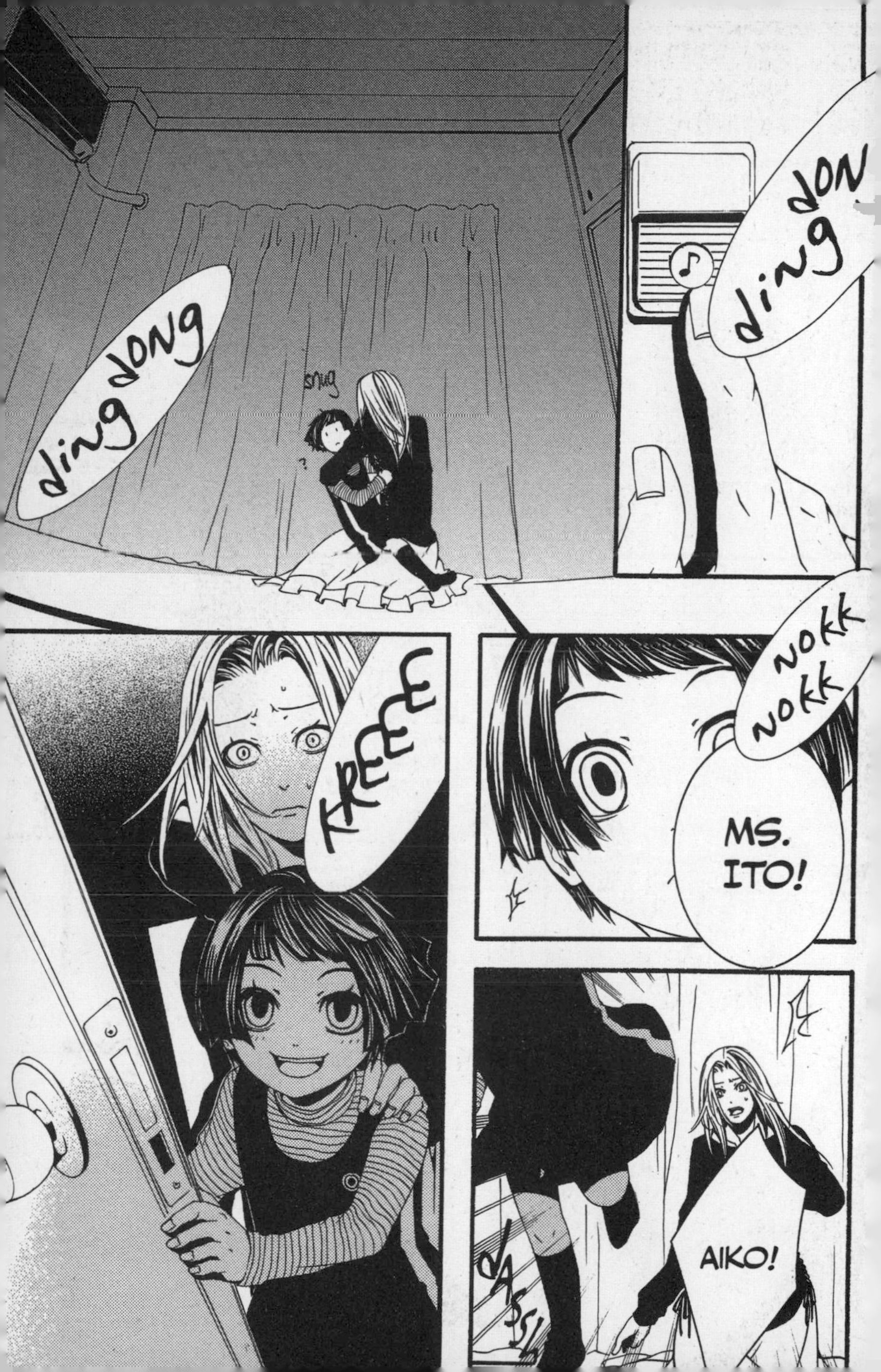
ding DON
ding DONG
snug
NOKK NOKK
MS. ITO!
DASH
AIKO!
KREEEE

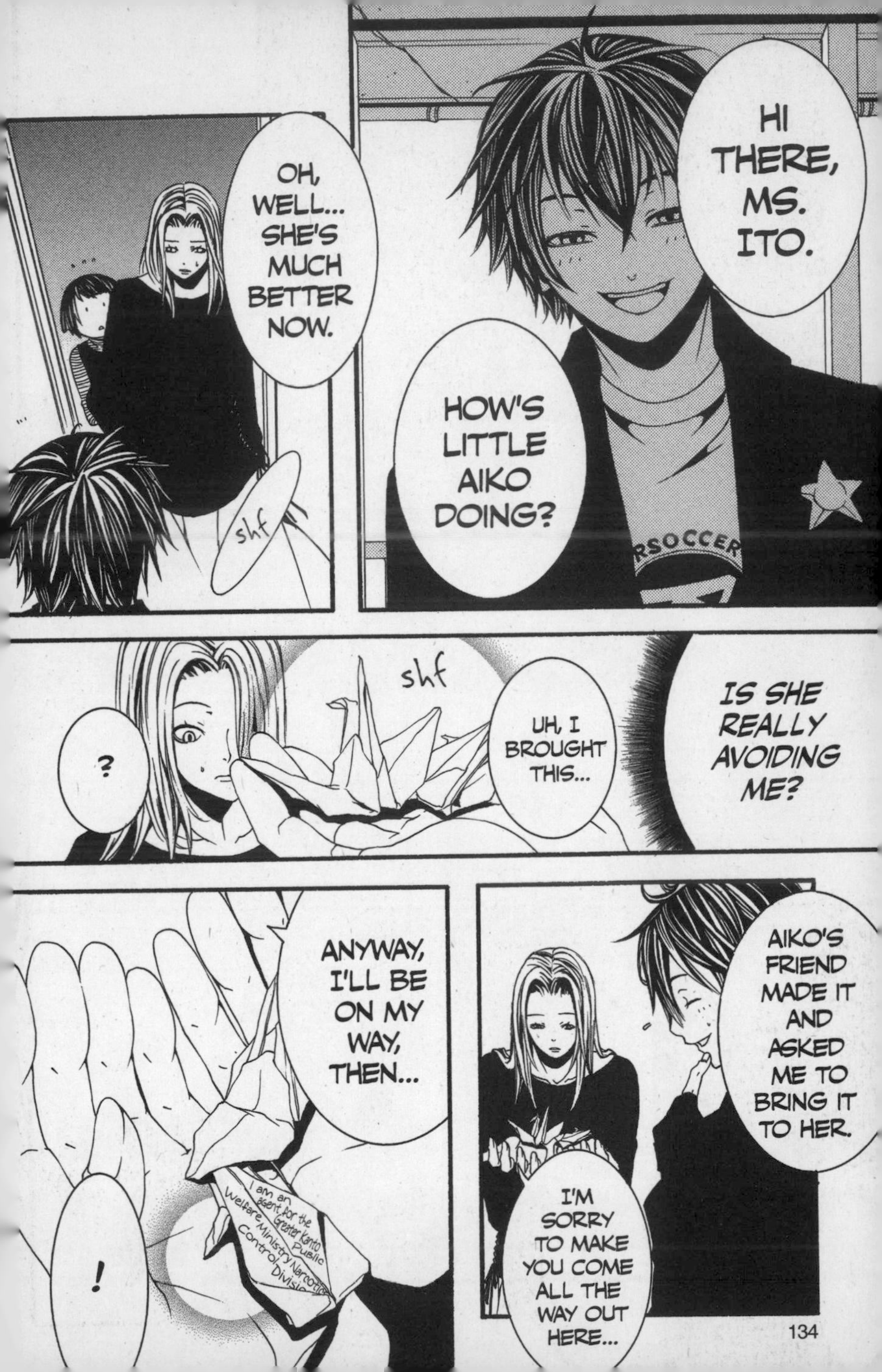
HI THERE, MS. ITO.
HOW'S LITTLE AIKO DOING?
OH, WELL... SHE'S MUCH BETTER NOW.
shf
IS SHE REALLY AVOIDING ME?
shf
UH, I BROUGHT THIS...
?
AIKO'S FRIEND MADE IT AND ASKED ME TO BRING IT TO HER.
I'M SORRY TO MAKE YOU COME ALL THE WAY OUT HERE...
ANYWAY, I'LL BE ON MY WAY, THEN...
I am an agent for the Greater Kanto Public Welfare Ministry Narcotic Control Divisi
!

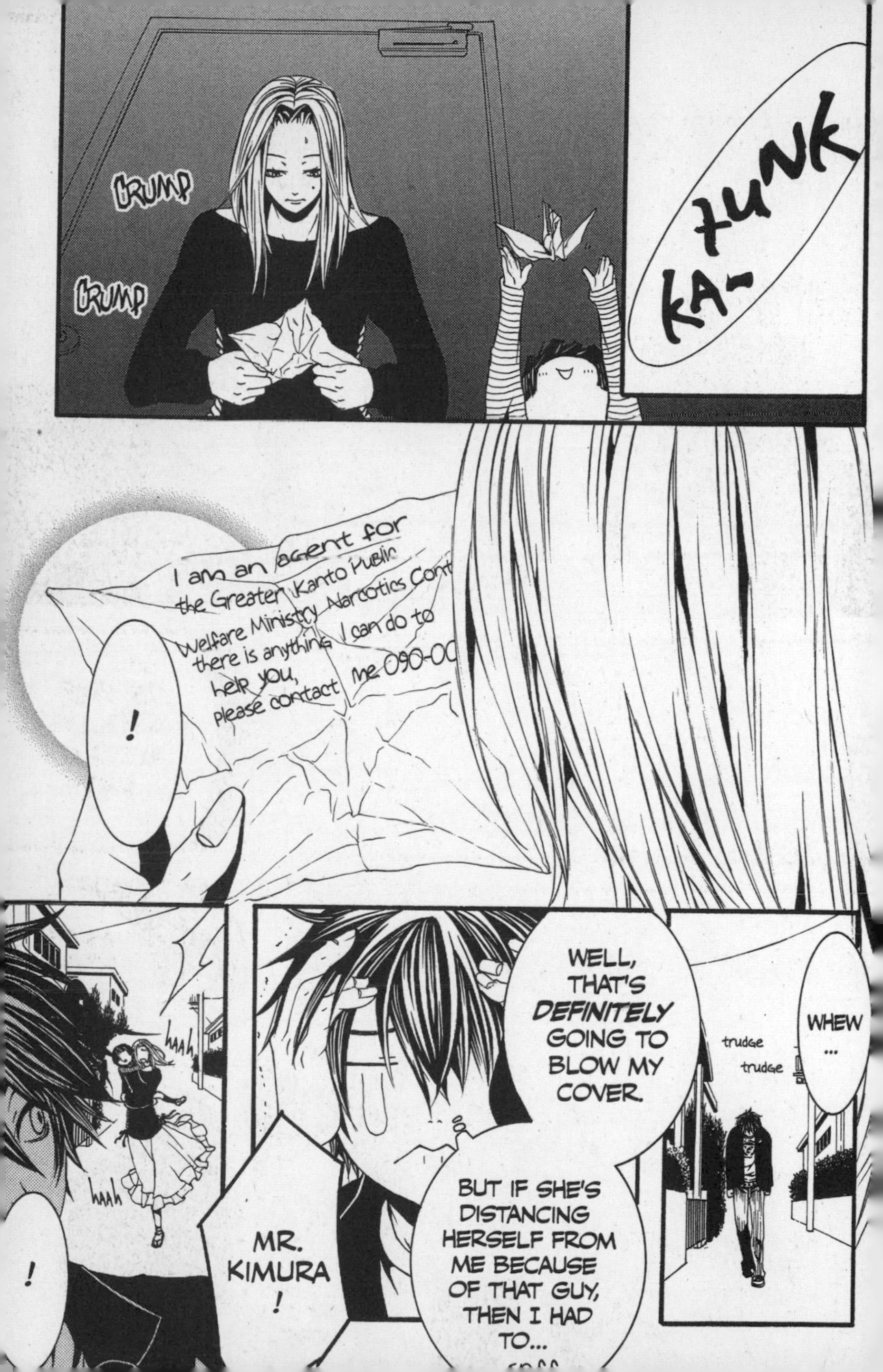
KA-ZUNK
CRUMP
CRUMP
I am an agent for
the Greater Kanto Public
Welfare Ministry Narcotics Cont
there is anything I can do to
help you,
please contact me 090-00
!
WHEW...
trudge
trudge
WELL, THAT'S *DEFINITELY* GOING TO BLOW MY COVER.
BUT IF SHE'S DISTANCING HERSELF FROM ME BECAUSE OF THAT GUY, THEN I HAD TO...
MR. KIMURA!
haah
haah
!

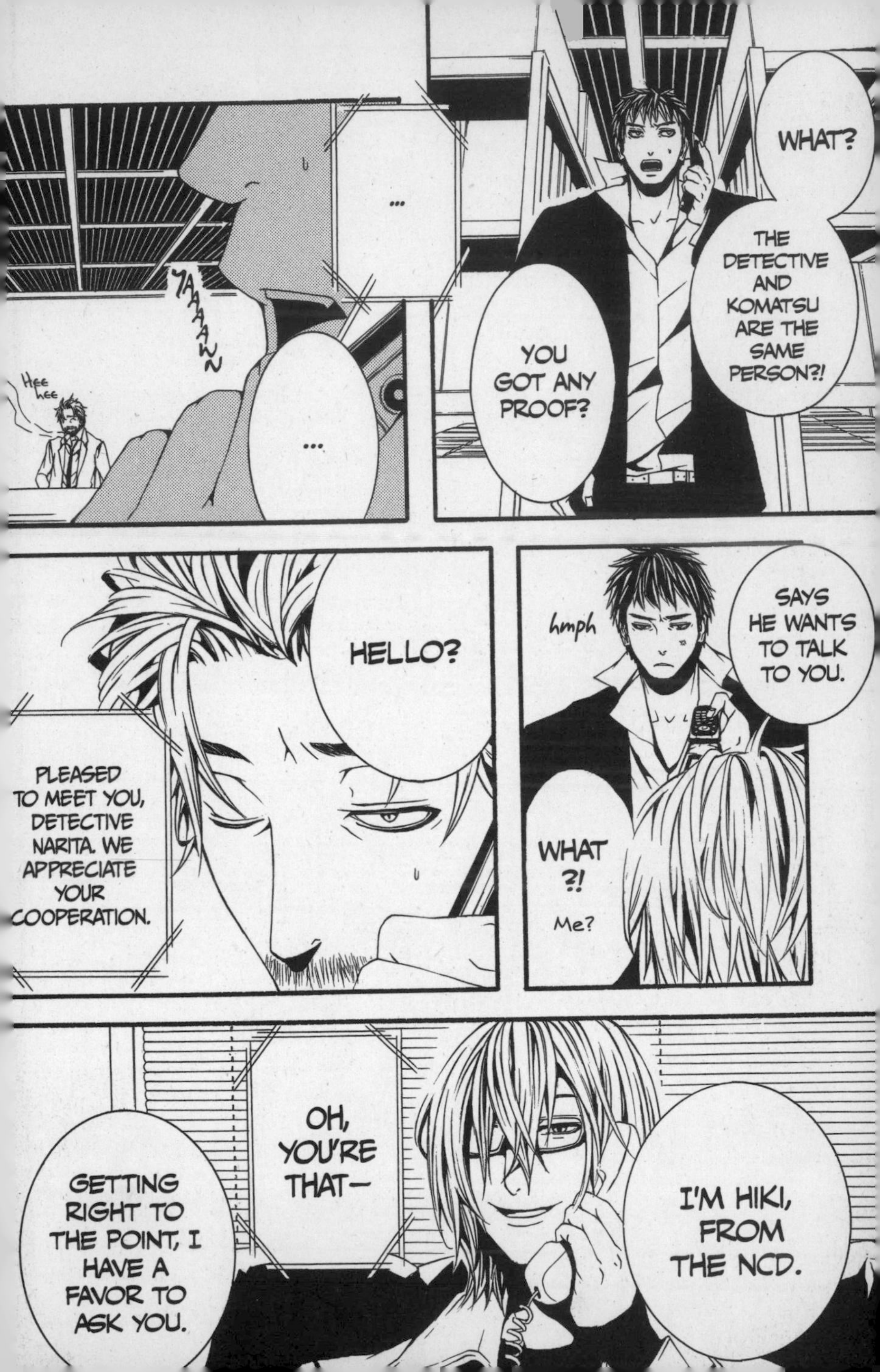
WHAT?
THE DETECTIVE AND KOMATSU ARE THE SAME PERSON?!
YOU GOT ANY PROOF?
...
YAAAAAWN
...
Hee hee
SAYS HE WANTS TO TALK TO YOU.
hmph
WHAT ?!
Me?
HELLO?
PLEASED TO MEET YOU, DETECTIVE NARITA. WE APPRECIATE YOUR COOPERATION.
I'M HIKI, FROM THE NCD.
OH, YOU'RE THAT—
GETTING RIGHT TO THE POINT, I HAVE A FAVOR TO ASK YOU.

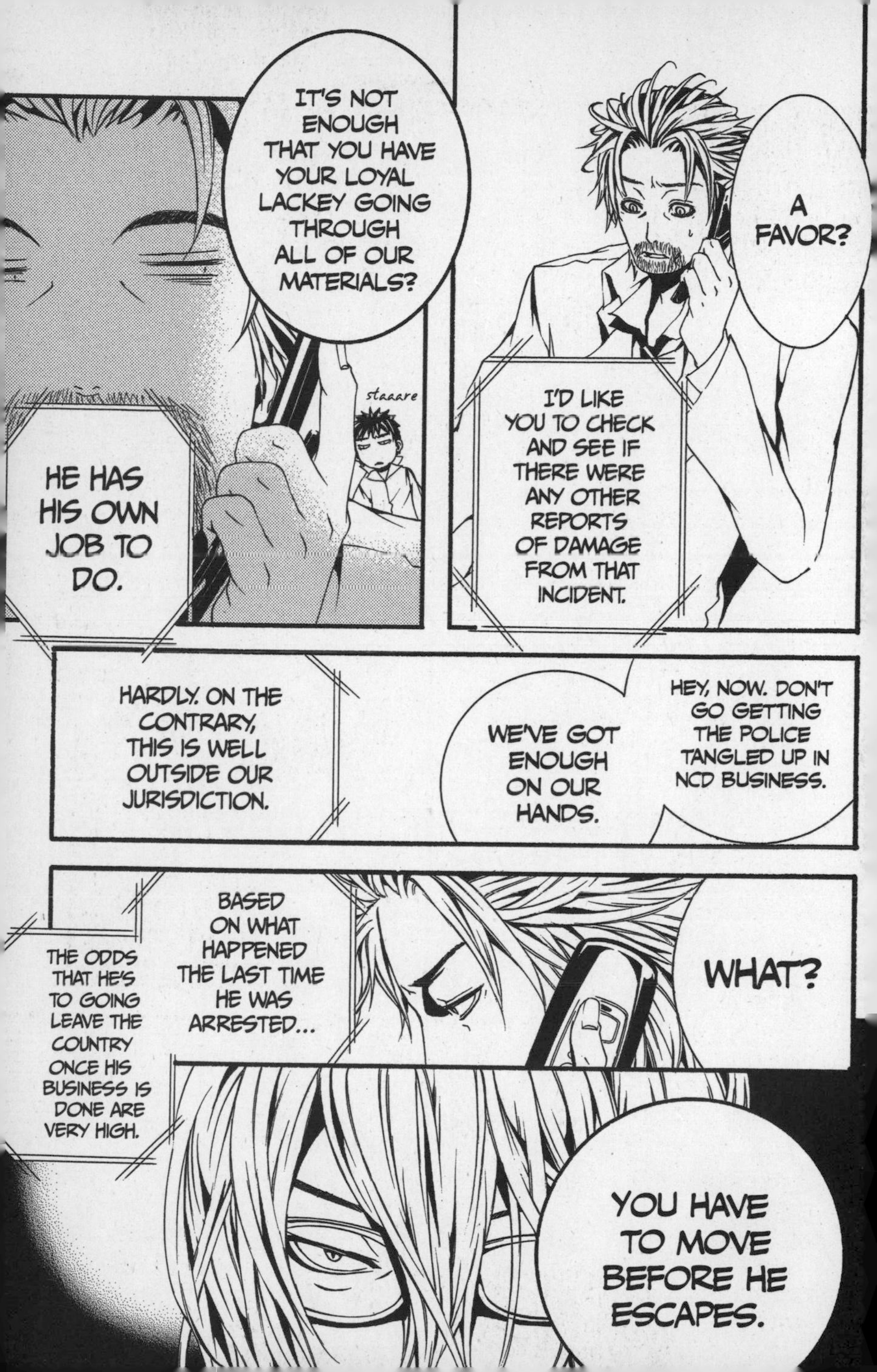
A FAVOR?
I'D LIKE YOU TO CHECK AND SEE IF THERE WERE ANY OTHER REPORTS OF DAMAGE FROM THAT INCIDENT.
IT'S NOT ENOUGH THAT YOU HAVE YOUR LOYAL LACKEY GOING THROUGH ALL OF OUR MATERIALS?
staaare
HE HAS HIS OWN JOB TO DO.
HEY, NOW. DON'T GO GETTING THE POLICE TANGLED UP IN NCD BUSINESS.
WE'VE GOT ENOUGH ON OUR HANDS.
HARDLY. ON THE CONTRARY, THIS IS WELL OUTSIDE OUR JURISDICTION.
WHAT?
BASED ON WHAT HAPPENED THE LAST TIME HE WAS ARRESTED...
THE ODDS THAT HE'S TO GOING LEAVE THE COUNTRY ONCE HIS BUSINESS IS DONE ARE VERY HIGH.
YOU HAVE TO MOVE BEFORE HE ESCAPES.

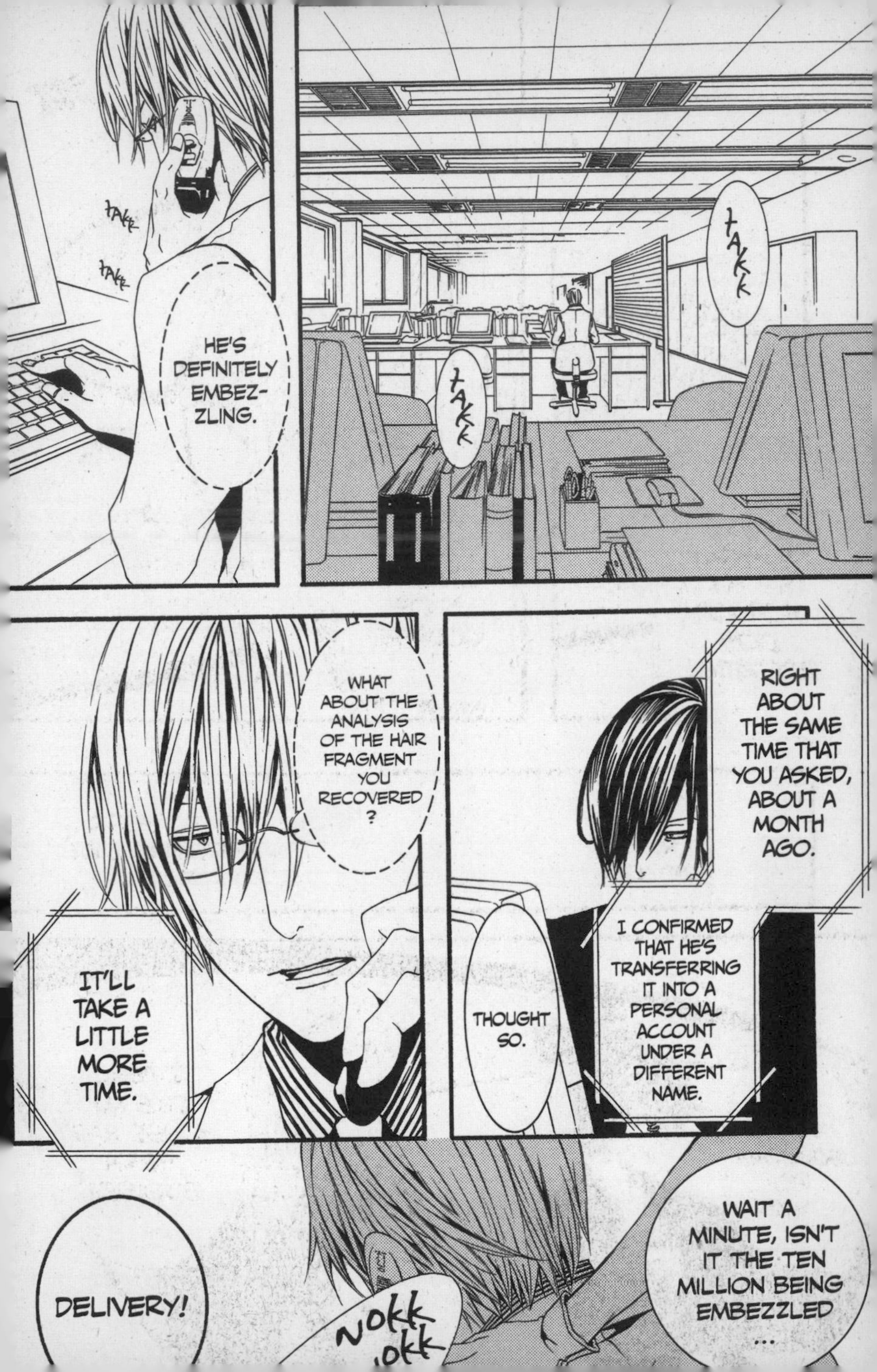
TAKK
TAKK
TAKK
TAKK
HE'S DEFINITELY EMBEZ-ZLING.
RIGHT ABOUT THE SAME TIME THAT YOU ASKED, ABOUT A MONTH AGO.
I CONFIRMED THAT HE'S TRANSFERRING IT INTO A PERSONAL ACCOUNT UNDER A DIFFERENT NAME.
THOUGHT SO.
WHAT ABOUT THE ANALYSIS OF THE HAIR FRAGMENT YOU RECOVERED?
IT'LL TAKE A LITTLE MORE TIME.
WAIT A MINUTE, ISN'T IT THE TEN MILLION BEING EMBEZZLED...
NOKK OKK
DELIVERY!

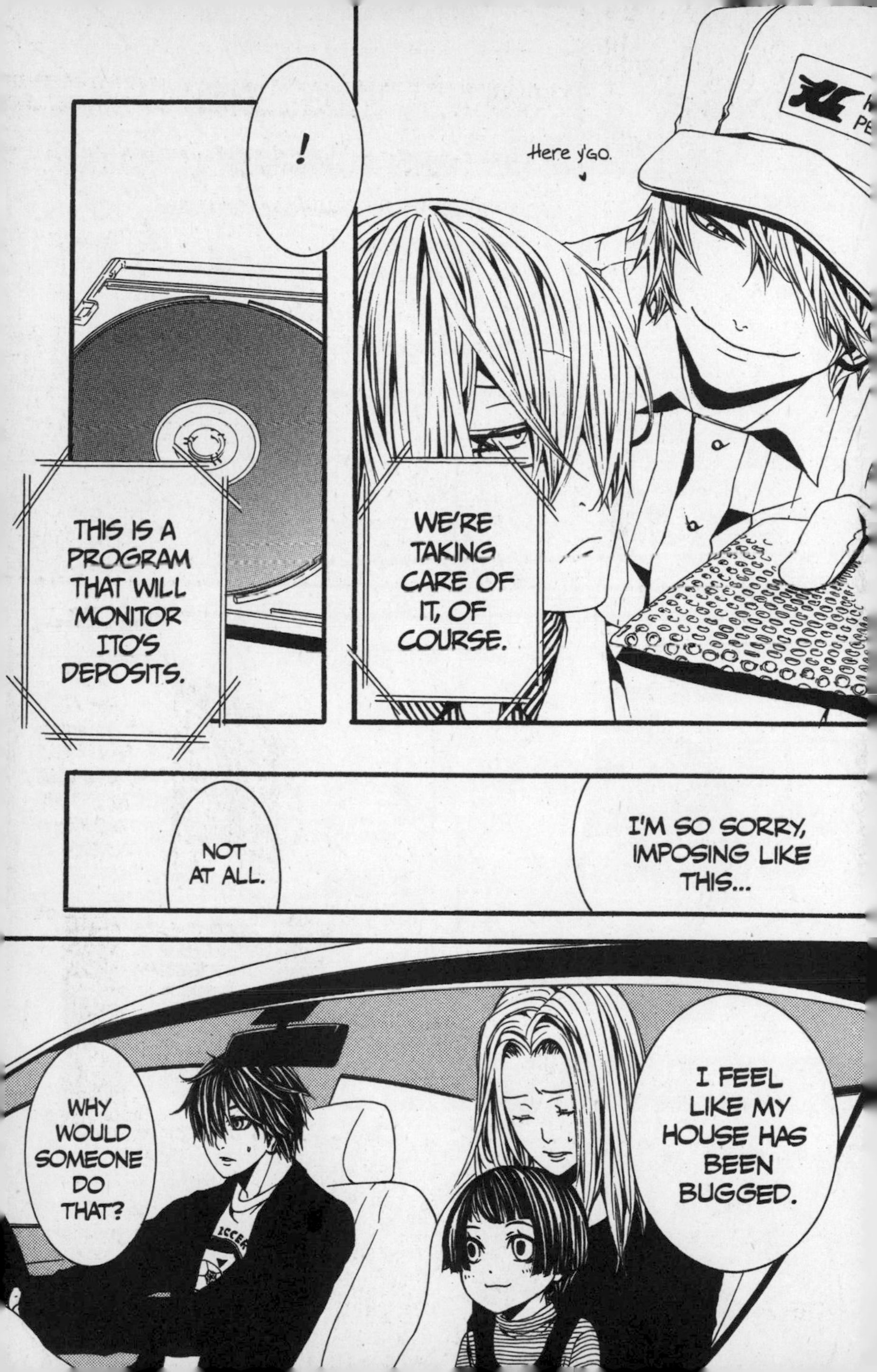
Here y'go.
WE'RE TAKING CARE OF IT, OF COURSE.
!
THIS IS A PROGRAM THAT WILL MONITOR ITO'S DEPOSITS.
I'M SO SORRY, IMPOSING LIKE THIS...
NOT AT ALL.
I FEEL LIKE MY HOUSE HAS BEEN BUGGED.
WHY WOULD SOMEONE DO THAT?

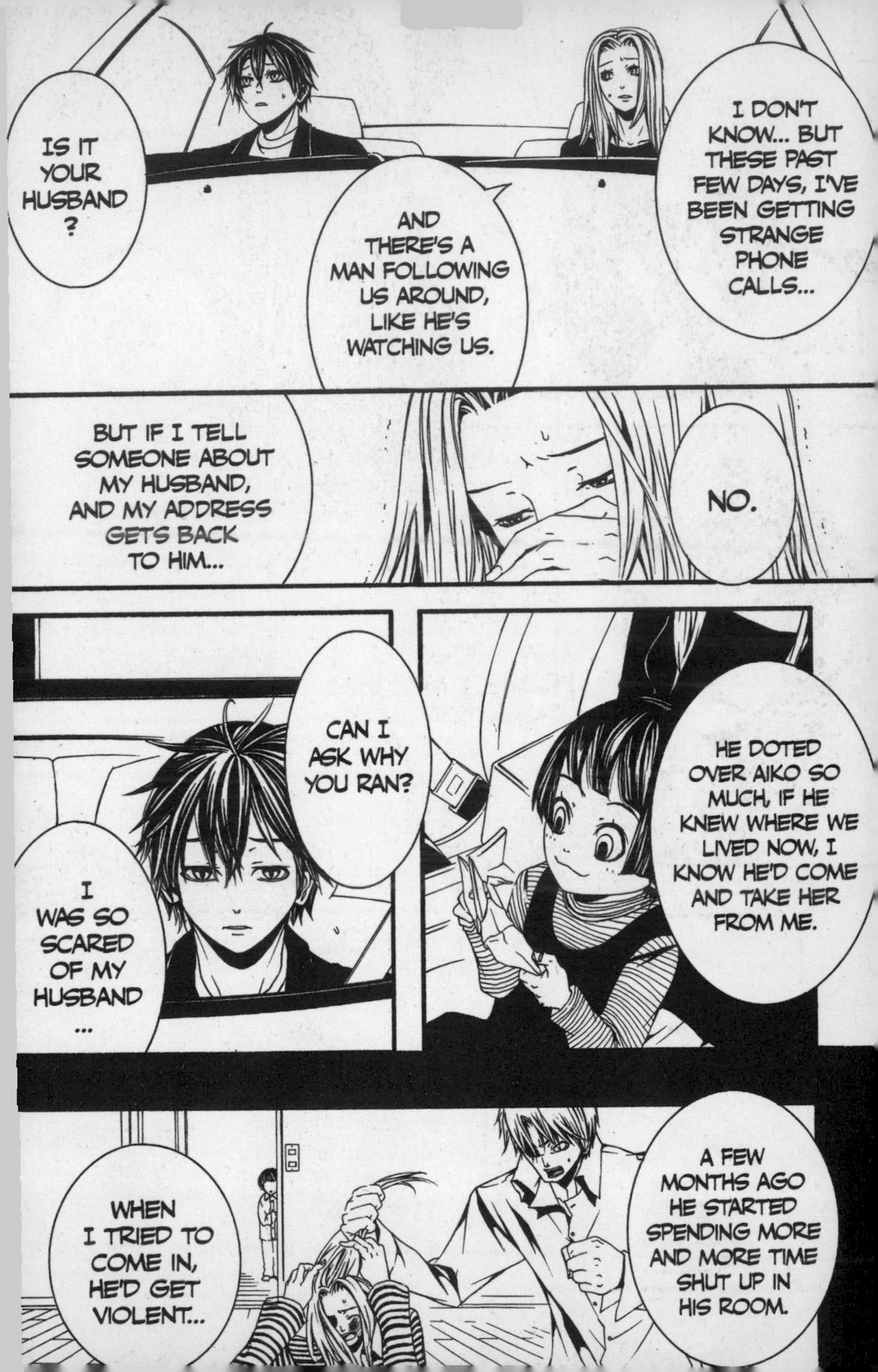
I DON'T KNOW... BUT THESE PAST FEW DAYS, I'VE BEEN GETTING STRANGE PHONE CALLS...
AND THERE'S A MAN FOLLOWING US AROUND, LIKE HE'S WATCHING US.
IS IT YOUR HUSBAND?
NO.
BUT IF I TELL SOMEONE ABOUT MY HUSBAND, AND MY ADDRESS GETS BACK TO HIM...
CAN I ASK WHY YOU RAN?
I WAS SO SCARED OF MY HUSBAND...
HE DOTED OVER AIKO SO MUCH, IF HE KNEW WHERE WE LIVED NOW, I KNOW HE'D COME AND TAKE HER FROM ME.
A FEW MONTHS AGO HE STARTED SPENDING MORE AND MORE TIME SHUT UP IN HIS ROOM.
WHEN I TRIED TO COME IN, HE'D GET VIOLENT...

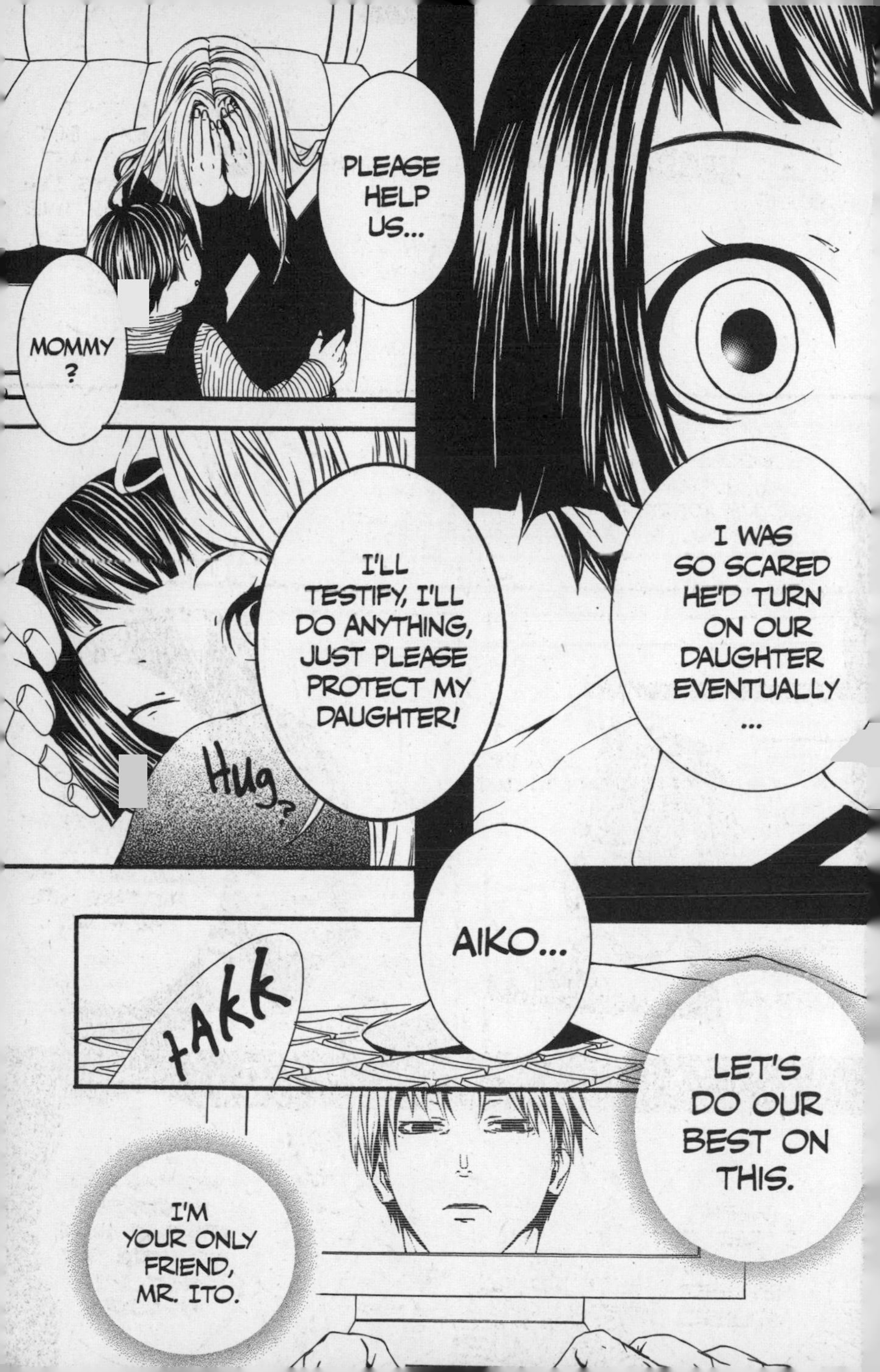
I WAS SO SCARED HE'D TURN ON OUR DAUGHTER EVENTUALLY ...
PLEASE HELP US...
MOMMY ?
I'LL TESTIFY, I'LL DO ANYTHING, JUST PLEASE PROTECT MY DAUGHTER!
Hug
AIKO...
takk
LET'S DO OUR BEST ON THIS.
I'M YOUR ONLY FRIEND, MR. ITO.

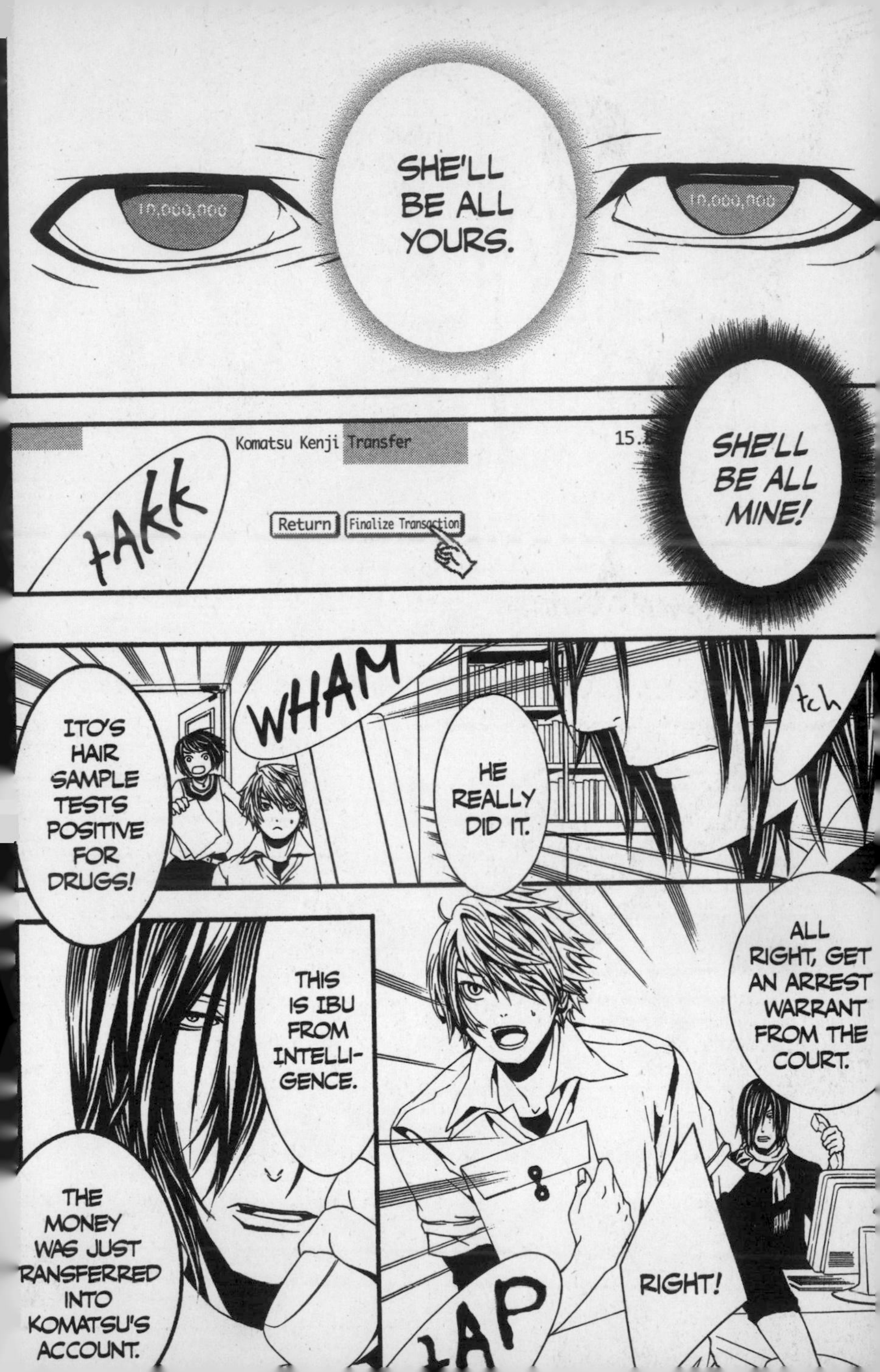
10,000,000
10,000,000
SHE'LL BE ALL YOURS.
SHE'LL BE ALL MINE!
Komatsu Kenji Transfer
Return
Finalize Transaction
tAkk
tch
HE REALLY DID IT.
WHAM
ITO'S HAIR SAMPLE TESTS POSITIVE FOR DRUGS!
ALL RIGHT, GET AN ARREST WARRANT FROM THE COURT.
RIGHT!
THIS IS IBU FROM INTELLIGENCE.
THE MONEY WAS JUST RANSFERRED INTO KOMATSU'S ACCOUNT.

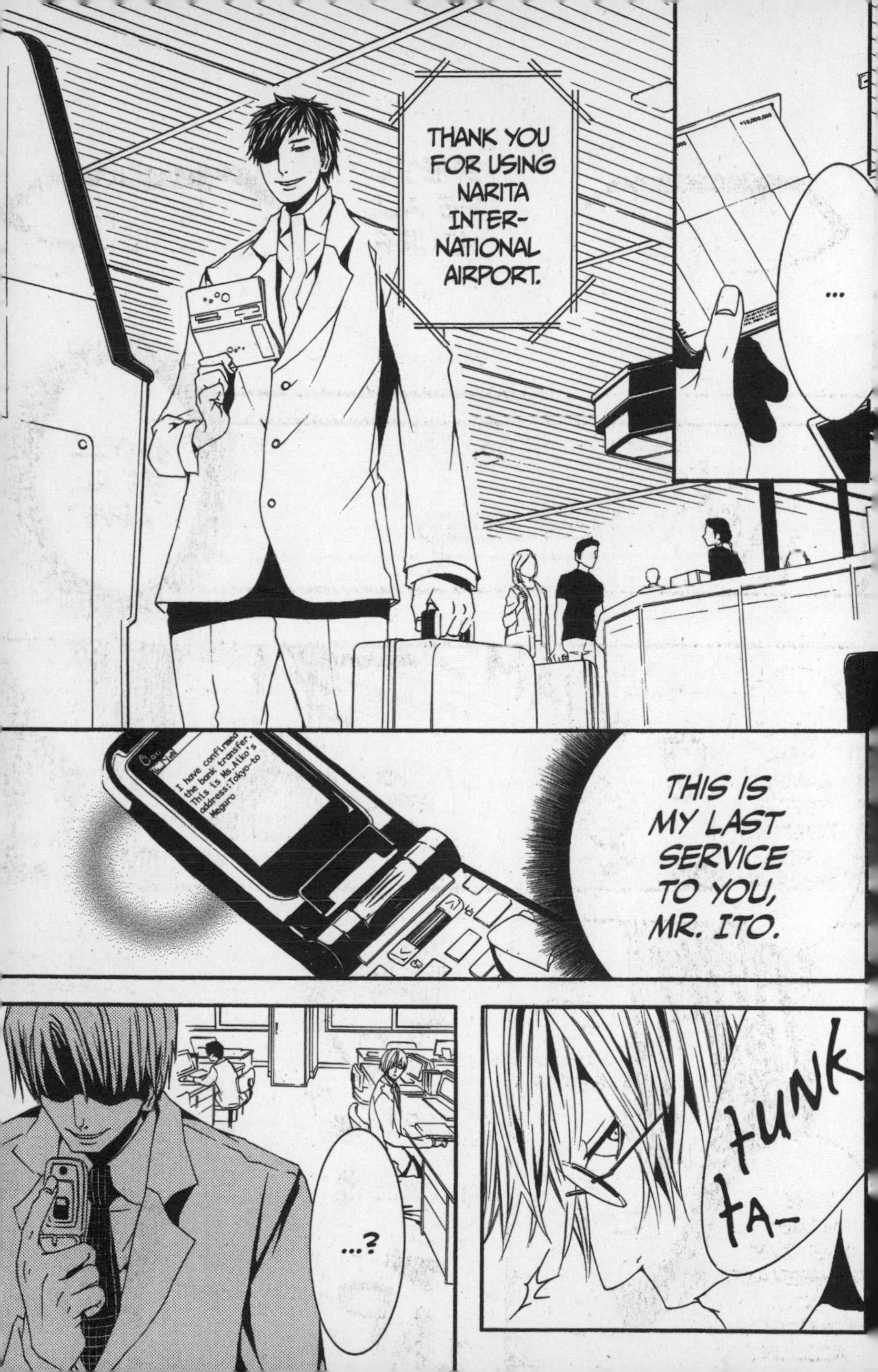
...
THANK YOU FOR USING NARITA INTER-NATIONAL AIRPORT.
I have confirmed the bank transfer. This is Ms.Aiko's address:Tokyo-to Meguro
THIS IS MY LAST SERVICE TO YOU, MR. ITO.
tunk ta-
...?

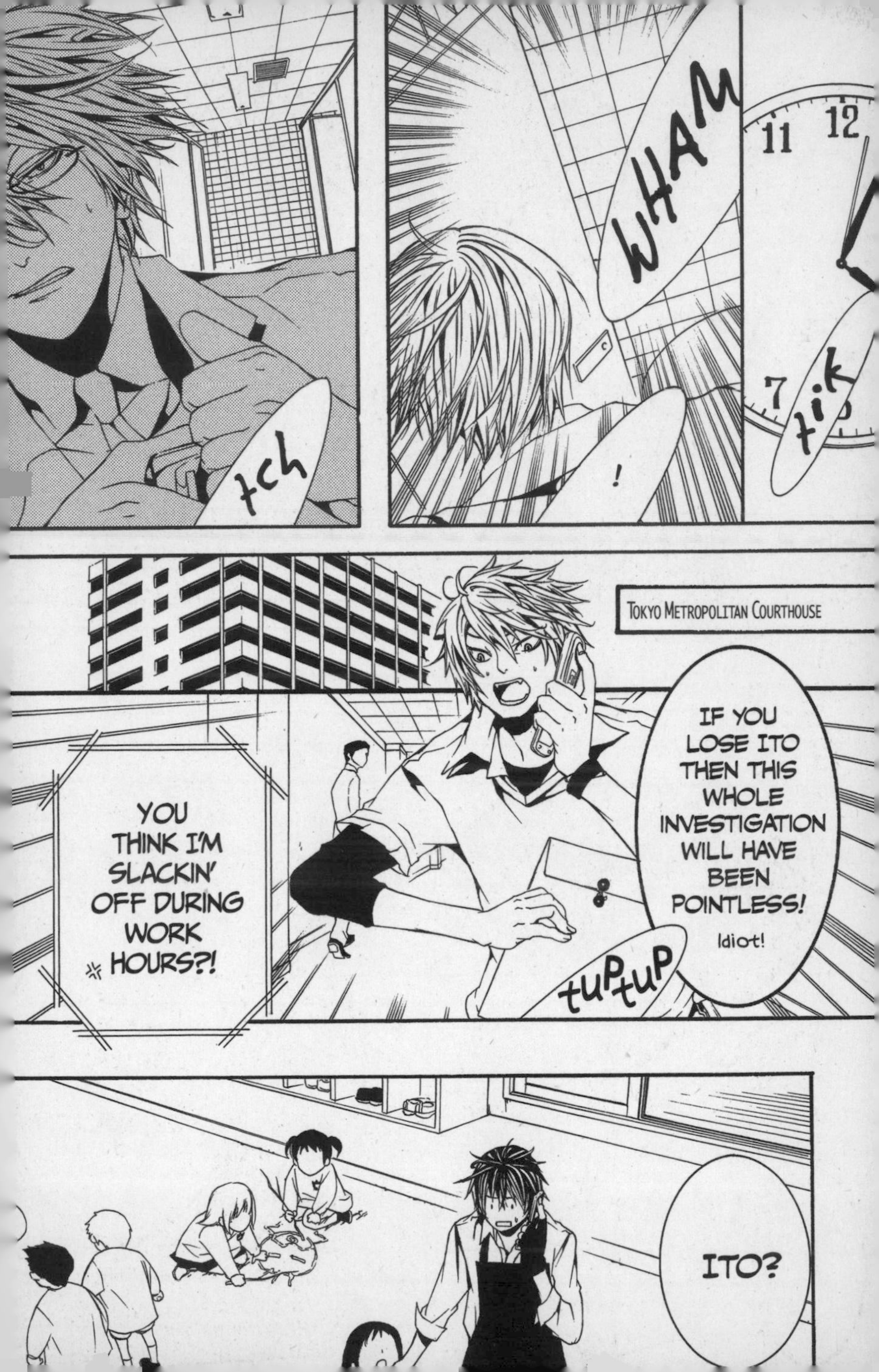
tik
WHAM
!
tch
TOKYO METROPOLITAN COURTHOUSE
IF YOU LOSE ITO THEN THIS WHOLE INVESTIGATION WILL HAVE BEEN POINTLESS!
Idiot!
tuptup
YOU THINK I'M SLACKIN' OFF DURING WORK HOURS?!
ITO?

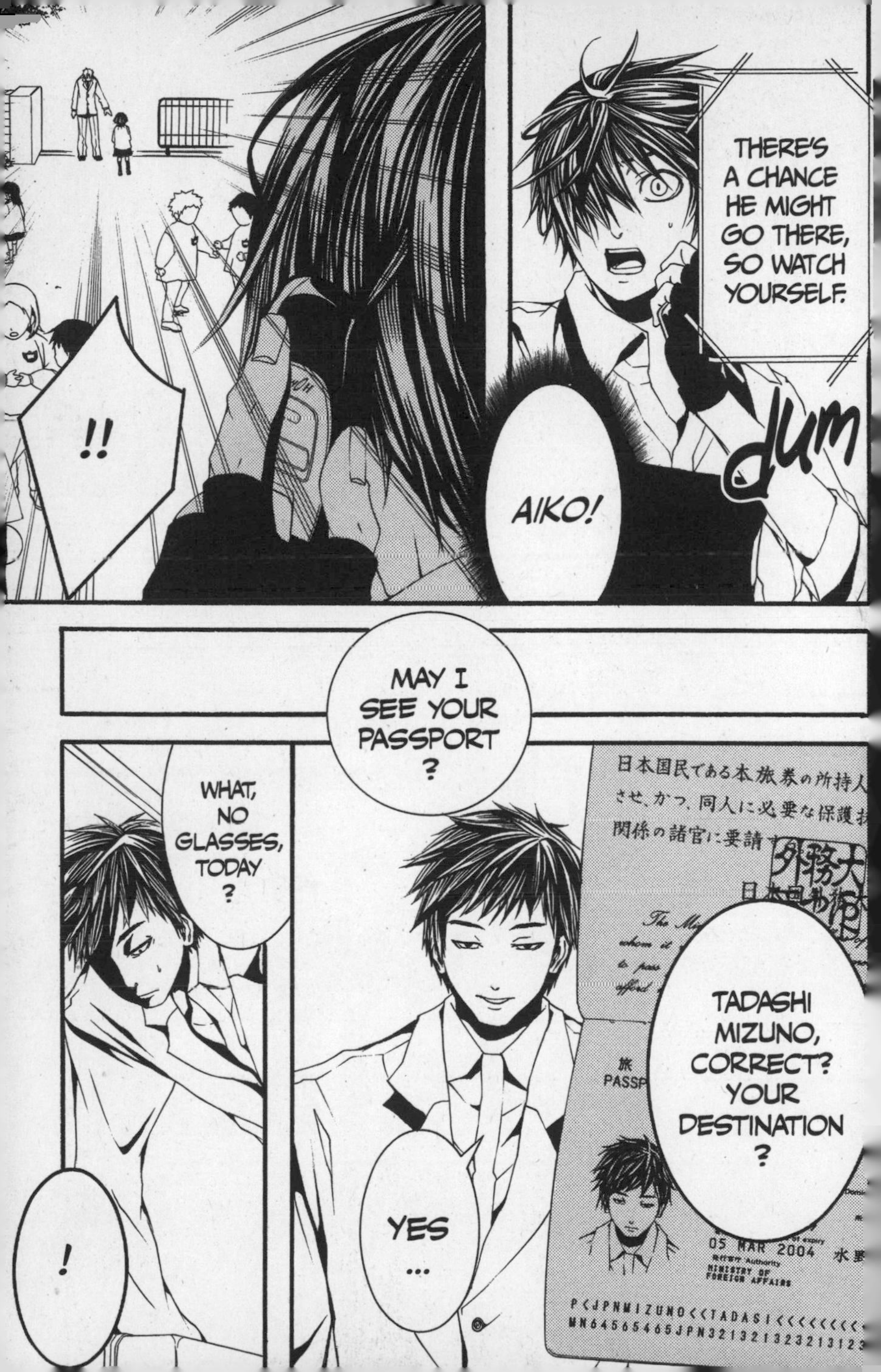
THERE'S A CHANCE HE MIGHT GO THERE, SO WATCH YOURSELF.
dum
AIKO!
!!
MAY I SEE YOUR PASSPORT?
日本国民である本旅券の所持人
関係の諸官に要請す
TADASHI MIZUNO, CORRECT? YOUR DESTINATION?
05 MAR 2004
MINISTRY OF FOREIGN AFFAIRS
YES...
WHAT, NO GLASSES, TODAY?
!

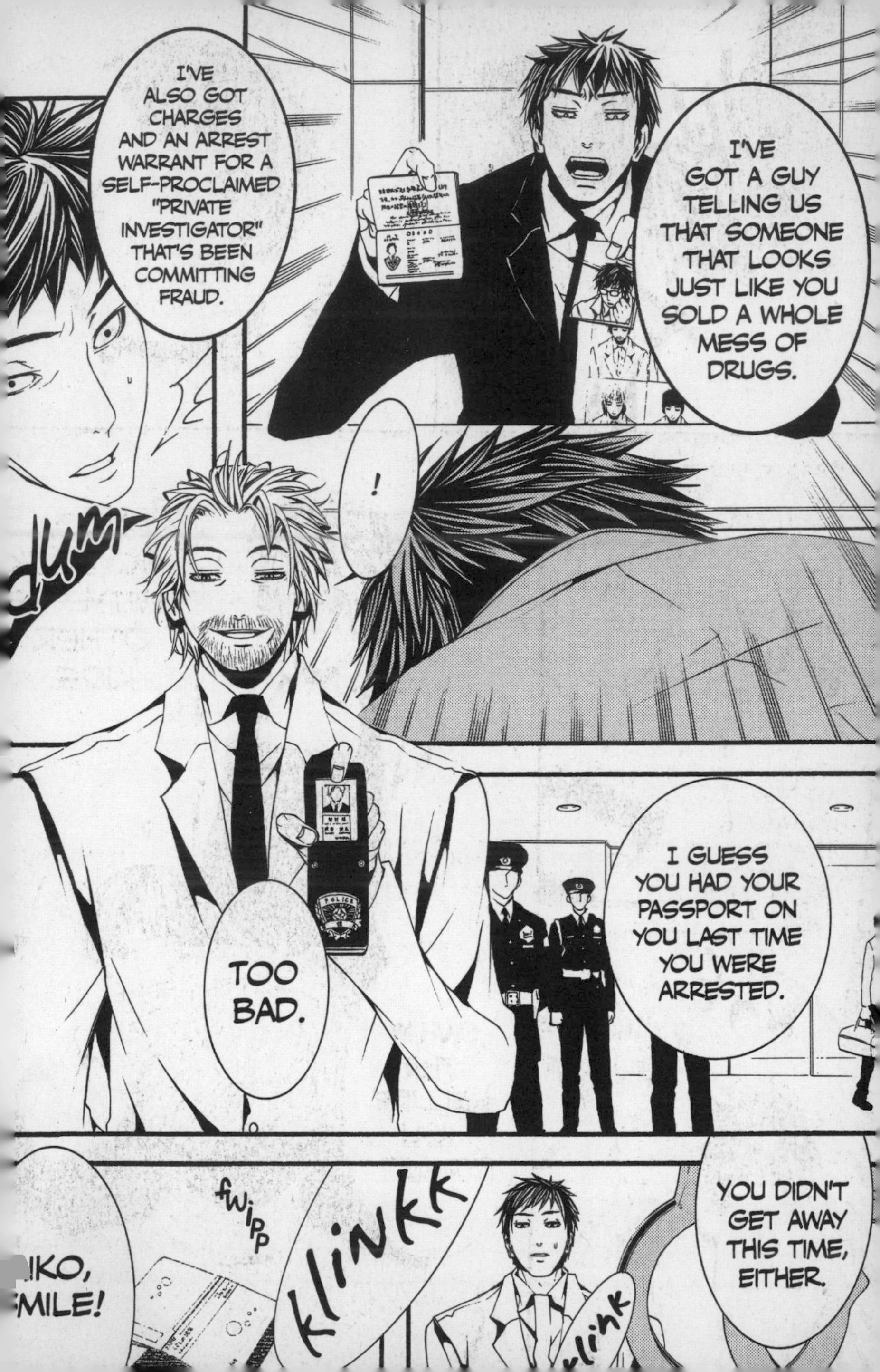
I'VE GOT A GUY TELLING US THAT SOMEONE THAT LOOKS JUST LIKE YOU SOLD A WHOLE MESS OF DRUGS.
I'VE ALSO GOT CHARGES AND AN ARREST WARRANT FOR A SELF-PROCLAIMED "PRIVATE INVESTIGATOR" THAT'S BEEN COMMITTING FRAUD.
dum
!
I GUESS YOU HAD YOUR PASSPORT ON YOU LAST TIME YOU WERE ARRESTED.
TOO BAD.
YOU DIDN'T GET AWAY THIS TIME, EITHER.
klink
klinkk
fwipp
IKO, MILE!

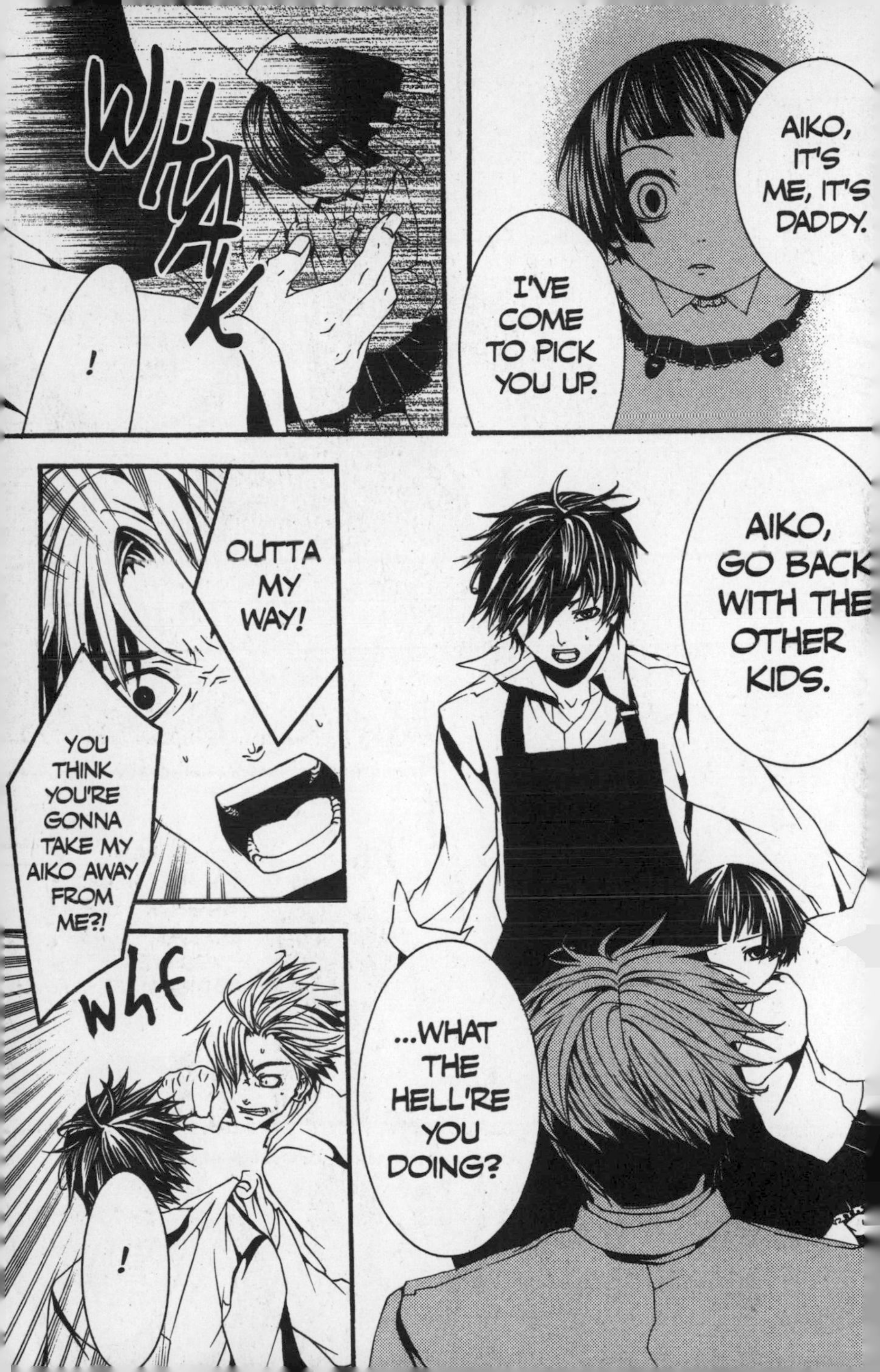
AIKO, IT'S ME, IT'S DADDY.
I'VE COME TO PICK YOU UP.
WHAK
!
AIKO, GO BACK WITH THE OTHER KIDS.
...WHAT THE HELL'RE YOU DOING?
OUTTA MY WAY!
YOU THINK YOU'RE GONNA TAKE MY AIKO AWAY FROM ME?!
WHF
!

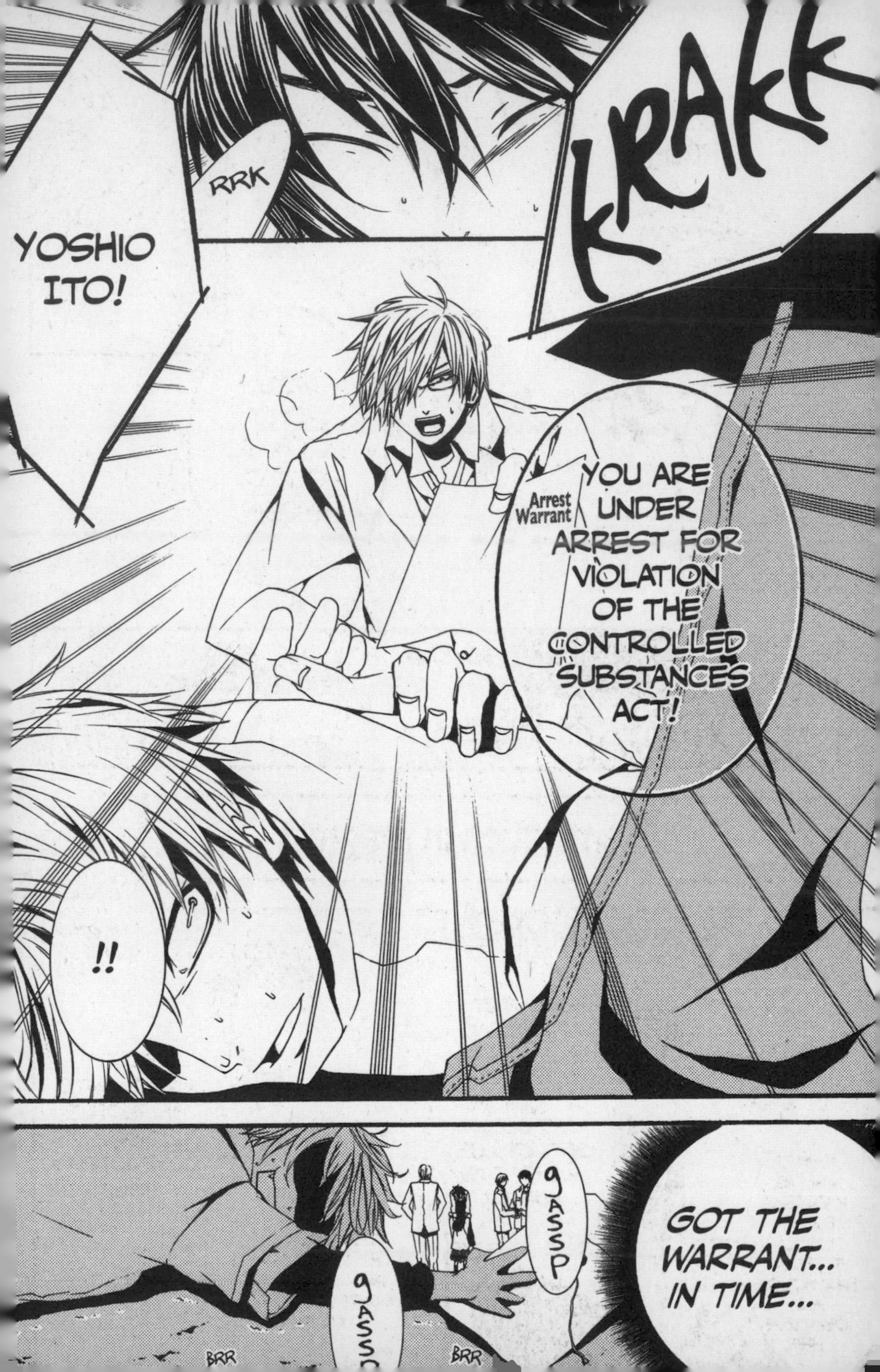
KRAKK
RRK
YOSHIO ITO!
Arrest Warrant
YOU ARE UNDER ARREST FOR VIOLATION OF THE CONTROLLED SUBSTANCES ACT!
!!
GOT THE WARRANT... IN TIME...
GASSP
GASS
BRR
BRR

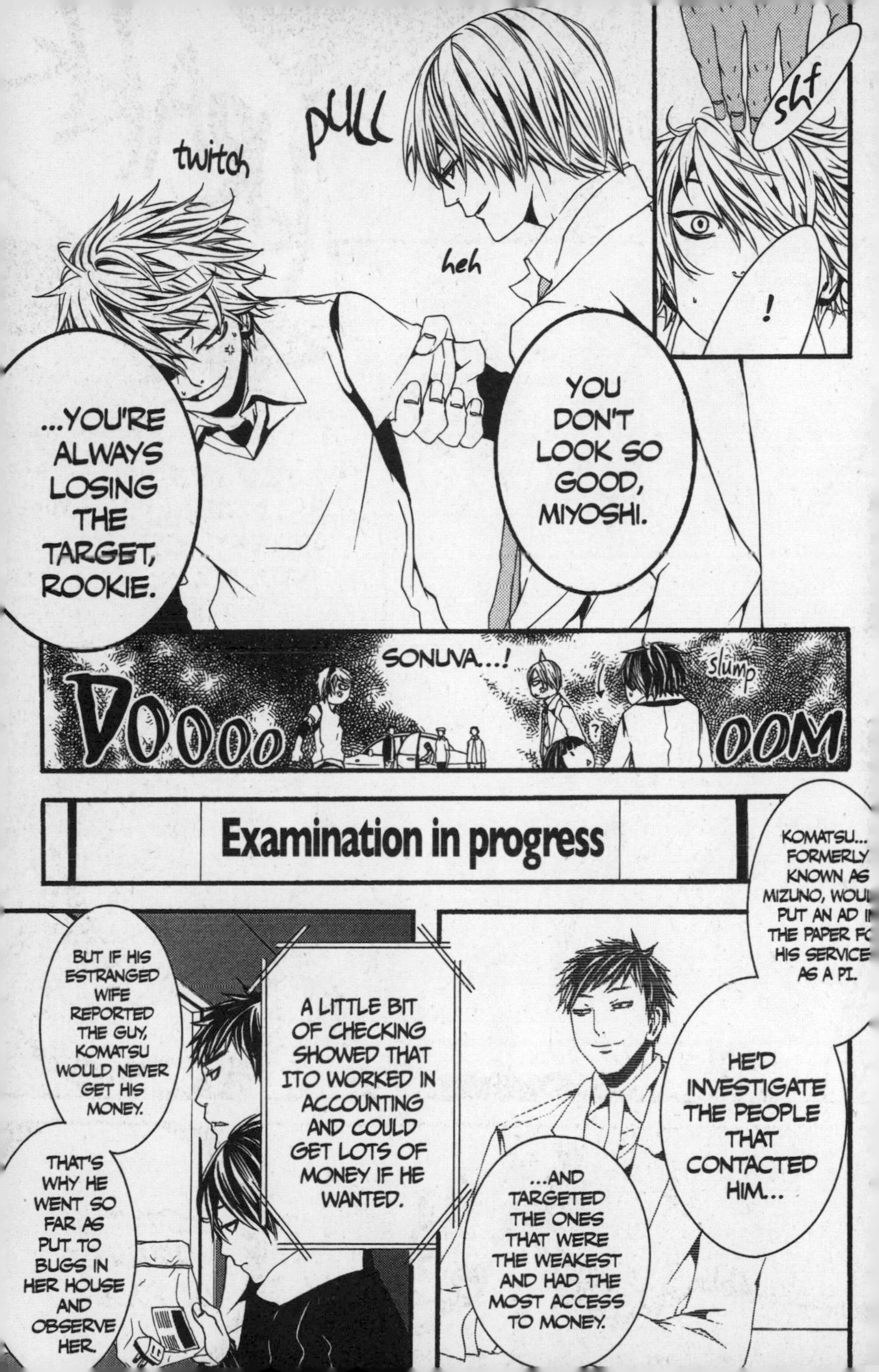
shf
!
pull
heh
twitch
YOU DON'T LOOK SO GOOD, MIYOSHI.
...YOU'RE ALWAYS LOSING THE TARGET, ROOKIE.
slump
SONUVA...!
DOOOOOOM
Examination in progress
KOMATSU... FORMERLY KNOWN AS MIZUNO, WOUL PUT AN AD I THE PAPER FO HIS SERVICE AS A PI.
HE'D INVESTIGATE THE PEOPLE THAT CONTACTED HIM...
...AND TARGETED THE ONES THAT WERE THE WEAKEST AND HAD THE MOST ACCESS TO MONEY.
A LITTLE BIT OF CHECKING SHOWED THAT ITO WORKED IN ACCOUNTING AND COULD GET LOTS OF MONEY IF HE WANTED.
BUT IF HIS ESTRANGED WIFE REPORTED THE GUY, KOMATSU WOULD NEVER GET HIS MONEY.
THAT'S WHY HE WENT SO FAR AS PUT TO BUGS IN HER HOUSE AND OBSERVE HER.

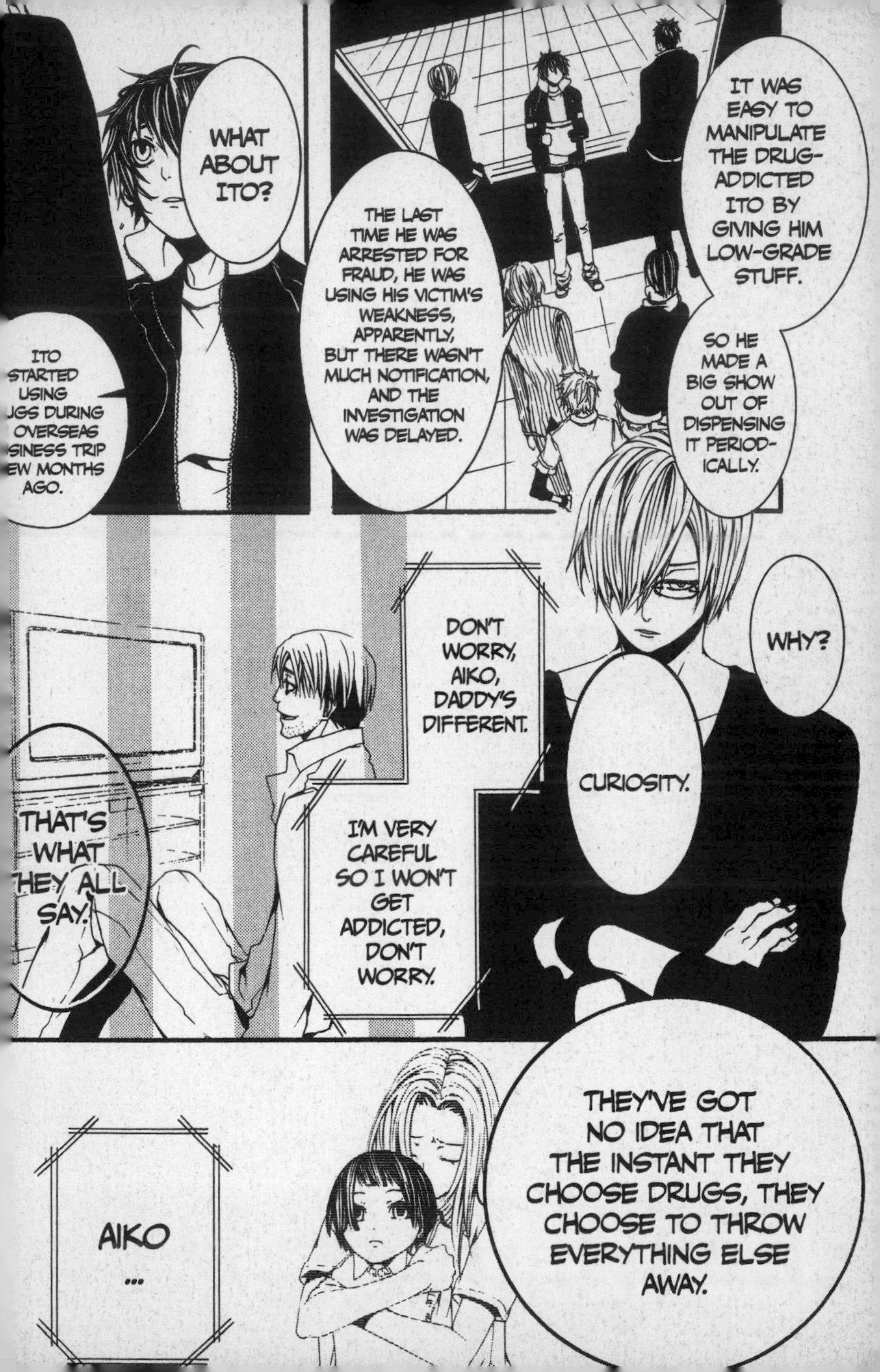
IT WAS EASY TO MANIPULATE THE DRUG-ADDICTED ITO BY GIVING HIM LOW-GRADE STUFF.
SO HE MADE A BIG SHOW OUT OF DISPENSING IT PERIODICALLY.
THE LAST TIME HE WAS ARRESTED FOR FRAUD, HE WAS USING HIS VICTIM'S WEAKNESS, APPARENTLY, BUT THERE WASN'T MUCH NOTIFICATION, AND THE INVESTIGATION WAS DELAYED.
WHAT ABOUT ITO?
ITO STARTED USING UGS DURING OVERSEAS SINESS TRIP EW MONTHS AGO.
WHY?
CURIOSITY.
DON'T WORRY, AIKO, DADDY'S DIFFERENT.
I'M VERY CAREFUL SO I WON'T GET ADDICTED, DON'T WORRY.
THAT'S WHAT HEY ALL SAY.
THEY'VE GOT NO IDEA THAT THE INSTANT THEY CHOOSE DRUGS, THEY CHOOSE TO THROW EVERYTHING ELSE AWAY.
AIKO ...

[switch]

スイッチ

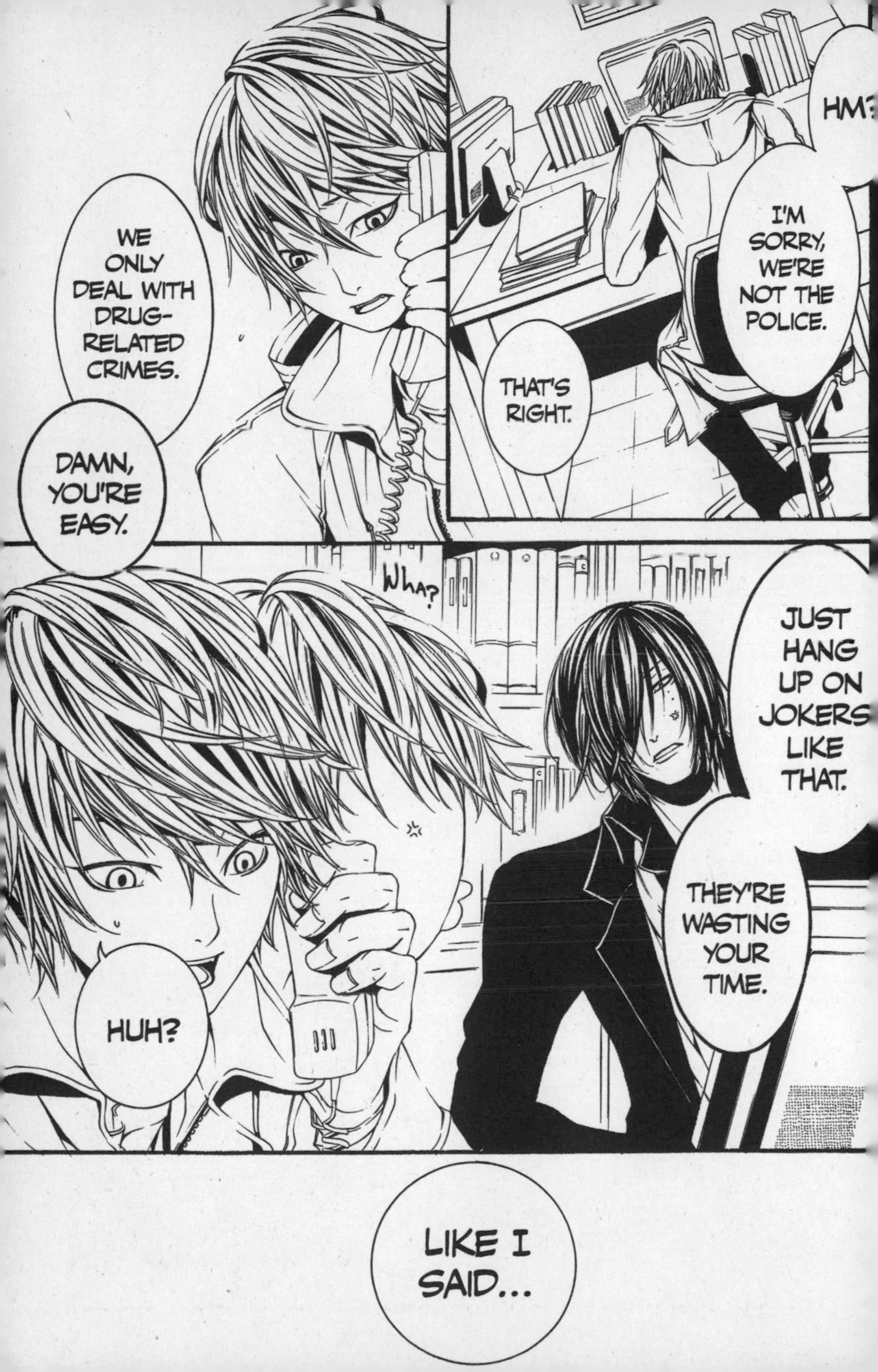
HM?
I'M SORRY, WE'RE NOT THE POLICE.
THAT'S RIGHT.
WE ONLY DEAL WITH DRUG-RELATED CRIMES.
DAMN, YOU'RE EASY.
JUST HANG UP ON JOKERS LIKE THAT.
Wha?
THEY'RE WASTING YOUR TIME.
HUH?
LIKE I SAID...

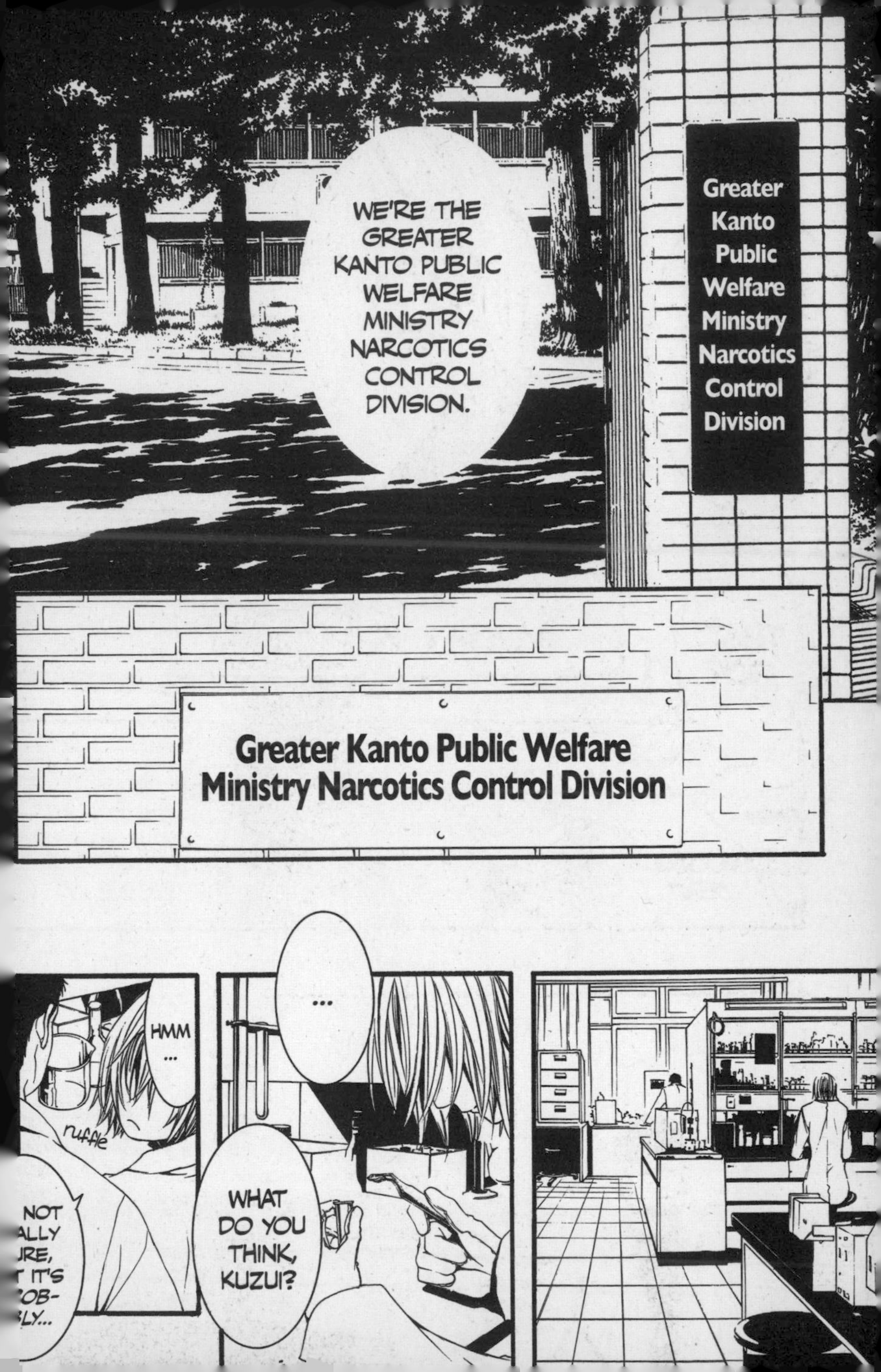
WE'RE THE GREATER KANTO PUBLIC WELFARE MINISTRY NARCOTICS CONTROL DIVISION.
Greater Kanto Public Welfare Ministry Narcotics Control Division
Greater Kanto Public Welfare Ministry Narcotics Control Division
...
WHAT DO YOU THINK, KUZUI?
HMM ...
ruffle
NOT ALLY URE, T IT'S OB- LY...

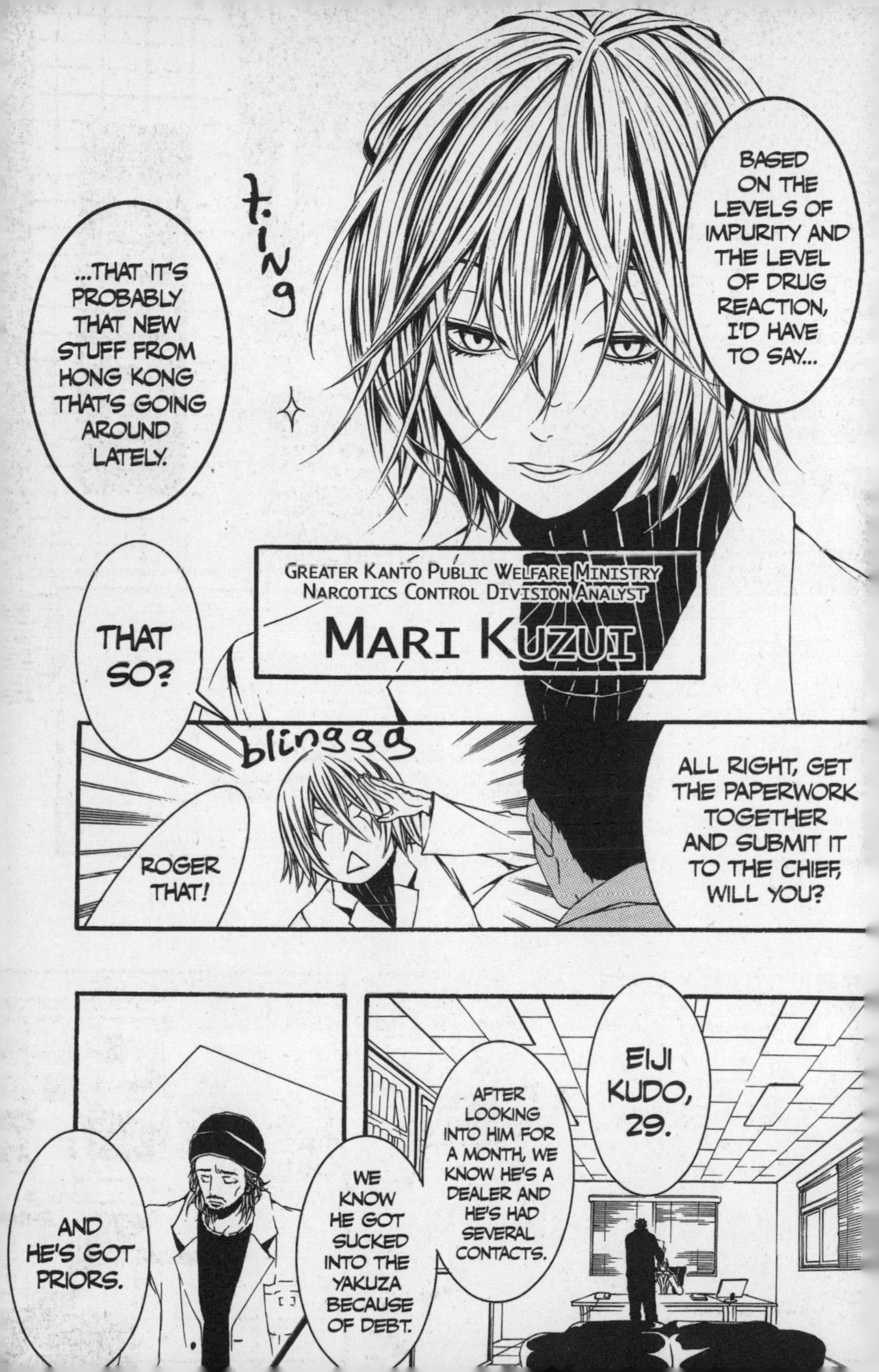
BASED ON THE LEVELS OF IMPURITY AND THE LEVEL OF DRUG REACTION, I'D HAVE TO SAY...
ting
...THAT IT'S PROBABLY THAT NEW STUFF FROM HONG KONG THAT'S GOING AROUND LATELY.
GREATER KANTO PUBLIC WELFARE MINISTRY NARCOTICS CONTROL DIVISION ANALYST
MARI KUZUI
THAT SO?
ALL RIGHT, GET THE PAPERWORK TOGETHER AND SUBMIT IT TO THE CHIEF, WILL YOU?
blinggg
ROGER THAT!
EIJI KUDO, 29.
AFTER LOOKING INTO HIM FOR A MONTH, WE KNOW HE'S A DEALER AND HE'S HAD SEVERAL CONTACTS.
WE KNOW HE GOT SUCKED INTO THE YAKUZA BECAUSE OF DEBT.
AND HE'S GOT PRIORS.

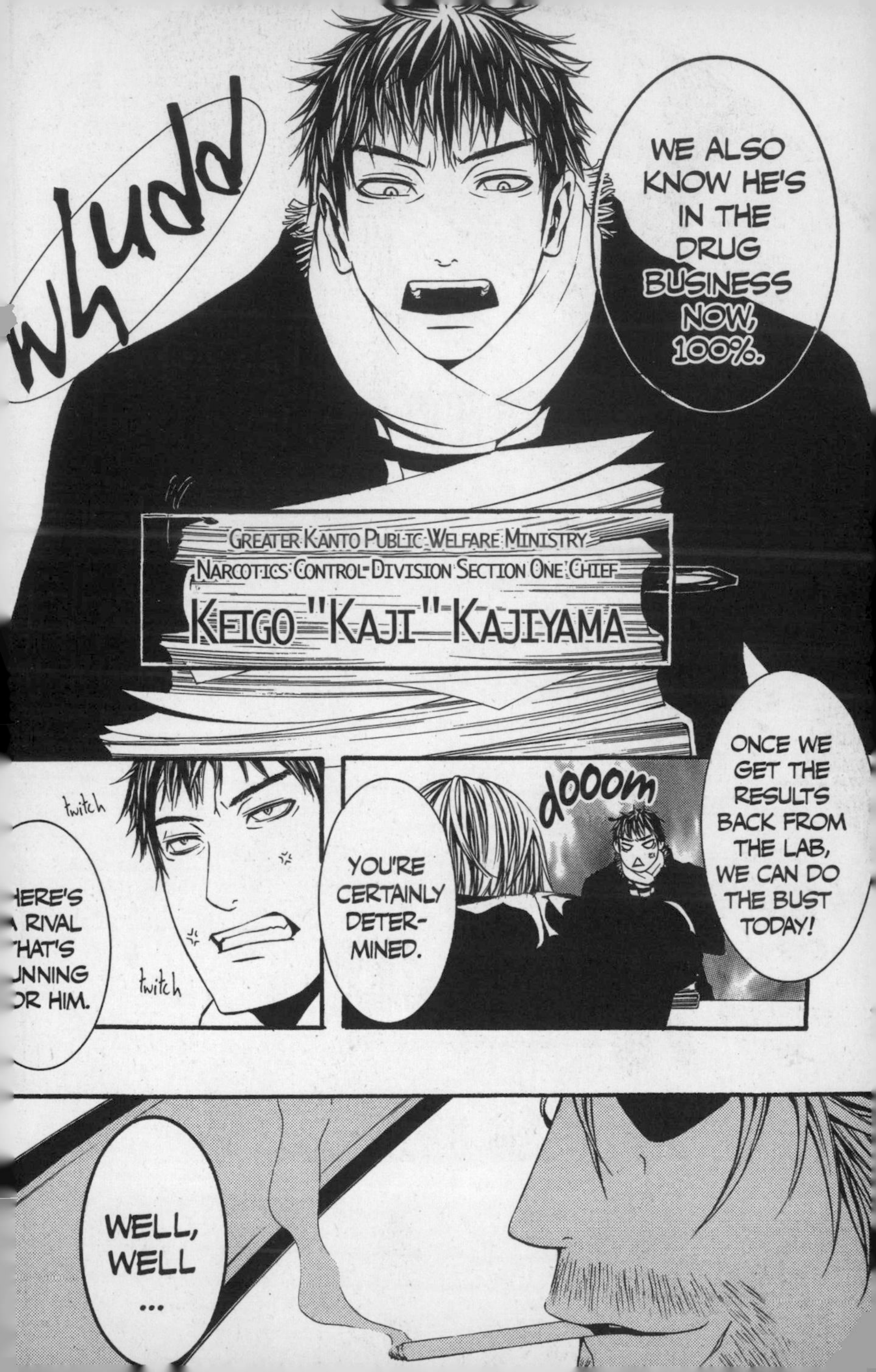
WE ALSO KNOW HE'S IN THE DRUG BUSINESS NOW, 100%.
whudd
GREATER KANTO PUBLIC WELFARE MINISTRY
NARCOTICS CONTROL DIVISION SECTION ONE CHIEF
KEIGO "KAJI" KAJIYAMA
ONCE WE GET THE RESULTS BACK FROM THE LAB, WE CAN DO THE BUST TODAY!
dooom
YOU'RE CERTAINLY DETER- MINED.
twitch
twitch
HERE'S RIVAL HAT'S UNNING OR HIM.
WELL, WELL ...

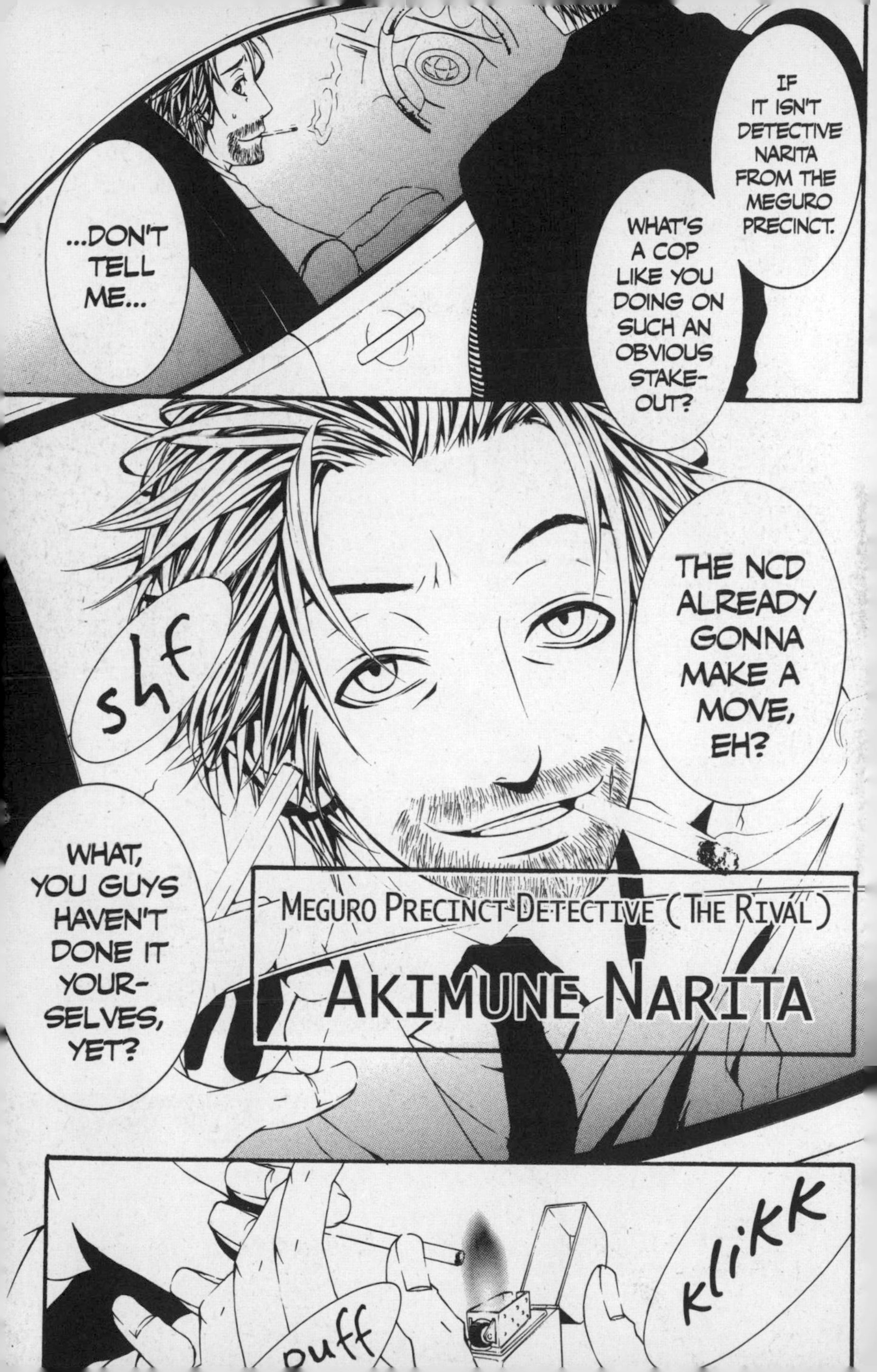
IF IT ISN'T DETECTIVE NARITA FROM THE MEGURO PRECINCT.
WHAT'S A COP LIKE YOU DOING ON SUCH AN OBVIOUS STAKE-OUT?
...DON'T TELL ME...
THE NCD ALREADY GONNA MAKE A MOVE, EH?
shf
MEGURO PRECINCT DETECTIVE (THE RIVAL)
AKIMUNE NARITA
WHAT, YOU GUYS HAVEN'T DONE IT YOUR-SELVES, YET?
klikk
puff

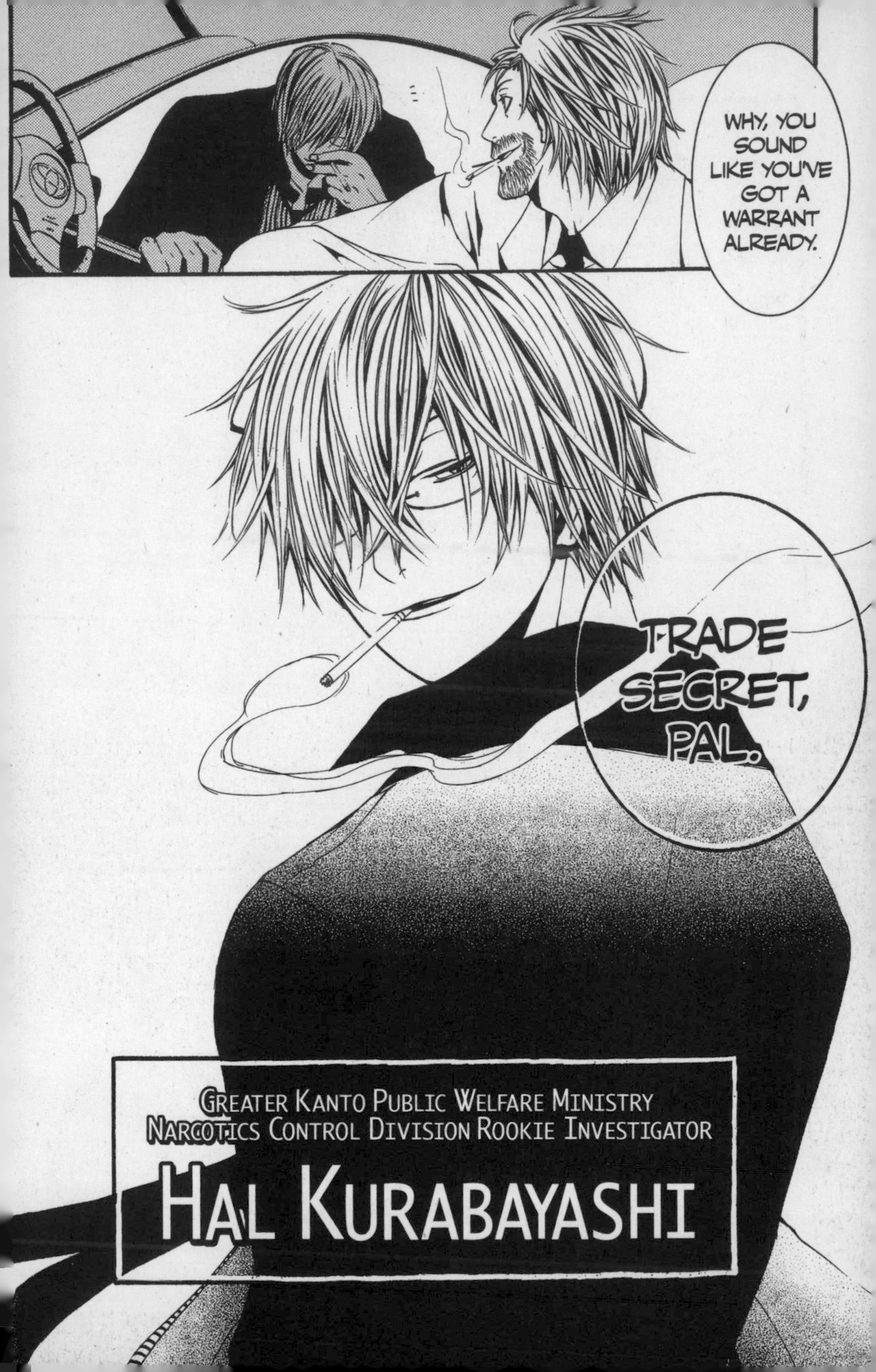
WHY, YOU SOUND LIKE YOU'VE GOT A WARRANT ALREADY.
TRADE SECRET, PAL.
GREATER KANTO PUBLIC WELFARE MINISTRY
NARCOTICS CONTROL DIVISION ROOKIE INVESTIGATOR
HAL KURABAYASHI

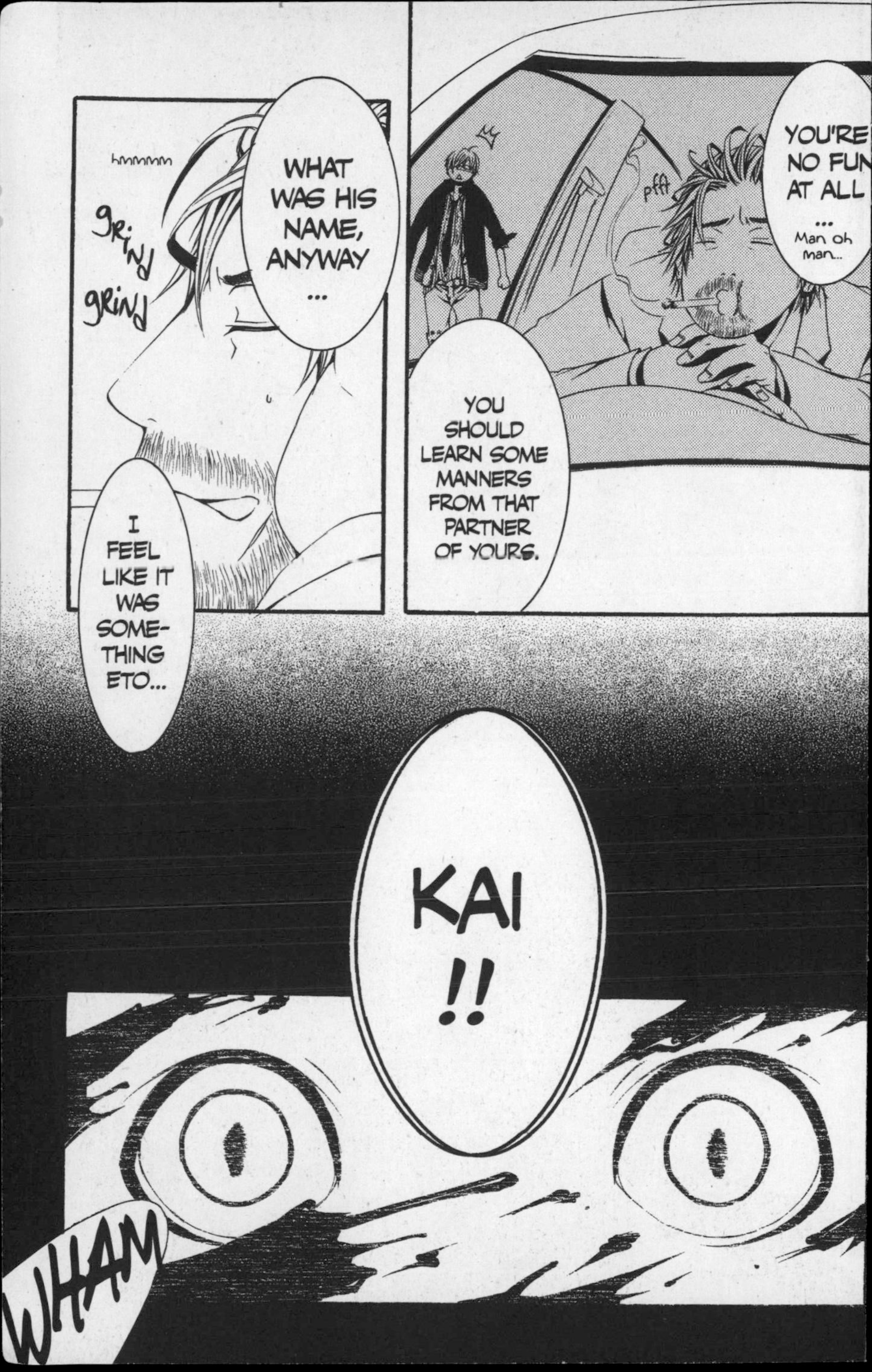
YOU'RE NO FUN AT ALL ... Man oh man...
pfft
YOU SHOULD LEARN SOME MANNERS FROM THAT PARTNER OF YOURS.
WHAT WAS HIS NAME, ANYWAY ...
hmmmm
grind grind
I FEEL LIKE IT WAS SOMETHING ETO...
KAI !!
WHAM

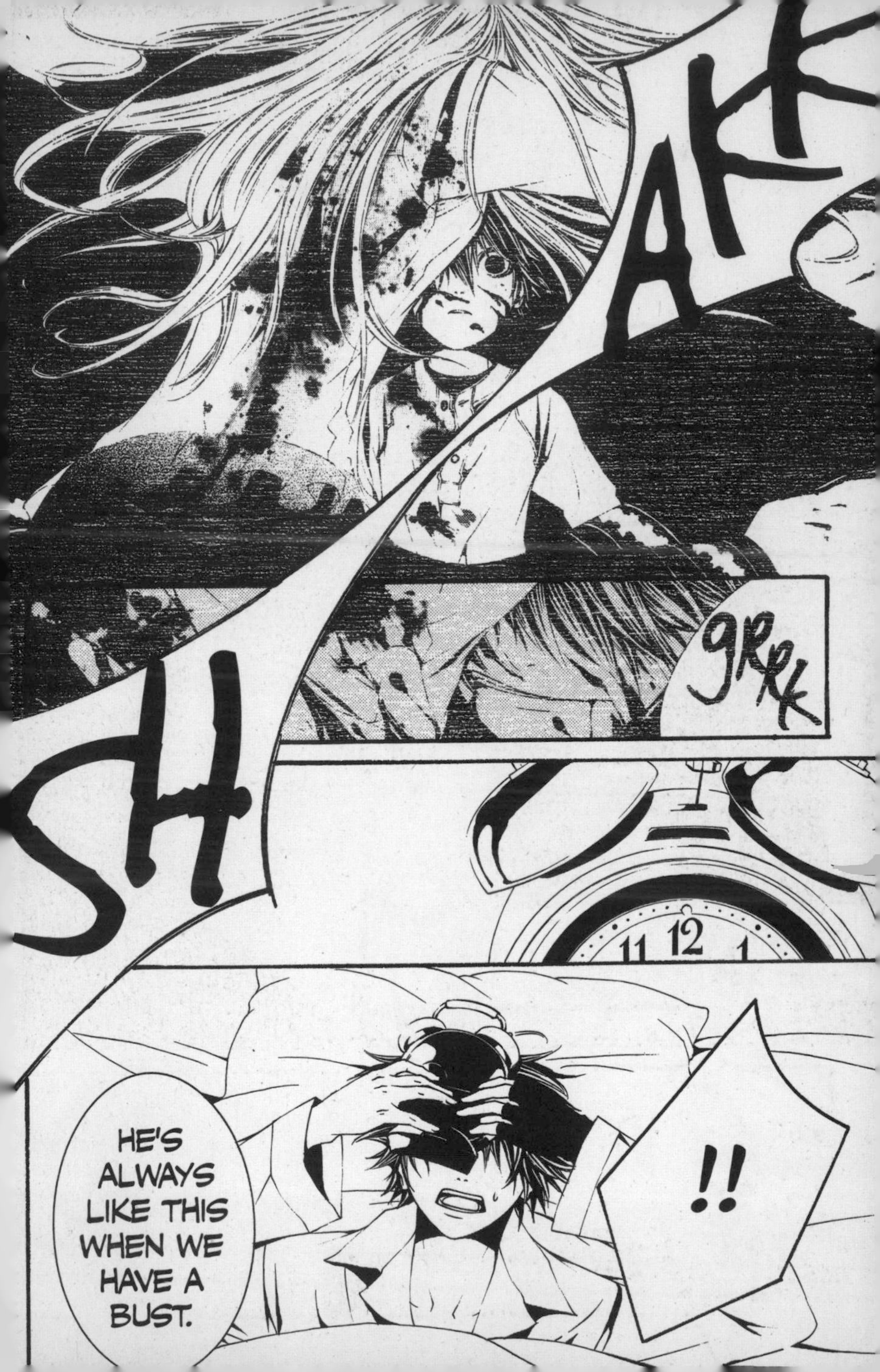
AH
gRRk
SH
!!
HE'S ALWAYS LIKE THIS WHEN WE HAVE A BUST.

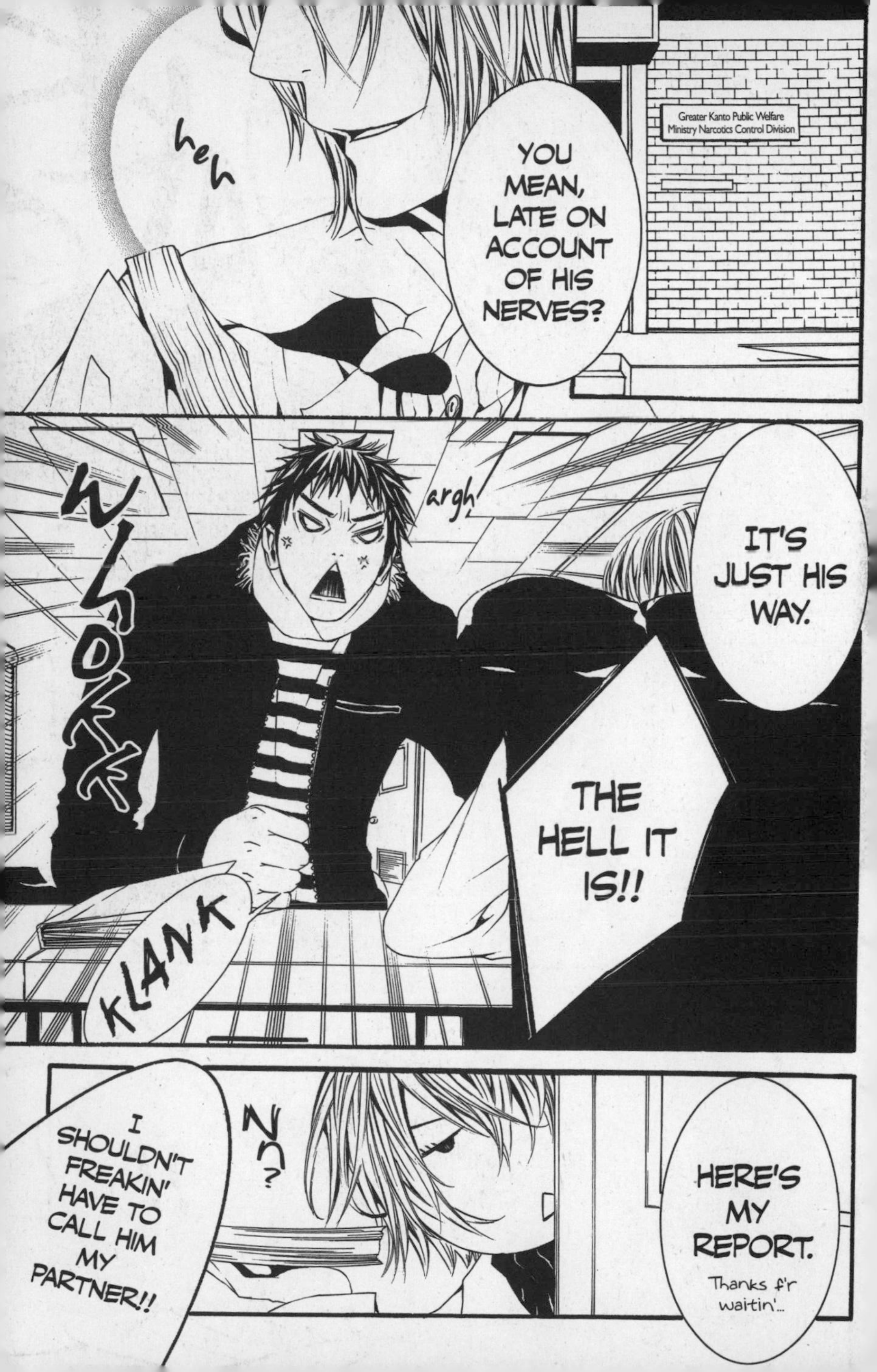
Greater Kanto Public Welfare Ministry Narcotics Control Division
YOU MEAN, LATE ON ACCOUNT OF HIS NERVES?
heh
IT'S JUST HIS WAY.
THE HELL IT IS!!
argh
KLANK
HERE'S MY REPORT.
Thanks f'r waitin'...
Nn?
I SHOULDN'T FREAKIN' HAVE TO CALL HIM MY PARTNER!!

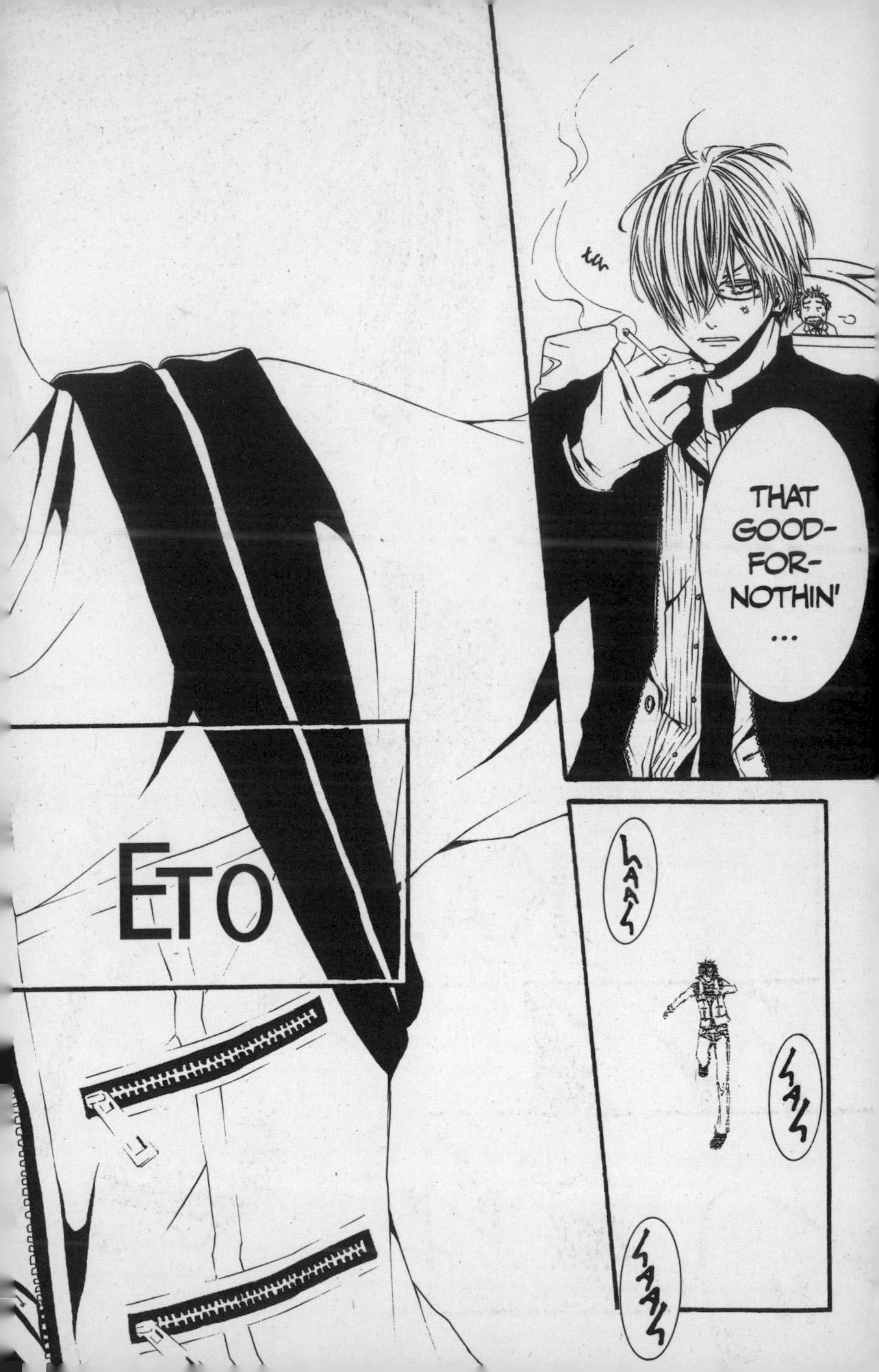
tch
THAT GOOD-FOR-NOTHIN'...
haah
haah
haah
ETO

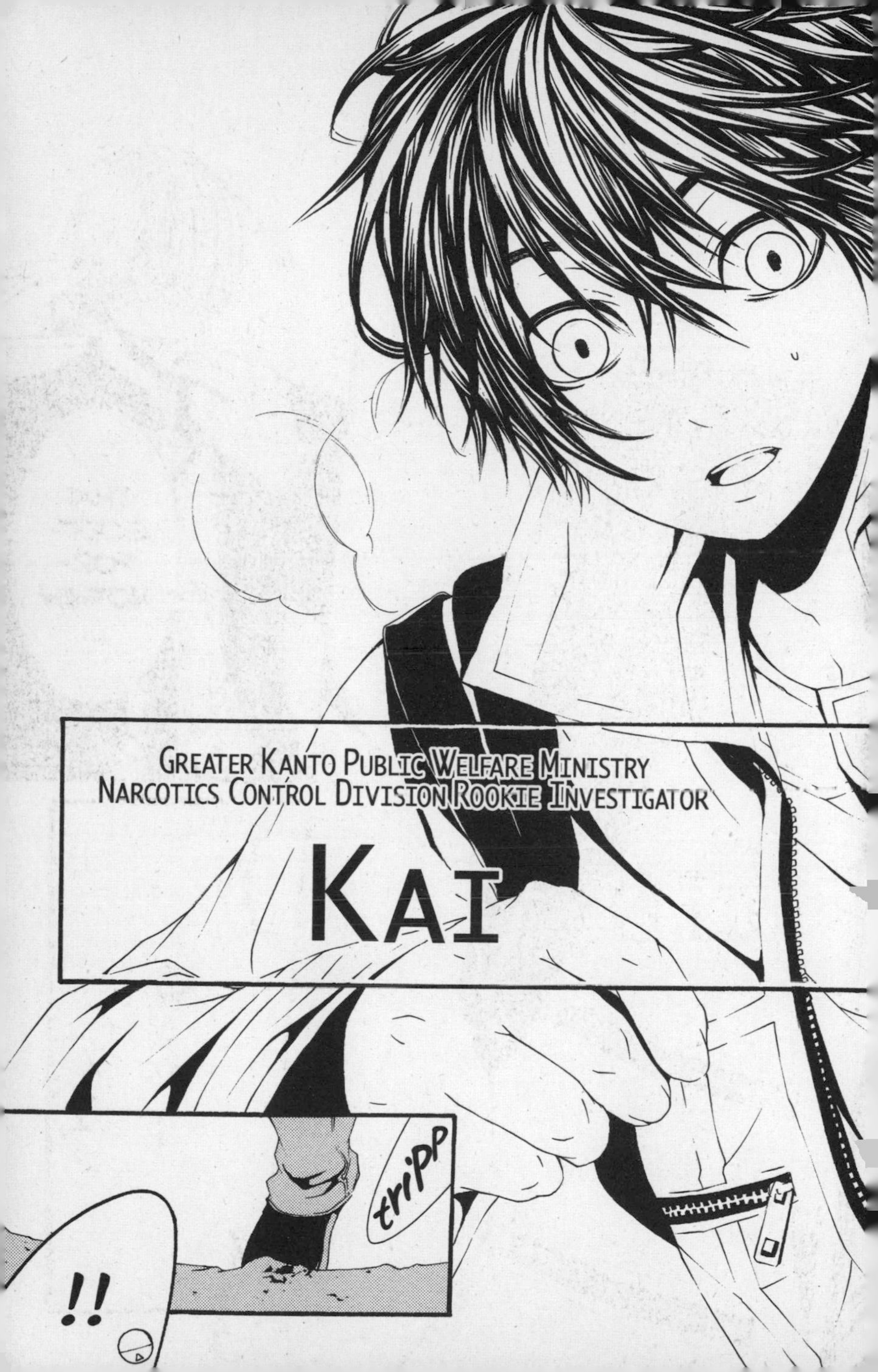
Greater Kanto Public Welfare Ministry
Narcotics Control Division Rookie Investigator
Kai
tripp
!!

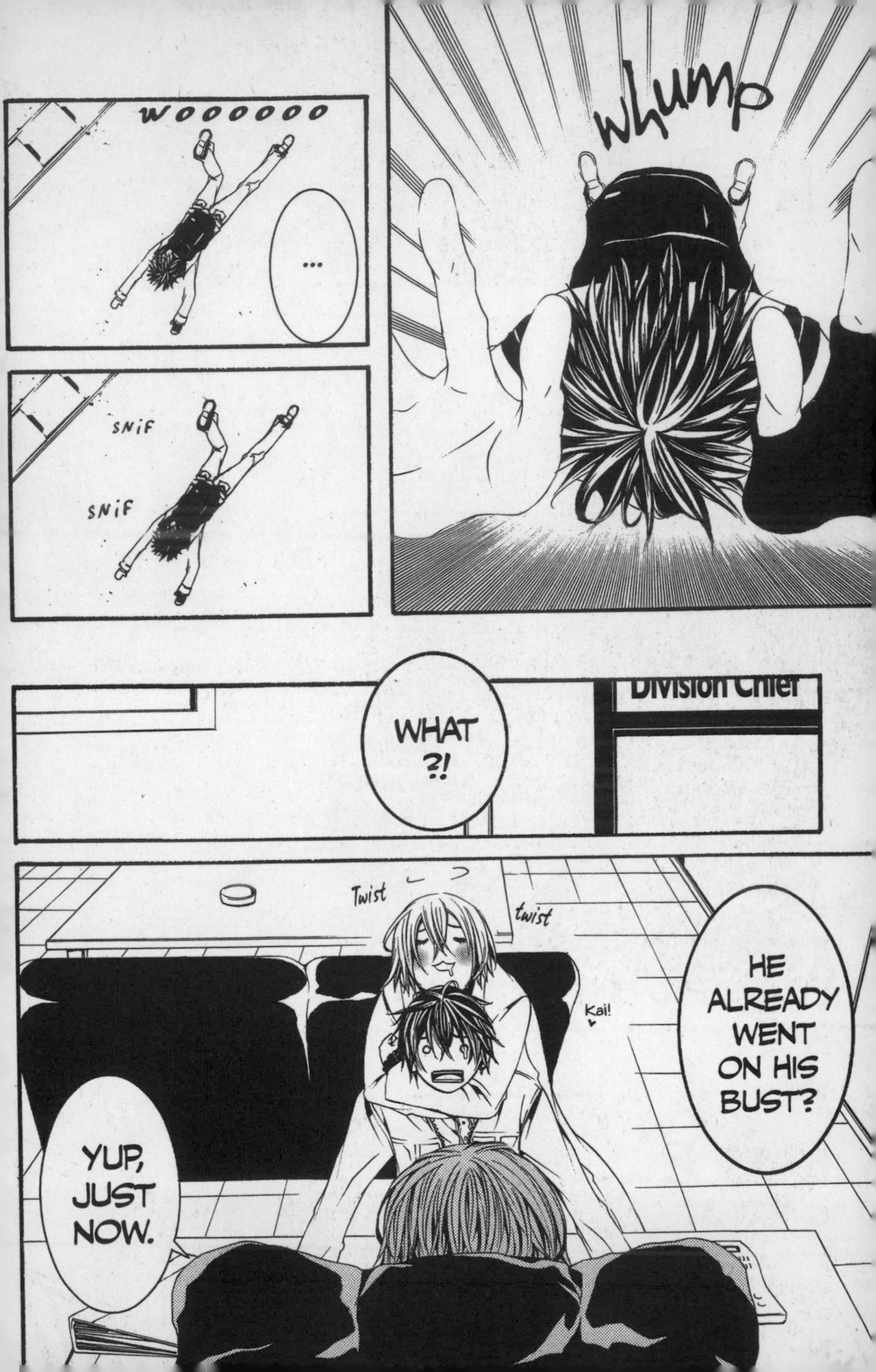

WHUMP
WOOOOOO
...
SNIF
SNIF
Division Chief
WHAT?!
HE ALREADY WENT ON HIS BUST?
twist
Kai!
Twist
YUP, JUST NOW.

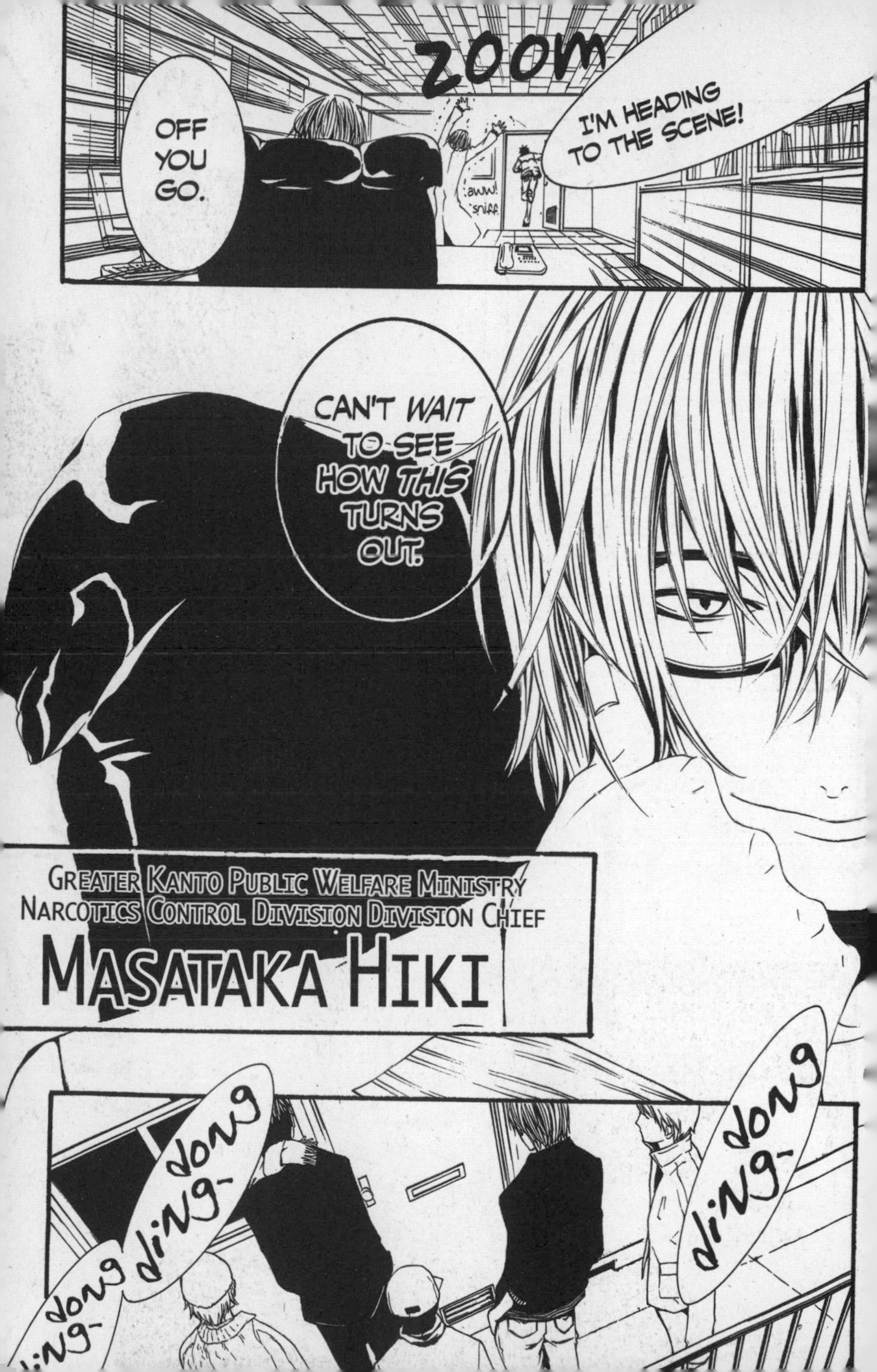
I'M HEADING TO THE SCENE!
ZOOM
aww! sniff.
OFF YOU GO.
CAN'T WAIT TO SEE HOW THIS TURNS OUT.
GREATER KANTO PUBLIC WELFARE MINISTRY NARCOTICS CONTROL DIVISION DIVISION CHIEF
MASATAKA HIKI
ding-dong
ding-dong
ding-dong

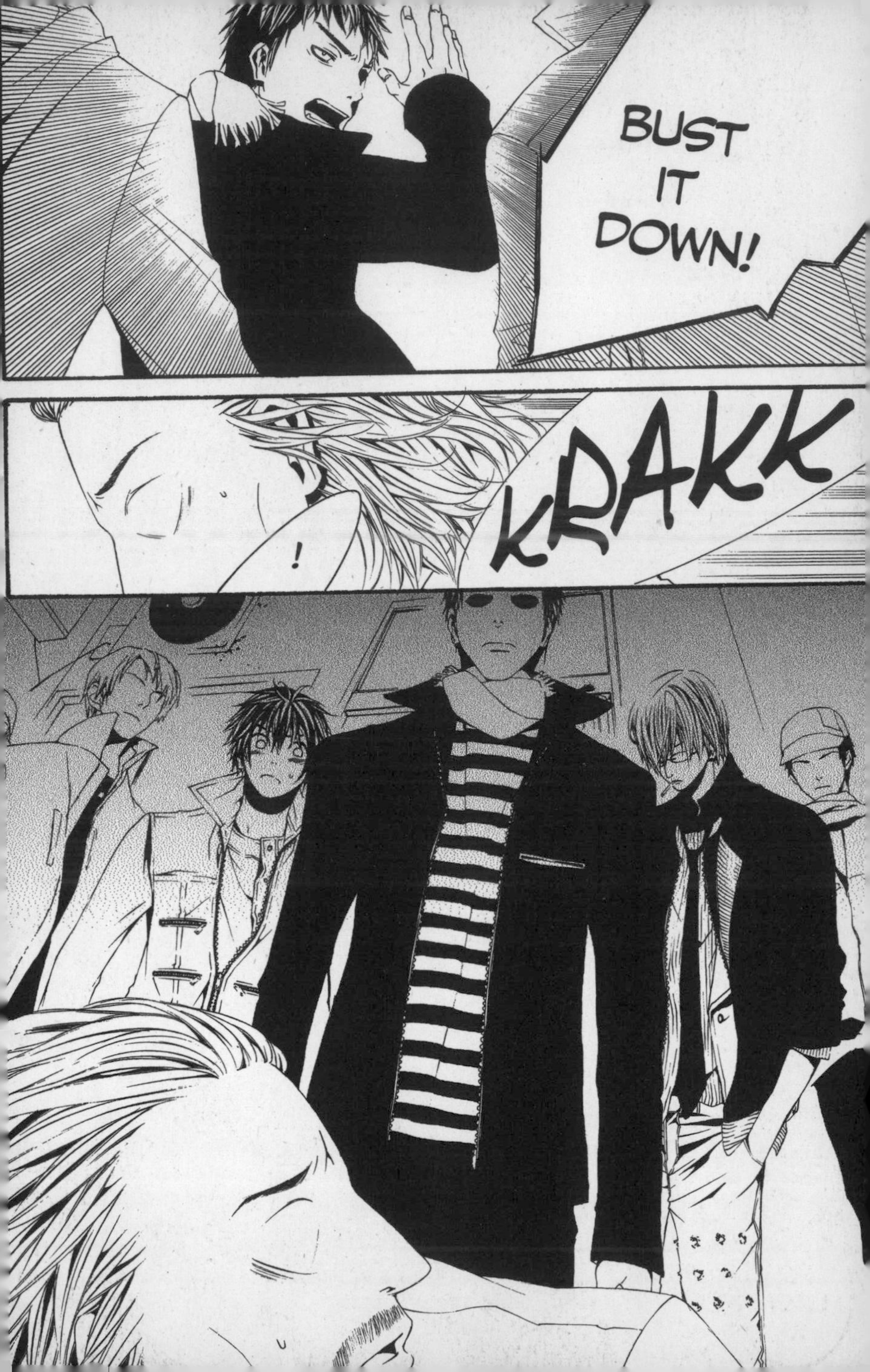
BUST IT DOWN!
KRAKK
!

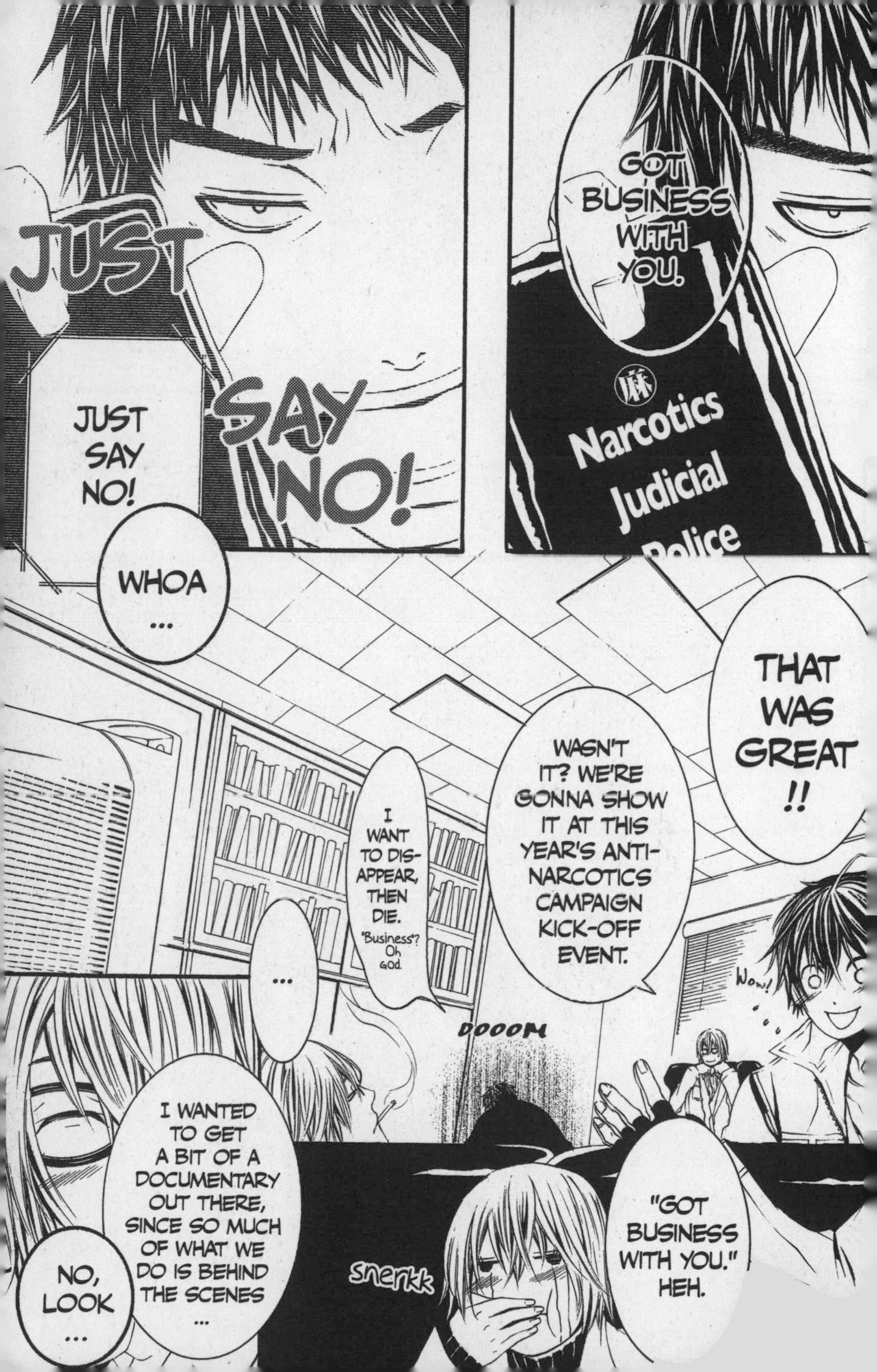
GOT BUSINESS WITH YOU.
麻
Narcotics Judicial Police
JUST SAY NO!
JUST SAY NO!
THAT WAS GREAT!!
WASN'T IT? WE'RE GONNA SHOW IT AT THIS YEAR'S ANTI-NARCOTICS CAMPAIGN KICK-OFF EVENT.
I WANT TO DIS-APPEAR, THEN DIE.
"Business"? Oh God.
WHOA ...
...
Wow!
DOOOM
"GOT BUSINESS WITH YOU." HEH.
snerkk
I WANTED TO GET A BIT OF A DOCUMENTARY OUT THERE, SINCE SO MUCH OF WHAT WE DO IS BEHIND THE SCENES ...
NO, LOOK ...

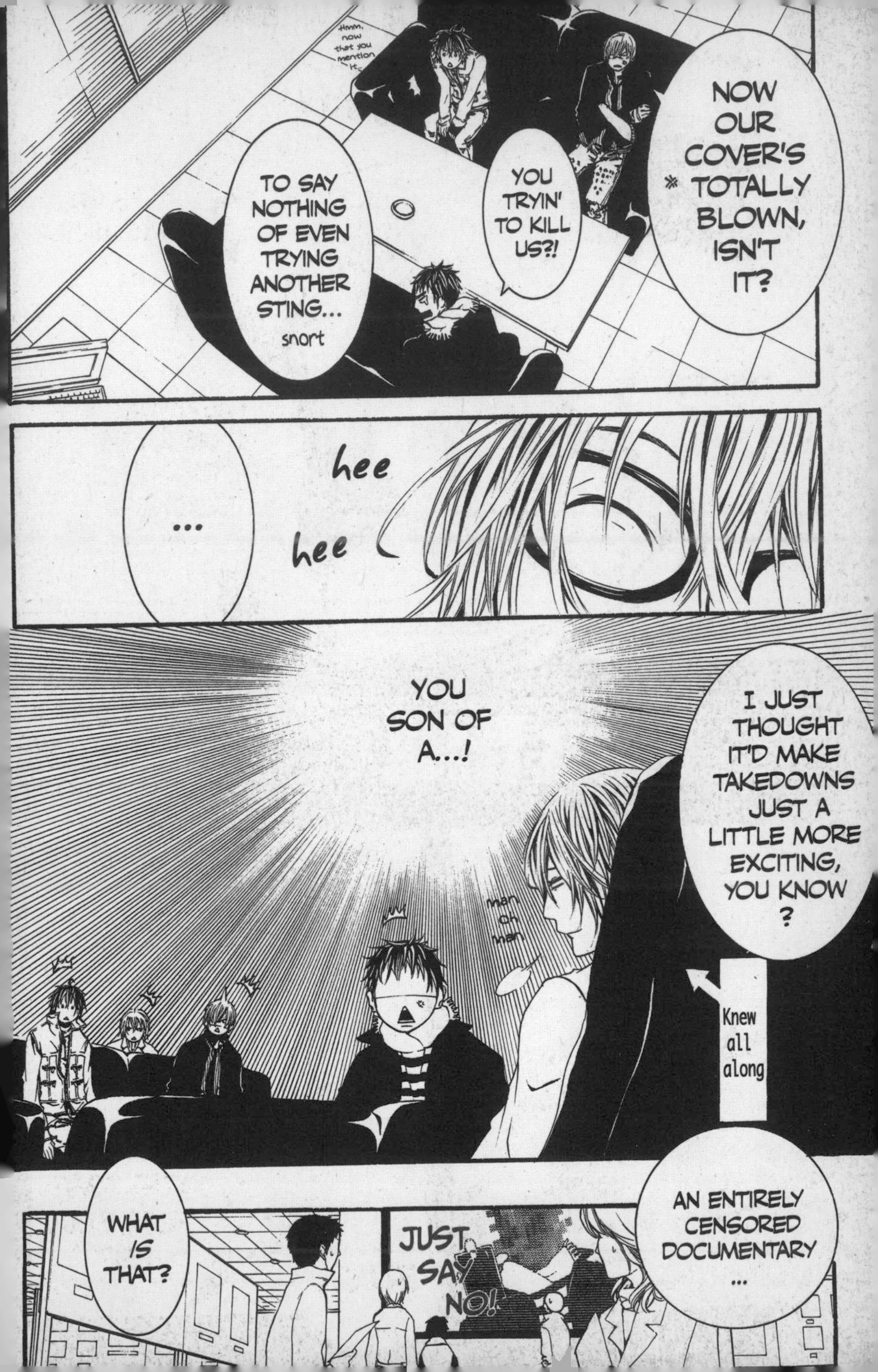
NOW OUR COVER'S ※ TOTALLY BLOWN, ISN'T IT?
Hmm, now that you mention it...
YOU TRYIN' TO KILL US?!
TO SAY NOTHING OF EVEN TRYING ANOTHER STING...
snort
hee
hee
...
I JUST THOUGHT IT'D MAKE TAKEDOWNS JUST A LITTLE MORE EXCITING, YOU KNOW?
Knew all along
man oh man
YOU SON OF A...!
AN ENTIRELY CENSORED DOCUMENTARY...
JUST SAY NO!
WHAT IS THAT?

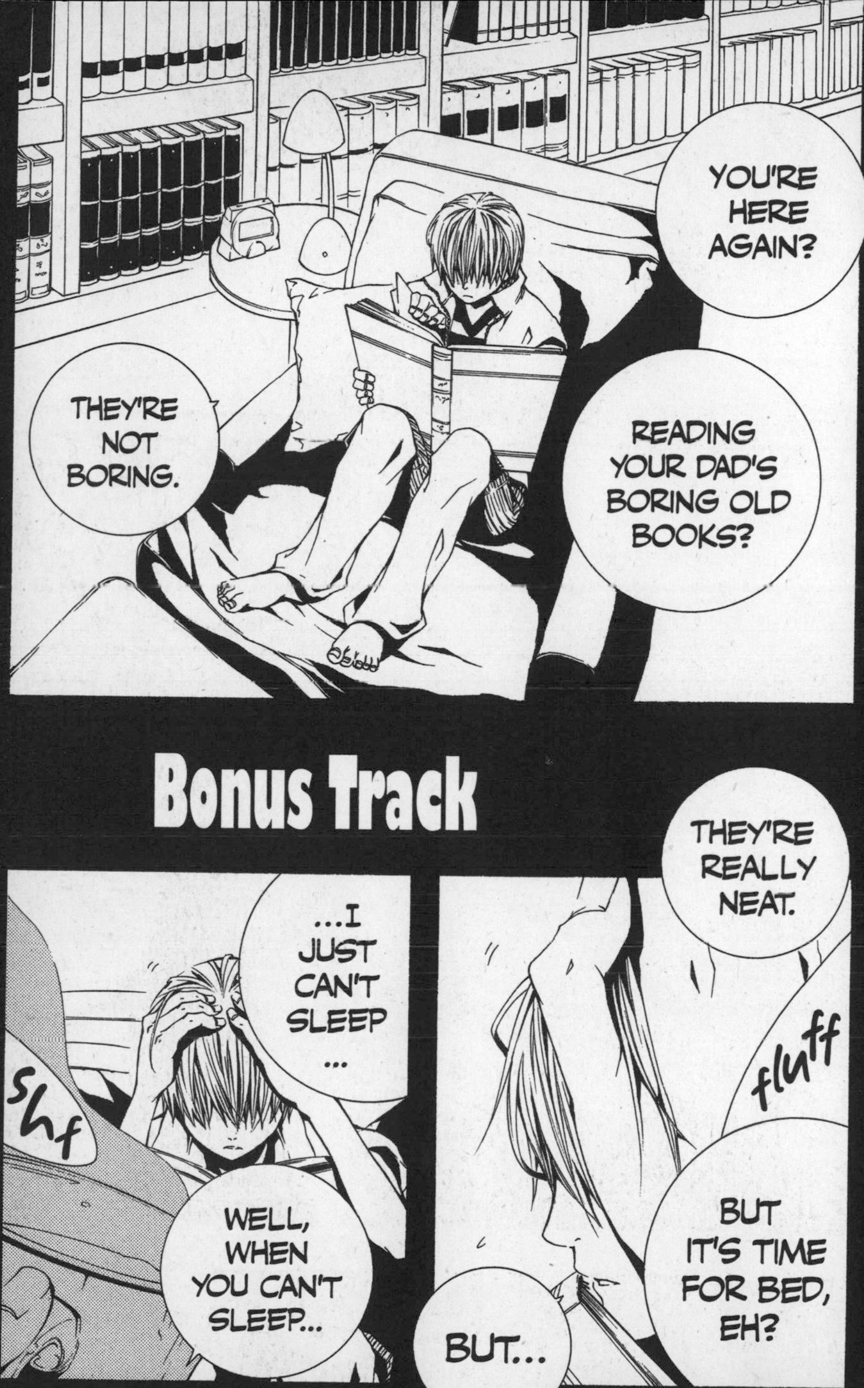
YOU'RE HERE AGAIN?
READING YOUR DAD'S BORING OLD BOOKS?
THEY'RE NOT BORING.
Bonus Track
THEY'RE REALLY NEAT.
fluff
BUT IT'S TIME FOR BED, EH?
BUT...
...I JUST CAN'T SLEEP ...
shf
WELL, WHEN YOU CAN'T SLEEP...

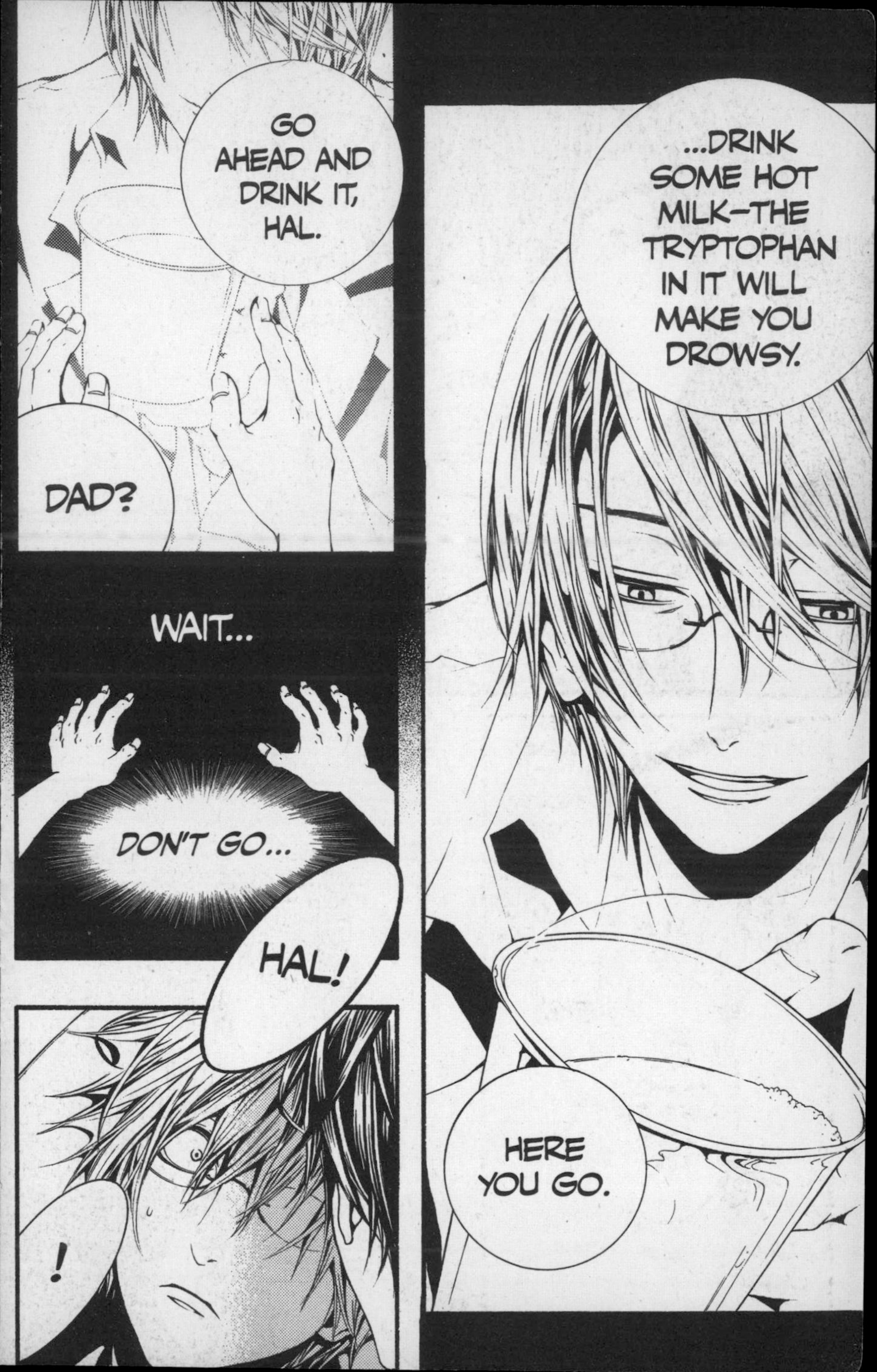
...DRINK SOME HOT MILK—THE TRYPTOPHAN IN IT WILL MAKE YOU DROWSY.
HERE YOU GO.
GO AHEAD AND DRINK IT, HAL.
DAD?
WAIT...
DON'T GO...
HAL!
!

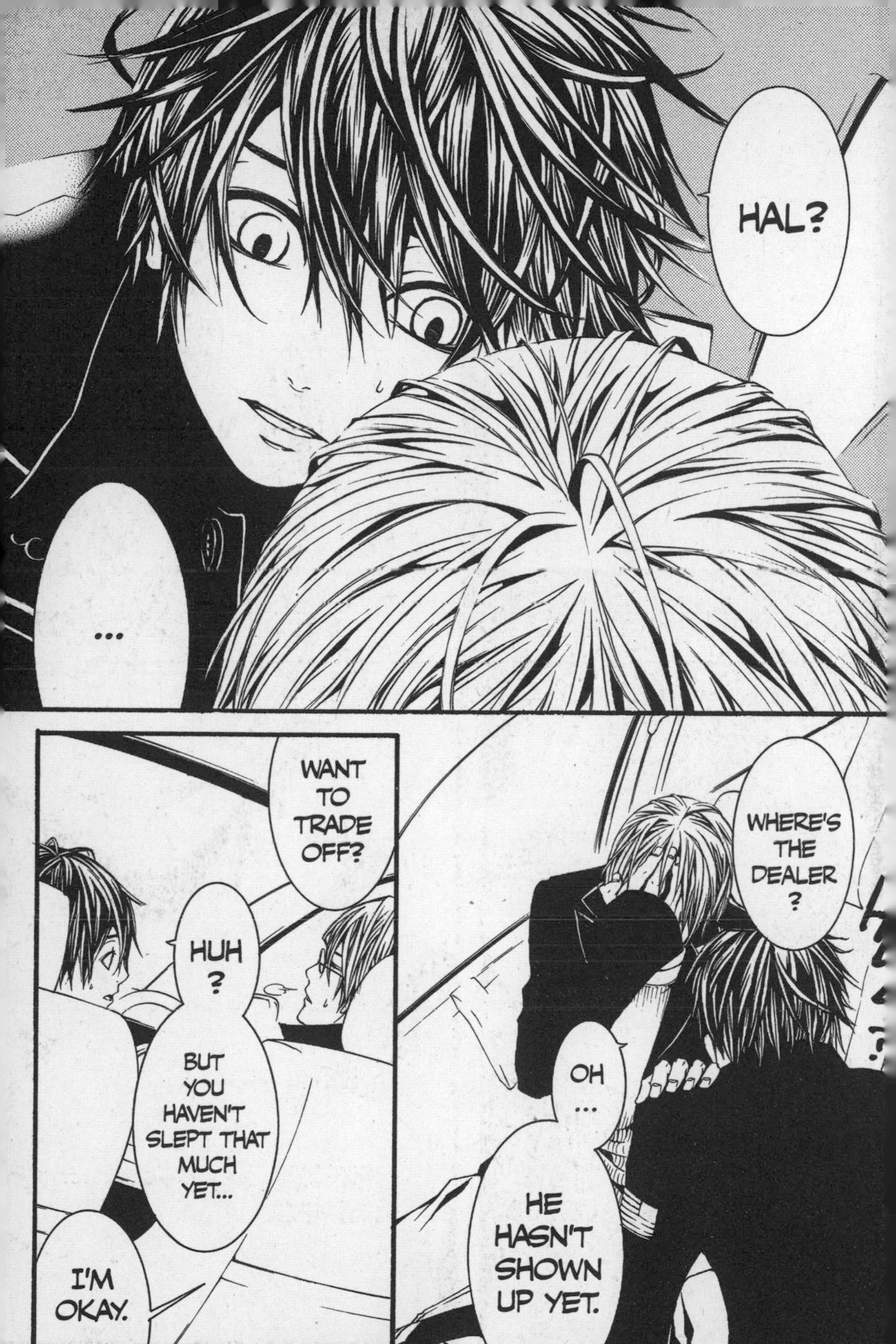
HAL?
...
WHERE'S THE DEALER?
OH...
HE HASN'T SHOWN UP YET.
WANT TO TRADE OFF?
HUH?
BUT YOU HAVEN'T SLEPT THAT MUCH YET...
I'M OKAY.

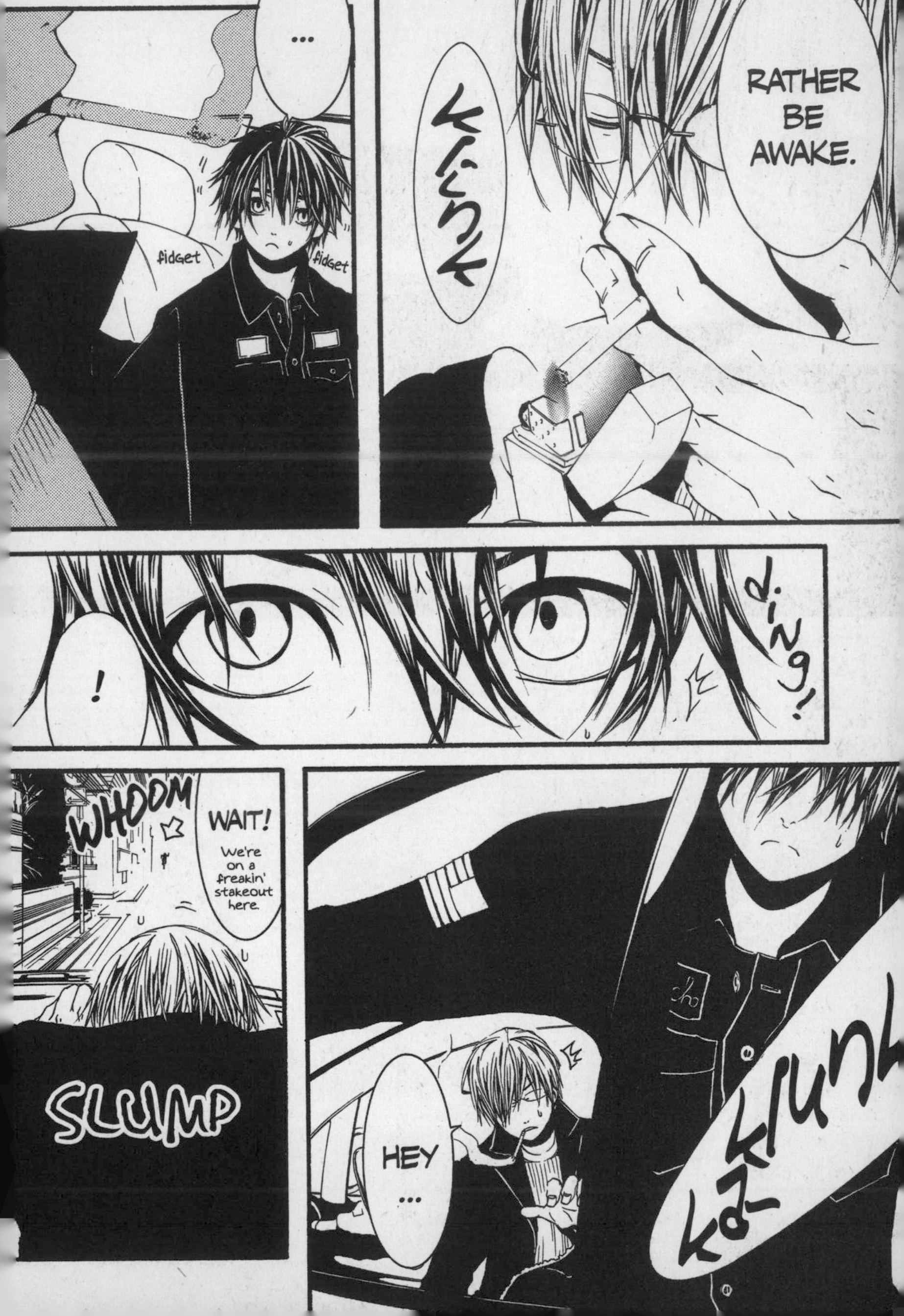
RATHER BE AWAKE.
...
fidget
fidget
ding!
!
ka-klunk
HEY ...
WAIT! We're on a freakin' stakeout here.
WHOOM
SLUMP

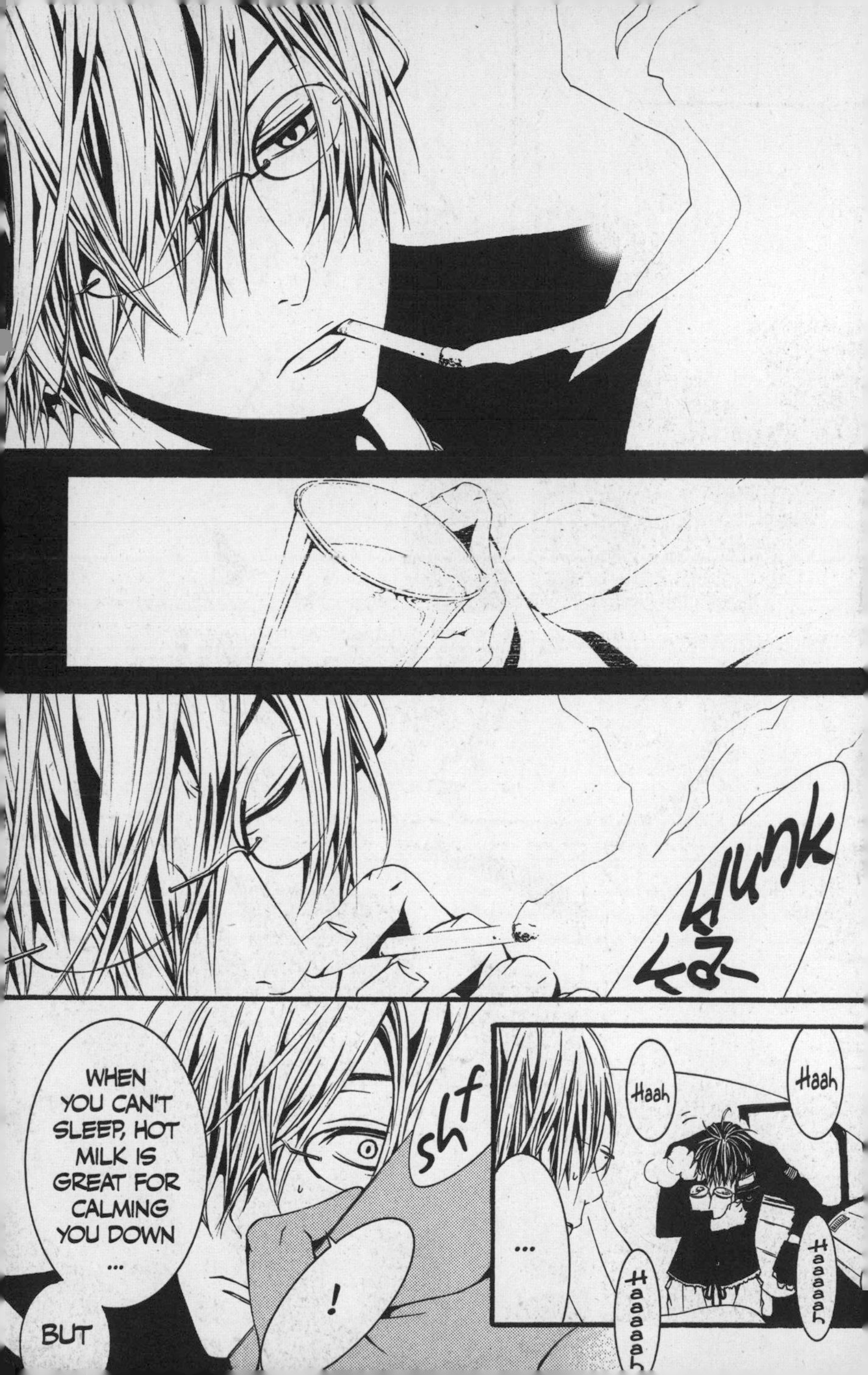
thunk
Haah
Haah
Haaaaah
Haaaaah
...
shf
WHEN YOU CAN'T SLEEP, HOT MILK IS GREAT FOR CALMING YOU DOWN ...
!
BUT

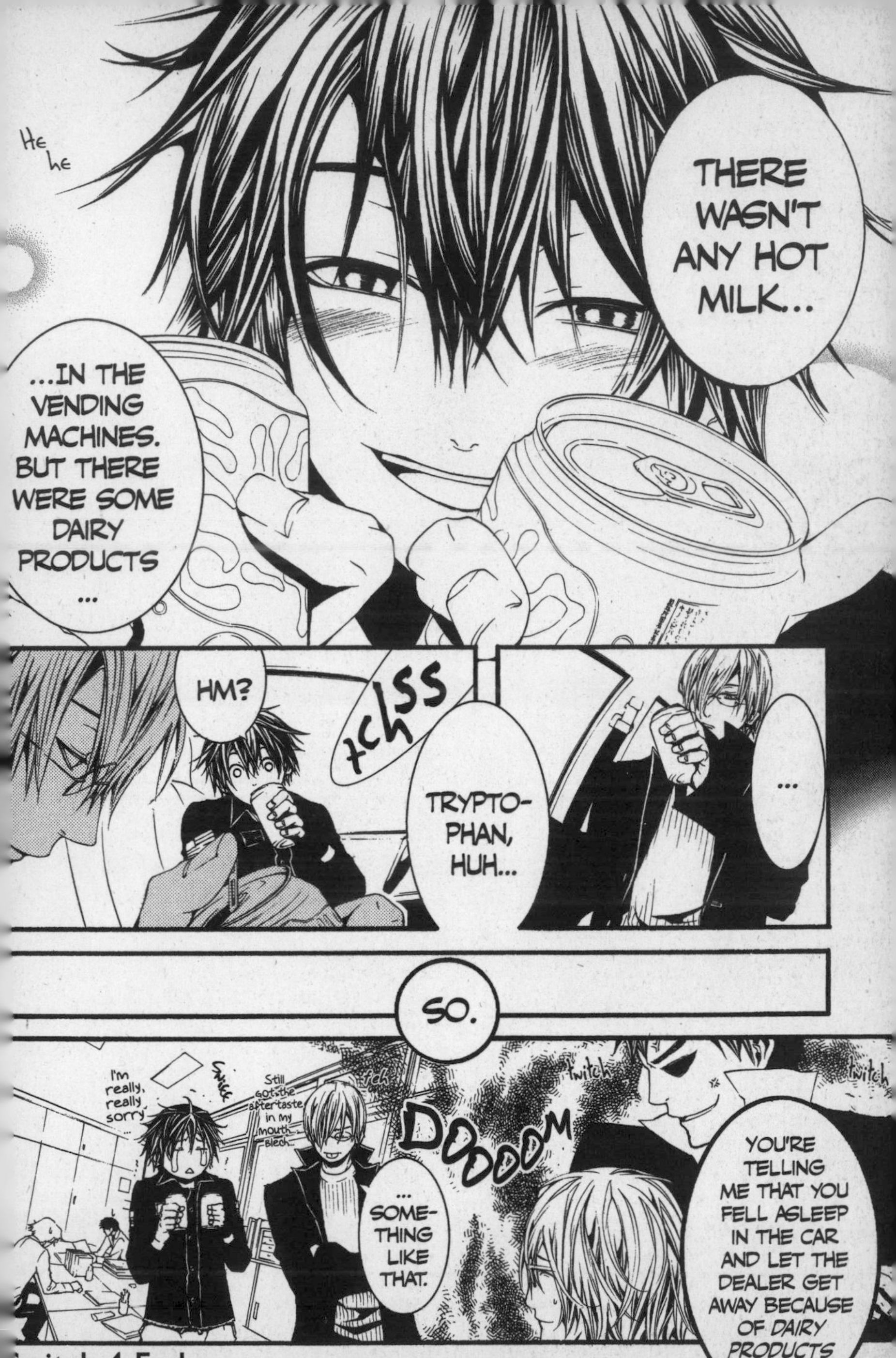
THERE WASN'T ANY HOT MILK...
...IN THE VENDING MACHINES. BUT THERE WERE SOME DAIRY PRODUCTS ...
He he
...
TRYPTO-PHAN, HUH...
tchSS
HM?
SO.
YOU'RE TELLING ME THAT YOU FELL ASLEEP IN THE CAR AND LET THE DEALER GET AWAY BECAUSE OF DAIRY PRODUCTS ?
twitch
twitch
DOOOOOM
... SOME-THING LIKE THAT.
tch
Still got the aftertaste in my mouth. Blech...
I'm really, really sorry ...

Twitch 4 End

A
WONDERFUL
CHAIR

CAN BE CONFIGURED
IN MANY WAYS

MESH

MOVEABLE

MOVEABLE

BACK
SUPPORT

MOVEABLE

naked ape

naked ape

They say that you spend about a third of your life sleeping, but I've been thinking about how long I spend sitting. I've calculated that I spend over ten hours a day sitting down. That's half my life, isn't it? So I went nuts and bought a really nice chair. This is really awesome. We're living in an age when chairs are totally designed for people who sit. We thank you very much, chairs!

naked ape is the collaboration of Tomomi Nakamura and Otoh Saki, who were born just three months apart. Nakamura, the artist, takes things at her own pace and feels no guilt for missing deadlines. Saki, the writer, also does cover design and inking and is called President by the assistants. naked ape's other works include *Black tar* and the ongoing futuristic crime thriller *DOLLS*.

SWITCH
Vol. 4

Story and Art by naked ape

Translation & English Adaptation/ Paul Tuttle Starr,
Translation by Design
Touch-up Art & Lettering/Evan Waldinger
Design/Sean Lee
Editor/Mike Montesa

Editor in Chief, Books/Alvin Lu
Editor in Chief, Magazines/Marc Weidenbaum
VP of Publishing Licensing/Rika Inouye
VP of Sales/Gonzalo Ferreyra
Sr. VP of Marketing/Liza Coppola
Publisher/Hyoe Narita

Published by VIZ Media, LLC
P.O. Box 77010
San Francisco, CA 94107

VIZ Media Edition
10 9 8 7 6 5 4 3 2 1
First printing, September 2008

www.viz.com   store.viz.com

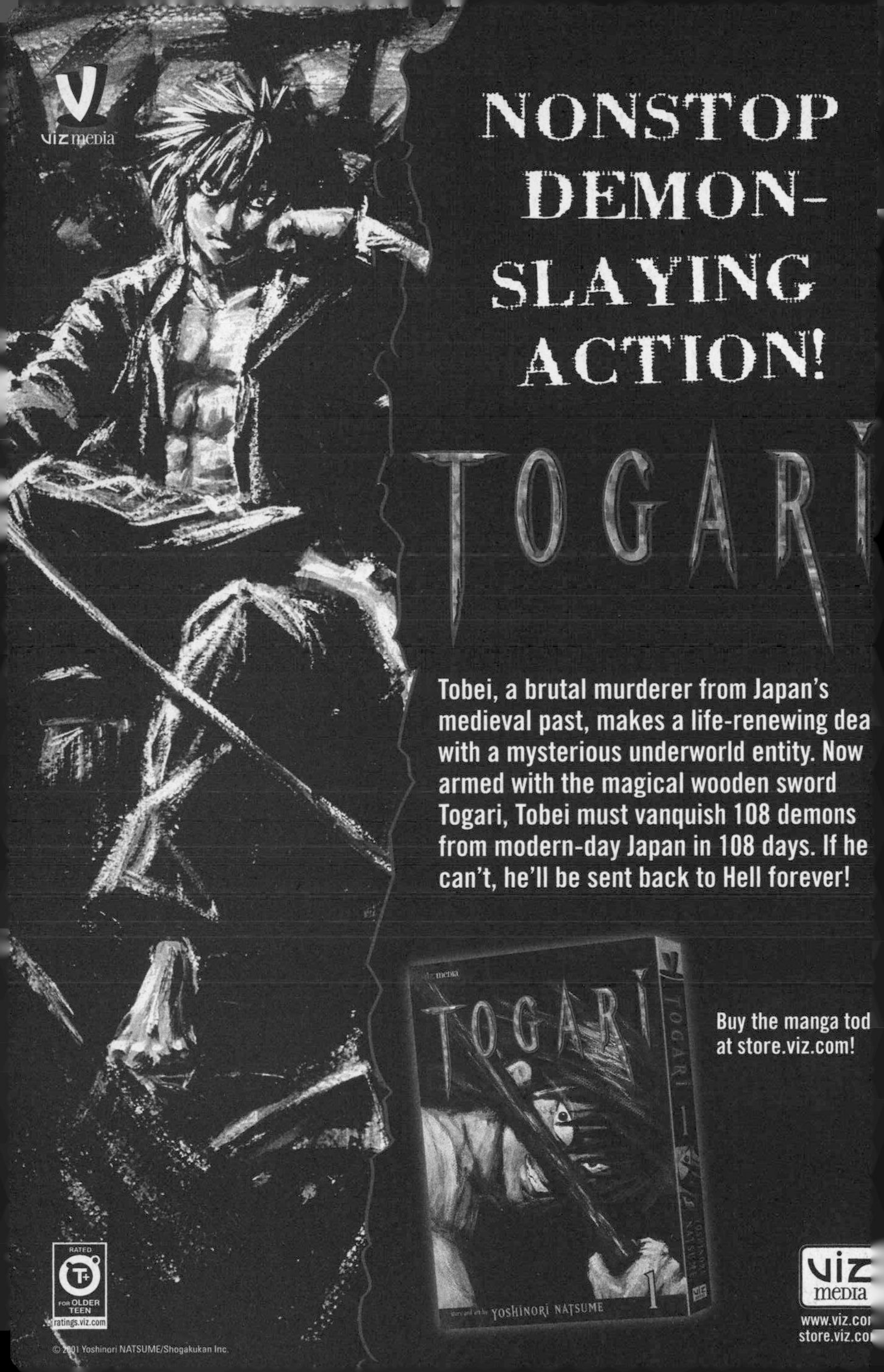
viz media
NONSTOP DEMON-SLAYING ACTION!
TOGARI
Tobei, a brutal murderer from Japan's medieval past, makes a life-renewing dea
with a mysterious underworld entity. Now armed with the magical wooden sword Togari, Tobei must vanquish 108 demons from modern-day Japan in 108 days. If he can't, he'll be sent back to Hell forever!
TOGARI
YOSHINORI NATSUME
Buy the manga tod
at store.viz.com!
RATED T+ FOR OLDER TEEN
ratings.viz.com
viz media
www.viz.co
store.viz.co
© 2001 Yoshinori NATSUME/Shogakukan Inc.

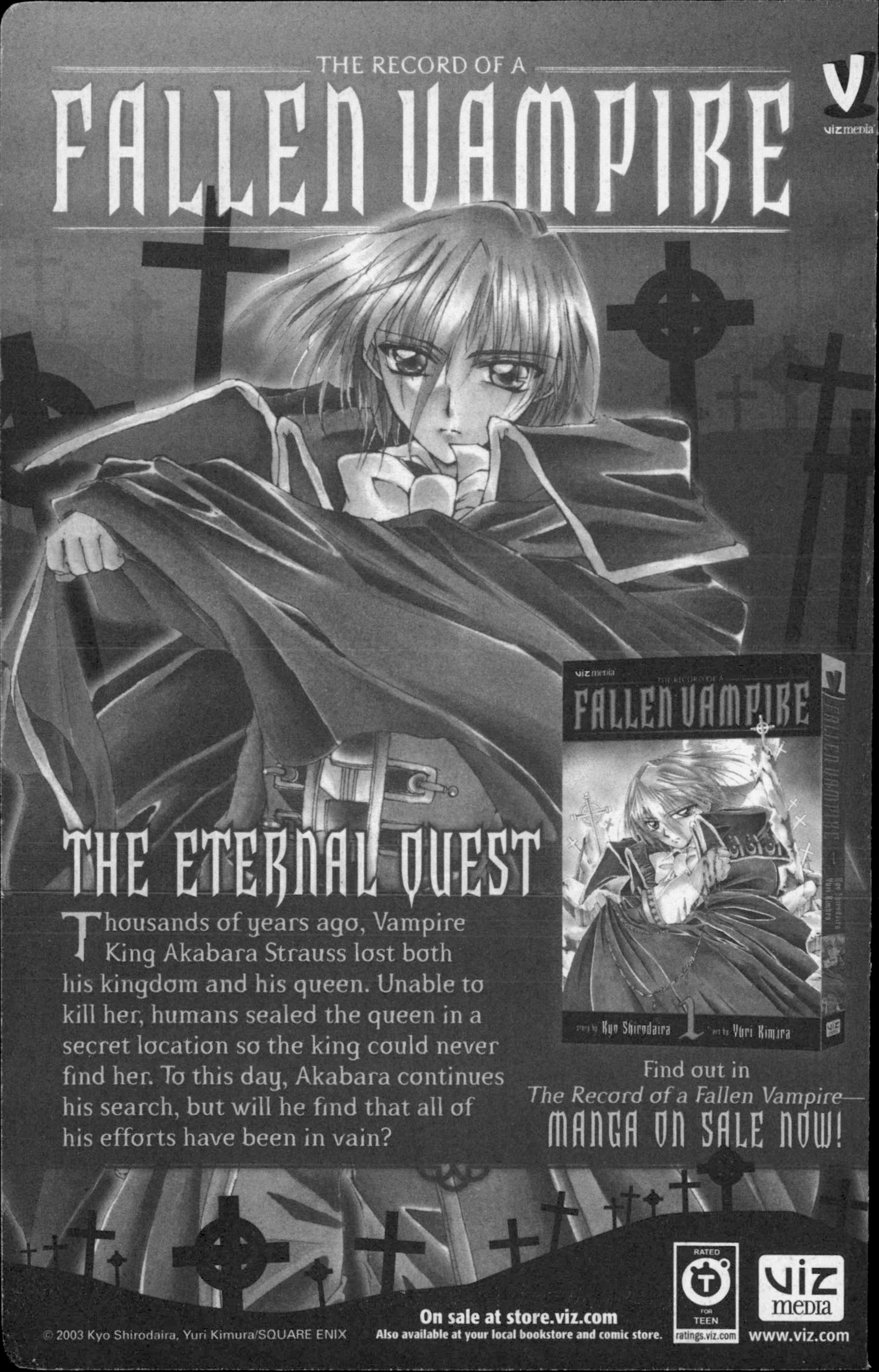
THE RECORD OF A
FALLEN VAMPIRE
viz media
viz media
THE RECORD OF A
FALLEN VAMPIRE
story by Kyo Shirodaira
1
art by Yuri Kimura
THE ETERNAL QUEST
Thousands of years ago, Vampire King Akabara Strauss lost both his kingdom and his queen. Unable to kill her, humans sealed the queen in a secret location so the king could never find her. To this day, Akabara continues his search, but will he find that all of his efforts have been in vain?
Find out in
The Record of a Fallen Vampire—
MANGA ON SALE NOW!
RATED
T
FOR
TEEN
ratings.viz.com
viz media
On sale at store.viz.com
Also available at your local bookstore and comic store.
www.viz.com
© 2003 Kyo Shirodaira, Yuri Kimura/SQUARE ENIX

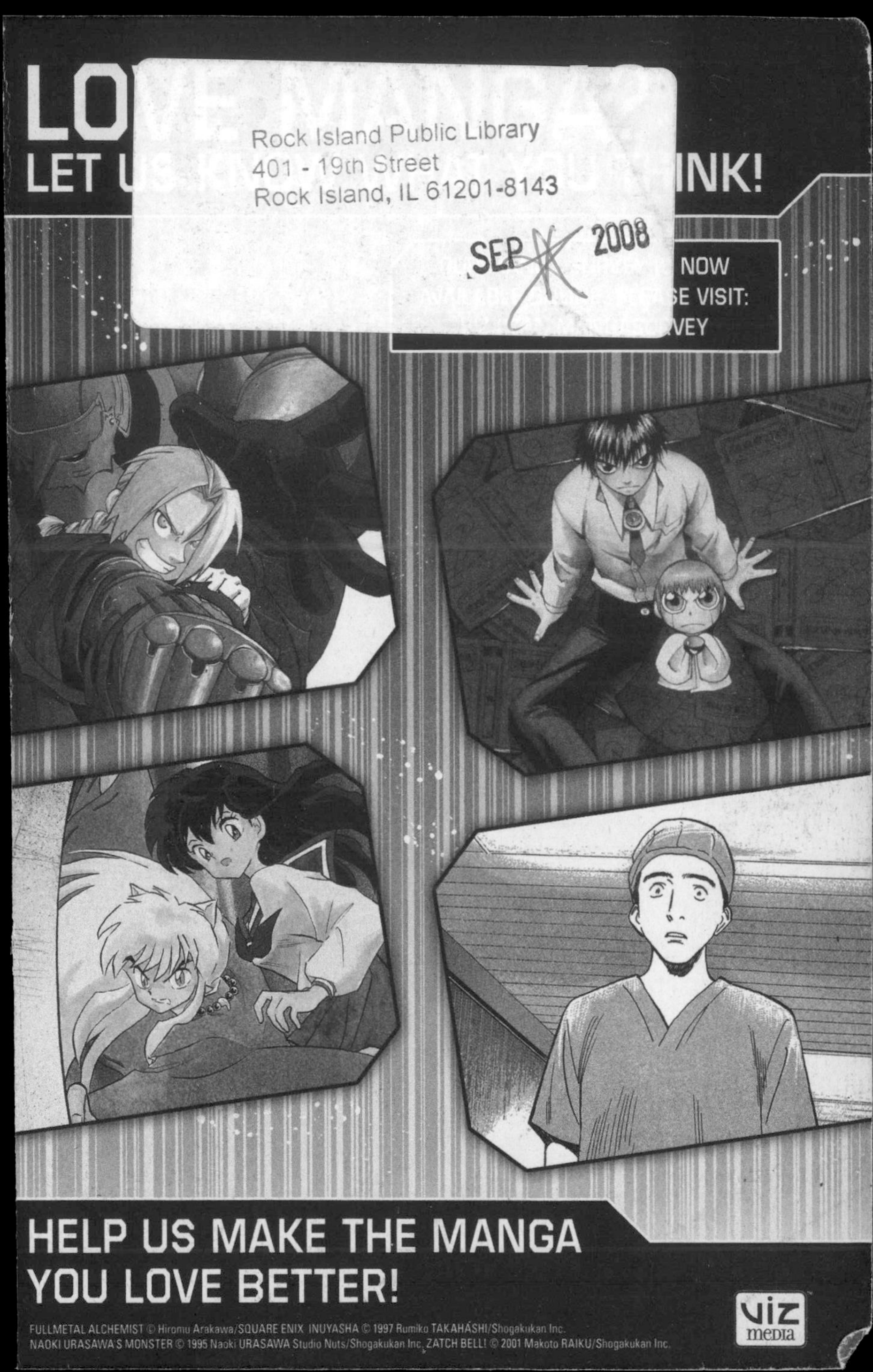